Ann Barry

EDINBURGH

Published 2000 by
ANN BARRY
103 Mayfield Road
Edinburgh
EH9 3AJ
Scotland

ISBN 0 9526441 2 6

A catalogue record for this book is available from the British Library.

Contents

Preface

Although long dormant, my association with the Cambridge Union dates back to my own student days. As a result, I owe thanks to many people who, over many years, have encouraged and helped me in this project. I take this opportunity of mentioning in particular: Terry Barringer, Colin Coates, Sandra Finding, Peter Freshwater, Nigel Hancock, Ronald Hyam, Gordon Johnson, Dermot Keogh, J.J. Lee, Elisabeth Leedham-Green, Stuart McLean, Ian Martin, Christopher Nott, Grace Owens, James Sturgis, Barry Thoday and the late Roland Thompson. I apologise to those whose names may be omitted. As always, my deepest thanks will be expressed in private. My scholarly debt to the many historians of Cambridge in whose steps I tread will, I hope, be evident from the text. Thanks are due to the members of the Modern History seminar at the University of Edinburgh and to the Historical Society of University College Cork for opportunities to discuss the project at earlier stages. My debt to the Master and Fellows of Magdalene College Cambridge goes far beyond the present work.

Thanks are due to the Cambridge Union Society and to Cambridge University Library for access to the records of the Union, and to the Master and Fellows of Trinity College and the staff of the Wren Library for permission to cite the Houghton MSS. I thank the staff of Edinburgh University Library. I also acknowledge with appreciation the remarkable resources of the National Library of Scotland. Illustrations are taken from *The Cambridge Scrapbook* (1859) and the *Graphic* (1886), both by unidentified artists. Sketches made by G.M. Brimelow in 1897 appeared in T.D. Atkinson with J.W. Clark, *Cambridge Described & Illustrated* (1898). Edwardian Cambridge was pleasantly captured by W.M. Keesey in *Cambridge: A Sketch Book* (1911).

King's College Chapel 1911

"Gone Up To Jesus":
A Note on Terminology

The present study is the product of three related interests. The first is a sometimes exasperated enthusiasm for Cambridge University, which is reflected in the four chapters that constitute Part One of the book. The second stems from a wish not simply to explore the history of the Cambridge Union as an institution, but from the desire to establish the extent to which its debates may be interpreted as evidence of opinion, both within the narrow world of student privilege and the wider community. The three chapters of Part Two discuss both aspects of the question. The debates on Ireland, which are the subject of the four chapters of Part Three, are explored in more detail and form part of a longer-term study of British perceptions, and misconceptions, of nineteenth-century Ireland. Perhaps the confidence is misplaced, but this study assumes that readers interested in Cambridge University during the nineteenth century will possess an outline knowledge of the history of Ireland in the same period, or should at least be familiar with the main events of what textbooks used to call the "Irish Question". By contrast, those who may approach the book from the other direction may be forgiven for feeling perplexed and alienated by the vocabulary and tribal traditions of an English university. Chapters Two and Three attempt an explanation, but those of us whose thought patterns have been shaped by modernity, whatever our national origins, will find much about Cambridge as it emerged from its *ancien régime* that we can never fully penetrate. A few preliminary notes on terminology may be useful.

Wherever possible, arcane vocabulary has been by-passed. For instance, Honours examinations are referred to as the Tripos (plural Triposes to indicate various subject degrees) because Cambridge still uses the term. Authorities generally trace its origins to a three-legged stool, but who sat on the stool and why, are matters of unresolved controversy beyond the realms of this enquiry. In mathematics, the top class of examination candidates were called Wranglers, but there seems no reason not to use here the internationally recognised equivalent, First Class. Officially the three Cambridge terms (that is, periods of formal study) are Michaelmas, Lent and Easter. Anyone steeped in the culture of Ireland will have some difficulty in recognising a Lent Term that starts in January and an Easter Term that finishes in June. The first and third terms were often referred to as the October and summer terms, and it seems simpler to refer to the middle period as the January or winter term. The process by which Oxbridge academics came to be called "dons" is as obscure as the etymology of the Tripos. Certainly nowadays few specimens of the breed radiate the *hauteur* of the Spanish grandees from whom the word derives, but it is used for its convenience. In reference to the colleges, the well-established terms of Master and Fellows are used, to refer respectively to the head of the institution and the academic staff or voting members. As Chapter Two seeks to clarify (or so it may be hoped), two colleges did not call their chief executive "Master", and a handful of the University's member institutions managed to evade calling themselves "colleges". Hence the collective term for the former was "Heads of Houses". One Oxford college, Christ Church, called its Fellows "Students", which causes confusion to this day, but happily that problem does not impinge here. We have enough.

Colleges are usually referred to by short title. Thus King's College is normally "King's" and so on. Again, Oxford demonstrates that there are levels of eccentricity undreamt of beside the Cam. Christ Church does not bear the label "College", but New College can never be correctly mentioned without it. The closest that Cambridge managed to fool outsiders was the transformation of the anciently-named St Peter's College to the more domestic Peterhouse. The unwary should however take note that Trinity Hall, a very small piece in the puzzle, is nothing to do with Trinity, which is a very large segment of Cambridge.

Some colleges endure yet further abbreviation. In colloquial usage, Corpus Christi and Sidney Sussex both drop their second element. By contrast, Gonville and Caius is simply "Caius". And here we come to further hurdles of pronunciation. John Keys (some prefer Kees) was inspired by the spirit of the Renaissance to re-found Gonville Hall in 1557. To proclaim his own enthusiasm for the new learning, he rendered his surname into Latin. Four and a half centuries later, the pronunciation obstinately preserves the original form. Another trap for the unwary is Magdalene, which even so notable a poet as Rupert Brooke rhymed with "dawdle in".[1] A plea in mitigation might point to Thurles and Youghal, Ballina and Drogheda (not to mention Dun Laoghaire) and mildly suggest that Cambridge is not unique. A note on the pronunciation of two of the surnames that appear in these pages may also be helpful. The intimidating William Whewell was known to students as "Billy Whistle" because – if we are to judge from Cambridge oral tradition – his name not only rhymed with "fuel" but its opening consonant preserved the aspiration characteristic of the North. Although there was nothing overtly religious about William Mackworth Praed, his surname was pronounced in a manner redolent of prayer, in the past tense.

From an Irish point of view, the nomenclature of the colleges is confusing both geographically and culturally. In the Cambridge context, Clare and Pembroke are colleges, whereas in Irish discourse they would refer respectively to a county and a ferry terminal. Life is too short to explain how Cambridge's Clare College and Ireland's Banner County can trace their name to the same medieval family. More confusing is the fact that the largest college at Cambridge, Trinity, bears the same name as the core institution of the University of Dublin. Like Oxford and Cambridge, Dublin's university was intended to become an institution that would embrace a range of component colleges. In the event, only the one college was ever founded. In the pages that follow, "Trinity" refers exclusively to the Cambridge college, while occasional allusions to its Dublin namesake are made in full. More generally, those familiar with Ireland may find it odd that names more often associated with churches and religious orders are in Cambridge routinely, and with little respect, applied in an aggressively secular context. It is said that a proud parent who announced that his son had gone up to Jesus received from friends in Ireland not congratulations on academic achievement but condolences in his bereavement.

Confusion in terminology extends to the central focus of this study, the Cambridge Union itself. No doubt this student debating society chose wisely when it turned its back on the cumbersome names of its predecessors, the Speculative and the Anticarnalist, but simplicity was achieved at the price of clarity. It was bad luck that "Union" should so very quickly have become a byword for revolutionary organisations. Social eminence seems to have obviated any identification with trades unions, but did not prevent occasional confusion, both then and since, with the local workhouse. A key-word search on the computerised index to *The Times* throws up an episode from 1841, "Insurrection at the Cambridge Union". The historian hurries away to the newspaper file half-hoping to find an O'Connellite confrontation, only to discover that the story refers to a mutiny by paupers against workhouse conditions. Right down to 1948, when the last vestiges of the Poor Law system gave place to the welfare state, down-and-outs occasionally arrived at England's oldest student debating society seeking food and refuge.

These are amusing confusions, but a central problem in terminology remains. The underlying factor in almost all Cambridge student debates on Ireland was the question of constitutional relationship between the two islands. In happier times, Erskine Childers made the Cambridge Union into a pun on that larger union brought about in 1801. In this study, the terms "union" (describing the structure of British-Irish government from 1801 to 1922) and "unionist" (a supporter of that relationship) are used sparingly and spelt in lower case, except in quotations.

The Cambridge Union elected three "junior" officers each term. Until 1852, the three were styled President, Treasurer and Secretary. In that year, the post of Treasurer was placed upon a longer-term basis and assigned to a senior member of the University. At student level, it was replaced by a new office, that of Vice-President. The three officers generally succeeded each other without much to-do. Here, as so often, the Cambridge ethos was different from that of Oxford, where the Union created four student posts, ensuring that progression to the Presidency often involved diamond-shaped electoral contests between the Librarian and Treasurer. In the first half-century of the Union's history, Presidents were as likely to be young BAs as undergraduates. Indeed, a few incumbents served a second term, although usually not consecutively: Charles Dilke in 1866 was the last. Members generally rose to the Presidency on the strength of their standing as public speakers, and the Society's silent and reactionary majority proved remarkably open-minded in electing candidates whose radical political beliefs were invariably rejected in the divisions that concluded each debate. One notable exception was William Smith O'Brien in 1831 who never spoke at all. Smith O'Brien came into residence at Cambridge as what we should now call a mature student, having already served a term as an MP at Westminster. It is a pity that he never addressed the Cambridge Union. Of course, had he done so he would at that stage of his career have preached the most rigid Toryism.

This study covers a period just short of one hundred years, from 1815 to 1914. Perhaps it may too easily imply that the century under review constituted a coherent unity, that Cambridge in the year of Waterloo was much the same as the Cambridge that marched off to the battle of the Marne. Common sense would prompt us to suspect that this could not be so. The University underwent major changes that effectively made the eighteen-sixties into a watershed, a caesura paralleled in the history of the Union by the construction of its permanent home in 1866. Veterans of the eighteen-twenties who attended the inaugural ceremony on that occasion spoke of a very different world that had existed forty years earlier. In the formal sense, members of the Union seem to have been largely indifferent to their Society's past. The sole attempt to appeal to a tradition on an Irish issue was the work of a visitor from Oxford, Swift MacNeill, who proposed the Union's first-ever motion on Home Rule in 1873 and arranged to return in 1913 to celebrate its fortieth anniversary. In reality, MacNeill's belief that he had carried the day back in 1873 was mistaken and his "tradition" was manufactured pretext designed to enable a Nationalist and Protestant member for a Donegal constituency to attack the legitimacy of Ulster unionism. Yet, as Chapters Two and Three will argue, the changes that seemed so seismic within Cambridge may appear to outsiders little more than minor modifications that barely changed the composition of the University in terms of class, gender or religious affiliation. It can hardly be doubted that even these reforms were purchased at the price of emphasising the appearance of changeless continuity, so that student debaters formed their ideas and thrashed out their disagreements within an academic microcosm that was dominated by a comfortable sense of continuity. In that sense at least, the Cambridge of 1914 was much the same as it had been a century before. Fundamentally, the conundrum is philosophical as much as historical: is it possible to attribute characteristics of any kind, including those of continuity, to an abstract institution? If there was stifling continuity in the traditions of the place, Cambridge was to some extent constantly refreshed by the counter-balancing enthusiasm of its annual infusion of youth. "The world was so interesting then", Leslie Stephen recalled of his undergraduate days forty years later.[2] That was a theme which animated Union debates from the time of George IV to the reign of George V. Nor should we forget that the Ireland that moved in and out of the Cambridge student world between 1815 and 1914 was also greatly changed and fundamentally the same.

One final word by way of disclaimer. Historians are not responsible for the material that they study. The English nationalist prejudice in the debate records of the Cambridge Union is capable of irritating an Irish reader, just as nineteenth-century Cambridge exudes a social exclusivity that is equally alien to a British author who had the good fortune to be born into a more democratic (and probably transient) age of wider access to higher education. In many respects, the first hundred years of the Cambridge Union belong to a remote era entirely alien to the twenty-first century world. Yet in others, some of the attitudes reflected in its debates remain to complicate relations between Britain and Ireland to this day.

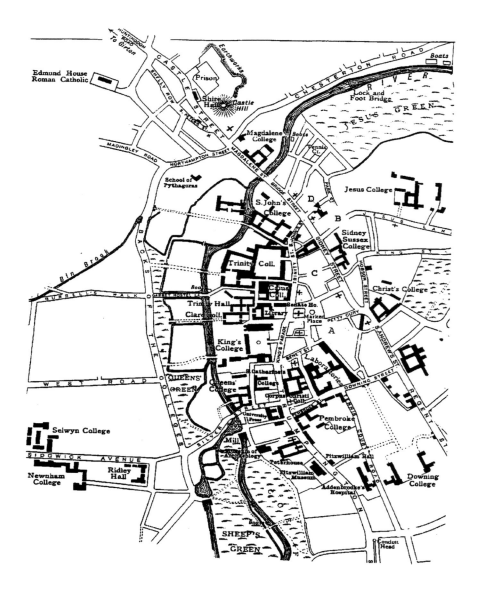

Map of Cambridge in 1897.

Successive locations of the Union are indicated: A = Petty Cury (1815-1831), B = Park Street (1831-1850), C = Green Street (1850-1866), D = Round Church Street

Part One

Cambridge in the

Nineteenth Century

The Cambridge Union from Round Church Street 1886

1: The Cambridge Union: Sources and Rivals

The Cambridge Union Society was founded in February 1815, the result of a merger, probably planned the previous year, of three smaller clubs which a later generation would have termed discussion groups. The idea of an openly constituted student society with its own premises was novel and bold in an English university, although the most important of the Union's three founding clubs, the Speculative, was probably an offshoot of a long-established town-and-gown debating society in Edinburgh. Renting its own accommodation meant that the Union did not have to restrict its membership, unlike most student clubs which met in undergraduate rooms and so were limited by the constraints of space. Its physical presence also offered some measure of independence from University and college authorities and made it less likely to collapse altogether in those years when, as happens to most student organisations, it descended into the doldrums. The Cambridge Union occupied rooms at the Red Lion Hotel in Petty Cury until 1831, when it decamped to premises at the rear of the Hoop Inn which were entered from Park Street off Jesus Lane. In 1850, there was a further move, this time to a converted chapel in Green Street. This proved inadequate, and was replaced in 1866 by a purpose-built debating chamber and club rooms on the present site in Round Church Street. The social amenities of the Union were enlarged by an additional wing erected in 1886.[1]

While the majority of its members probably regarded the Union primarily as a convenient place to read newspapers, the purpose of the Society was to organise debates so that its members might practise public speaking. The notion that young men might hold opinions of their own on any subject did not sit easily with the ethos of Cambridge University in the early nineteenth century. Worse still, the idea that they might express such opinions in a semi-public forum was deeply disturbing to those who wielded political authority in the era of the Napoleonic wars. In 1817, no less a personage than the Vice-Chancellor himself arrived at the Red Lion to interrupt a meeting of the Union and forbid all further debates. As Chapter Five will argue, a society with its own premises could find ways of evading this formal prohibition. Thus a student who sympathised with Greek resistance to Turkish rule could simply move that the Union subscribe to a newspaper published in Athens, and proceed to deliver a speech in general support of the Hellenic cause. Consequently, in 1821 the University decided to permit open debating under restrictions designed to prevent discussion of current politics.[2] These, too, could be circumvented, since the arguments in favour of the Greeks establishing their independence in 1799, which was a legitimate subject for discussion under the "twenty-five year" rule, were remarkably close to those that still applied in 1824, the year in which the subject was debated. The restrictions were abandoned in 1830, although a fastidious faction deplored the overt politicisation of Union debates, and the Society was if anything weakened by their partial secession for about a decade.

If one feature of its activities was that the "strength of the English language was put to the test," as a commentator wrote of the debate on Home Rule in 1893,[3] the Cambridge Union could at least claim to have indirectly enlarged its vocabulary. The term "Union" was adopted in other universities, for instance at Oxford in 1826 and Edinburgh in 1889. These were clubs primarily dedicated to debating, but thereafter on campuses throughout Britain and Ireland, and in Commonwealth countries overseas, the term "student union" came to refer to recreational facilities automatically available to all undergraduates upon their enrolment at the university. It needs to be stressed that this was never the case at Cambridge, where the Union was – and remains – a private society charging its own subscription. In the mid-nineteenth century, this was probably equal to about two percent of the total expenditure of the average undergraduate – small enough to be a worthwhile investment for those who wanted access to club facilities or debates, but sufficiently large to constitute a substantial item of economy for those who did not. It is unlikely that the Cambridge Union ever attracted more than one-third of each annual intake of freshmen to the University, and it did not reach even that level of participation until the late eighteen-eighties, after the completion of the additional wing that substantially expanded its social amenities. Given the prestige of the Society, and the general level of prosperity that was necessary in a Cambridge undergraduate, the low rate of membership is a little puzzling. The Union always had its detractors, and some students were congenital non-joiners. Parnell, for instance, never became a member, and in addition was beaten up because he declined to subscribe to the Magdalene Boat Club.[4]

By and large, Cambridge undergraduates in the nineteenth century had little sense of political solidarity within the University. Appendix One shows that from time to time undergraduates were aroused by collective grievances, with some of the largest debates in the nineteenth century taking place not on Home Rule but on issues such as an attempt to ban boating through Grantchester Meadows. However, the Union did not see itself as a representative body entitled to negotiate with the University authorities on behalf of the student community. On a very few occasions, the Cambridge Union sought to fill the gap in overall student organisation by taking the initiative to convene open meetings of all junior members of the University. Some of these were largely formal, as in 1892 in response to an invitation from the students of the

University of Dublin to send delegates to the celebrations of the three-hundredth anniversary of Trinity College.[5] More notable was the open debate in 1897, discussed in Chapter Three, in which twelve hundred undergraduates condemned any moves towards admitting women to Cambridge degrees. In 1885, an open meeting was convened with the aim of condemning the decision of the University soccer and rugby clubs for deciding to arrogate to themselves the right of awarding "Blues", a mark of sporting distinction hitherto monopolised by cricketers, athletes and – of course – oarsmen. A motion demanding that the assorted footballers "bring themselves again into harmony with those unwritten laws by which the social relations of members of this University are governed" was rejected by 707 votes to 466.[6] It says something for the late Victorian mindset that the rowing man who proposed the motion was about to stand for parliament as a Liberal, and would become an enthusiastic supporter of Irish Home Rule.

It may seem questionable to suggest that the debates of such a narrowly constituted society can be usefully studied as evidence of English attitudes to Ireland in the nineteenth century. Student debates, doubters will object, rarely reflect informed opinion, and those held at Cambridge can hardly be claimed to be representative of the wider community. The University was an elite institution, virtually closed to all but the wealthy and notably unwelcoming to anyone not a member of the Church of England (not to mention its exclusion of women). Moreover, as a private club, the Cambridge Union probably did not reflect even that unrepresentative elite. Not only was membership confined to a minority of the undergraduate population, but many probably joined the Union mainly for its club facilities. Thus debates were patronised by a minority of a minority of a student body that was itself drawn from a highly restricted social elite. Furthermore, it may be suspected that a vote on a motion in a debating society is evidence merely of the effectiveness of oratory: that the unformed minds of the young could easily be seduced by the brittle brilliance of a clever speech.

Chapters Two to Four relate the Union and its Irish debates to the wider context of Cambridge University. Chapters Five and Six outline the history of the first hundred years of the Cambridge Union, while Chapter Seven argues that the debate records provide consistent evidence of opinion, and even that they can be related to shifts in attitude in the wider population. The debates themselves are discussed in the remaining chapters. Chapter Eight covers the years from 1816 to 1885. The interpretation of the proceedings in the first half of the nineteenth century is not always straightforward. In the early decades, there was a taste for debates on cultural issues, originally because the Union was strongly discouraged from discussing current affairs. In the absence of detailed debate reports, it is sometimes difficult to reconstruct the way in which such motions were interpreted. One example is the seemingly innocent debate in 1827 on whether legislation was a more effective means of discouraging cruelty to animals than Coleridge's *Rime of the Ancient Mariner*, with its bleak warning of the dire consequences of shooting an albatross. A surviving account indicates that some members chose to interpret this ostensibly precious topic as a demand for political concession in Ireland because the first act of parliament banning cruelty to animals had been carried by an Irish MP, "Humanity Dick" Martin, who also supported Catholic Emancipation.[7] However, by the eighteen-sixties, the culture of debates had changed to a more modern tone. "You seem so absorbed in politics that you have no time for literature," a veteran of the eighteen-twenties chided his successors of 1866.[8] By 1885, the Union had regularly come to grips with three fundamental issues in Irish politics, Church, Land and Home Rule.

The most obvious reason for breaking the analysis at 1886 is that Home Rule ceased to be merely a subject for abstract debate once Gladstone placed it upon the agenda of Westminster politics. In addition, two elements specific to Cambridge make 1886 a landmark year. First, as a direct by-product of the Home Rule crisis, the Cambridge Union began the practice of inviting distinguished public figures – including Irish Nationalists – as visiting speakers. Prior to 1914, visitors were usually limited to one debate in each term, but the practice enabled Cambridge undergraduates to listen to Irish Nationalists such as John Redmond and John Dillon. Although the innovation in 1886 was controversial, it seems to have been rapidly and tacitly accepted as an appropriate way of shoring up the perennially under-represented Catholic and Nationalist viewpoint in Union debates. Secondly, the eighteen-eighties saw the development of university journalism, including the reporting of debates. Cambridge journalism could be vigorous and outspoken, but its Union correspondents took lightly any implied responsibility to accuracy or fairness. None the less, the *Cambridge Review* and the *Granta* are useful in unravelling puzzling aspects of the formal record, and from their pages it is possible to recover something of the lost world that was swept away in 1914. Chapter Nine traces the consideration of Irish issues from the tense atmosphere of the Home Rule crisis of 1886 through to dwindling and even mocking discussions of the later eighteen-nineties. Chapter Ten shows how shifting attitudes, probably associated with a slightly changing Cambridge, came to accept even Home Rule in the Edwardian period.

The first printed record of Union debates was compiled in 1817, when the Society was defending its right to free speech against the University authorities.[9] The list was incomplete, since a page had been accidentally torn out of the minutes, creating a blank in the record for much of 1815-1816. The first surviving minute book dates from 1823, and internal numbering suggests that the original volume was missing as early as 1828.[10] After the resumption of formal debating, the Union published each year until 1834 a steadily lengthening account of its deliberations, which listed motions, speakers and votes back to 1815. The interruption of the publication of an annual report seems to be one of the indications of the malaise into which the Society fell in the eighteen-thirties. Brief printed reports listed debates year-by-year from 1837 to 1841, and a regular series was resumed from 1843. The annual listing of the debates was accompanied by the reports of the Vice-Presidents, who were responsible for day-to-day club facilities and (until 1902) for the organisation of debates as well. Thus with the exception of the incomplete record for the first year of the Union's history, it is possible to reconstruct a full programme of debates for the whole period.

Other sources of information for the history of the Cambridge Union are scattered, but a few merit special mention. In 1866, the inauguration of the Union's permanent home in Round Church Street was marked by a ceremony at which several veterans of the early years spoke nostalgically of their recollections. As a fund-raising exercise, the proceedings were printed, along with a selection of contemporary press comment. This valuable source was mindlessly recycled in 1878 as *A Short History of the Cambridge Union*, by J.F. Skipper, whose powers of historical selection may be measured from the fact that he managed to spread just four paragraphs over sixteen pages. Skipper added some additional information, much of which was unfortunately wrong. Finally, in 1953, an ex-President, Percy Cradock (later British ambassador in Beijing) produced a history of the Union down to 1939, in a dual capacity as author and editor. Cradock contributed an evocative account that concluded with the solemn adjournment of the debate planned for 22 January 1901 in honour of Queen Victoria, who had died earlier that day. The second part of the book comprised the reminiscences of ten subsequent Presidents, three of whom (Wilson Harris, future editor of the *Spectator* and the lawyers Arnold McNair and Norman Birkett) held office prior to 1914.[11] Biographies of Union activists sometimes provide further scraps of information, especially if the biographer was also active in the Society. Thus Leslie Stephen, a frequent contributor to debates, chronicled the activities of his brother Fitzjames in the Union, while F.W. Maitland, President in 1873, performed the same service for Leslie himself. G.O. Trevelyan, President in 1861, similarly laid stress on the Union career of his uncle, Macaulay.[12]

Reconstructing Macaulay's bombastic notes for a speech on the character of George III, Trevelyan commented that the absence of a Hansard record for the Cambridge Union was "an omission which, as time went on, some among its orators had no reason to regret". Attempts to produce a verbatim record were few and mercifully unsuccessful. William Mackworth Praed conflated and reconstructed the speaking styles of several of his contemporaries to produce an extended account of an imaginary debate on parliamentary reform, set in 1823. The speeches were interwoven with staccato verse assessments. One orator was summarised as "Public debts/ epithets/ Foul and filthy, good and great/ Glorious wars/ British tars/ Beat and bruise/ Parlez-vous/ Frenzy, frown/ Commons, Crown/ Ass and pannier/ Rule Britannia!/ How I love a loud debate!"[13] A proposal in 1829 to print the opening speeches for and against each motion was not even pressed to a vote.[14] Eighty years later, when a prospectus for a new undergraduate journal promised "verbatim reports of Union debates", the *Granta* exclaimed: "By the dust of our ancestors!"[15] The historian who has endured the Hansard records of the real parliaments of Westminster and Ottawa can agree that it is possible to have too much of a good thing. Recalling that Leslie Stephen, one of the greatest intellects to contribute to Union debates, once took pride in denouncing the prime minister of the day as "a contemptible sneak",[16] the historian can be reconciled to the absence of a full record of proceedings. Although one of the veterans speaking in 1866 warned undergraduates that "you must not content yourselves with merely reproducing the articles in the daily newspapers",[17] there can be little doubt that the content of Union debates was often derivative. The *Granta* commented in 1898 that one anti-Home Rule speaker "reminds us of a *Times* leading article" and advised him "to study the *Daily Mail*".[18] Of a debate on agrarian issues in Ireland in 1902, it complained that "arguments fresh at eight o'clock became aged and decrepit at half-past eleven".[19]

It is only fair to note that young men of about twenty years of age had little alternative but to recycle the arguments of their elders. Leslie Stephen gave a glimpse of the Union grappling with the American Civil War, and a warning of the fate of the speaker who laid claim to special authority. "A youth surrounds himself with a vague halo of semi-official splendour on the strength of a relation having been, say, British Minister at a South American republic." Speaking "with great solemnity", one hand grasping the lapel of his frock coat, he confides "his serious doubts as to our relations with the United States", hinting "that from information which he is not at liberty to divulge (this is a dark hint at the before-mentioned Minister)", there was reason to fear that the United States government had already issued orders for the invasion of Canada. This display of pomposity, we may be relieved to read, is "received with a roar of laughter" from an audience of "honourable members" unconvinced by the speaker's pretension.[20] By contrast, the value of personal experience and an original point of view may also be assessed from the contribution in 1889 of a freshman from Belfast who "proved that Home Rule ought not to be granted because an Orange friend of his was able to aim straighter with a pistol than any Home Ruler he had ever met".[21]

We owe the survival of such gems to the reporting of Union debates by the slightly donnish *Cambridge Review*, established in 1879, and the breezily undergraduate *Granta*, which followed in 1889. The first debate reports in the *Cambridge Review* did little more than provide a list of speakers, but gradually attempts were made to convey the atmosphere of discussion as well as brief digests of speeches. When the *Review* experimented in 1887 with a livelier type of reporting, criticism was so severe that coverage of Union affairs was briefly abandoned altogether.[22] In October 1888, however, it returned to the informal style that would be maintained at least until the First World War. From its inception in January 1889, the *Granta* also gave generous space to Union debates. There were alternate periods of collaboration and tension between Union activists and the *Granta's* managers. During the magazine's first term, a Union debate on student journalism was organised as a publicity stunt.[23] Yet the relationship between student orators and student journalists was a sensitive one. "Publishing any proceeding of the Society beyond a debate, the result, and the names of the Speakers" was for long an offence against the Union's Laws, punishable by a fine of one guinea. Undergraduate journalism was usually unsigned, making it unlikely that the provision was ever enforced, but even to be suspected of being the Union correspondent of the *Granta* could arouse hostility: at least one sparkling debater missed the Presidency because he was thought to be the perpetrator of the magazine's barbed comments.[24] The Ulsterman E.W. MacBride, the friend of the crack-shot Orangeman quoted above, became so incensed at his portrayal in the columns of the *Granta* that he threatened in 1892 to move a motion of censure.[25] There was a major confrontation in 1897, after the *Granta* had published an exposé of undergraduate politics entitled "Tammany at the Union". In revenge, the Union Committee formally proposed the expenditure of one shilling a week on two copies of the offending magazine, with the contemptuous intention of destroying its circulation by making it available free in the Society's newspaper room.[26] (In normal times, the Union purchased copies of the *Granta* at the end of each term in order to bind them for permanent preservation.) Thus the portrayal of Union debates in the pages of the *Granta* and, to a lesser extent, in other shorter-lived publications, was the product of a symbiosis between student journalists and student orators, held together by some degree of mutual tension.

Not only did these reports fall considerably short of a Hansard record, but they tended to draw inspiration from the *Essence of Parliament* by "Toby MP" that appeared in the weekly pages of *Punch*. The publication by another student newspaper, the *Gownsman*, of an anthology of its Union columns in book form led the *Granta* to comment that "most of the reports are quite naturally more of a nature of general criticisms than of analysis of arguments".[27] The comment was fair, although it was a case of the pot abusing the

pigmentation of the kettle. When Noel Compton-Burnett defended British rule
in Ireland in 1908, the *Granta* abstained from summarising his remarks, simply
reporting that he "struck attitudes famous in Assyriology and minced and
simpered".[28] However effete his body language, the brother of the redoubtable
Dame Ivy went to his death on the Western Front a decade later, and there is a
certain poignancy that his thoughts on Irish government, if thoughts they were,
should be so totally lost. Moreover, even when attempts were made at serious
summary of a speaker's argument, brevity of reporting made for inadequate
coverage. Here, for instance, are two versions of an undergraduate speech
against Home Rule in 1893. According to the *Cambridge Review*, the speaker

> pointed out some more dangers in the proposed scheme. The case of
> Ireland was exceptional owing to its proximity, and the natural
> aspirations of that country were incompatible with our own safety.[29]

The *Granta* noted that the same speaker

> made some very sensible points, showing that the Federal system is not
> applicable to Ireland. The weight of responsibility lies, not with those
> who defend old institutions, but [with] those who set up new.[30]

The extracts suggest a rejection of the case for Home Rule that was thoughtful
and coherent, but incompletely summarised. In this case, it would have been of
immense interest to have had a full transcript, for the speaker was the twenty-
two year-old Erskine Childers, whose subsequent conversion to Home Rule was
a step on the road through Dominion status to outright republicanism. By the
time of his execution by a Free State firing squad in the Irish Civil War, Childers
had travelled a very long way from the despatch box of the Cambridge Union.
Yet in some respects, his thinking remained consistent, notably in his rejection
of any form of federation between Ireland and Britain.[31] The attempt to
reconstruct the arguments advanced by Childers against Home Rule in 1893
underlines the limitations of student journalism as a historical source and points
instead to consideration of the debates as, at best, evidence of group opinion.
The historian's consolation at the inadequacy of this form of evidence must
surely be that few indeed were the Union orators whose views merit special
analysis.

The Cambridge Union has been overshadowed by two other societies in
England's ancient universities: the Oxford Union and the Cambridge Apostles.
In both instances, it may be argued that the implied comparison has been
exaggerated.

By the twentieth century, the Oxford Union was by far the better known of the two institutions.[32] Bumptiously self-satisfied young politicians might be accused of an "Oxford Union" manner. Ronald Searle once caricatured a sadly serious young man as Secretary of the Cambridge Union,[33] but otherwise no particular quality, good or bad, was associated with the older of the two student debating societies. Even a stern critic of the incubus of the alleged "Oxbridge conspiracy" on British life accepts the stereotype that the Cambridge Union has been "more sober, in both senses of the word, than its celebrated rival, and more measured", because its members know "how to let off steam, without, for the most part, going daft".[34]

However, the relationship was not always so unequal. We have it from no less an authority than John Stuart Mill that in the eighteen-twenties, the Cambridge Union was "an arena where what were then thought extreme opinions, in politics and philosophy, were weekly asserted, face to face with their opposites, before audiences consisting of the *élite* of Cambridge youth". Thus the Cambridge society was already "at the height of its reputation" when a "United Debating Society" was formed at Oxford in 1823.[35] Cambridge promptly recognised a kindred body, and extended honorary membership to the Oxford subscribers. Unfortunately, this generous gesture was not formally notified to the sister university, whose debaters only learnt of the privilege early in 1825. Their secretary, "Soapy Sam" Wilberforce, hastened to assure the Cambridge Union that the arrangement was reciprocal. However, the following year, Cambridge learnt that the "original Oxford debating society" had been "dissolved, and another formed under the name of the 'Oxford Union'". Reciprocal membership was quickly re-established, an arrangement that was extended in 1832 to include the University of Dublin Literary and Historical Society.[36] Whatever their subsequent respective reputations, the Oxford Union derived its name from the successful Cambridge forerunner.

The relative vitality of the two Unions in their early years may be gauged from descriptions of the first joint debate. In November 1829, a delegation from Cambridge visited Oxford. This was the year of the first Oxford-Cambridge boat race and just two years after the start of an annual intervarsity cricket fixture, suggesting that the excursion was part of a developing "Oxbridge" culture. However, the clash of both ideas and debating styles showed Cambridge to be superior in status and confidence. The subject chosen by the Cambridge debaters was an apparently innocuous motion arguing that Shelley was a better poet than Byron. The selection of this poetic issue had two advantages. First, it helped the three Cambridge representatives, all members of Trinity College, to secure the necessary permission to absent themselves from the university during term-time, apparently because they managed to convey the impression to the Master of Trinity, Christopher

Wordsworth, that they intended to defend the poetry of his brother, William.[37] Secondly, under its innocent cover, a motion in favour of an atheist made possible a wide-ranging attack on inherited institutions:

> as Shelley had been expelled from Oxford and treated with much blind injustice, it would be a very grand thing for us to go to Oxford and raise a debate upon his character and powers.[38]

Cambridge was represented by Monckton Milnes, Arthur Hallam (all-too-soon to be immortalised himself in Tennyson's *In Memoriam*) and by a third speaker, Thomas Sunderland, a thundering orator and unbalanced personality who later succumbed to persistent mental illness. Nearly forty years later, an Oxford man could still recall "the astounding vigour of that Cambridge onslaught". Only Henry Manning, future cardinal of the Catholic Church, ventured to speak for the amoral Byron, but "we had not a chance of resistance....It was an universal *sauve qui peut* – a skedaddle." Manning himself equally found "the irruption of the three Cambridge orators" an unforgettable experience:

> We Oxford men were precise, orderly, and morbidly afraid of excess in word or manner. Both Monckton Milnes and Arthur Hallam took us aback by the boldness and freedom of their manner.

Sunderland's oratory completed the rout. "It had never been seen or heard before among us: we cowered like birds and ran like sheep." The recollections of 1866 were not simply the product of the "fragrant and sweet" nostalgia that Manning found "very dear as life is drawing to its close".[39] (He was to live for another twenty-six years.) There is supporting contemporary evidence from the diary of one Oxford student in 1829: "Cambridge men came & all spoke – rather astounding to us".[40]

That astonished diarist was perhaps more than any other person if not responsible for, at least symbolic of the process by which the Oxford Union overtook its sister society in prestige. "The man that *took* me most," Milnes reported of his visit, "was the young Gladstone of Liverpool – I am sure a very superior person."[41] According to legend, it was Gladstone's devastating attack on the Reform Bill in the Oxford Union that prompted the Duke of Newcastle to install him in the House of Commons as MP for the pocket borough of Newark. There is, indeed, an equivalent, if anticlimactic story for Cambridge, where J.W. Blakesley was said to have been invited to become the Tory candidate for the borough seat on the strength of his anti-Reform speeches in the Union. There the parallel ends. Technically reformed but energetically corrupt, the borough of Cambridge was in nobody's pocket. Blakesley's criticisms of Reform stemmed not from Toryism but from his own version of liberal principles. Had he accepted the Tory invitation to stand, he would not have been elected.[42]

None the less, the claim that Gladstone's installation for Newark "was the fruit of his famous anti-reform speech at the Oxford Union"[43] represents a simplification on the part of John Morley, who was also a veteran of the society. The Duke of Newcastle acted on the recommendation of his son, Lord Lincoln, who was not ready to enter parliament himself. Gladstone and Lincoln had been friends since their Eton days. "I have now known him for several years", Lincoln assured his father, praising Gladstone's "honest unflinching integrity of character combined with talents far above the common stamp even of those who are called clever men".[44] The most the Oxford Union speech can explain is *how* and *when* Gladstone came to enter parliament through the patronage of a grandee whom he had never met. It is possible that if the Duke's offer had not been made, Gladstone would have proceeded to ordination in the Anglican Church, and so disqualified himself from election to the House of Commons. Others may suspect that politics would have diverted his path anyway. By modern values, the slave-owning Gladstones were multi-millionaires and, like his father and politically untalented brother, Gladstone would have found little difficulty in getting into parliament even if he had never opened his mouth in an Oxford debate.

To a remarkable extent, prominence in the Cambridge Union rarely ensured a fast-track to subsequent employment of any kind. A.G. Gardiner speculated that it "was probably the fame of his political debating in the Union" that secured William Vernon Harcourt the offer of employment in 1849 as a leader-writer on the *Morning Chronicle* (which happened to be owned by that same Lord Lincoln who had launched the career of Gladstone).[45] However, Gardiner's own account suggests that Harcourt owed his appointment to his membership of the Apostles, a society that did cultivate access to powerful patrons in the wider world. The notion of the Union as a training ground for statesmen probably flourished in part because the myth appealed to the vanity of its more ambitious members. Thackeray (whose sole contribution to a Union debate was an embarrassment) poked fun at students "who used to ape statesmen at the spouting-clubs, and who believed as a fact that Government always had an eye on the University for the selection of orators for the House of Commons".[46] Almost the only authenticated example of a door being specially opened to a President of the Cambridge Union comes from the memoirs of the Labour peer, Lord Pethick-Lawrence, who was given a personal tour of Joseph Chamberlain's orchid house by its proud owner, presumably in recognition of the fact that his son Austen had been an officer of the Society.[47]

The Oxford Union basked in the reflected brilliance of Gladstone's career, which was part of the growing supremacy of Oxford itself in mid-nineteenth-century British politics. Henry Fawcett noted in 1866 that the outgoing Liberal cabinet had included "nine first-class Oxford men, and not one who had taken high honours at Cambridge".[48] As Fawcett added, the political eclipse of Cambridge was a relatively recent phenomenon, and explanation must presumably be sought in wider elite preferences, for Oxford in general and Christ Church in particular. In one sense, the decline of the Cambridge grip upon political power was curious since, until the establishment of new Honours degrees in the eighteen-sixties, the chief feature distinguishing its curriculum from that of Oxford was its emphasis upon mathematics. Cambridge University, one of its partisans claimed, was just as good as Oxford for classics, "only at Cambridge you are dosed with mathematics into the bargain".[49] Thus Cambridge might have been thought to offer the more appropriate training for the government of a nation of shopkeepers. Yet both Peel and Gladstone, two of the greatest financial reformers of the century, were both products of Christ Church. Some reformers felt that the problem lay not so much in the inclusion of mathematics in the Cambridge degree as in the competitive spirit with which it was taught, which virtually required students wishing to secure a good degree to resort to expensive "coaches" to prepare them for examinations. Archdeacon Hare in 1843 described "the practice of private tuition, and the use of emulation as the one great spur to the acquirement of knowledge" as "the two great evils in our system" that were responsible for the fact "that our position relatively to Oxford has altered so much in the last twenty years".[50]

Cambridge could claim seven prime ministers in the first two-thirds of the nineteenth century: Pitt, Perceval, Ripon, Grey, Melbourne, Aberdeen and Palmerston. An eighth, Russell, would have preferred Cambridge but was sent to Edinburgh because his father believed that "nothing was learned in the English universities" and that "the sciences of horse-racing, fox-hunting, and giving extravagant entertainments" constituted "the chief studies of our youth at Cambridge".[51] All seven of those Cambridge prime ministers belong to the period before the establishment of the Union, although Palmerston cut his political teeth in one of its forerunners, the Speculative.

On the face of it, the Cambridge Union did nothing to continue the tradition of nurturing prime ministers, while its Oxford counterpart proved much more successful in harnessing future statesmen. Gladstone and Asquith were both Presidents, Salisbury held Union office and it was only the outbreak of war in 1914 that aborted the rise of Harold Macmillan. By contrast, the Cambridge Union is associated with the good losers, near-misses and glorious failures who might have become prime minister but somehow did not. Austen Chamberlain managed a unique double, rising no higher than Vice-President at Cambridge and ending his career as the only Conservative Party leader in modern times not to make it to Ten Downing Street. Two Presidents, Harcourt and Dilke, may be added to the list of lost prime ministers, to be lengthened in the twentieth century by R.A. Butler. Yet the comparison may flatter the junior society. Gladstone's third cabinet contained no fewer than three former Presidents of the Cambridge Union. As Wilson Harris put it, "if the average has been equal the peaks at Cambridge have never been as high".[52]

None the less, the Cambridge Union can claim some giants and a number of notable figures. Thomas Babington Macaulay was roundly criticised by his enemy, the poet and politician Winthrop Mackworth Praed, for inefficiency during his term at Treasurer in 1823, but within a decade he was directing the educational budget of Bengal to the support of teaching in English. Edwin Montagu, President in 1902, was the Secretary of State whose political reforms in 1919 helped realise Macaulay's prediction that Indian independence would mark the proudest day in English history. In this, Montagu may be thought to have atoned for his part in a campaign to block the election of C.R. Reddy, from Mysore, who was in line to become the first Asian President of the Cambridge Union in 1906, a remarkably odd excursion into colour prejudice for a Jew. [53]

Cambridge Presidents who went on to cabinet rank included C.P. Villiers, who held office in Palmerston's second ministry and R.A. Cross, Disraeli's Home Secretary in the eighteen-seventies. Charles Dilke, Harcourt and G.O. Trevelyan served under Gladstone. One of the greatest political crises in Victorian history, the Hyde Park riots of 1866, pitted head to head two Cambridge Union veterans of forty years earlier: the Home Secretary, Spencer Walpole (President in 1827) and the leader of the Reform League, Edmond Beales (Secretary in 1824). In a later generation came C.F.G. Masterman, whose Liberal credentials are hardly enhanced by his perpetration of a notably insensitive and racist joke in a Union debate on Ireland in 1897, and Lord Edmond Fitzmaurice. F.H. Maugham, who impugned the integrity of Parnell in a Union debate in 1889, served as Lord Chancellor in the cabinet that handed the Treaty Ports to de Valera fifty years later. Other Cambridge Union activists who made their mark in politics prior to 1914 included Macaulay, Charles Buller, the third Earl Grey, Beresford Hope, Lord John Manners, Hugh Childers, Henry Fawcett, Austen Chamberlain and Reginald McKenna. The Attlee cabinet of 1945, one of the most notable in modern British history, included four veterans of the Cambridge Union. Pethick-Lawrence and Noel-Baker were former Presidents. A talent for making enemies ensured that Hugh Dalton was never elected to office. The fourth and perhaps most distinguished of them all was J.C. Ede of Christ's College, who spoke frequently in the Union before lack of money forced him to abandon Cambridge. Ede was something of a figure of a fun, a scholarship boy from Surrey, rare enough in the University and rarer still in the Union: the *Granta* dismissively reported that unless it noted to the contrary, it was to be assumed that Mr Ede spoke on every occasion.[54] So far as his aloof contemporaries were concerned, he had vanished into the grim world of elementary school-teaching, but he did not disappear for good. He became a Labour MP, and adopted the name Chuter-Ede. As a junior minister in Churchill's wartime coalition he helped shape the 1944 Education Act, ensuring to others the opportunities that he had been unable to grasp himself. After the war, he served for six years in Attlee's cabinet and proved himself to be a great reforming Home Secretary.

Presidents of the Cambridge Union also included two notable economists, A.C. Pigou and J.M. Keynes. It would surely be hard to identify anyone who exercised a greater intellectual influence over the economic life of the Western world in the half century from the nineteen-thirties than J.M. Keynes (President in 1905). A respectable crop of historians includes J.R.M. Butler, F.J.A. Hort, F.W. Maitland and J.R. Tanner, in addition to Macaulay himself. A.W. Verrall and Walter Raleigh helped make English Literature a serious subject of study. Former Presidents turned into schoolmasters with remarkable regularity. The bleak figure of Benjamin Hall Kennedy (President in 1825) ruled over Shrewsbury, before returning to Cambridge as Professor of Classics, leaving as his legacy Kennedy's *Latin Primer*. H.M. Butler and J.E.C. Welldon were headmasters of Harrow; E.E. Bowen gave the school its famous song, *Forty Years On*.

The extent to which the Cambridge Union shaped their talents and personalities is open to doubt. Whenever Leslie Stephen encountered the claim that an English public school had "produced" a famous former pupil, he mentally substituted the phrase "failed to extinguish".[55] Samuel Butler, headmaster of Shrewsbury, held that the Union did "fatal mischief" to first-rate intellects,[56] a claim somewhat underlined by the fact that he was succeeded by Kennedy. In later life, Cecil Raikes regretted that his success in the Union had been "rather dearly bought", blaming his failure to gain a First on the time it consumed.[57] The argument advanced by Seeley for the teaching of politics in his inaugural lecture as Professor of History carried the heavy implication that the subject needed to be lifted above the Union.[58] It was equally rare to find the "Union" style of oratory, if such a thing existed, cropping up in later life. In a famous speech to the University Senate in 1897, Maitland lampooned a proposal to establish an independent degree-granting institution to satisfy the demands of women studying at both Cambridge and Oxford, nicknaming it the "Bletchley Junction Academy" – a reference to the intersecting point of the branch railways linking the two university towns. Maitland's speech has delighted historians, but it did not make much impact on Cambridge male chauvinism in 1897.[59]

Indeed, the effectiveness of the Cambridge Union as a political training ground may be measured by the fact that none of the three post-1815 graduates of the University to become prime minister ever took part in its debates. Henry Campbell-Bannerman was "not one of the academically brilliant and ambitious young men, shining lights of the Union".[60] Indeed, he was not even a silent member of the Society, unlike Arthur Balfour and Stanley Baldwin. Balfour presided over an intellectual clique that met in his rooms at Trinity and showed "an unusual disregard, and almost contempt for politics". A contemporary recalled that he "was emphatically not one of those show young men who come from the Union ... and take their place as it were by right in the House of Commons". Rather young Balfour was fast-tracked into parliament by right of membership of the aristocratic Cecil clan. He delayed two years before he made his maiden speech, and spoke only then because of the insistent pressure of a politically-minded aunt.[61] It may not be just coincidence that Balfour's near-contemporary at Christ Church, Lord Rosebery, should have been the exception in the Oxford list of nineteenth-century prime ministers. Although he had been a keen debater at Eton, Rosebery "never made an appearance on the larger stage". His biographer, Lord Crewe, himself at Cambridge in the eighteen-eighties, could only comment that "these things are greatly ruled by fashion, and in some periods at both the great Universities it is not the fashion to attend the Union".[62]

The non-participation of Cambridge's other future prime minister, Stanley Baldwin, is even more mysterious, for he had taken part in sixth-form debates at Harrow and had proclaimed to his headmaster, H.M. Butler, that he intended to enter parliament. This may have been a piece of defiance, since as a schoolboy Baldwin had fallen foul of school discipline, and suffered the indignity of a flogging. His crime was the writing of pornography, which was a sin against morality, compounded by the fact that he had sent a copy to Eton, which was an even greater offence against the good name of Harrow. Baldwin fled to Cambridge, only to find that Butler was translated to the Mastership of his own college, Trinity. The flogging headmaster was the first of seven members of the Butler dynasty to become Presidents of the Cambridge Union, and perhaps the association discouraged any desire that Baldwin might have entertained to make a mark in university debates. He was equally undemonstrative in the college debating society, the Magpie and Stump, which expelled him for failing to speak. Baldwin compounded his humiliations by emerging from Cambridge with a very poor degree, prompting his father's acerbic remark: "I hope you won't get a Third in life."[63] He made his maiden speech in the Union in 1920 as Financial Secretary to the Treasury. It was in character that when he returned in 1924, as prime minister, it was to warn undergraduates that "when we come to big things we do not need rhetoric", a quality to which he attributed both the French and Russian revolutions. His host on that occasion was the last of the seven Butler Presidents, "Rab", through whom Baldwin took vicarious revenge by insisting on buying him a seamy novel from the railway station bookstall.[64]

Nor can the Cambridge Union lay claim to the three Commonwealth statesmen who passed through the University in the quarter century before 1914. Smuts was too poor to join and also too busy: he took both parts of the Law Tripos in the same year but still managed a Double First. Nehru, who was a member of the Union, was not impressed by what he heard. S.M. Bruce, later prime minister of Australia, directed his energies to the river and rowed in the 1904 Boat Race.

Since a three-year subscription conferred membership for life, Cambridge Union representation in high places grew by accretion. In 1895, both Archbishops were life members, Maclagan of York having spoken on Church issues in the eighteen-fifties, while Benson of Canterbury had somehow stretched his straitened finances to become a silent member. At the general election of that year, no fewer than sixty members of the Society were returned to the House of Commons, among them the Speaker, W.C. Gully, who had been President in 1855. (One of the Union's few Irish members, William Ewart, industrialist and Conservative MP for North Belfast, had died in 1889. Unlike Oxford, Cambridge did not produce gentlemanly Protestant Home Rulers, other than Parnell himself.) Union officers thought the size of the delegation "a matter of congratulation to both Societies",[65] but in reality it merely reflected the general inter-connection between Cambridge and the social elite. As the political spectrum widened, so the Union's Westminster representation declined, to 42 in 1910, and 38 by 1914. Overall, student debates merit study as a record of opinion, not as a means of discovering how brilliant young proconsuls prepared themselves for predestined positions of leadership and still less as a process by which "striplings settled questions spoiled by men". Lytton was not alone in his tongue-in-cheek appreciation. As a report in 1908 cheerfully put it, the Union had "with its customary thoroughness, managed to settle many of the problems which continue to worry the leading statesmen and politicians of the country".[66]

These reservations no doubt apply equally to Oxford, but by the beginning of the twentieth century, the Oxford Union had undoubtedly outstripped its older counterpart in general esteem. Perhaps this was because in 1902, the office of prime minister had been held for 21 of the preceding 22 years by two of its former officers. In 1900, the Oxford President, Raymond Asquith, described the custom of "having to go over to Cambridge to speak to their Union" as "one of the most boring things one has to do". Writing with the easy arrogance of a Balliol man whose father was often hailed (correctly as it turned out) as a future prime minister, he treated the experience with distaste:

It is a detestable place to speak in, and the Cambridge orators are as repulsive a crew as I have ever seen: not one of them speaks English – I don't mean the idiom, but the dialect: they all have the manner and accent of Welsh missionaries.

Raymond Asquith was in Cambridge to oppose the proposition that "the British nation is incompetent to govern Alien Races", in which the Union agreed with him with a large majority. The only Cambridge man whom he liked was "a pure-bred Boer called Van Zijl but even he has a strong Glasgow accent".[67] Van Zijl, like Smuts a few years earlier, had come from Stellenbosch, and would return to a career in politics and on the South African bench. It was to his credit that he was not deterred by the prevailing climate of jingoism that swept Britain at the time of the Boer War, but went out of his way to denounce imperial policy in South Africa. It was equally to the credit of the Cambridge Union that although its members never once endorsed his strictures, Van Zijl was elected President in 1901. Raymond Asquith notwithstanding, there was something to be said for the "Welsh missionary" spirit of the Cambridge Union.

By the late twentieth century, the apparent contrast between the two societies remained: Oxford Union Presidents Edward Heath, Jeremy Thorpe, Michael Foot and William Hague rose to the leadership of their parties; Cambridge Union Presidents Douglas Hurd and Kenneth Clarke did not. Yet even for Oxford, the peaks were becoming less Himalayan. In the half-century following 1945, as Britain entered its egalitarian age, no fewer than eight prime ministers were graduates of Oxford. Six of these had little or no connection with the Union – Thatcher, of course, because women were not eligible for membership in her time. Douglas-Home played cricket, Blair was a member of a rock group. Oddly enough, it is a single debate that explains why the Oxford Union retained its folkloric supremacy throughout the twentieth century despite failing to keep pace with its own university as a nursery of political leaders.

On 9 February 1933, Oxford hit the headlines when its Union resolved by 275 votes to 153 that "this House will in no circumstances fight for its King and Country".[68] The newsworthiness of the debate owed something to the fact that the Nazis had come to power ten days earlier although at that stage both Hitler's intentions and his grip on power still seemed uncertain. Much of the publicity was generated by such critics as the correspondent of the *Daily Telegraph* who denounced the vote as "an outrage upon the memory of those who gave their lives in the Great War". Hooligans invaded the debating chamber and ripped the record from the minute book, inspired perhaps by a manifesto issued by Randolph Churchill demanding that the motion be formally expunged from the Society's records. There is good reason to sympathise with the contemporary allegation that Winston's unpopular son had seized a patriotic "opportunity for self-advertisement", although he was supported by Quintin Hogg and, surprisingly, by Frank Pakenham, who as Earl of Longford would make a cerebral and herbivorous contribution to post-war public life. The campaign did indeed compel the Oxford Union to debate a motion one month later to expunge the King and Country debate from its records, but by this time undergraduate opinion had hardened in the face of external pressure. Churchill even attempted to withdraw his proposition, which was massively rejected by 750 votes to 138. There were elements of the precious in the whole affair: at least one of those who voted against the motion in resentment against outside intrusion to expunge the record had taken part in the assault on the minute book. There was also a certain amount of undergraduate light-heartedness, including at least one stink bomb. It was hard not to laugh when a speaker portentously announced, "I am not Hitler", and tensions were diffused when the formal reading of a report announced that the Society's Library had purchased the autobiography of the heavyweight boxer Gene Tunney, *A Man Must Fight*.

Martin Ceadel concludes his charming and thoughtful study of the episode by chiding his readers for devoting so much of their time to such a trivial issue. This is a little harsh on the students of Oxford, whose frivolity of manner probably masked deeper seriousness of purpose. Yet this is not to claim that any special significance should be attributed to the King and Country debate. Winston Churchill claimed that as a result of this "ever-shameful resolution .... in Germany, in Russia, in Italy, in Japan, the idea of a decadent, degenerate Britain took deep root and swayed many calculations".[69] As its wording reveals, Churchill's interpretation was hardly impartial. Randolph's defiance of a hostile Union constituted a rare occasion on which this highly prodigal son actually gained his father's unqualified admiration. Even without the element of paternal loyalty, Winston Churchill had every reason to portray the nineteen-thirties as an epoch in which he had stood alone against a misguided and defeatist elite. A.J.P. Taylor, a historian prone to magnify the causal significance of bizarre snippets, firmly insisted that there is no documentary evidence that any foreign government took the debate seriously, although this view may owe something to his personal observation that the Oxford Union was "silly".[70] The most that can be said is that if the dictators did indeed base their bid for global domination on assumptions drawn from a debate at the Oxford Union, we need not be surprised at their failure.

The controversy over the King and Country debate was a tribute to the leading position that the Oxford Union had come to hold in the public imagination. The Cambridge Union had passed a similar motion by an almost identical vote in 1927 without causing a national uproar, although it rejected the notion of "peace at any price" in a much larger vote, 304 to 222, in 1928.[71] While a refusal to hang the Kaiser back in 1919 had generated "several letters from shocked correspondents",[72] by and large the British public had the sense to disregard the views of Cambridge undergraduates. The truth was that their opinion mirrored that of the wider community in its confusion. The Cambridge Union endorsed pacifist motions in 1936 and 1937, but also demanded armed intervention in the Spanish Civil War.[73] The Cambridge response to the outcry over the Oxford debate of 1933 was a move to debate a motion refusing to fight for King and Harper, whose garage premises inconveniently adjoined the Union building.[74]

The other society which has tended to overshadow the Cambridge Union is barely known in the wider world, but looms large in studies of British intellectual history.[75] Founded in 1820, the "Conversazione Society" quickly became known as "the Apostles". The nickname is usually assumed to refer to its limitation to twelve resident members, a number that in fact it did not always maintain, but it may contain an echo of its original dedication to evangelical Christianity. Its founder devoted his career to a campaign to establish an Anglican diocese in southern Europe, and his political skills and career focus were sufficient to get him installed as its first bishop. Later Apostles revered the memory of George Tomlinson, bishop of Gibraltar, but it is unlikely that they would have found him congenial company. Around 1824, under the influence of the more theologically questioning spirit of F.D. Maurice, the society changed in character, incidentally abandoning its original base in St John's to become associated with Trinity and, much later, with King's.

The Apostles met every Saturday night in members' college rooms, and attendance was obligatory. They consumed sardines on toast ("whales"), listened to a member reading a learned paper, and then took turns on the "hearthrug" – there had to be a hearthrug – to discuss what had been said, with the intention of evolving a proposition upon which all would vote. The Apostles developed anthropologically formidable rituals of collective identity. The external world was held not to exist, so that non-members could be dismissed as "phenomena". Members did not resign, but "took wings" (usually on leaving Cambridge) to become "angels". Potential recruits, referred to as "embryos", were carefully vetted by existing Apostles, but only learnt of the society's existence on being notified of their "birth". Apostles never discussed the society with outsiders, although an individual's membership could be inferred by the realisation of the fact that he was always unable to accept invitations on a Saturday night.[76] Secrecy gradually became an obsession, especially after 1855 when H.J. Roby (or, as he was known in Apostolic tradition, h.j.roby) responded to news of his birth with a refusal to waste his time on such activities.[77] At one level, "the Apostles were a typical undergraduate debating club and typically silly".[78] Thus James Clerk Maxwell announced that while logicians had identified seven syllogisms, "he had himself discovered 135". Unfortunately, "the great majority could not be expressed in human language, and even if expressed were not susceptible of any meaning".[79] A critic in 1864 acknowledged that a few able minds had passed through the ranks of the society, "but as regards national thought or progress, its annals might be cut out of the intellectual history of England without being missed".[80] It was certainly believed in Cambridge that the Apostles did not manufacture genius but rather were "very successful in catching celebrities",[81] taking care to hatch only those embryos who were already marked out for academic success.

Such criticisms miss the point that the Apostles operated at a level of seriousness far above that of the average student discussion group. Henry Sidgwick, one of its greatest figures, defined their essential creed as "a belief that we can learn, and a determination that we will learn, from people of the most opposite opinions".[82] There was a world of difference between this high-minded sentiment and the joviality of the debating club in Sidgwick's own college in the same decade, which resolved in 1866 "that any person who ventured singly to differ from the intellect of the Society did not deserve a fair hearing".[83] A few notable Apostles, such as Bertrand Russell and Leonard Woolf,[84] paid tribute to the role of the society in their education, and especially to the lack of restriction or inhibition in its discussions.

A paper delivered by G.E. Moore on sex in 1894 highlights both the strengths and weaknesses of the Apostles.[85] Moore argued that love must be mutual, a definition that ruled out sexual intercourse, since "one party is active, the other passive". Thus "for a man and woman who truly love one another copulation will be disagreeable, yet, they will share this as they share other trials and troubles". It was important that a husband should not become addicted to sex for its own sake, and commit "that monstrous unnatural vice of copulating with a woman more often than is necessary for begetting children". Moore's biographer suggests that all this may have been a tongue-in-cheek sending-up of Apostolic omniscience, although it is in line with Moore's general prurience. What is certain is, that for good or ill, Moore would not have got away with a such a discourse at the Union. (The Union did not bend the taboo banning the discussion of sex until the nineteen-twenties, turning its attention to birth control in 1924 and 1927. Even then – to quote Flanders and Swann – members invited two bishops to show them the way, but not even Their Graces of Exeter and Hereford could persuade the young men of Cambridge that sex ought to be confined to procreation.[86]) As Leslie Stephen had written of the Union, "there is nothing which the British youth detects so soon and despises so much as an affectation of premature wisdom".[87] Moore's paper may or may not have been wise, but it was certainly premature since it evidently reflected a total absence of any sexual experience.

Thus the implied comparison between the solemnity of the Apostles and the frivolity of the Union does not tell the whole story. The secrecy surrounding the Apostles, partly defensive but also quietly arrogant, added to their mystique, especially when coupled with their rumoured questioning of all established beliefs. The Apostles became associated with the breaking of two of the great taboos, homosexuality in the era of Lytton Strachey and treachery through the later membership of Guy Burgess and Anthony Blunt.

Of course, by no means every Apostle was so interesting or original as to be a homosexual or a Soviet spy, and many disappeared into modest careers after taking their wings. Although collectively they represent a convenient example of an intellectual elite worthy of study,[88] the Apostles were neither exclusively nor comprehensively representative of the greatest brains that passed through Cambridge. Alfred Lyttelton, who was elected in 1878, was already recognised as England's greatest all-round amateur sportsman, but nobody ever saw him as a penetrating contributor to Apostolic debate. As a contemporary tactfully put it, Lyttelton "did not allow the influence of these discussions to tell permanently upon his mind".[89]

On the other hand, the Apostles almost certainly vetted and rejected Monty Rhodes James, perhaps the most erudite undergraduate of all time, who was a member of an Apostolic feeder organisation, the Chitchat Club at King's.[90] They also passed over Leslie Stephen, who had hoped to follow his brother, Fitzjames, into their ranks. Most striking of all, the omission of Macaulay, a great mind and still more sparkling conversationalist, was so inexplicable that one chronicler assumed that the Conversazione Society could not have been formed until after he had left Cambridge.[91] Above all, recruitment was heavily biased towards the larger and more fashionable colleges. Although it was an article of faith among the Apostles that they were unconfined by space and time, their information network did not manage to leap the few hundred yards required to locate the interesting mind of Charles Kingsley at Magdalene or the penetrating intellect of Jan Christiaan Smuts in Christ's.

By arrogating to themselves the status of a closed elite, the Apostles scored in prestige over the Union, even if the latter gave opportunities to others to claim, and sometimes to prove, a measure of intellectual ability and verbal cogency. Leslie Stephen found it a salve for the disappointment at his exclusion from their ranks. "My own intellectual ambition was satisfied by an effort or two [in fact, nine] before the more popular audience of the Union."[92] Both societies were capable of being "typically silly", but the Apostles had the advantage of meeting behind closed doors. Thus A.H. Hughes-Gibb, a typical Union President of the Edwardian years, could be cheerfully cut down to size by the *Granta* under the nickname of Huge-Gibe, but the "chaff" with which William Vernon Harcourt confounded James Fitzjames Stephen was recalled as the giant combat of Apostolic genius.[93] The Apostles, too, manipulated another advantage over the Union. Some, at least, of the "angels" remained active as well-wishers to the younger men, taking an interest (for whatever motive) in newly hatched embryos and providing a network of contacts that could help launch a promising career in Bloomsbury. The supporting role of its "angels" probably explains why the Apostles, alone among Cambridge student clubs, managed to endure without the institutional underpinning of its own premises. By contrast, lacking any such support network of former Presidents, the Union was seen as the culmination of adolescence, whereas membership of the Apostles was the first step in adult life. This can be seen in some biographies, especially those written by pious relatives anxious to deny that the revered subject ever engaged in childish amusements. Henry Sidgwick's family devoted several pages to his role as the Apostles' unofficial "Pope", but just an aside to his Presidency of the Union.[94] Richard Chenevix Trench's grieving family went a step further, insisting that Carlyle's statement that Trench had been a member of "a Debating Society called the Union" was "apparently a mistake" for the Apostles.[95]

If the Apostles can be stripped of some of their mystique, and the Union forgiven some of its occasional frivolity, the two societies may be seen at least in parallel, in an overlapping and sometimes even symbiotic relationship. The Union had grown out of the Speculative, an essay-reading club that had met in its members' rooms, mainly in St John's and Trinity. If not an outright revival, the Apostles were at least occupying well-established but temporarily vacant ground. Individual Apostles were also often active in the Union. By August 1914, the Apostles had elected 224 members in numbered sequence. Of these, 41 rose to the Presidency and a further twelve held other Union offices.[96] If the Cambridge Apostles merit collective study as an intellectual elite, it is worth noting that almost one quarter of them were officers of the Union – and others can be traced in the records of debate. The relationship waxed and waned throughout the nineteenth century. The crucial transition of the Conversazione Society to intellectual openness between 1823 and 1826 was associated with an influx of prominent Union personalities. The link was broken for a time after 1830 when influential Apostles seceded in protest against the Union's defiance of the ban on discussing contemporary politics. Although young Henry Hallam was "made for a debater .... his co-apostles threw cold water on his taste"[97] and discouraged him from speaking in the Union. There followed a remarkable period of convergence: between Apostle number 126, elected in 1851, and Apostle number 157, elected in 1863, there were thirteen Presidents of the Union, seven of them commemorated in the *Dictionary of National Biography*. Thereafter, the relationship was steady rather than intense, although a number of the more distinguished Cambridge names of the next quarter-century appear on both lists. During the two decades after the election in 1891 of the Ulsterman,

Malcolm MacNaghten, already an ex-President, only two Apostles became Presidents of the Union, although one of those was J.M. Keynes. As the undergraduate population increased, so Union debates increasingly came to resemble mass meetings, while by contrast the Apostles abandoned their earlier reluctance to elect shy individuals. Thus the culture of the two organisations moved in different directions. This divergence makes even more striking the fact that during the sixty-five years between 1825 and 1890, roughly one President of the Union in every five was an Apostle. It is surely this inter-relationship, rather than the list of Union veterans who became MPs, which was a matter of congratulation to both societies.

It is not necessary to believe that the Oxford Union launched Gladstone and encouraged Hitler. Nor is it essential to envisage the meetings of the Cambridge Apostles as youthful genius in combat with eternal mysteries. Above all, it is not for their wisdom and foresight that the debates of the Cambridge Union merit attention. We shall look in vain for great insights from young men on the verge of adulthood and boys emerging from adolescence as they flash the plumage of their derivative prejudices. Yet a case can be made that their debates can tell us something about levels of interest and divisions of opinion on the issues of the time, not just among the young men of Cambridge but more widely in what most people call "the real world". The Apostles, of course, denied that any such thing existed. In this, they merely took to extremes an attitude of unworldliness that surrounded them. To appreciate the significance of debates at the Union, we must begin by exploring that strange and remote planet, the University of Cambridge.

2:   The Town and the University

The great achievement of the University of Cambridge between 1815 and 1914 was that it managed to reform itself, in many respects fundamentally and in almost all, unwillingly, while conveying the impression through its buildings and its rituals that it was both unchanging and timeless.[1] Since in extreme manifestations, the University came close to being a spiritual concept, it is best to start with its physical location of the East Anglian market town of Cambridge. "Imagine the most irregular town that *can* be imagined, streets of the very crookedest kind, twisting about like those in a nightmare, and not infrequently bringing you back to the same point you started from," wrote Charles Bristed, an American student of the eighteen-forties. "Among these narrow, ugly, and dirty streets, are tumbled in ... as if it were at random ... some of the most beautiful academical buildings in the world."[2] For much of the nineteenth century, the town of Cambridge barely exceeded its medieval limits, roughly the core area of the colleges today. The modern inner suburb of Chesterton was described in 1827 as a "beautiful romantic village about two miles from Cambridge". (Indeed, the villagers of Chesterton were still celebrating May Day according to the old calendar a century after it had been reformed in 1752.) When the concept of "resident member" was introduced to the governance of the University in 1856, the category was defined as those living within a mile and a half of Great St Mary's church. In the eighteen-seventies, the first college for women located itself at Girton in the confident belief that a distance of two miles from the town would secure it in a permanent state of purdah. Although the population of Cambridge, 11,000 in 1811, had doubled by 1831 and would double again by the twentieth century, there was always an undercurrent of academic opinion that assumed that the town existed solely to service the University. In 1902, the Union debated a motion that "the University of Cambridge exercises a detrimental influence on the Town". Predictably it rejected the charge, although by just two votes – but only 56 members bothered to take part. "The town, of course, did not count at all."[3]

The urban environment of Cambridge contributed little that was conducive to a scholarly lifestyle. In 1826, "a few superior house fronts" in the centre of the town projected "a certain air of dilapidated dignity", but overall the streetscape was "mean", a reflection of the lack of "good building materials" in the locality. As the century progressed, the principal streets were rebuilt in mass-produced, railway-hauled brick and the town came to value its appearance: "not even Solomon in all his glory is arrayed like the window-boxes in Trinity Street", wrote an observer in May 1895. But if the architecture improved, nothing could be done about the climate. "It can certainly rain at Cambridge", grumbled Thackeray in 1829. Everywhere in the town there was water, water running in ditches, water stagnant in open drains, water in droplets in the damp unhealthy air. Generations of students laughed at the joke about the undergraduate who was pulled from a gutter and then appealed for help in rescuing the man beneath him.[4] Students were even drowned, especially in the days before street-lighting: in 1818 a young Scots aristocrat actually died of exposure after falling drunk into a ditch on Parker's Piece. Nor was sluggish drainage a mere physical hazard. Within a month of the founding of the Union in 1815, Cambridge was swept "by a fever of some kind", probably typhoid, and the University actually closed down for a term. At first, William Whewell at Trinity was not particularly bothered, reporting that there were "several men ill, but not one of my acquaintance; and besides, the disorder appears to be local, and has been confined to one or two of the smaller colleges". Jesus College was suffering because of "the stagnant and putrid waters in its neighbours", but Jesus was a quarter of a mile away and "not one man in Trinity or St John's" had fallen sick.[5] His tone changed when the disease struck on his own staircase. The 1815 epidemic was not the last public health threat to Cambridge. In 1832, a Union business meeting resolved to contribute twenty guineas to the local Board of Health "in the event of the cholera morbus reaching the town".[6] Even the country's intellectual elite was slow to grasp the notion of prevention as the key to public health.

Of course, no contemporary British town was a sanitary paradise. The most that can be said is that they were probably more salubrious than their continental equivalents. A French Countess visiting Trinity in 1832 expressed surprise at the absence of people relieving themselves in the corners of the Great Court.[7] Yet local customs were not much of an improvement. As late as the eighteen-nineties, a rectangular patch of grass in Trinity's Whewell's Court was known as "the billiard table" on account of six strategically placed pockets of shingle "for emptying pails" (and, no doubt, chamber pots).[8] In a mock election campaign in 1892, Erskine Childers promised "a measure for the better housing of the denser population of Whewell's Court" where about one hundred undergraduates were crammed into a narrow plot of land.[9] And Whewell's Court was no medieval slum, but the personal project of, and ultimately memorial to, the poor boy from Lancaster who rose via the Presidency of the Union to become a terrifying Master of his college.

Accustomed to fast-flowing Pennine streams, Whewell was struck when he arrived in Cambridge in 1812 by "the narrow dirty Cam".[10] Southey had been even more explicit a few years earlier. "The Cam, a lazy stream, winds behind the town and through the college walks, collecting filth as it goes."[11] It was unfair to attribute moral shortcomings to the Cam. The problem was the mismatch between a small river and a large, low-lying drainage basin. Cambridge, thirty miles from tidal water, is barely thirty feet above sea level. By contrast, Oxford, at twice the distance, is six times higher and cleansed by the longest river in England. Many Oxford-based companies and utilities use "Thames Valley" in their titles, but hardly anyone would call the saucer-shaped country to the south of Cambridge a "valley", let alone apply the word to the flat Fens to the north. In the eighteenth century, Oxford had given its river the poetic name of "Isis", but it was not until the end of the nineteenth that Cambridge began grudgingly to borrow the by-name of the Cam's headwaters, the Granta. To cap it all, the slow-moving Cam was more likely to freeze in winter than the free-flowing Thames, preventing vitally-needed coal from reaching both town and gown. The last such crisis actually occurred early in 1845, a few months before the arrival of the railway.

As the nineteenth century progressed, the state of the Cam steadily worsened. One reason lay downstream in the Fens. An unexpected by-product of the large-scale drainage projects from the seventeenth century was the shrinkage of the peaty soils, followed by renewed flooding. By 1830, the solution had been found in the installation of steam-engines capable of pumping the water into the rivers and drainage canals that ran into them. For the people of the Fens, this was a brilliant solution, celebrated in verse on the engine house at Pymore:

> These *Fens* have oft times been by *Water* drown'd,
> Science a remedy in *Water* found.
> The power of *Steam* she said shall be employ'd
> The *Destroyer* by *itself* destroy'd.

Hence the Cam was "a sleepy river" as it flowed through Cambridge "on its way to wriggle through the broad level of the Fens".[12] The Cam is only twelve feet above sea level at Waterbeach, five miles north of Cambridge. The more effectively its lower reaches were employed to drain the Fens, the less capacity it could provide upstream.

The problem was worsened by the insanitary irresponsibility of the growing local population who used the river as "a charnel-house for the carcasses of almost all the dead dogs, cats, sheep, and pigs that have died in Cambridge during the year".[13] Everyone agreed that the state of the river was a scandal. The largest-ever expression of unanimity in a Union debate occurred in 1887, when all 171 members present agreed that the Cam was "a disgrace to the authorities and a serious danger to the health of the community".[14] Above all, it is a tribute either to the propriety or the hardiness of the Victorians that so few of them mentioned the fact that the river stank of sewage.[15] Indeed, it continued to do so until the middle of the eighteen-nineties, when an expensive main drainage scheme at first did little more than redistribute the smell.[16] Given the state of the Cam, the popularity of rowing in nineteenth-century Cambridge becomes all the harder to understand. Organised boat racing began near Midsummer Common, below the town sluice which presumably filtered some of the filth, although races later moved further downriver. The late-Victorian enthusiasm for male nude bathing located itself discreetly upriver, although not necessarily upwind, from the town. Punting through the colleges was virtually unknown before the installation of the sewerage scheme, even though it had long been popular on the Thames. If, for much of the nineteenth century, Cambridge University strikes us as intellectually stagnant, it must be remembered that even its location was a backwater.

The draining of the Fens had created a vast geometrical landscape, prompting one Cambridge don to wonder whether it was "fancy ... that sees in the scenery of Cambridgeshire something of affinity to the studies of mathematics and astronomy in which the University has conquered such wide fields?"[17] Tennyson drew a less flattering connection, likening the "uninteresting" curriculum to the "disgustingly level" countryside.[18] Few praised the Cambridgeshire landscape. Thackeray thought it "ugly in the extreme", while to James Stephen, Professor of Modern History, it was "a prodigy of ugliness, to which nature and art have each contributed their share".[19] The poet John Moultrie called nearby Madingley, "sole village from the plague / of ugliness, in that drear land exempt".[20] Madingley probably escaped censure because it is located on rising ground. The term is carefully chosen for, as Leslie Stephen put it, "what is facetiously called a hill in these parts" was no more than a "barely perceptible swelling in the ground which serves as a pedestal for a windmill".[21] Perhaps the one redeeming feature of the Cambridge area was the glorious sunsets, especially after a shower of rain. Whewell described one in October 1849, the year that Professor Stephen was tramping the "unpleasant roads" planning his course of lectures: the "gloomy drizzle" gave place to "the most brilliant blue, wet sky that you can conceive, with tawny gold-edged clouds, looking as if they had been combed out of the wet rain-clouds".[22] But Cambridgeshire owed its wonderful sunsets to the inconvenient fact that its dull, flat landscape left room for plenty of sky.

Although a massive over-simplification, it is helpful to think of the University as a federation of colleges. In 1815, there were sixteen of them, all bearing the heavy imprint of the distant past. Every college required its Fellows to be celibate (or, at least, unmarried), despite the fact that the rest of the Anglican world had come to terms with clerical wedlock 250 years earlier. The denunciation of celibacy in 1766 as "a Remnant of Popery: a Doctrine fit only to be taught & maintained in the court of the Whore of Babylon" (as the Pope was unflatteringly called) had been insufficient to bring about change.[23] The sexual imperative did have the advantage of ensuring a steady turnover among younger Fellows, many of whom left as soon as they could obtain a "college living" (a patronage appointment to a rural rectory). The preparation of the young clerical academic for pastoral work was not ideal. "After a few years spent in lecturing, he could become a country parson and try how far his knowledge of the Greek drama or the planetary theory would qualify him to edify the agricultural labourer."[24] The other side of the coin was that effective power remained concentrated in the conservative hands of long-term bachelors. Significantly, when the ban on married Fellows finally disappeared in 1882, "you could not say that there was a general rush to the altar".[25]

A seventeenth college, Downing, had been chartered in 1800, after a lawsuit aimed at blocking its founder's bequest that had dragged on for half a century.[26] The establishment of the first college for over two centuries offered the opportunity for some cautious educational experiments, such as fellowships devoted to law and medicine, free from the requirement of ordination in the Church of England. Lacking both prestige and cash, Downing did not admit students until 1820, and found them difficult to attract. Bulwer Lytton, who certainly did not live frugally at Trinity Hall, remembered the early Downing undergraduates for their extravagance.[27] This quality was shown by one of the first intake, Charles de Thierry, who "bought" the North Island of New Zealand from two visiting Maori chiefs. Even more remarkably, he attempted, unsuccessfully of course, to take possession of his fiefdom and ended his days as a music teacher in Auckland.[28]

It is probably no accident that Downing was the last fully-fledged college to be added to the University for a century and a half, and that no serious attempt was made to establish new foundations of any kind for three-quarters of a century. Invited in 1843 to comment on a plan to establish a cut-price institution to train missionaries for the colonies, Whewell probably had Downing in mind when he warned of "the very serious expense of erecting a new college ... the formidable charges of purchase money of the ground" not to mention "building chapel, hall, and lodging-rooms" (the order is revealing) and paying salaries to teachers and administrators.[29] Significantly, the mid-twentieth-century expansion of colleges – the twelve years from 1954 saw the biggest wave of new foundations at Cambridge since the decade of the Black Death – came at a time when the main burden of the academic payroll had been transferred to the University itself. The sluggish development (if not virtual failure) of Downing ensured not simply that the question of reform in Cambridge would remain largely in the hands of the colleges, but in the hands of colleges that were themselves mired in conservatism.

Exasperated reformers were sometimes driven to conclude that "Henry VIII would have done a service to education if he had swept the colleges away with the monasteries".[30] Yet only once did the Union make the effort to contemplate the notion of the University without colleges, in 1900 when it rejected by 88 votes to 16 the motion that "in the constitution of an ideal University, Colleges should have no place".[31] Even then, the topic was probably chosen to accommodate a visiting debating team from Edinburgh, where a collegiate system had never been seriously attempted. The *Student's Guide to the University of Cambridge* (written for students, not by them) did not bother to describe how the University worked, since the subject was "difficult to understand" and "of no practical importance to the student".[32] An undergraduate of 1902 recalled that he "was barely conscious of the existence of a Vice-Chancellor".[33] For the ordinary undergraduate, it was his college that dominated daily life and academic studies.

The *Student's Guide* divided the colleges into two categories, the two giants and the rest. In 1866, the two largest colleges, Trinity and St John's, contained about eight hundred students, while "taken together" the other fifteen collectively accounted for the rest, about one thousand.[34] College rivalries were already ferocious in the early nineteenth century – Caius, for instance, was dismissed by a Johnian ecclesiastic as "always a conceited and seldom a successful society" – and were reinforced by the culture of mindless institutional patriotism that transferred itself to Cambridge from the reinvigorated mid-Victorian public schools. F.M. Cornford in 1908 sardonically regarded "College Feeling" as the key element that distinguished Cambridge from a series of boarding houses, "for in a boarding-house hatred is concentrated, not upon rival establishments, but upon the other members of the same establishment".[35] In contrast to more recent times, it was possible for undergraduates to move from one college to another, in pursuit either of better opportunities or lower standards. There was a well-trodden path from St John's to tiny Sidney Sussex (described in mid-century as "almost a colony of second-rate Johnians"),[36] while a Master of Trinity dismissed Magdalene (the only college located beyond the town's principal bridge) as a "transpontine Institution for fallen undergraduates".[37] Yet it is a measure of academic insularity that in a century which saw the mass outpouring of people to found whole new nations overseas, the technical Cambridge term for movement between colleges was "migration".

In the early decades of the nineteenth century, inter-collegiate hostility was particularly directed against St John's, which had been dominant until about 1800. "Johnians" were nicknamed "pigs", for no obvious reason. In an orgy of unfunny humour, their college was known as the "Piggery", a dull Johnian could expect to be punningly dismissed as a "boar", and members of the college asked whether they had tried to make their ears into silk purses. When part of St John's was painted a garish red, wags dubbed the colour a pigment.[38] Mercifully, St John's gradually ceased to be such a focus for jealous wit. In 1847 the college lost prestige by unsuccessfully opposing the candidature of the Prince Consort in the only contested election in modern times for the honorary post of Chancellor. Student numbers began to fall, a trend which a caustic Trinity aristocrat attributed to the fact that the lower classes had decided to emigrate to Australia instead. In the later part of the nineteenth century, St John's was hit especially hard by falling income during the agricultural depression, and other colleges drew level.[39]

The eclipse of St John's left Trinity as the pre-eminent college. In 1899, the Union even debated a motion declaring that "the excessive size of Trinity College is disastrous to itself and prejudicial to the best interests of the University",[40] but the claim was brushed aside by a flood of Trinity oratory, backed no doubt by a Trinity block vote. There were times in the nineteenth century when Trinity behaved more like a university within a university: in the eighteen-forties, Trinity had more students than Yale.[41] By and large, the University as a whole benefited from Trinity's independence and initiative. A reforming Fellow of Christ's declared in 1850 that Cambridge owed a debt to its largest college for "keeping alive the flame of scholarship in the University".[42]

It was not that Trinity was invariably a hotbed of radicalism. In early life, William Whewell was a fervent reformer, and once even took sardonic pleasure at the sight of a short-sighted senior fellow "trying to open a door on the side where the hinges were".[43] As so often happens in the human lifespan, Whewell eventually reached a point where he had reformed if not the universe then at least the University to his own satisfaction, and he denounced his own juniors as "a set of school-boys" when they sought to go further.[44] His successor as Master invoked sarcasm to crush dissent: "we are none of us infallible, not even the youngest".[45] As an undergraduate, Bertrand Russell regarded H.M. Butler and the two most senior Fellows of Trinity "merely as figures as fun", but after securing his own fellowship, he came to regard them as "serious forces for evil".[46] However, by virtue of its size, Trinity was almost the only college in Cambridge to contain enough reform-minded spirits not to be cowed and marginalised, as undoubtedly happened in the smaller societies. Two Fellows of Trinity were particularly important in bringing about the major reforms of the eighteen-sixties. Henry Sidgwick is celebrated in English intellectual history for courageously resigning his Fellowship in 1869 on grounds of religious doubt. Less well known is Coutts Trotter, who operated chiefly and very skilfully in the field of college politics. Like William Whewell in an earlier generation, both had been President of the Union.

It helped that Trinity was wealthy enough to back new initiatives. The first serious scheme to tax the colleges for the benefit of the University, drawn up in 1880, proposed that Trinity should contribute £229 out of every £1000 raised – more than 32 times the amount required from impoverished Magdalene. As early as 1868, the college of Isaac Newton reserved a fellowship for the teaching of the Cinderella subject of Natural Science. (Half a century later, one of the senior fellows regarded as evil by Bertrand Russell continued to express his resentment at the innovation by referring to scientists as "naturals", the Shakespearian word for a fool.[47]) Wealth went hand-in-hand with self-confidence: from 1836 Trinity insisted that candidates for admission actually pass an entrance examination. Not surprisingly, members of Trinity thought themselves a cut above the rest of the University. Henry Campbell-Bannerman gave ironic expression to this sentiment shortly before his death in 1908:

> When he and his Trinity friends walked about Cambridge, they were of course aware that there were other oldish buildings somewhat resembling their own and saw other men walking about clad in garments of a similar description, but as to who they were and what were their occupations and who tenanted those other buildings they were quite indifferent and had no desire to know.[48]

An undergraduate satire of 1914 imagined the President of the Union, Gordon Butler, describing his Committee as "good fellows in their way, but not Trinity men". His father, H.M. Butler, was suspected of believing that God was a former student of the college.[49]

Social relations were broader but probably less intense in the two largest colleges. "On the one hand, they bring a much larger number of men together; on the other hand, they do not bring them so close together."[50] Arthur Benson, a former Eton schoolmaster, thought they had "no real college spirit", because "the different schools which supply a big college form each its own set there". An undergraduate from a major public school "falls into his respective set, lives under the traditions and in the gossip of his old school, and gets to know hardly any one from other schools". The rest were excluded "and really get very little good out of the place".[51] For some, like Arthur Balfour, Trinity was large enough to absorb their social energies and ambitions, but others used the college as a springboard to achieve prominence in the University at large. F.W. Lawrence recalled that when he stood for office in the Union, he benefited from both college and old school support: "I probably got the votes of most of the Trinity men and also those of old Etonians from all over the University."[52] He later married the suffragette Emmeline Pethick, hyphenated her surname with his own and moved to the Left, despite the fact that he had opposed socialism in Union debates. An idealist, he was something of an exotic figure in the Labour Party, but evidently he had nothing to learn about the politics of the block vote.

One reminiscence of late-Victorian Cambridge reckoned that few undergraduates "were *habitués* of more than three or four colleges at most" and that some "had never entered half the colleges".[53] The Union acted as an important solvent, as Lord Powys, told its members in 1866: "it serves to keep alive the great catholic idea of a University amidst the independence and isolation of the several colleges". With a nod to the recently terminated American Civil War, he added that "it prevents your states rights making you unmindful of your federal obligations".[54] College micro-cultures dictated different intensities of relationship with the Union. Trinity was large enough both to dominate for long periods and to sustain an internal life of its own: H.M. Butler hoped to make its own debating society, the Magpie and Stump, into a serious-minded counterweight if not an outright alternative to the Union.[55] The fact that it was a Master of St John's who had been the Vice-Chancellor who tried to close down the Union in 1817 probably coloured the relationship until Wood's death in 1839. In that period, only four Johnians were elected to the Presidency, as against 22 from Trinity. Nine other Johnians held the lesser offices of Secretary or Treasurer without proceeding to the chair, which suggests that they may have been warned off taking too prominent a role. Later, however, it was St John's that in 1864 sold the Union the site for its permanent home in Round Church Street. In the eighteen-eighties, W.E. Heitland, as a tutor at St John's, allowed Alfred Mond to give time to Union debates that he should have devoted to his studies.[56] Mond's Cambridge enthusiasm for Irish Home Rule transferred to a more general sympathy for small nations: when he became MP for Swansea in 1910, opponents mocked both his opinions and his German accent by attributing to him the slogan "Vales for the Velsh". Unfortunately, his investment of time in debates was at the cost of academic achievement: the future founder of ICI failed the Natural Sciences Tripos and had to retreat to Edinburgh to learn his chemistry. By the eighteen-nineties, St John's was said to be "'running' the Union".[57]

In the smaller colleges, personal influence could be even stronger. John Perkins, tutor at Downing, was an enthusiast for the Union. During his twenty-five years in office, this struggling college produced no fewer than eight Presidents of the Union. The Downing dynasty came to an end in 1887 when Perkins took charge of the college's finances and switched his energies to discouraging tenants on its farms from shooting foxes.[58] The reverse process seems to have been at work in Magdalene, which produced five Presidents between 1829 and 1853, but no more until the future archbishop, Michael Ramsey, in 1926. The gap largely coincides with the reign of the Honourable and Reverend Latimer Neville who, as a recent historian has unkindly remarked, "slumbered" in the Master's Lodge for half a century after Magdalene's hereditary Visitor, who happened to be his father, had discerned academic qualities undetected by the Tripos examiners and appointed him to head the college in 1853.[59] Peer pressure might also be a factor in a small college. As a freshman at King's, Oscar Browning "was solemnly warned that if I continued to speak at the Union I should be sent to Coventry. I did continue to speak, and the penalty was inflicted".[60] While in later life Browning became an unctuous and unappetising character, there is no reason to think that his ostracism was the product of personal unpopularity, since he not only became President of the Union but was also elected to the select society of the Apostles. King's in 1856, still virtually a preserve of Eton and smarting under imposed reforms, was probably a special case in its hostility to the outside world. In mid-century Christ's, it was unusual to join the Union. Trinity Hall, although one of the smallest colleges, produced a steady trickle of Presidents, probably because of its tradition of training lawyers. Elsewhere, the dynamics of the relationship with the Union are probably impossible to discover. Pembroke produced its first President in 1824, its second more than seventy years later and then five more by 1914. It would be an over-simplification to claim that students who could afford the subscription became members of the Union and those who could not did not join. College culture played a role as well.

Just as the physical location of Cambridge as a dank country town helped to shape a conservative academic community, so the physical dominance of the colleges made it difficult to locate the University as an institution. With the exception of its handsome Senate House, the University in 1815 was almost as invisible a presence as the Holy Spirit that it was intended to serve. In many respects, the Senate House was an improbable symbol of an English and a Protestant university, not least in having been designed on the model of a pagan temple by James Gibbs, who was both a Scotsman and a Catholic. It was in any case used principally for the transaction of formal business and the conduct of examinations. It was inconvenient for the latter purpose, not least because for much of the nineteenth century, major examinations were held in the middle of winter: "as temples had no chimneys, and as a stove or fire of any kind might disfigure the building, we are obliged to take the weather as it happens to be," Whewell complained after spending a frozen ten-hour day as an examiner in 1820.[61]

The University also occupied an adjoining huddle of medieval buildings, the Old Schools. These were inadequate for the housing of any kind of secretariat, even after the acquisition of adjoining and equally ancient buildings from King's in 1829, although this purchase made possible the construction of a separate University Library building a decade later. In 1899, a senior official sought to add administrative offices to the University's want list since "we practically have none at present".[62] Hence the frequently invoked metaphor of Cambridge as a federation, which enabled Bristed to explain to his American readers in 1852 that the relationship between the University and the Colleges resembled that of "our Federal Government in relation to the separate States".[63] Indeed, when in 1836 Britain's first explicitly federal university was created by the shot-gun merger of two colleges in London, one Utilitarian and the other Anglican, the resulting University of London was explicitly described as "a Board of Examiners ... to perform all the functions of the Examiners in the Senate House in Cambridge".[64] London University's principal office block is called the Senate House to this day.

Leslie Stephen pushed the metaphor too far when he claimed that in the first half of the nineteenth century, Oxford and Cambridge were "not universities at all but federated groups of colleges".[65] As in the United States, the central government had the long-term potential to outstrip the component parts. While in comparison with the colleges, the University might have seemed physically insignificant in the early nineteenth century, its responsibilities were by no means unimportant. Most notably it was the University that conferred degrees and operated the examinations that led to them. Moreover, the apparent dominance of the colleges in 1815 was a by-product of a very narrow degree curriculum confined to classics and mathematics. Two fixed disciplines based upon a handful of set texts could be taught by small numbers of college Fellows recycling what they had ingested themselves perhaps decades earlier. College teaching had its limitations, and undergraduates ambitious of graduating with high honours regularly went outside to seek out specialist coaches. (This process, which added greatly to the cost of a Cambridge education, was regarded by reformers as a blot on the University. Ironically, it also assisted impecunious but able students to qualify for a degree and then pay off their debts from the fees gained by teaching their successors.) In short, even under the old curriculum, the dominance of the colleges was not as secure as it sometimes seemed. As reform slowly made headway in the second half of the nineteenth century, a broader range of degree subjects strengthened the hand of the University as individual colleges found it impossible to keep up with the provision of new teaching.

The most notable example was the rise of science. In the first half of the nineteenth century, "night descended on science study at Cambridge"[66] and the dawn came but slowly. A Natural Sciences Tripos was established in 1851, but at first it was only open to those who had already graduated, that is to those who had won their spurs in mathematics and classics. Consequently, in its early years there were usually more examiners than candidates. Natural Sciences became a fully independent degree subject in 1861, when just three students proceeded to the BA Honours; the numbers had risen to 194 by 1910.[67] No university is on oath when fund-raising, and the claim made in 1899 that half the published scientific research in the United Kingdom owed its origins, directly or indirectly, to Cambridge must be regarded as indicative rather than precisely accurate.[68] Not only did the University support science, its great success story of the late nineteenth-century, but science in return strengthened the position of the University against the colleges. Most of them could not afford to provide expensive laboratories and experimental equipment: tiny Sidney Sussex heroically tried, but even mighty Trinity abandoned the attempt.[69] In large measure, science teaching had to be a University and not a college activity, with the necessary funding either pooled or begged from outside. As the first public appeal for cash put it in 1899, "it is to the University, and the University alone, as distinguished from the Colleges of Cambridge, that we must look for expansion and effort in this direction".[70]

To a remarkable extent, until the very beginning of the twentieth century, the physical planning of Cambridge University remained dominated by medieval piety. Five of the older colleges had inherited monastic buildings or their ruined sites, while the Augustinian Friary in Benet Street eventually became the University's Botanic Garden. The gardens were relocated to a site on the southern outskirts between 1844 and 1852, and the Austin Friars site became the New Museums, an unplanned jumble of laboratories and science departments. By 1900, several quarts of unattractive construction had been squeezed into this pint-pot site. Luckily, it was the slow development of Downing – for in Cambridge, a hundred years was but a day – that proved fortuitous both for Cambridge science and for the physical manifestation of the University. A century after its foundation, the college was still only "an unfortunate torso"[71] within its magnificent precinct. In 1902, the University bought an adjoining block of land from Downing in order to extend the facilities of the New Museums site. Thus Cambridge was able to avoid the physical separation of old and new studies that was to occur in Edinburgh, where lack of space in the central area forced the development of a distinct suburban campus for its Science Faculty. None the less, Cambridge quickly faced the challenge of two cultures, at least in University politics. In Cornford's typology of academic parties, the scientists were the Adullamites, cave-dwelling conspirators, "not refined, like classical men" but "dangerous, because they know what they want; and that is, all the money there is going".[72] If the most obvious physical manifestation of the University in 1815 had been the ceremonial Senate House, by 1914 it was the science precinct of the New Museums and its growing overspill, the Downing site.

The other potential weapon in the University's locker was its professorships. In 1815, Cambridge already possessed Chairs in subjects that could not be easily integrated into a curriculum dominated by classics and mathematics. During the first half of the nineteenth century, most of them made little impact: "if all the professorships had been abolished, no difference would have been perceived by the ordinary student".[73] Index references in Winstanley's *Early Victorian Cambridge* summarise the problem: "Professors, neglect of duty by... decline in attendance at their lectures .... insufficiency of their stipends ... absenteeism of ...". An extreme example in 1815 was Richard Watson, Professor of Divinity, who solved the competing claims of his Cambridge Chair and his Welsh bishopric by residing in the "delightful country" of the Lake District. The "Right Reverend time server" admitted that he had been absent from Cambridge "above twenty years" but defended himself by claiming that he had "set a spirited example of husbandry" by planting larch trees on the slopes of Windermere, an activity not normally associated with the study of theology. Watson also insisted that he had "honourably provided" for his family. The adverb may be queried, since his "intention of retiring, in great measure, from public life", upon which he had resolved in 1789, had not been accompanied by resignation from either his bishopric or his Chair. We may perhaps feel some sympathy in regard to the former, since Llandaff was a notoriously poor diocese: an earlier Cambridge don, on being exiled there, had sardonically referred to himself as the Bishop of Aff, because the land had all gone. The richly endowed Regius Chair of Divinity, on the other hand, was capable of financing whole forests of larch trees.[74]

With an absentee pluralist such as Watson as the benchmark, Cambridge professorships could only become more effective as the nineteenth century progressed. William Smyth delivered identical lectures in the Chair of History for three decades until he finally published them in 1840 and retreated into silence. His account of the French Revolution "always drew an audience, because it was known from previous experience that in the course of it he would burst into tears upon mentioning the melancholy fate of Marie Antoinette".[75] His successor, James Stephen, supplied competent scholarship, in the face of some narrow controversy over the orthodoxy of his religious beliefs. In the eighteen-sixties, Charles Kingsley tried with surprising success to make the Chair of Modern History into a springboard for moral education:

> again and again, as the audience dispersed, a hearer has said, "Kingsley is right – I'll turn over a new leaf, so help me God." And many a lad did it too.[76]

His successor, J.R. Seeley, apologised for "a somewhat exaggerated view" of his role, but aimed to oust the Union from control of political education in the University.[77] Undoubtedly there remained some professors who did not give Cambridge their undivided time: C.V. Stanford, appointed to the Chair of Music in 1887, spent much of his time at the Royal College in London and in later years was unkindly said to have delivered his Cambridge lectures at the railway station.[78] Stanford claimed that it was an unavoidable absence from Cambridge that compelled him in 1887 to launch a fiery attack on the officers of the Union for alleged partiality to the cause of Irish Home Rule. Arthur Quiller-Couch, Professor of English Literature from 1912, simultaneously held office as mayor of the Cornish town of Fowey. Yet even if half-timers, these dynamic personalities were not absentees, and they can be counterbalanced by the physicists, Clerk Maxwell, Lord Rayleigh and J.J. Thomson, who made the Cavendish Laboratories into an international centre for scientific research.

In institutional terms, the importance of the University, in comparison with the colleges, grew throughout the nineteenth century. Consequently, it is important to be more specific in identifying exactly who is meant in allusions to "the University". The term may variously refer to the executive officers who spoke on its behalf, to the senior members who embodied its collective values and with glacial slowness shaped its response to new challenges, to the shifting and endlessly renewing population of junior members, ranging from the serious to the raucous, and to various combinations of all three.

At the head of the University's institutional structure was the Chancellor, the one official who was expected to be an absentee and encouraged to be a cipher. The role of the Chancellor was to protect the University's interests in high places and radiate slightly distant aristocratic lustre upon its activities. In 1815 the post was held by William Frederick, Duke of Gloucester, whose popularity rested mainly upon the fact that he was George III's nephew rather than one of the king's unsavoury sons. Although the University had bestowed a Doctorate of Laws upon him when he was just twenty years of age, the *Dictionary of National Biography* is more realistic in its tactful observation that the Duke's "intellectual powers were by no means of a high order". Indeed, given the shuddering memories in Cambridge of the hyperactive political control exercised by one of his eighteenth-century predecessors, the Duke of Newcastle, a ruthless Whig party boss, it is likely that "Silly Billy's" limited attainments were seen as an asset. However, even if he did not get in the way, the Duke was not much use in a crisis. In 1834, when Dissenters petitioned the House of Lords for the right to take Cambridge degrees, its Chancellor "did a wise thing": realising that he lacked the ability to defend the University's position, he simply stayed away from the debate.[79] When Union partisans petitioned him against the suppression of debates in 1817, they would have known that they were engaging in a publicity exercise and not a serious request for his intervention.

Indeed, it is a measure of the resistance of Cambridge to internal reform that later Chancellors felt called upon to play a positive role in bringing about change. Prince Albert was a valuable intermediary between dons and politicians at the time of the first Royal Commission into higher education at Oxbridge, in 1851, an initiative that Cambridge conservatives compared to the worst assaults on civil rights in the blackest days of English history. Albert's successor, the seventh Duke of Devonshire, was a rare example of an aristocrat who bothered to exert himself in the examination hall, achieving a double First in mathematics and classics. He funded the development of scientific research: the Cavendish laboratories commemorate the Devonshire family name. He was followed in office by the equally generous eighth Duke, better known as the Lord Hartington of late-Victorian politics. The process that transformed Cambridge "from a rather indifferent academy into a great University"[80] was supported by the profits of the aristocratic entrepreneurship that developed industrial Barrow and seaside Eastbourne on the Devonshire estates. Hartington was a wooden performer in public. Commissioned to perform the opening ceremony for a new building in 1889, he was congratulated by a reporter for having "successfully repeated what he had been told to say". Yet it was the aloof Harty-Tarty who summoned an informal meeting of leading University figures in 1903 to break the news that public opinion regarded them as "devoted to bygone ideals" and out of touch with contemporary education.[81]

The resident head of the University was the Vice-Chancellor, chosen in rotation from among the Masters of the various colleges, who were collectively known by the neutral term, "Heads of Houses". (Two colleges did not use the term "Master", while in a further riot of anarchic eccentricity, several did not formally call themselves colleges at all.)[82] By convention, the vice-chancellorship was held for one year and was bestowed upon the most senior Head who had not previously held the office. It would have been hard to have devised a system that more effectively combined administrative discontinuity with strategic conservatism. Because most Masters reigned over their Colleges for decades, and had long since served as Vice-Chancellor, the most senior Head who had never held the office was often the most junior Master of all. Since Masterships were by no means sinecures, the custom meant that a relative newcomer was required to cope with two demanding new jobs in short order. A quarter of a century after his installation as Master of Trinity in 1820, Christopher Wordsworth looked back in horror at the thought that he had been "at all in a fit condition to undertake two such offices at once".[83] If his compromise solution to permit the Union to resume its debates but not to discuss current events seems bizarre, we need to remember that this was just one of the many issues he was required to tackle. Moreover, the absence of an effective University secretariat meant that the Vice-Chancellor had to be his own chief clerk. In addition to chairing committees, licensing lodgings, presiding over examinations, adjudicating prizes and dealing with problems of discipline – some of which involved questions of policy – he was also responsible for "ordering and superintending every repair, making every payment, and keeping, verifying, and balancing the entire account of receipt and expenditure during his year in office".[84] Almost the only benefit in imposing this demanding office upon a relative junior was that a young man's digestion was more likely to survive the punishing round of official entertaining that was integral to the post.[85]

In the circumstances, it is hardly surprising that in nineteenth-century Cambridge, a reforming Vice-Chancellor was virtually a contradiction in terms, for the incumbent usually lacked both the seniority and the time to pursue a serious agenda for change. An energetic Vice-Chancellor, like James Wood in 1816-17, might make a point of upholding the University's privileges, or he might pursue some crusade of his own. William Whewell, for instance, took a unilateral decision in 1855 to re-organise the art collections in the Fitzwilliam Museum in order to remove all hint of nudity from the main tourist route through the picture gallery.[86] Even that controversial initiative can be explained partly as an unbalanced response to bereavement – his wife had recently died, accentuating the grip of his Victorian belief in female purity – and by the fact that Whewell was holding office for a second time, and so knew his way around the rituals of administration.

Unusually, Whewell had in fact enjoyed his first stint as Vice-Chancellor, back in 1843, partly because he was a demonically efficient administrator, but also because he had reconciled himself to abandoning serious scholarly work during his year of office. Even so, he quickly came to terms with the limits of his power. "I have tried to suppress pigeon-shooting in the outskirts of the town, uproar in the Senate-house galleries, and dinners at taverns", he wrote. As for reform, anything that could be done "must *in the University* be done with great caution, and must be of a nature as to take effect slowly".[87] If that was the conclusion of an energetic and self-confident reformer, it is no wonder that the average inexperienced and overworked Vice-Chancellor relied upon the advice of his predecessors, who were unlikely to embrace radical departures from their own record. An opportunity for consultation occurred each Sunday when the Heads of Houses gathered in Great St Mary's, the University church, sitting together in a reserved section, nicknamed Golgotha, the place of skulls, "a name which the appearance of its occupants renders particularly fitting".[88]

The informal cabinet of the Heads of the Houses was not the only check upon the powers of the Vice-Chancellor. Proposals for change had to be accepted by a wider constituency of senior members in the University Senate (and, until 1856, by a steering committee called the Caput which resembled the United Nations Security Council, in that any single member could veto a proposal before it was brought to a vote). Unlike the Union, which did at least combine the processes of debating and voting, the Senate usually separated the discussion of an issue from any proposal to take action. Special meetings, called Congregations, were held to consider elegantly worded Latin propositions, called Graces. These were often challenged, leading to a division between Placets, those pleased with the proposal, and Non-Placets, those displeased. As a result, the Congregations might be dominated by voters with little knowledge of the arguments behind a proposal for change.

This shortcoming was compounded by another peculiar feature of the University's constitution, that membership of the Senate was open to all Masters of Arts. Moreover, the MA was obtained not by higher study and further examination but by the simple process of buying the degree four years after graduating as a Bachelor of Arts. Thereafter, subject only to payment of a registration fee, any graduate of the University could retain the right to a say in ultimate policy-making and, with it, a powerful sense of belonging. "It is a trivial matter...", wrote one MA on a visit to Cambridge in 1863, "walking through streets and college grounds in one's Master's gown; but there is a powerful charm in the symbolism of the thing: it is a visible sign of membership, of being at home."[89] The doggedness with which Cambridge conservatives resisted the admission of Dissenters to all degrees is partly explained by the fact that to have let them in would have been tantamount to abandoning the Anglican purity of university government. Since Masters of Arts of the University of Cambridge enjoyed the privilege of a second vote at parliamentary elections (and continued to do so until 1949), very many of them made a point of maintaining their formal connection: for instance, there was an exceptionally high turn-out of non-residents at the general election of 1826, when Palmerston was challenged in his University seat for supporting Catholic Emancipation.[90]

Modern universities, which regard good alumni relations as a prerequisite for successful fund-raising, might be tempted to admire a constitution that gave graduates such an influential role in the running of the institution. By turning every graduate into an ambassador, Cambridge gave itself a lifeline to the outer world: "the more the University extended its knowledge of its work by keeping up its connection with non-resident members," one of them argued in 1878, "the more it would extend its influence throughout the country".[91] The theory was fine, but all too often the process operated in reverse, the graduate vote freezing the University in an ice-block of nostalgia. "The non-residents ... loved the University, they loved their colleges."[92] Love is blind and sees no faults. Worse still, by far the largest single category of Cambridge graduates were Anglican clergy, who had plenty of time to come and vote and were motivated by nostalgia coupled with ferocious antipathy to change, Dissenters and ambitious women. A polemical Nonconformist in 1837 described "the lean curate in his dirty white handkerchief, and with a cadaverous face" and "the rubicund shovel-hatted long-gaitered incumbent from his fat benefice", arriving in horse-drawn vehicles straight out of the Old Testament which "vomited their clerical freight" in front of the Senate House.[93]   Advances in technology made the problem even worse.

Historians of the nineteenth century conventionally associate the growth of railways with the spread of liberal ideas. This was not wholly the case in Cambridge. When the railway reached Cambridge in 1845, the University succeeded in keeping the station at an inconvenient distance from the colleges. In 1851 an unusually reactionary Vice-Chancellor, George Corrie, complained that Sunday excursion trains were "as distasteful to the authorities of the University as they must be offensive to Almighty God".[94]   (Corrie's objection was that low fares were "likely to tempt persons who, having no regard for Sunday themselves, would inflict their presence on this University on that day of rest". Stripped of his Sabbatarian prejudices, Corrie might well be regarded as the first prophet to warn against the tourist pollution that threatens the Cambridge of today.) As the University grew, so the railway station became an ever more irritating bottleneck, as when hundreds of undergraduates returned for the summer term of 1890 to be "welcomed by two porters and nearly as many hansoms". Unluckily for Victorian Cambridge, even an inconvenient railway service made its open Senate even more accessible to rock-headed conservatives. Within twenty years, five branch lines converged on the town, and three more upon nearby Ely. "The district around Cambridge is generally supplied with parsons from the University, who can be brought up when the Church is in danger", reported Leslie Stephen after the Senate voted in 1866 to refuse a benefaction for a lectureship in that most subversive of subjects, the history of the United States. To study American history might be to discover that a country could flourish without State intervention in matters of belief and "when the Church is having its foundations sapped ... it would be easier to argue with a herd of swine than British parsons". Progressives shuddered whenever they saw the Senate House full of rustic clerics in "ancient and shiny silk gowns, elaborate white ties and shabby hats", knowing that the intruders had travelled not simply back to Cambridge but back in time to engage in a nostalgic protest against the modern world before hurrying off to old haunts to enquire about the fortunes of the college boat.[95] Non-resident voters helped to keep compulsory Greek in the curriculum right down to 1914, defending the language of the New Testament and the eternal integrity of their own education against those who timidly suggested that the growing horde of scientists might usefully study French or German. Clerical MAs were prominent in the massive explosion of male chauvinism that rejected any move towards the admission of women to Cambridge degrees in 1897. When the same issue was fought out again in 1921, it was a Suffolk vicar who incited a mob of male undergraduates to sack the feminist stronghold of Newnham College.[96]

It was not even that incursions of non-residents necessarily tipped the balance, for on several notable occasions their influx simply reinforced the conservatism of the local academic community. Their significance probably lay in the fact of their very existence. Like the House of Lords in national politics, they were out there, ready to be summoned by the jungle drums, as in the characteristic form of a letter from the Master of Sidney to the *Morning Post* in 1878 warning that "the revolutionary party" had seized control of the University and rallying the MAs to defend "such rights as yet remain to them".[97] It was disheartening to reformers to contemplate the irrational tide ready to sweep aside as irresponsible radicalism any "scheme unanimously agreed upon by experts after a two years' exhaustive consideration of thirty-five or more alternative proposals".[98] A.C. Benson, author of the words of *Land of Hope and Glory*, was hardly a dangerous radical, but even he grumbled in 1906 at the educational shortcomings of a Cambridge that was still only partly reformed:

> If the more liberal residents try to get rid of the intolerable tyranny of compulsory classics, a band of earnest, conventional people streams up from the country and outvotes them ... obviously believing, that education is in danger.

As a result, "the intellectual education of the average Englishman is sacrificed to an antiquated humanist system, administered by unimaginative and pedantic people".[99] When an Edwardian visitor enquired how the University was governed, it is not surprising that he received the answer, "Very badly".[100]

Is the indictment of a blinkered and conservative Cambridge a fair one? In 1904, defenders of compulsory Greek argued that its abolition would have "disastrous effects not only on the University, but on the higher intellectual life of the country".[101] Our response is to laugh, but since few of us can read Greek, we ought to declare a personal interest in the controversy. No doubt the advantages of studying Greek duplicated the advantages of learning Latin, and its study took up time which would have been better used in mastering German, the language of most new ideas in nineteenth-century Europe. None the less, there might still be something in Whewell's view that a mathematician who knew no Greek was "a mere mathematician; and such a one is not an educated man".[102] Leslie Stephen mocked those who opposed the introduction of new subjects into the Cambridge curriculum. "To teach a youth philosophy would be to train him in talking humbug; and history or the physical sciences meant mere cramming with facts."[103] This makes fine polemic, but candour requires us to admit that the criticism has sometimes proved true, and perhaps more often than merely sometimes. Those of us who fear for the ability of twenty-first century students to express themselves in the English language should hesitate before condemning those who defended educational standards in an earlier age.

It is easy, too, to mock the ragbag curriculum of the Cambridge pass degree. In 1822, William Paley's *Evidences of Christianity* was introduced as a compulsory text. Enterprising publishers quickly spotted a market for a crib, and ninety years later undergraduates were still handing over three shillings and sixpence for "a potted Paley"[104] which they mechanically ingested for examinations, even though theological debate had moved far beyond Paley's simplistic attempts to defend Holy Writ by rational argument. Yet, stripped of the clerical cobwebs, the inclusion of Paley can be seen as an attempt to create what modern higher education jargon calls a "transferable skill". Even in Edwardian times, the major career path for pass degree graduates led to ordination in the Church of England. Exposure to Paley, even potted Paley, was at least a step towards preparing them for the Anglican pastiche of the real world. The Cambridge pass degree can be condemned as a jumble of unrelated bits and pieces, but it can also be seen as a precursor of the interdisciplinarity that is the modern hallmark of a true and rounded education. Was it any more absurd to require Cambridge pass degree students to mug up their Paley than it was, in Malcolm Bradbury's fictional University of Watermouth, to insist that nobody could graduate without a credit in Sociology? And if we condemn Cambridge for a moribund century of pumping out potted Paley, we should at least recall that Charles Darwin regarded the mental training involved in studying the *Evidences of Christianity* as the most useful part of his Cambridge experience, even if this was not saying very much. The damning charge against the University's reliance upon a single textbook was that it was an exercise in mere rote learning and not a training in independent thought. J.M. Kemble found this out the hard way when he decided to "crumple up" Paley's arguments in an examination, and was failed for his pains.[105]

It may be that the real indictment of nineteenth-century Cambridge is not that it resisted change, but rather than it carried through extensive and radical reform in a manner that perversely encouraged its own products to believe that they could ignore inconvenient modernity. The allegation is worth formulating, simply to highlight the fact that it provides its own defence. It is unlikely that Cambridge would be a world-ranking university today if it had not re-invented itself so effectively in the second half of the nineteenth century. That process of renewal would have been impossible without the heavy camouflage of continuing tradition. Frontal assaults by Royal Commissions and Select Committees were necessary triggers to the process of reform, but the detailed work had to be carried out by sappers within the walls. As Cambridge faced its last great upheaval of change in 1882, a moderate conservative warned reformers against creating an institution "more immediately suited to the needs of the moment, but dissociated from the memories of the past, and so deprived ... of the guarantee of stability ... which a connection with those memories would secure".[106] The price of achieving substantive change was the continued toleration of much that was nonsensical but reassuring.

The overall result was that as a community of senior members, the University of Cambridge often seemed to be bounded neither by place nor time. This in turn subtly affected the world view of the junior members, and is an essential context for analysing Union debates. By the late twentieth century, change had become so constant that those who wished to stand still were expected to make a special case. In nineteenth-century Cambridge the pattern was precisely reversed. Opposing structural reform of the University in 1878, the articulate reactionary E.H. Perowne warned that "if safeguards against change were removed", Cambridge would fall victim to "the disease of incessant restlessness".[107] There was no suggestion in this of any obligation to respond to the needs of the times. Indeed, the reverse was the case, for the every ritual of the place spoke complacently of a closed world exempt from any need to change. A.C. Benson caught the atmosphere of a small college gathering for formal dinner: "the lighted windows of the Hall gleam with the ancient armorial glass, from staircase after staircase come troops of alert, gowned figures, while overhead, above all the pleasant stir and murmur of life, hang in the dark sky the unchanging stars".[108] Almost a century later, that remains an evocative cameo of Magdalene at twenty-five past seven on a winter's night. It was not surprising that for many Cambridge men, the practices of the University should seem as fixed as the stars in the sky.

The Union was part of the blind acceptance of a comfortable world. Although many of the key Cambridge reformers – Whewell, Thirlwall, Sidgwick, Trotter and Maitland among them – were Union veterans, its members only occasionally became excited by University affairs and certainly claimed no special right to contribute to decision-making. Debates on purely academic issues rarely attracted large audiences. A motion calling for radical reform of the Senate as the University's governing body was rejected in October 1900 by 60 votes to 49, a thin enough turn-out for the autumn term, with barely half as many members voting as in the two previous debates, on the Khaki election and Joseph Chamberlain's policy in South Africa. On the whole, undergraduates accepted that by enrolling at Cambridge they had sacrificed any right to be treated as adults (and most of course were not, since the age of majority was 21). It sometimes seemed that the University of Cambridge was a seamless web of complacency that united the oldest Master of Arts, ignoring the modern world in his country rectory, with the youngest freshman, denouncing all forms of change at the Union despatch box. "A University gave a man all through his life the sense that he belonged to a great community", declared Arthur Balfour in 1897.[109] Chapter Three explores how three of the major challenges to the old Cambridge impinged upon the undergraduate world.

Precocious self-advertisement at the Union despatch box

3:   The Undergraduate World

As a community of junior members, Cambridge was essentially an undergraduate university.[1] True, there were always those who stayed in residence after taking the Bachelor of Arts degree, and young graduates played an important part in the Union throughout the nineteenth century. F.J.A. Hort and Henry Sidgwick were already junior Fellows of Trinity when they were elected to the Presidency in 1852 and 1861, while G.M. Trevelyan contributed to debates in 1898, during his fifth year in Cambridge. (The restriction of the Presidency to the first twelve terms of residence, which has underscored the relationship between the Union and the irresponsibility of gilded youth, was a development of the nineteen-twenties: Selwyn Lloyd, in 1927, was the last fifth-year incumbent.) However, Cambridge was slow to develop anything like a modern postgraduate student community. Most resident BAs were engaged in more of the same: reading for the additional Triposes that began to appear from the eighteen-fifties, and competing for prizes and college fellowships. "I don't like our Fellowship Examination system", wrote Sidgwick on the basis of his experience at Trinity, which did at least operate a formal competition. "[I]t keeps men reading away at the old things in a kind of restless, unprofitable way, and wasting the valuable time in which they might be preparing themselves for work in life".[2] Fellowship examinations placed very little emphasis upon the candidate's potential for the advancement of learning. Not until 1894 did Cambridge adopt the category of "research student" (just in time to admit the physicist Ernest Rutherford from New Zealand). The University had long awarded higher doctorates, in Divinity and Law (to which Letters and Science were added in 1878)[3] but these marked the apex of a scholarly career. Exceptions were few: "Silly Billy" was given an honorary doctorate at the age of 20 because he was a royal duke, and M.R. James was deemed to have earned one by the time he was 32 because he was a high-flying polymath. Otherwise, the notion of a doctorate as an apprenticeship ticket at the start of an academic career was alien to nineteenth-century Cambridge. When the PhD was grudgingly introduced in 1919, it was largely on the assumption that it would appeal mainly to Americans.

    In 1815, it would have been difficult to generalise about Cambridge undergraduates as a single body. For instance, until 1851, students at King's formed a special sub-group, exercising the right to take their degrees "without the bore of the Senate-House examination"[4] – an arrangement based, it seems, on a misunderstanding of a fifteenth-century charter. Noblemen also had the right to proceed to degrees without taking any examinations, although this privilege was curtailed in 1825.[5]

The standard model Cambridge undergraduate was the pensioner. To apply such a term to active young men may seem yet another example of perverse eccentricity but, in this case, Cambridge usage can be defended. "Pensioner" was derived from the Latin verb meaning "to pay", and was an entirely appropriate description of students who paid fees. The English language would have developed on more logical lines had it called people in receipt of regular payments "pensionees". Alongside the pensioners were the scholars, so called because they qualified (increasingly on merit, but sometimes by virtue of birth in a particular county or attendance at a particular school) for financial support from their college. Beyond college awards beckoned a tempting range of lusciously-funded and highly competitive University scholarships. For poorer students, however, the route into the University was generally not through scholarships but by enrolling as the cut-price version of the pensioner and becoming a sizar. Originally, sizars had been admitted on condition of undertaking menial tasks, such as waiting on their social superiors at table. Most of the more galling requirements had disappeared by the nineteenth century, but sizars still paid much reduced fees. "The Sizar must of course occupy a position of inferiority, as one avowedly poor in the company of richer men; but on the other hand, the very avowal of his poverty secures him from many temptations."[6] St John's had a particularly generous record of supporting sizars, diverting to their support income from special bequests for which there were no eligible claimants. The Cornishman Leonard Courtney, a future Liberal Unionist MP, gained his Cambridge education in this way between 1851 and 1855. Although it became obvious that Courtney was going to graduate with high Honours, St John's delayed electing him a scholar of the college, even though a scholarship conveyed more prestige, simply because he would have been disadvantaged financially. After the expected First Class degree, Courtney's former schoolmaster suggested that he should "take part in the debates of the Union" as a preparation for a career at the Bar: as a sizar it would have been virtually out of the question for him to disgorge the necessary subscription.[7]

At the other end of the scale, in 1815 the de-luxe model Cambridge undergraduate was the Fellow-Commoner. Nicknamed "Empty Bottles" in tribute to their average mental capacity,[8] Fellow-Commoners paid top-up fees which gave them the right to wear gorgeous academic gowns and to dine at High Table with the Fellows of their colleges. By no means all of them valued the opportunities for cultivated discourse that this latter privilege offered. Arthur Balfour recalled that in Trinity in the eighteen-sixties, when the system was approaching its demise, a casual observer "would have seen the upper end of the High Table wholly occupied by Masters of Arts in their black gowns, while undergraduates in blue and silver sat massed together below them", since "they preferred each other's company to that of their elders and betters".[9] A former Trinity student was surprised to observe "several noblemen's sons sitting at the undergraduates' table" when he revisited the College in 1868, as the system sputtered to its end.[10] The breed died out soon afterwards. In the earlier period, dress was even employed to differentiate sub-castes among the Empty Bottles: Cap Fellow-Commoners would strive to establish aristocratic descent in order to move up to the more coveted status of Hat Fellow-Commoners, who were exempt from the requirement of wearing academic headgear.[11] Sensitive problems arose when the occasional continental aristocrat had to be placed within this strange hierarchy.[12]

The disappearance of the most extreme distinctions by the late nineteenth century does not in itself mean that a uniform undergraduate body emerged. The more seriously Cambridge came to take both intellectual and sporting pursuits, the more varied were the personalities attracted to the University. In any case, as in most modernising societies, the elimination of inherited rank was associated with the rise of acquired status in the student community. One expression of this set of values was the *Granta's* weekly series, "Those In Authority", which half-solemnly chronicled the lives and exploits of various twenty-something young men prominent in University clubs. The undergraduate world of 1900 was subtly riddled with hierarchy, some of it projected upwards from the prefect system of the public schools. Contemporary memoirs indicate that the President of the Union commanded huge prestige, although E.S. Montagu was thought to be taking matters a little far by flying a flag to show that he was in residence.[13] However, in 1905, soon after his term of office, the Union began to collect and display photographs of ex-Presidents.

Undergraduates were *in statu pupillari*, their membership of the University making them subject to a code of discipline actively enforced on the streets of Cambridge by the University's own police force, the proctors. Even the geologist Adam Sedgwick, one of the most notable intellects of the nineteenth century, took his turn on patrol, accompanied by constables called bull-dogs, "taking cigars out of the mouths of dissolute young men".[14] It was the responsibility of the proctors to ensure that undergraduates wore academic dress as they walked the streets after dark. On arriving in Cambridge by stage coach in 1828, Alfred Tennyson was deposited in Trumpington Street and promptly challenged by the proctor: "What are you doing without your cap and gown, sir, at this time of night?" The future poet laureate, as yet innocent of University regulations, belligerently replied: "I should like to know what business it can be of yours, sir."[15] It was a remarkable example of institutional inertia that the proctors continued until 1965 to enforce the wearing of academic dress in the streets at night, imposing fines of six shillings and eightpence upon defaulters.

The University's authority extended far into the civic life of the town, imposing its own licensing system on lodging houses from 1818, and even retaining the power to arrest and imprison suspected prostitutes (with the emphasis upon "suspected") until a national outcry in 1891 put an end to the "special jurisdiction". When astronomer J.C. Adams, who discovered the planet Neptune, took his turn as a proctor, a wit assured him that he would not be observing the constellation Virgo.[16] It is hardly necessary to add that, while in theory all undergraduates were equal before the proctors, in practice the authority of the University was exercised with more discretion against its more aristocratic members. Viewed through a more recent historical experience of Student Power, it may seem difficult to appreciate that one of the reasons why the Cambridge Union won its battle for free speech was that its most prominent champions were young men co-opted into the University hierarchy on the basis of the automatic prestige of their birth.

It is difficult now to reconstruct the complicated patterns of authority within which the pre-1914 Cambridge undergraduate lived. In a curious way, the Victorian social pyramid bent back on itself in a kind of fourth dimension. The *Student's Guide* advised that lodging houses possessed one advantage over rooms in college: "the servant can be summoned at any time by pulling a bell-rope", whereas support staff in the colleges, "gyps" and bedmakers, "make their rounds at fixed hours".[17] However, come ten o'clock at night (or even nine o'clock in some digs), lodging-house keepers were bound by the terms of their University licence to turn the key and lock their charges in for the night. No doubt the *Granta* was being in tongue-in-cheek when it included a Magdalene bedmaker among "Those in Authority" in 1904, in tribute to her completion of sixty years of service. Still, at the heart of student pupil status, there was an ambiguity in the composite relationships of masters and servants, in which the latter sometimes acted as gaolers to the former. In the eighteen-nineties, the Senior Porter at Trinity conducted himself with such regal bearing that undergraduates seriously believed him to be an illegitimate son of the Prince of Wales.[18] Naturally, it became a matter of honour for adventurous undergraduates to evade the rules, but it is striking that the existence of the whole system of academic discipline was accepted with very little question. In 1883, the Union condemned the proctorial system, by 173 votes to 56 but, ten years later, members roundly rejected a motion condemning the phrase *in statu pupillari* as "strong evidence of a system which is at once intolerant and intolerable", with only 58 members troubling to vote. In 1892, a far larger house had deplored "any attempt to abolish the Special Jurisdiction of the Vice-Chancellor" over the town of Cambridge by a massive 192 votes to 41. A motion calling for the abolition of the University's system of discipline was rejected in 1901 by 44 votes to 28.[19] If Cambridge undergraduates voted consistently against self-government for Ireland, they showed themselves even more enthusiastic in kissing their own fetters.

The continued maintenance of this system of social discipline is all the more remarkable given the overall growth of the student population in the century after 1815. In round terms, Cambridge contained about one thousand undergraduates around 1820, two thousand by the middle of the eighteen-sixties, rising to three thousand by 1889. The Boer War was probably responsible for a slight dip in 1900, but numbers climbed again, touching 3,700 in 1909.[20] Then as now, the standard undergraduate course lasted for three years. George Stephen, who graduated in 1814, recalled that "the first year at Cambridge was delightful – the second, wearisome – the third, detestable". However, the student population fluctuated throughout the academic year. Until 1881, Tripos (Honours degree) examinations were held in January, after ten terms of residence. Consequently most freshmen arrived in October, but others made their first appearance later in the year: Tennyson's misunderstanding with the proctors occurred in February. Undergraduates also came and went more or less as they chose. Although Parnell was notionally a Cambridge undergraduate for four years between 1865 and 1869, in fact he was absent for six of his possible twelve terms, a fact that throws into some doubt all those biographies that portray him as an idle and directionless young man incapable of making friends among the English.[21]

The growth of the University is best charted through matriculations, the number of new students admitted to Cambridge in each academic year. New entrants to the University hovered just below the 300 mark between 1814 and 1817, but then climbed steeply, to pass 400 in 1819. In the eighteen-twenties, four colleges – Corpus, Jesus, St John's and Trinity – responded to the pressure of numbers with new buildings, and in three of them the still-surviving name "New Court" bears witness to the fact that this was the first construction boom that the University had seen since the seventeenth century. Thereafter, matriculations remained steady, not to say stagnant, at around 400 each year until the middle of the eighteen-sixties, when there was another steep climb. William Whewell was pressing Trinity into building again by 1859, and other colleges soon followed. The Union's permanent home in Round Church Street belongs to this period, its members (who chose their architect by ballot) having the doubtful honour of being the first to bring Alfred Waterhouse to Cambridge. He quickly left his heavy mark elsewhere, most notably upon Caius and Pembroke. Matriculations broke the 600 mark in 1869, passed 700 in 1877 and were above 900 by 1884. The Union again responded to pressure of numbers by adding a new wing to its building in 1886. In 1887 and 1890, the University actually gained slightly over a thousand new students, but numbers stabilised again before a final burst from 1907 onwards pushed matriculations close to 1200 a year.[22]

The increase in student numbers in the eighteen-twenties probably helps to explain the rise of organised sports: a Cambridge University cricket club was founded in 1820, and the inter-college rowing competition (the "Bumps") began in 1827, with five Colleges now large enough to provide teams, Trinity typically entering three.[23] The surge was part of a wider interest in higher education. University College, London began in 1826 and its Anglican rival, King's, started to take shape in 1829. They were followed by the miniature northern Oxbridge at Durham in 1832, founded "to supply a cheaper place of education for North-Country clergymen than the two old Universities".[24] At the same time, St David's College Lampeter opened to train clergy for Wales on a small scale, while in Scotland the forerunners of Strathclyde and Heriot-Watt Universities started life as technical institutes. Other rivals were mooted. In 1826 Earl Fitzwilliam pledged £50,000 to a project to establish a university in York as a response "to the overflow of students" at Oxford and Cambridge.[25] If Cambridge suddenly grew, it was partly in self-defence.

Yet thereafter, although the population of England and Wales rose from twelve million in 1820 to twenty million by 1860, the numbers annually entering Cambridge remained the same for more than three decades. The Union debate on Catholic Emancipation in 1829 set a record for numbers voting that was not broken until 1866 (although there is good reason to think that the 1829 division was packed). Matriculations at Oxford were also static, and at identical levels. As late as 1860, the University of London (a project to which the Cambridge Union showed a marked absence of goodwill)[26] was still producing fewer than one hundred graduates a year.[27] Twenty years after the founding of Durham University, a friendly Cambridge commentator could write that "it answers its purpose pretty well" but "one seldom hears much about it".[28] Owens College, the forerunner of the University of Manchester, did not open its doors until 1851, and the beginnings of the great provincial universities in Newcastle, Leeds, Birmingham, Bristol, Sheffield and Liverpool all belong to the decade after 1871. One of the most dynamic periods of British history, between 1820 and 1870, was marked by a declining rate of participation in higher education, at least so far as English students were concerned.

Except for medicine at the Scottish universities – a field in which for much of the nineteenth century, Cambridge barely attempted to compete – there was little in the way of higher education elsewhere in the island group to tempt an English student. In Ireland, the University of Dublin was the "sleeping sister", while Queen's College Galway only just escaped closure in 1873.[29] There was a Presbyterian atmosphere about Queen's College Belfast which probably made it as unattractive to students from England as it proved to be to the Catholic hierarchy.[30] Queen's College Cork opened in 1849 with 115 students. In its early years, the College shared its entrance with the local prison, and classes had to be abandoned on days appointed for public hangings. Student numbers at Cork hit 280 in 1878 before falling away to 106 in 1896. "Where Finbarr taught," said its motto in an appeal to a local saint, "let Munster learn." In a famously patronising comment, Macaulay praised its buildings as worthy to stand in the High Street of Oxford, but nobody expected Cork to poach students from the two English universities.[31]

The Union was a subscription society and it never accounted for a majority of Cambridge undergraduates. At the time of the construction of the new building in 1866, there were hopes of increasing membership to at least fifty percent of the student population.[32] However, as late as 1884, little more than twenty percent of the new intake to the University joined the Union. Enlargement of the building in 1886 made the Society more attractive, but even so, by the first decade of the twentieth century, it was recruiting just 35 percent of each freshman year.[33] Even though it attracted only a minority of the total student population, the increasing membership still tended to shift the Union's primary focus away from debating towards a more general function as a club and social centre. Of the 300 members joining annually by the eighteen-nineties, only a handful could realistically expect to make their mark as orators. Oddly enough, as will be discussed in Chapter Seven, the increased size of the student population produced an unexpectedly inverse effect on the style of speaking in debates: the declamations of the earlier period were replaced, as audiences became larger, with a more conversational style of (sometimes) common-sense exposition.

While the Cambridge population probably represented an effective cross-section of the country's elite, it could hardly be claimed as a significant numerical sample. In 1860, about one eighteen-year old English male in every five hundred enrolled at Cambridge. Although the doors widened in the decades that followed, by Edwardian times the ratio was still no more than one in three hundred. In one important respect, however, the sample probably became slightly more representative. The removal of the Anglican monopoly over the BA degree in 1856 evidently did not create an immediate Nonconformist rush to Cambridge: in 1858 and 1859, matriculations actually dipped below 400 for the first time since 1823. However, the formal ending in 1871 of the Anglican monopoly over all degrees except those in Divinity was part of a changing climate that made the University more welcoming to Protestants who were not part of the Church of England, although much less so to Catholics. Hard statistics are lacking, but the change does seem to have been reflected in the division of political opinion in Union debates during the later period.

The rapid growth of student numbers after 1870 can still be seen in the brick and stone of Cambridge. Essentially, the colleges expanded so that they continued to dominate the landscape of a growing University. Emmanuel abandoned plans to merge with Christ's; St Catharine's escaped the embrace of King's. Nothing came of the suggestion made by Lord Edmond Fitzmaurice, a former President of the Union, that Sidney Sussex should be closed down.[34] Yet the architecture obscures one of the might-have-beens of late-Victorian Cambridge, the possibility that the University might have swamped its federal components by direct admission of undergraduates independently of the colleges. The idea of creating a cut-price category of non-collegiate students had been discussed for two decades before it was reluctantly accepted in 1869.[35] Reformers sought to emulate the come-all-ye admissions policies of the Scottish universities which sought the widest possible basis of entry (per capita of population, Scotland had almost six times as many university places as England) but allowed students to proceed towards graduation at their own pace – an element of flexibility not offered in Cambridge. Undergraduates admitted directly to the University and living in lodgings around the town would save money by avoiding college charges and the accompanying temptations to fast living. Moreover, advocates of change could piously argue, the plan was a return to medieval practice, to the way Cambridge had operated before the colleges had sprung up and decentralised admissions. In Cambridge, it is always helpful to quote precedent, and the more antique, the better.

Thus from 1869 there was a faint possibility that Cambridge might have evolved into something like a giant American state university, with the colleges declining into exotic fraternity houses. Such a development would probably have emphasised the potential role of the Union as a central focus for student life in a radically changed university. But the experiment made only a muted impact upon Cambridge. Part of the answer for this was the town itself. The 1881 census showed that its population ranked about sixtieth among British towns and cities: Cambridge was simply not large enough for a programme that relied on the availability of lodgings in private houses. In addition, the non-collegiate experiment had to compete on two fronts, without the University and within. London University was by now well established, and the seeds were being sown that would grow into major provincial universities, all of which set their faces against any form of sectarian privilege from the outset. The intending student seeking higher education that was secular, innovative and relatively cheap had the luxury of an increasing range of choice. Inside Cambridge, the colleges also fought the challenge. Although the agricultural depression hit their income from endowments, many colleges managed to scrape together the cash for new buildings: indeed, increased income from student fees was an attractive alternative to decreasing rents from farms. Moreover, colleges could offer the intangible advantages of prestige and sociability not available to the isolated "Non-Colls". They were indeed more expensive, but they could – and some aggressively did – offer compensations such as scholarships and better access to career opportunities in the Church of England. Non-collegiate students were never especially numerous, and the ambitious among them defected to mainstream colleges as soon as they had displayed academic or sporting qualities that would make them a marketable human commodity. The first two Non-Colls to become President of the Union were both snapped up by mainstream colleges: A.G. Tweedie in 1877 by Caius and J.H.B. Masterman in 1893 by St John's. Of 203 undergraduates admitted through this route by 1876, 103 had moved to colleges, and a third of the others left without taking a degree.[36] Twenty years later, Gladstone responded to a request for a message of goodwill by hailing the Non-Colls as "a standing reserve established in favour of the Colleges", whose depredations were "a perpetual drain upon its best ingredients".[37] The impact of the great statesman's good wishes on morale is not recorded.

Far from swamping the existing structure, the Non-Colls were quickly compelled to emulate it, forming a shadow college of their own. This came about partly because colleges formed an essential part both of University teaching and the structure of discipline. A non-college could not be headed by a Master, but significantly the official appointed to supervise non-collegiate students was styled the "Censor", after the functionary who had regulated morals in ancient Rome. In 1874, a meeting place for Non-Colls was established at a house in Trumpington Street, close to the Fitzwilliam Museum. In 1892, this became known as Fitzwilliam Hall, and later Fitzwilliam House. Unusually for Cambridge, the name was adopted without any corresponding benefaction or patronage, probably because it bestowed a comfortably aristocratic and medieval aura. Organisation along sub-collegiate lines was also a form of social self-defence: the Union had twice in 1868 voted its disapproval of the non-collegiate experiment.[38]

Alongside the Fitzwilliam scheme, there were three specific attempts to create bargain-basement sub-colleges, recognised by the University as "hostels" – in the often quoted analogy of the American federal system, a form of territorial status short of statehood. The first of these, Selwyn College, proved unexpectedly controversial, largely because it was intended as an Anglican foundation and was thus seen as a clerical riposte to the opening of the University at large to Nonconformists. Unusually, the Selwyn project provoked no fewer than three Union debates between its initial proposal in 1878 (which was condemned by 64 votes to 34) and its opening in 1882, when it was grudgingly accepted by 86 votes to 74, after the rejection of an amendment insisting that it "should be compelled to take the name of Selwyn Hostel".[39] Like

Alaska and Hawaii, and at about the same speed, Selwyn and Fitzwilliam eventually progressed to full statehood, formally becoming colleges of Cambridge University in 1957 and 1966 respectively.

Two other hostels were less successful. Cavendish College combined economy – it was famous for its exceptionally narrow beds – with the experiment of opening the University to boys in their mid-teens. An over-ambitious project, Cavendish ran up considerable debts, partly in the construction of a building likened to a fever hospital on a site even more remote from downtown Cambridge than its inconveniently remote railway station. A sardonic reporter described the arrival of nine freshmen at Cavendish in 1889 as "alarmingly rapid growth". In reality, the project was going nowhere and it closed in 1892.[40] A commercial venture, Ayerst's Hostel, collapsed four years later. Homerton, a teacher-training college, took over the Cavendish buildings, while Ayerst's premises, although not its hostel status, were acquired by St Edmund's House, Cambridge's first post-Reformation Catholic institution.

Overall, non-collegiate students made only a marginal contribution to the Union. As a subscription society, it offered an obvious area for economy in the eyes of students who had opted for a cheaper form of education, especially after 1874 when Non-Colls acquired a social centre of their own. None the less, at various times in the eighteen-seventies and -eighties, clusters of them contributed regularly to Union debates, in some years outnumbering speakers from most of the mainstream colleges. However, this new breed of student did not bring a wholly new voice to Union debates. The one and only Cavendish speaker made his maiden speech in defence of the House of Lords, while the first two contributions from Selwyn opposed a motion that Ireland should be governed by the Irish. The case of J.H.B. Masterman is revealing. His home address, Rotherfield Hall, Sussex, does not suggest social deprivation. The problem for the Masterman family lay in the need to put six sons through Cambridge within little more than decade: even for a country gentleman, the expense was daunting. Three of the Masterman brothers became Presidents of the Union, one of them continuing to a place in Asquith's cabinet.

The non-collegiate experiment was a characteristic example of the way in which the undergraduate world of Cambridge was modified in the half-century before 1914. Changes that seemed radical in principle often turned out to have only a blunted impact on the ethos and operation of the University. By 1870, Cambridge had undergone a major overhaul, and the outlines of the modern University were apparent. Yet in one wholly new area of challenge, the admission of women, and two continuing areas of resistance, the role of classics in the curriculum and the dominance of the Anglican Church, Cambridge succeeded in disguising and blocking change. In a modern academic community, organised student opinion would be insistent and uncompromising in its demand for reform. The Cambridge Union was more likely to be found in the last ditch of opposition.

The first British census, in 1801, had recorded the University of Cambridge as having a population of 803 males and 8 females, the latter being wives of Heads of Houses, the only college dignitaries then allowed to marry.[41] Otherwise, for much of the nineteenth century, Cambridge was a bastion of masculinity. "We ... rigidly exclude the female sex," wrote Leslie Stephen from Trinity Hall in 1865, "so that I have not spoken to a lady for three weeks."[42] So fixed is the modern assumption that everyone should be engaged in continuous sexual self-expression that it is difficult to come to terms with the asexuality of Cambridge in an earlier epoch. True, it was not overheated imagination that caused the proctors to scour the streets for loose women. In the early nineteenth century, the artisan suburb of Barnwell was nicknamed "New Zealand", apparently because it provided sexual delights rivalling those of Polynesia.[43] Yet celibacy was the predominant characteristic of student life. "As for women," wrote Hugh Dalton of the Edwardian years, "most of us, while undergraduates, did not take much serious or sustained interest in them".[44] A character in E.F. Benson's Cambridge novel set in the same era remarked that although he was twenty, "I've never kissed a girl yet, let alone the other thing"[45] – although this record of abstinence perhaps reflected E.F. Benson's own priorities. G.E. Moore's uninformed theorising about copulation confirms that Cambridge students were ill-equipped to respond to the invasion of their world by the opposite sex. Lacking the experience that might enable them to appreciate women as normal people, they fell back on the twin images of the angelic and the threatening.

Two colleges catering for women students emerged soon after 1870. Neither Girton nor Newnham was officially part of the University, the former having started life in 1869 at Hitchin, a strategic location that gave it a choice of potential university affiliations, being as close to London as to Cambridge. The development of two institutions incidentally permitted women students to replicate the essential Cambridge experience of inter-college rivalry on the hockey field: an unusually boisterous dance at Girton in 1919 was excused on the grounds that "we do not win the Newnham match every day!"[46] However, Girton and Newnham were the product not so much of a double tide of female emancipation as of a deep split in tactics. Emily Davies, the founder of Girton, wanted women to batter their way into the existing male world on their merits, whereas for the group around Henry Sidgwick, the Newnham project was part of a wider agenda of educational subversion. The difference can be seen in architectural terms: Girton, in its secluded village, built a chapel; Newnham, just across the Backs, was defiantly secular. Girton, it was said, wore stays [corsets]; Newnham did not.[47] The two projects did not always enjoy smooth co-existence:

on one occasion Sidgwick noted the reception of a letter from Miss Davies which "mentioned affably that I was the serpent that was eating out her vitals".[48] In fairness, it must be said that Sidgwick and his allies, operating inside the University, did their best to frustrate Miss Davies and her plans, and the absence of charity was by no means one-sided. Charles Kingsley, Professor of History, described Emily Davies as "a bad woman", adding: "She would have been a better woman if she had married and had children."[49]

Although Sidgwick was a former President of the Union, and Emily Davies was sister of another, undergraduate debaters of the eighteen-sixties were not in the vanguard of support for the higher education of women. Motions calling for their admission to university degrees and professional diplomas were defeated by 59 votes to 19 in 1863 and 67 votes to 21 in 1867, the minority consistent at 24 percent.[50] In 1868 an attempt to express "admiration" for "the efforts of Women to establish for themselves Colleges, on the principles of those existing for Men" was rejected by 33 votes to 19. However, the following year the Union undertook by 78 votes to 26 to watch "with interest and sympathy the career of the Ladies' College at Hitchin", after rejecting an amendment to substitute "amusement". Thereafter the Union did not turn its attention to Newnham and Girton until 1893 when the Ulsterman MacBride, never one to pull his punches, proposed that they were "useless and dangerous and ought to be abolished". The motion was not altogether serious, but in any case it was defeated by 145 votes to 86.[51]

Official Cambridge attempted to absorb the women, as it was absorbing the Non-Colls, by simultaneously accommodating and ignoring them. Unfortunately, compromises that satisfied senior members had the capacity to alarm their juniors, who were more likely to view women as direct competitors. Three major landmarks in the decade after 1881 saw undergraduate opinion, at least as reflected in Union debates, hardening into defensive masculinity. In 1881, women were permitted to sit Tripos examinations on a "let's-pretend" basis. The real results, for the men, were announced first. Until 1909 candidates in classics and mathematics were not simply grouped into degree classes, but placed in order of merit within them as well. Then a separate list was read out to report where the women would have been ranked, had they been taking the examination as anything other than a courtesy. Unfortunately for the male sense of enlightened compromise, the women failed to enter into the dilettante spirit of the exercise. Some began to appear alongside, although of course not actually *within*, the First Class. Worse still, in 1887 Miss Ramsay of Girton out-performed all the official candidates in the Classics Tripos, while in 1890 Miss Fawcett of Newnham similarly outranked all the male mathematicians.[52] "Newnham celebrated Miss Fawcett's victory ... by unlimited cocoa on Saturday night", reported one unregenerate chauvinist. Miss Ramsay's future was quickly settled. The recently returned Master of Trinity, H.M. Butler, was a widower tackling a job in which it was generally thought that possession of a wife was an essential qualification. Within a year, he had persuaded the brilliant young Girtonian to become his bride.[53] It is something of a challenge to our notions of Victorian prudery to reflect that a very senior academic in his mid-fifties was able to woo a first-year postgraduate (as Miss Ramsay would have been had she been awarded her degree) without being accused of harassment. The marriage was a success. Butler survived to his eighties, increasingly reminding one irritated observer of William Blake's conception of the Almighty.[54] Cynics attributed his longevity and rude health to his wife's conversion to Christian Science and her consequent refusal to allow medical practitioners to come near him.[55] Two sons of the marriage became Presidents of the Union.

Miss Ramsay's good fortune was a happy story, but it did not solve the problem of brilliant women who passed Honours examinations without receiving a Cambridge degree. They could not all marry the Master of Trinity.[56] It became apparent, at least to some, that if women could triumph in the unfeminine endurance test of Tripos examinations, it was illogical to refuse them the unladylike outcome of taking a degree. Indeed, for women who defied convention and wished to earn their own living, the refusal of the degree was an unfair handicap.

This common-sense view did not find universal favour among members of the Union. Their shifting attitudes towards feminist issues form a useful counterpart to analysis of opinion on the Irish question. Tables Nine and Ten compare Cambridge Union debates on the extension of the franchise to women with divisions on the same issue in the House of Commons. Comparison is possible since this was one of the few issues on which MPs were usually given a free vote, beyond the constraints of whips and party loyalties. The comparison indicates that there was more resistance in the Cambridge Union to a recognition of women's rights than there was at Westminster, with levels of opposition among undergraduates tending to conform to those of Conservative MPs – despite the fact that thirty to forty percent of any Cambridge Union audience identified with the Liberals. Young men, it would seem, felt more threatened by assertive females than did their elders. Furthermore, attitudes towards women see-sawed, from cautious endorsement of the abstract principle of female higher education, through reluctance to abandon the male bastion of Cambridge to outright gusts of chauvinist resistance when the challenge from women became too frightening. By the time the issue of women's degrees reached crisis point in 1897, male undergraduate opinion had hardened into outright, even frenzied rejection. By contrast, throughout the last two decades of the century, the Union was steadily opposed to Home Rule, but both the intensity and the proportionate size of that opposition tended to decline. By 1897 Ireland had ceased to be viewed as a major threat.

Initially, Union debates show a student body responding with cautious ambivalence to the demands of women. In 1877 and 1879, the Union supported two motions in favour of the higher education of women, although neither referred specifically to Cambridge. The divisions, of 73 votes to 36 and 85 votes to 58, suggest a consistent measure of approval (67 and 59 percent). Significant, however, was the failure of an amendment in the debate of May 1879 that sought to toughen up support for the higher education of women "especially as preparing the way for the removal of their political and professional disabilities". This was rejected by 75 votes to 33: only half the men sympathetic to the principle of higher education for women were prepared to see it as a vehicle for more general emancipation. Earlier, in 1876, a motion stating that it was "desirable that women should be admitted to the study and practice of medicine" had been rejected by 73 votes to 53.[57] Medicine was no occupation for ladies.

Ambivalent attitudes continued into the eighteen-eighties. In May 1880 and May 1887, the Union actually voted in favour of the admission of women to Cambridge degrees, again by narrow but consistent majorities of 54 and 52 percent (109 votes to 92; 71 votes to 65). In both cases, this cautious endorsement proved to be a false dawn as the pace of feminisation, in the form of admission to examinations and the success of Miss Ramsay, moved too rapidly for the young male ego. In March 1881 there was a violent spasm of rejection after the University formally agreed to allow women to sit Tripos examinations, regularising previous ad hoc arrangements dependent upon the goodwill of individual boards of examiners. A motion that not only approved the opening of examinations to women but bluntly hoped that "it is only a step towards granting them degrees" was rejected in a well-attended debate by 166 votes to 102. The 62 percent majority of March 1881 recalled the 69 percent opposition to general emancipation in May 1879.[58]

The sense of threat can also be seen in the debate of February 1888, which revealed a complete shift of attitudes in the nine months since the narrow acceptance of a motion disapproving "of the continued refusal of Degrees to properly qualified women students".[59] In the interval, Miss Ramsay had shown herself much too well qualified in the Classics Tripos, and young men responded by pulling up the drawbridge. Moreover, the 1888 motion spoke of admitting women not simply to degrees but to "academical rank" or, in other words, a role in the running of Cambridge. It was soundly rejected by 135 votes to 55. For the next decade, the swing away from the women's cause was continuous. A carefully worded motion specifying nothing more than the BA degree was narrowly rejected by 102 votes to 90 in 1889, and a more sweeping proposition thrown out by 59 votes to 35 in 1891.[60] The triumph of Miss Fawcett in the Mathematics Tripos probably accounts for the sharp fall in sympathy between the two debates. One speaker who supported the women's cause in both debates was Lord Corry, son of the Earl of Belmore, of Castle Coole in Fermanagh: the Irish ascendancy was not always a voice for reaction at Cambridge. More generally, the Union condemned "the granting of any further 'rights' to women" by 74 votes to 52 in 1889, viewed "with dismay the advance of feminine despotism" in 1891 by 85 votes to 57 and condemned all moves towards female suffrage in 1894 by 62 votes to 25.[61] The 37 percent minority of 1891 was replicated in 1896, when a division of 157 against 87 again dismissed the argument for women's degrees, despite the advocacy of F.W. Lawrence, better known as the future champion of the suffragettes, Lord Pethick-Lawrence.[62]

The admission of women to the Bachelor of Arts degree was not as straightforward as it might now seem. The BA led straight to the MA, which conferred full membership of the University, the "academical rank" that carried with it the right to participate in its government. Furthermore, Cambridge MAs formed a parliamentary constituency, and in the eighteen-nineties only visionaries thought that women should have the right to elect MPs. (The Union rejected women's suffrage on 28 of the 31 occasions that it debated the idea between 1866 and 1914. The exceptions were majorities of 3 in a division of 225 in 1908, of 4 out of 394 in 1911, and a single vote among 145 members in the very last peacetime debates in June 1914, all three interspersed with unambiguously anti-feminist majorities.) In short, the question of women's degrees was – as Sidgwick had foreseen – part of a wider issue of the role of women in society.

In 1897, the University came up with a proposal worthy of its origins as a school of medieval theology. Women were to be given the title of the BA degree, but not the degree itself, thereby stamping the product but avoiding the complications of full membership of the University. The response to this mild, almost craven, compromise was a massive explosion of masculine anger: the proposal was rejected by almost three-to-one in a vote by over 2,300 MAs.[63] An unofficial referendum, plus petitions and counter-petitions, among undergraduates also attracted mass participation and produced an even more remarkable rejection by more than seven-to-one. One measure of the sense of crisis was the decision to throw open the Union debate to all resident junior members of the University. Hundreds had to be turned away, and at one point it was feared that the gallery of the debating chamber was about to collapse. The President of the University Boat Club was so unfamiliar with Union procedure that he began his remarks, "Ladies and Gentlemen" but, despite his unpolished oratory, the motion was passed by 1083 votes to 138.[64] If hardly the most glorious moment in the history of the Cambridge Union, the vote – when compared with the 157-89 rejection of women's degrees the previous year in a debate confined to members only – did at least suggest that Union activists were marginally less reactionary than the student body as a whole.

The episode now seems so bizarre that it is worth pointing out that there were indeed arguments against the proposal, even if they do not strike us as especially good ones. Some felt that "women are not undeveloped men".[65] After centuries in which the two sexes had operated in separate spheres, it was not immediately obvious that the higher education of women should take the same form as that of men, a view to which some later feminists might feel sympathy if from a wholly different starting point. An ex-President of the Union stated as fact that women did better than men in the study of history and languages, but were "far behind" in classics, mathematics and natural sciences. The implication – which has lingered until recent times – was that the female mind flourishes in a riot of creativity but cannot cope with subjects that require intellectual rigour: "women's talents are different to men's".[66] The *Granta's* cartoonist was less subtle, portraying Cambridge as a seminary for young ladies: "Cooking & Plain Sewing Extra".[67] Others saw that admission to degrees would entail the breaking of all barriers, "an inevitable step towards a mixed University", a term that became a coded reference to "a matrimonial agency".[68] Cambridge was surely too important for such a reckless experiment, while "any man of sense would see that a large number of subjects do not lend themselves to treatment in mixed classes".[69] Rowing men saw the degree as only one part of a Cambridge education – for some of them perhaps not even that – and feared the loss of sporting types to Oxford. "What we should gain in women, we should lose in men."[70] Strangely enough, when Oxford subsequently decided that it did not wish to be the home of this particular lost cause, the rowing men did not noticeably swing to the female cause.

The movement to admit women to universities was part of the late-Victorian boom in higher education. Unfortunately, one feature of rapid expansion was that resources did not keep abreast of numbers. In this, at least, the modern academic can empathise. "University Lecture Rooms and Laboratories are crowded enough in all conscience".[71] Even the Union's most prominent supporter of Home Rule for Ireland, Thomas McDonnell, was persuaded by the argument that there was "no room" in Cambridge for any more women, although he did not explain why this constraint ruled out a simple act of justice for those who were already there. "Girton and Newnham are full. Where could they go?" A heckler helpfully nominated Downing.[72]

Even accepting that there were practical obstacles to any large-scale influx of women into Cambridge, it is impossible to ignore the fact that the core opposition to the proposal rested upon threatened masculinity. Essentially, the difficulty experienced by Cambridge men in accommodating the arrival of

Cambridge women lay in their own inability to reconcile, or break free from, two wholly different perceptions of females, one seeing them as angels and the other fearing them as harpies. The elevation of women above the sordid level of ordinary life made possible the superficial pun that in perfection there could be no degree.[73] The architecture of the Cambridge Union captured this notion, permitting "ladies" to view debates from the gallery, so constituting an "upper house".[74] Indeed, the first occasion on which the Union had discussed any issue relating to women was a motion in 1837 declaring that their presence as spectators at parliamentary debates would raise the tone of the House of Commons.[75] The restrictive use of the term "ladies" can be seen in contrast to a statement from an internal Union report of 1892, which declared that "a small increase in the staff of women" had improved the efficiency of "the work of daily cleaning".[76] Ladies were ethereal creatures, located not simply above the debaters but above the issues debated. Thus their presence in large numbers in 1897 at a debate on the report of the Irish Financial Commission was sufficiently unexpected to be remarked upon by (male) student journalists. "We were surprised to see more than 120 ladies assemble in the gallery to listen to a debate of so technical a nature," remarked the puzzled *Cambridge Review*.[77] This was, after all, the decade of *The Importance of Being Earnest*, in which Miss Prism advises little Cecily to omit the Fall of the Rupee from her study of economics because the episode was "somewhat too sensational".

When women did not conform to the angelic ideal, they became a terrifying threat. "The harpies are upon us" – so ran the opening words of the *Granta's* call to resistance in 1897.[78] Two comments by ex-Presidents in the Union debate of that year are revealing. One revealed a profound insecurity in rejecting the argument that it was inconsistent to allow women to take examinations but not receive degrees: "If I give a beggar my coat, he has no right to demand my trousers." Another made macho reference to the divisions in student opinion revealed by the rival petitions. "Our opponents say we are animals. I would rather represent 2000 animals than 300 vegetables."[79]

It is only fair to note that a succeeding student generation quickly came to repent these excesses. The Union approved the granting of Cambridge degrees for women narrowly (by 131 votes to 121) in 1905 and emphatically (by 147 votes to 55) in 1909. However, the change of heart did not extend to a wish to invite women into participation in Union debates.[80] At the inauguration of the Union's new wing in 1886, there had been some jocular allusions to the likelihood that women might soon be admitted to membership.[81] Miss Ramsay probably set that possibility back by a quarter of a century. Even then, a proposal to open Union membership to members of Girton and Newnham was rejected in 1912 by a two-to-one majority (127 votes to 63). "The shy man would be driven out of the Union by the change", warned a future Cambridge don, while an ex-President called upon members "to resist the evil encroachment of the feminist movement, which would have the effect of unsexing women".[82] As late as 1935, it was considered witty to argue that the sort of women who would wish to join the Union would not be the sort of women the Union would want, an attitude redolent of Groucho Marx if less likely to amuse posterity.[83]

The rest of the story may be told quickly, even if it does not report any rapid process of change. In 1921, in the last great festival of the backwoodsmen, women were once again refused full membership of Cambridge University, but on this occasion the mystical compromise of 1897 was allowed to slip through. The titular degree fell short of the real BA (Cantab.) and was susceptible to indelicate abbreviation, but it was a belated victory of a kind.[84] Full and unvarnished degrees were eventually conceded in 1948. The Union was less precipitate, and did not get around to admitting women to membership until 1963. The first woman President was elected in 1967. In 1991, she received a peerage as Baroness Mallalieu and became prominent as a defender of fox-hunting. The first female ex-President to enter parliament was elected for a marginal seat in 1974, almost a century and a half after Gladstone had used the Oxford Union as the launch-pad for his political career. In 1996, she too went to the Lords as Baroness Hayman, and the following year became a junior minister in the Blair Labour government. Thus the Cambridge Union just managed to make its mark on the political history of women in twentieth-century Britain.

There is, of course, no way of knowing whether Cambridge Union attitudes to Ireland would have been altered had women contributed to debates. What does seem clear is that young Cambridge males were indulging in large-scale denial of the obvious presence of women around them. In some respects, they showed more openness towards the claims of distant Ireland.

By 1870, the dominance of mathematics and classics in the Cambridge curriculum that had marked the first half of the nineteenth century was being challenged by a range of newer subjects. Tripos (Honours degree) examinations in moral sciences (philosophy) and natural sciences began in 1851. Law followed in 1858, history in 1875, medieval and modern languages in 1886, mechanical sciences (the engagingly primitive Cambridge term for engineering) in 1894 and economics in 1905. Arthur Balfour was one student who was glad that his undergraduate career did not begin until 1865. "At Cambridge, till within a comparatively short time of my going there, academic honours could scarcely be reached except by the well-worn road of classical learning and advanced mathematics." He flourished in the study of philosophy: "neither in classics nor in mathematics could I hope to do more than admire other people's work ignorantly and from afar."[85]

Despite the broadening of degree studies, mathematics and classics retained their prestige, the latter still entrenched with insidious privilege in the curriculum. Essentially, the indictment of their earlier dominance had been twofold: concentration upon just two disciplines had created a culture that was both restrictive and aridly competitive. Leslie Stephen had parodied the narrowness of the University's approach to study during the first half of the nineteenth century:

> Cambridge virtually said to its pupils, "Is this a treatise upon geometry or algebra? No. Is it, then, a treatise upon Greek or Latin grammar, or on the grammatical construction of classical authors? No. Then commit it to the flames, for it contains nothing worthy of your study."[86]

Successful candidates in these two prestige subjects continued to be arranged, not simply in degree classes, but in strict order of merit until 1909, eighty years after a critic had complained that Tripos examinations were discussed in "the slang of the race-course". "The love of *excelling*, not the love of *excellence*, is made the basis of our studies".[87]

At its best, mathematics was a stimulating discipline. It was reported of Parnell, who does not seem to have been overly bookish, that "when he had been given the ordinary solution of a problem, would generally set about to find whether it could not be solved equally well by some other method".[88] A President of the Union of the eighteen-nineties was even more enthusiastic. Through mathematics, F.W. Lawrence encountered "beauty, order, and harmony", indeed a sense of communion with God.[89] In more prosaic spirit, in 1901 the Union rejected by 59 votes to 42 a motion declaring mathematics "inadequate" as a mental training.[90]

The rationale for the study of classics was less clear-cut, and indeed placed a Christian and conservative university in the curious position of basing its education upon pagan and republican Greece and Rome. It was contended that the study of languages possessing systems of grammar and reflecting concepts of thought so different from the modern world was an essential foundation for the writing of good English. "The old-fashioned test of an English sentence – will it translate? – still stands after we have lost the trick of translation", as Evelyn Waugh was to put it.[91] For all its high-minded veneration of the ancient world, Cambridge Latin could be racy and even mildly indecent. One don chortled for sixty years over a blunder in translation made by a fellow undergraduate, who confused "merx" (merchandise) with "meretrix" (prostitute), while another was delighted with the suggestion that the highly inconvenient fashion accessory, the ladies' bustle, might be translated as "superbum".[92]

By the end of the nineteenth century, champions of the new degree subjects were starting to assert parity of esteem with the old. E.W. MacBride, the scientist from Belfast, even had the hardihood to ask the Union to support the abolition of the Classics Tripos in 1891. He "succeeded in thoroughly annoying his opponents" but was defeated by 102 votes to 25.[93] MacBride's motion was a piece of philistine aggression: classics was as valid a discipline of study as physics and chemistry. The reason for hostility lay in its privileged status: even after the shake-up of the curriculum, permission to proceed to any Tripos examination continued to depend upon a basic knowledge not only of Latin but of Greek as well. Greek had become compulsory with the creation in 1822 of the Previous Examination (or "Little-Go"). Originally conceived as a retrospective entrance test, the Little-Go became a hurdle that every undergraduate had to surmount before proceeding to more specialist study. The case for compulsory Latin as a foundation for a general education was respectable, and could even be pleaded as an essential qualification for scientists: not only was Latin the linguistic expression of logical thought, but it was useful in the study of botany. The case for a second classical language was much less impressive, since a knowledge of Greek mainly duplicated the advantages gained from studying Latin. It took six assaults over 48 years before Greek, still resisting, finally fell on its sword in 1920.

However, even in the early twentieth century, as the University was becoming a more serious place, over half the undergraduate population did not sit for Honours in any subject, and around one fifth left without taking a degree of any kind.[94] The Master of Magdalene, who was well placed to comment, stated in 1914 that many of the last category "had come up to have a good time, and did not care to read or work hard".[95] In their defence, it has to be said that the Pass degree was stale and unstimulating. The sterile dominance of the classical culture can be seen even in the fact that Pass degree candidates were long known as "Poll Men", from the Greek *hoi polloi*, the rabble. The *Student's Guide* claimed that "those persons are not always to be believed who say that they got no good at Cambridge, that they only forgot what they had learnt", bravely adding that it was "possible that they learnt something without being conscious of it".[96] One of the sternest critics of this vacuous nonsense was A.C. Benson, a Fellow of Magdalene and himself a former classics master at Eton. "The defenders of the classical system say that it fortifies the mind and makes it a strong and vigorous instrument", he wrote in 1906. "Where is the proof of it?" The evidence pointed in the other direction: it was "difficult to imagine a condition of greater vacuity than that in which a man leaves the University after taking a pass degree" thanks to its "contemptible, smattering" content.[97]

King's led the way in discouraging any undergraduates who did not propose to aim for Honours. The Union was less demanding. In 1878, a motion calling for the abolition of the Pass degrees was thrown out by a massive 84 votes to 6. On the positive side, in 1879, a motion in favour of the creation of an Honours degree in modern languages was backed by 62 votes to 15. However, by and large there was little undergraduate interest in, or enthusiasm for, major syllabus reform. Some of the new degree subjects made only a muted impact. In the eighteen-eighties, Cambridge was "dimly conscious" of the existence of a School of Modern Languages. At "irregular intervals", there were "spasms of anxiety to find out whether the existence is more than nominal", but "the fit is of short duration, and is followed by no malignant after-effects". [98]

The conservatism of the University (and especially of its easily mobilised parsonic reserve) in the defence of compulsory Greek was characteristic. More surprising was the lack of enthusiasm for change shown in Union debates, since one of the arguments of the reformers was that most students only went through the motions of mastering Greek, deriving no real benefit from the experience. It was one thing for Sir Richard Jebb to claim that Greek "was the most perfect vehicle for expression which the world has known".[99] He was, after all, Professor of Greek. Members of the Union might not have been very good at Greek, but they rallied to its defence. A 61 percent vote in its favour out of a division of 94 students in 1877 was startlingly similar to the 59 percent majority when 157 members took part in a similar debate in 1904. A larger turn-out the following year saw the support for Greek slip to 55 percent in a division of 267. This was three times the turn-out on the same issue in 1913, when Greek gained a 54 percent victory.[100] Remarkably, the Cambridge Union came to terms with Irish Home Rule more rapidly than it felt able to abandon a classical language which few of its members really understood.

Despite the rebuke of Monckton Milnes in 1866 that political debates were squeezing out literature, the Union provided opportunities for intellectual discussion of subjects that were long absent from the formal programme of the University. Although a debate in 1892 disapproved, by 36 votes to 29, of the idea of an Honours degree in English,[101] the Union was probably the largest and most long-lasting forum for the discussion of literature in nineteenth-century Cambridge. The future Professor of Ecclesiastical History, F.J.A. Hort, proposed in 1849 that Macaulay's *History of England* was "utterly wanting in the most essential characteristics of a great history". Hort was sharing the benefits of the new course in moral sciences, but as there were only four students enrolled for the degree, in this case the Union was performing a wider educational function. His motion triggered a lively debate, leading to the conclusion that members did not like Macaulay's political opinions but regarded his book as one "the master-pieces of English Historical Literature".[102] Later in the century, literary debates became rarer and even pedestrian. In 1888, the Union listened to Ignatius Donnelly expound his theory that Francis Bacon wrote the plays of Shakespeare, and disagreed with him by 131 votes to 101.[103] However, although when literary issues went out of fashion as subjects for formal debate, they erupted from time to time in business meetings as members argued about purchases for the

Society's Library. In the early decades, the Union took its role so seriously that even the acquisition by its Library of material as frivolous as the novels of Walter Scott was a matter for controversy.[104] Later, there were campaigns to block the purchase of the poems of Walt Whitman, Oscar Wilde had to be referred to a referendum of all members, and Zola was contested through a series of business meetings, novel by novel.[105]

The broadening of the University degree syllabus in the nineteenth century was thus undercut by the continued entrenchment of both ancient languages as essential preconditions for study. This in turn perpetuated the narrow range of schools which could most effectively prepare candidates for entry to Cambridge and so added considerably to the obstacles faced by those from outside the social elite. Occasionally a day school, such as King Edward's Birmingham in the eighteen-forties, would mount a challenge through the excellence of its classical teaching, but in practice the emphasis upon Greek and Latin was a form of restrictive practice to ensure that the top prizes at Cambridge continued to be dominated by former pupils of the public schools. "Take them away," wrote Bristed in 1852, "and you would take away four of the first five men in every classical Tripos."[106] One of the founders of Cheltenham explained in 1841 that a public school education "appeared to be to a certain extent necessary to future success" at the universities, since "honours were almost invariably carried away by those who had been educated at our great public schools".[107] The cumulative result of all this was the creation of a vast constituency, stretching from the youngest freshman to the oldest country parson, ready to spring to the defence of an educational ritual in which they had themselves invested so heavily.

The reforms of 1856 and 1871 opened first the BA and then almost all other degrees of Cambridge University to non-members of the Church of England. However, for the average undergraduate, the downfall of Anglican supremacy was masked by the fact that the University was an invisible entity obscured by the concrete presence of the colleges. The colleges, too, were forced to concede the outworks of Anglican privilege: Fellows were no longer required to take Holy Orders, and the Royal Commission of 1881 even removed religious tests for Masterships. The Master of Corpus ingenuously protested that such a change would be contrary "to the intention of the pious founder and benefactors of the college", conveniently overlooking the complication that most of those worthies lived in the Middle Ages and would have regarded the Church of England as schismatic and heretical.[108]

Out-argued and out-gunned, the conservatives in their colleges fell back on the citadel of Anglican identity, compulsory chapel. A recent historian estimates that it took the First World War to eradicate this deeply entrenched aspect of Cambridge culture, especially in the smaller colleges where social control over the young was at its most rigid.[109] For instance, at Magdalene in Parnell's time, undergraduates were expected to attend chapel twice on Sundays in addition to their weekday obligations. Like most of his contemporaries, Parnell paid a steady trickle of fines for missing chapel services.[110] Whether he rejected the system as a whole, we cannot tell. Certainly the first elected office he held after leaving Cambridge was his membership of the Synod of the Church of Ireland. In larger colleges, and especially in Trinity, there is plenty of evidence that compulsory chapel produced a mutinous and irreverent congregation, punctuated occasionally by more organised protests. The best known of these took the form of a Society for the Prevention of Cruelty to Undergraduates, which in 1838 issued spurious class lists, arranging the Fellows of Trinity in order of their own attendance. An undergraduate from New South Wales was expelled after being caught distributing this "blasphemous anti-Chapel" publication, a disapproving Fellow noting that it was "comical enough that the youth came from Botany Bay". By coincidence, the SPCU awarded its prize for the most diligent chapel attendance to a Trinity tutor, Charles Perry, who nine years later became first bishop of Melbourne.[111]

Cambridge attitudes (but not those of Magdalene) seem to have shifted in the period between 1864 and 1872. The Union debated compulsory chapel attendance on five occasions, moving from initial approval of the institution by 108 votes to 83 to condemnation in 1868 by 92 votes to 42, a shift in attitudes which paralleled the sudden drop in enthusiasm for the Irish Church.[112] As late as 1862, Trinity was still upholding the principle that all members of the college should attend a common act of worship, whatever their own beliefs. That year, the issue arose with the proposed admission of a Hindu, but assurances were given that he "would be regular ... in his attendance at chapel".[113] Henry Sidgwick's well-publicised resignation from his Fellowship in 1869 on grounds of religious doubt was probably an indirect blow to the institution, not least because Trinity was at pains to find a means to hold on to this self-proclaimed agnostic. By the eighteen-nineties, non-attendance in Trinity led to a civil interview with the Dean but "no punishment was ever inflicted".[114] None the less, when F.M. Cornford tried to secure formal abolition of the practice in 1904, he was almost contemptuously out-manoeuvred by its defenders. The experience helped spur Cornford into writing his *Microcosmographia Academica*, still a biting and illuminating guide to the politics of conservatism. "There must be some rules", Cornford wrote in mocking parody of the defence of compulsory chapel, and "the object of rules is to relieve the younger men of the burdensome feeling of moral or religious obligation". Chapel attendance reminded students of their ecclesiastical duties while simultaneously inoculating them against undue religious enthusiasm.[115] It also got them out of bed in the morning.

Gradually, some colleges became a little more flexible towards chapel attendance, prepared to excuse Nonconformists on grounds of conscience. In 1886, Wilfrid Blunt met a King's undergraduate who had been excused chapel after converting to Buddhism, although his notion of practising his new faith seemed centred on the consumption of near-fatal amounts of hashish.[116] In 1908, Hugh Dalton secured exemption as an agnostic, but the college made him wait until his twenty-first birthday before conceding the privilege. Dalton celebrated by appearing outside King's College Chapel on his first Sunday morning of freedom, clad in pyjamas and dressing gown, and compounding his offence by cavorting on the grass, sacred space from which undergraduates were barred. But King's was a notoriously eccentric place and no notice was taken of Dalton's triumphalism.[117]

Overall, exceptions to the rule of chapel attendance were marginal, exotic and seemed to have been confined to the larger and more forward-looking colleges. The Anglican monopoly over Cambridge had been broken in 1871 but, forty years later, its spell was still sufficiently self-assertive to force undergraduates out of bed in the morning. Some Nonconformists secured exemption, but for others social pressure to attend Anglican worship probably gave no great theological offence. It was notorious that upwardly-mobile Dissenting families usually conformed to the Church of England after a couple of generations anyway: one of their spokesmen had assured Anglicans in 1864 that they would "capture nine out of ten of those who enter the University as Nonconformists".[118] Of course, the prevailing atmosphere of Anglicanism was far less welcoming to Catholics, as Chapter Four will discuss.

It is tempting to illustrate the changing nature of Cambridge in the century after 1815 by contrasting two Union personalities, eighty years apart, who came from the Lancashire town of Ulverston, on the southern fringe of the Lake District. Thomas Sunderland came to Cambridge in 1825 from Rugby School. The son of the prosperous "squarson" Rector of Ulverston, Sunderland was a formidable orator but a slightly unhinged personality whose opinions boxed the political compass from the Jacobite to Jacobin. Thackeray enjoyed his speeches but thought Sunderland "too fond of treating us with draughts of Tom Paine".[119] As was not uncommon in the days before the office acquired a special glamour, he declined the Presidency in 1827. Norman Birkett attended a local school in Barrow and worked in his father's shop before coming to Cambridge in 1907. The family were Wesleyans, and young Birkett intended his university education to be the prelude to the Methodist ministry. He was active as a lay preacher during his undergraduate years, but eventually opted for a brilliant career at the Bar. While sitting the entrance examination at Emmanuel, Birkett was asked if he had any ambition at Cambridge. He replied: "To be President of the Union."[120]

The eighty years from the Anglican and public-school Sunderland to the Methodist and shop-keeping Birkett is a measure of the denominational change in nineteenth-century Cambridge, but it may flatter the extent to which the University had opened its doors socially. Birkett's father was no mere tradesman, but the leading shopkeeper in Ulverston. At his death in 1913, he left an impressive estate of £15,000. His son had to economise to meet the additional expenses of hospitality that fell upon him as President of the Union, but he was never seriously short of cash:

> We thought it a natural thing that there should always be plenty of coal for our fires, plenty of food for our tables ... that we could go abroad in the vacation ... that tobacco and wine should be within reach of modest incomes, that an occasional Norfolk jacket and flannels should not create a minor financial crisis.[121]

The recollection came from Birkett. The sentiment (if not the fashion) would have been appropriate to Sunderland.

If the changes in gender, curriculum and religion achieved by Cambridge in the nineteenth century were less than total, and were obscured by rituals of continuity, they were at least more substantial than any alteration in the social composition of the University. Cambridge had always found the means for the occasional poor boy to secure an education. The two protagonists in the legendary confrontation that put an end to Union debates in 1817 were both from Lancashire: the father of the Vice-Chancellor, James Wood, had been a weaver; Whewell, the defiant President, was the son of a carpenter. Their success did not encourage them to challenge the system. Wood died in 1839 leaving over £50,000 – making him a millionaire in today's terms. Thackeray portrayed Whewell as Dr Crump. "He does not disguise his own origin, but brags of it with considerable self-gratulation. ... The argument being, that this is a capital world for beggars, because he, being a beggar, has managed to get on horseback."[122] Thackeray's sneer was close to the mark: we cannot believe that every Wood and every Whewell was plucked from obscurity to academic triumph at Cambridge. In reality, even those two careers owed a good deal to luck. Wood was not simply the son of a weaver, but the son of a weaver who enjoyed teaching algebra; Whewell happened to live close to an endowed grammar school with scholarships to Cambridge, but even he had to rely on a public subscription to finance his education. Whewell's own contribution to the development of the University unwittingly helped to narrow its social range by increasing its intellectual demands, while standing firm on the requirement of not one, but two, classical languages. Cambridge did not notably widen its social intake in the century after 1815. If anything, it may even have become more restricted.

Few working class families could afford to support a teenage boy at school to the age of eighteen, not to mention the negative cost of the loss of his earning power.[123] In the circumstances, estimates of the minimum cost of a Cambridge education become almost irrelevant. In 1866, the *Student's Guide* put the lowest estimate, for a sizar, at £115 a year. Others thought the minimum annual cost at between £125 and £150.[124] The average weekly wage for a farm labourer in England and Wales was about fourteen shillings (£0.70). Assuming full-time, year-round employment (which was unlikely), "Hodge" might accumulate an annual income of about £36. By this point, the calculations have become fantastic: by saving ten percent of his income for one hundred years, he might put a son through Cambridge. Most farm workers lived on or below the poverty line. Even the aristocrats of labour, the engine drivers, earned at most around £90 a year. Four years' gross income equalled the cost of three years' study at Cambridge.

In the vocabulary of Victorian Cambridge, a poor student was someone from the same social background as the majority of undergraduates, who happened to have less money. E.W. Benson was the grandson of an army officer who – according to family legend – had squandered his fortune through high living as a hanger-on to Silly Billy, the Duke of Gloucester. His father was never successful as a manufacturer in Birmingham, and it was his widow who struggled to send the future Archbishop to Cambridge in 1848. He managed "to get through his first year upon something over £90" but in later life "spoke feelingly of the miseries he endured through living with a large circle of more or less wealthy friends".[125] Poverty was a highly relative concept viewed through the prism of a very narrow social band. "The working-class boy at Cambridge before the twentieth century is as rare as a needle in a haystack."[126] Benson was unusual, and probably unwise, in joining the Union. In mid-century, a three-year "Life" subscription cost £6.6 shillings, around two percent of the total basic cost of a Cambridge education, and an obvious area of economy for the impecunious.

Social change came slowly. In 1890, the new County Councils were given the power to make grants to needy students. Between 1896 and 1899, 26 male undergraduates at Cambridge were so assisted, about one percent of the total. Their fathers included a bootmaker, a bridle cutter, a tailor and a wharf foreman – but others were more middle-class, and two of the young men were doctors' sons who had attended Shrewsbury.[127] Wilson Harris believed that when he came to Cambridge in 1902, "hardly one undergraduate was being educated at no cost to his parents".[128] If there were exceptions, they demonstrated only that it was not the sons of weavers and carpenters who benefited from Cambridge's curious combination of a progressive emphasis upon merit with a conservative attitude to the curriculum. In the eighteen-nineties, it was widely believed that the six brilliant Llewelyn Davies brothers had all won scholarships large enough to put them through school and university at no cost to their father.[129] In 1907, it was said of the President of the Union, Edward Selwyn, that "the income he derives from his scholarships would just fail to liquidate the National Debt".[130] For John Llewelyn Davies, a noted theologian and former President of the Union, it was no doubt a relief to be spared the cost of educating his offspring from the stipend of an Anglican living in Westmorland. The Etonian Edward Selwyn was also a clergyman's son. Scholarships smoothed their passage through Cambridge, but they were not necessary to make Cambridge possible.

Nor can it be said that Cambridge rushed to widen the chink in its door. In May 1911, the Union decided by 55 votes to 47 that it "would welcome facilities for the introduction of working men into the privileges of the University". The tone of the motion alone falls short of an endorsement of social revolution. As late as March 1914, the Union "decided, not unnaturally, that the older Universities were adequately fulfilling their duties to the Nation".[131] Dons were even less radical than undergraduates. "I utterly abominate the idea of swamping us with poor beggarly students who ought to be tinkers & tailors", grumbled Joseph Romilly – who always voted Liberal – in 1853. Sixty years later, Arthur Benson complained of an undergraduate who had "an accent like a slum" and wondered: "is it any use such a man coming here?" The objectionable student hailed not from one of Britain's industrial cities, but from the bucolic Norfolk town of King's Lynn.[132] It was a short step to the snobbish exclusionism that drew an Archbishop's rebuke upon the Dean of St Paul's in 1921. W.R. Inge, a product of Eton and former Cambridge professor, protested against the intrusion of the lower orders into the educational preserves of their betters:

> In the past the public school man has been exposed only to the natural competition of his own class, recruited [i.e. added to] very sparingly from below. But now our sons have to meet the artificial competition deliberately created by the Government, who are educating the children of the working man, *at our expense*, in order that they may take the bread out of our children's mouths.[133]

Archbishop Davidson replied that the Church of England was "whole-heartedly in favour of all such facilities being placed within the reach of those who can use them" and that it would "continue to do its best to throw open as widely as possible our country's educational doors".[134] This was a wholly bizarre interpretation of the clerical role in Cambridge for the previous hundred years, and was perhaps motivated in part by a shrewd appreciation of the disparity between falling clerical incomes and the continuing social aspirations of the clergy. The old culture of classics and privilege would die hard. Even in the changing circumstances of the nineteen-twenties, as Fellows of St John's scraped together funding to support the son of an engine driver, one of them punned that the young man might have to come up *in loco parentis*.[135] It was a very English joke, but Cambridge was a very English university.

4: Cambridge, Catholicism and the Irish

Socially, intellectually, by gender and by religion, nineteenth-century Cambridge was a restricted universe. The University was also constricted in national identity, English rather than British and certainly not an international community. Two students from the United States, Charles Bristed in the eighteen-forties and William Everett in the eighteen-sixties, found their experience so unusual that they actually wrote Yank-at-Cambridge books about it. By the late nineteenth century, a few colleges had crossed the colour line, but they were hardly typical: a cartoon in a May Week magazine of 1894, "A Lecture at Christ's", is remarkable for the crudity of its racism.[1] Given the narrowness of the starting point, a multi-racial Cambridge was perhaps too large a jump. Most of the University's students had long been "drawn almost exclusively from England and Wales" and the ethos and outlook of the place remained stubbornly English.[2] William Wordsworth, who graduated in 1791, was moved by the thought that Edmund Spenser, "moving through his clouded heaven", had trodden the same courtyards two centuries earlier. "I called him Brother, Englishman, and Friend!"   Charles Kingsley imbued his fictional Chartist student, Alton Locke, with an unlikely moment of inspiration on stumbling across oarsmen racing on the Cam. "My blood boiled over, and fierce tears swelled into my eyes; for I, too, was a man, and an Englishman." A conservative polemicist of 1866 was on safe ground in his assumption of inter-connected identities when he denounced a proposal for a lectureship in American history as "opposed to all English feeling, all academic feeling, and all Church feeling".[3]

Until recent times, "English" was often used as a synonym for "British", even by upper-class Scots,[4] and the usage remains entrenched through such derivatives as "Anglo-American". In Cambridge, by contrast, "English" usually meant "pertaining to England". Even Scots and Welsh were semi-outsiders. Cambridge had been a pace-setter in Reformation times because its North Sea trade gave it direct links with Germany. Yet in striking contrast, there was no obvious academic link with Scotland's east-coast university towns, Edinburgh, St Andrews and Aberdeen. Sidney Sussex claims that in John Young, it can boast the first Scotsman ever to take a Cambridge degree; Venn more cautiously accepts him as one of the first.[5]   Since Young graduated in 1606, when Cambridge University was already four centuries old, Scots cannot have been a common element. Nor had Cambridge anything comparable to the

Snell Exhibition at Oxford, which financed a steady stream of able Scots from Glasgow to Balliol from the time of Adam Smith.

However, by the nineteenth century, there were "plenty of them",[6] as J.F.M. Wright recalled with distaste: indeed, two of the three future prime ministers who attended the university in the century after 1815 were from north of the Border. Yet there is little evidence of a distinctively Scots contribution to Cambridge. Some came by way of the Scottish universities, but for much of the nineteenth century these were in effect junior colleges: in the eighteen-forties, Glasgow University was "regarded as a preparatory school".[7] Critics alleged that because students at Scottish universities were younger than their English counterparts, they were drilled by rote so that they found it difficult to adjust even to such a measure of intellectual openness as could be found in the Cambridge curriculum. Wright warned that "if you fall in with a Scot, you get hold of a bore of a pedant" full of "a pompous rigmarole, about the wealth, honours, and erudition of Aberdeen, St. Andrew's, Dumfries, Glasgow and Edinbro!". In his opinion, Scots' "pretensions to superiority" were evidence only of "their comparative ignorance".[8]

Such hostility was rare: by and large, the Scots faded into the background. Even those with Scots surnames were often heavily anglicised. The Scottishness of the family of John Moultrie, a poet in the eighteen-twenties who wrote about the Union, had been filtered through three generations in South Carolina. His Loyalist father had removed to England, completing the son's acculturation with an Eton education. (Fort Moultrie, in Charleston Harbour, commemorated a patriot uncle and was to be one of the flashpoints that triggered the American Civil War.) George Corrie, Master of Jesus, one of Cambridge's most rigid conservatives, was a Scot by descent, but the son of an Anglican clergyman in Rutland. The ultimate adjective in his formidable vocabulary of denunciation was "un-English". The philosopher J.E. McTaggart, President of the Union in 1890, came from a Wiltshire family called Ellis, who had changed their surname as a condition of an inheritance.[9]

At least a sprinkling of the more prominent Cambridge Scots came from aristocratic and gentry backgrounds, as would be expected from the cost of an English university education. They included Charles Maitland, probable co-founder of the Union, Arthur Balfour and the Marquess of Queensberry, codifier of the rules of boxing and persecutor of Oscar Wilde. Scots aristocrats who became Presidents of the Union included W.F. Campbell in 1847 (later Lord Stratheden and Campbell), Lord Aberdeen's son Arthur Gordon in 1849 and W.F. Scott (later Lord Polwarth) in 1885. They barely differed from their English counterparts. Some aristocratic Scots were members of the Episcopal Church, a minority group in Scotland and very much a lairds' sect. When Lawrence Dundas managed to drown himself after getting drunk in 1818, he was commemorated with a memorial in a local Anglican church. Even if Presbyterians, they came from a social background that found it easy enough to emulate Queen Victoria's movement between the two established churches. Scotsmen of this type differed little from the English elite in outlook and behaviour. The young Marquess of Huntly was beaten within an inch of his life outside Holy Trinity church taking part in a traditional Fifth of November fight between Town and Gown in 1866.[10]

It is revealing that the Union never once debated the Ten Years' controversy that preceded the Disruption of the Kirk in 1843, although it did discuss a passing dispute in 1871 over the decision of the Archbishop of York to hold an Anglican service in Scotland. The only serious debate on a Scottish issue in one hundred years resulted in an uncharacteristic expression of sympathy for the crofters in 1885, a degree of goodwill not extended to their Irish counterparts. On the rare occasions when the Union subsequently turned its attention light-heartedly northwards, few members bothered to attend. In 1902, a small gathering agreed that "the Scotch take life too seriously". In 1911, the handful present had the good taste to reject the proposition that "the nature of the Scot is abhorrent".[11]

It has been calculated that in the century after 1540, seven times as many Welshmen had headed for Oxford as for Cambridge.[12] Oxford was more convenient, and in Jesus College it had an institution with a notably strong Welsh identity. Cambridge was remote and offered no such base. Magdalene had briefly seemed set to become the Welsh college in the sixteenth century until a racist Master determinedly drove them out.[13] St John's reserved some of its endowments for the education of natives of the Principality. It was at St John's in 1598 that the future Archbishop of York, John Williams, had made it his first task to overcome the "National Defect" of his Welsh accent.[14] The inter-varsity contrast continued into the nineteenth century: Cambridge had nothing to compare with the Dafydd, the society dedicated to the promotion of Welsh culture, founded at Oxford in 1886.[15] As with the Scots, those who seemed Welsh could turn out to be Englishmen in disguise: John Llewelyn Davies, twice President of the Union, was the product of a Sussex vicarage. Another theologian, and a genuine Welshman, was Rowland Williams, who in 1839 actually managed to persuade the Union that Ireland was owed a debt of justice by the English. Although Williams was tipped to become the first Welsh-speaking bishop since the Reformation until he became notorious for his contribution to *Essays and Reviews*, he had come to Cambridge from Eton. There he had narrowly escaped death when he was literally scalped in an English public school initiation ritual.[16]

Two Welshmen who reached the Presidency went on to become Liberal MPs, their careers going down with the eclipse of Lloyd George. Ellis J.

Griffiths was President in 1886 and Ernest Evans, an Aberystwyth graduate, in 1909.[17] The Union debated the disestablishment of the Anglican Church in Wales on seven occasions between 1886 and 1914. Evans proposed the only motion that was carried, by 88 votes to 71, despite its peremptory demand for "Immediate Disestablishment". More typical and revealingly worded was the passage, in January 1913, in an almost mirror-image division of 83 votes to 62, of a resolution declaring that proposed legislation "for the Disestablishment of the Church in Wales is both unjust in itself and contrary to the best interests of the Nation". The motion did not specify the Nation whose interests were ill-served, but the division was very similar to the vote of 84 against 68 that had rejected a motion in 1904 sympathising with the "Welsh revolt", the refusal of Welsh local authorities to administer the terms of the 1902 Education Act in protest against privileges granted to Anglican schools.[18] Edwardian Cambridge seems to have been closely divided on those occasions when it actually thought about Welsh issues, but on balance the Union subscribed to the legendary encyclopaedia heading: "Wales, see England".

The first recorded bequest to Cambridge University was made in 1256 by a cleric who was anxious to ensure that masses would be said for his soul. The gift came from William de Kilkenny, who was a court bureaucrat as well as bishop of nearby Ely. Was he Irish? The *Dictionary of National Biography* was not sure: William spent his career serving the king in England and it could not be proved that he had ever lived in Ireland. Even if he was Irish by birth, was he so by ethnicity? His family were Anglo-Norman incomers. As the Duke of Wellington so succinctly put it, being born in a stable did not make you a horse.[19] The enigma of definition lies at the heart of any consideration of the Irish at Cambridge.

However they may be defined, the Irish were not especially numerous in nineteenth-century Cambridge. The 1798 uprisings had been enough to persuade the Irish executive not to take up Archbishop Robinson's endowment for a university at Armagh, since the policy of union with Great Britain explicitly pointed to encouraging the gentry to seek their education at Oxford and Cambridge.[20] It seems unlikely that many did so. Trinity College Dublin offered a more convenient and cheaper alternative, as can be seen by its overproduction of clergy, medical doctors and lawyers, far beyond Ireland's capacity to absorb. A study of 1290 undergraduates admitted to Jesus College Cambridge between 1849 and 1885 identified 818 as coming from public schools (or institutions modelled on them). Of these, precisely three came from Ireland – as compared with thirty from similar schools in Australia and New Zealand.[21] Of course, other Irish came by way of English schools. Parnell had attended private cramming establishments in Somerset and Derbyshire, while one major school, Cheltenham, was established partly to serve a genteel Irish community who chose to overwinter at an English spa town.

Even if statistics existed, it is likely that any attempt to secure reliable figures for Irish Protestants at Cambridge would break down on the rock of self-identification, especially among families that owned estates on both sides of the Irish Channel. Did the Lansdownes belong to Wiltshire or to Kerry? Were the Fitzwilliams from Yorkshire or from Wicklow? Palmerston, son of an Irish peer, was annoyed to find himself regarded as "a Paddy"[22] (as he put it) during his time at Edinburgh University, because he came from an indisputably English family that had acquired Irish property and an Irish title as a sideline. Augustus Stafford O'Brien, who became a Fellow Commoner at St John's in 1829, owned estates in Northamptonshire and at Cratloe overlooking the Shannon in the west of Ireland: he had himself rowed to services in Limerick cathedral in a six-oared barge. Stafford O'Brien could be coldly realistic about Irish life, but was also capable of lapsing into flights of fancy:

> Ireland is the only country that *might be*. America will be, Italy has been, Belgium can't be, England (I suppose) is; but darling Ireland might be...

Did his devotion to this "delicious mixture of possible and uncertain" mean that he saw himself as Irish? In the eighteen-forties, he associated with the romantic political group known as Young England. In 1847, he dropped his second surname because people confused him with the Young Irelander, Smith O'Brien.[23] An even more complex individual response came from Kenelm Digby, who graduated in 1819. Son of the Dean of Clonfert, and member of a family long settled in Ireland, Digby found the medievalism of Cambridge fascinating, and eventually converted to Catholicism − but he spent his later life in England.[24] Thomas and Michael McDonnell, who championed Irish causes around the turn of the century, were Londoners and former pupils of St Paul's School. Their identification with Ireland was in some measure an act of personal choice. Winston Churchill and Michael Collins rarely agreed, but both regarded Erskine Childers as a renegade Englishman. Despite his English antecedents, Childers opted to identify with his mother's Irish relations. By contrast, Parnell, although probably influenced by his American mother, did not choose to adopt her nationality.[25] Henry Lynch proposed a motion in favour of Home Rule at the Union in 1882. Was he Irish? His father had grown up on the family estate near Ballinrobe in Mayo and attended Trinity College Dublin. He had then joined an expedition exploring the Euphrates, settled in London as Consul-General for Persia, and sent his son to Eton.[26] Similar examples are noted in later chapters. The enduring triumph of the nationalist tradition of 1916 has been to obliterate those who identified themselves as simultaneously Irish and British, as was probably the self-image of young Lynch. Yet because these Irish-British not only existed, but naturally formed cross-channel marriage alliances, there were also many English families who felt links to Ireland. One of the most popular characters among inter-war Cambridge dons bore the splendidly English name of Aubrey Attwater. In 1914, he made what sounds like a gauche contribution to a debate on Ulster and was crushingly reported by the *Granta*. "Mr Attwater told us about his relations in Ireland, and knows a lot about the country."[27] There must have been many young Cambridge men who similarly felt an identification with Ireland and (perhaps less constructively) a qualification to pronounce upon its destiny.

Young Irish aristocrats at Cambridge showed characteristics which observers attributed to national identity, including some that made them a larger-than-life nuisance. The Earl of Mount Charles, son of the Prince Regent's mistress Lady Conyngham, became persuaded that a fellow-passenger on a stagecoach to London in 1816 was a ringleader of the labourers' revolt in the Isle of Ely. The accused, a Fenland farmer, denied the allegation with such acerbity that Mount Charles produced a pair of pistols and issued a challenge to a duel, an action that was not only an absurdity, but a social solecism, since duelling was the preserve of gentlemen. Contemporary opinion, however, accepted that Mount Charles had conducted himself "after the ancient fashion of his countrymen", thereby attributing an ethnic quality to an immigrant family.[28] A drunken party on St Patrick's night in 1834 produced a riot of vandalism in Trinity. The offenders included Lord Claude Hamilton, two members of the Ponsonby family, a Conyngham and Lord John Beresford, later Marquess of Waterford, all aggressively asserting their version of Irishness.[29] The following year, a Fellow of Trinity "wisely gave a great dinner to his Irish Pupils, it being St Patrick's Day".[30] In the eyes of English observers, Irish impetuosity could also take a more generous form. Joseph Romilly was the University official responsible for the administration of degrees. Thanks to the special relationship with the University of Dublin, graduates of the sleeping sister could be "incorporated" and so acquire a parallel Cambridge degree. In 1845, Romilly carried out this procedure for William Baxter, a Dublin graduate and a schoolmaster at Cheltenham. To his surprise, Baxter showed his appreciation with the gift of a magnificent salmon from the Severn − "very like a warm-hearted Irishman," Romilly commented. "I have shown equal attention to hundreds of others without any expression of gratitude."[31] It is striking that Romilly should have automatically transmuted a personal gesture into an example of national character. His own forebears were French Protestants (a life-long friend, Adam Sedgwick, attributed Romilly's geniality to the "French blood in his veins") while Baxter's were presumably Scots, a people whom conventional stereotype (on equally fragile evidence) did not associate with generosity.

The reporting of Union debates in University magazines after 1886 makes it possible to identify at least some of those who spoke as Irishmen: most were evidently Protestants, and not surprisingly, most of those were unionists. Two tentative conclusions may be suggested in regard to their contribution to discussion of Irish issues. The first is that there is little evidence that their first-hand testimony exercised much impact, perhaps because in background and outlook, they were remarkably similar to their English contemporaries, and so were often simply duplicating metropolitan prejudices. (It is only fair to add that Indian nationalists made equally little headway in the Union, and probably for diametrically opposite reasons). The second is that because Cambridge remained predominantly Anglican and extremely expensive, it is unlikely that many of its Irish Protestant students came from the Ulster Presbyterian commercial community. For Episcopalians, Oxford and Cambridge were the outworks of Trinity College Dublin, while for Northern Presbyterians, Edinburgh and Glasgow were the outer orbit of Queen's Belfast, the most successful of the three colleges established in 1845. If E.W. MacBride appears frequently in these pages, it is not merely because he was outrageously quotable, but because he spoke with a voice that was rarely heard. Indeed, as the strength of Ulster intransigence emerged in 1912, it became clear that neither the British political elite nor nationalist Ireland had any real appreciation of the force it was suddenly confronting.

If Irish Protestants were probably a minor presence in nineteenth-century Cambridge, Catholics of any variety were even rarer. In the first half of the century, the University was little more than a glorified Anglican seminary and Catholics were barred from taking a degree; in 1867, as Cambridge began to open its doors, the Church itself adopted a negative attitude.[32] Since Cambridge was not one of the growing industrial centres, there was little to attract Irish immigration. The small community that formed in the poor district of Barnwell was probably a by-product of seasonal migration of harvest workers, who probably included the "very ragged miserable Paddies" observed by a Fellow of Trinity, Joseph Romilly, at Cambridge railway station in August 1852. The Irish had been, however, sufficiently numerous in 1841 to defend the construction of the first Catholic chapel from a mob of undergraduates who celebrated the Fifth of November by attempting to root out its foundations.[33] Britain's only census of religious practice, in 1851, reported that attendance at Mass accounted for a shade under one percent of all church-going in Cambridge. The Catholic presence was just large enough to seem mildly threatening in Protestant demonology. Religious crises were one aspect of undergraduate life, and by 1884 it was estimated that 149 Cambridge men had converted over eight decades.[34] The threat was emphasised in the local skyline by the construction, between 1885 and 1890, of the imposing Gothic church in Hills Road. Often called the "Catholic cathedral", the church was in fact far larger than its congregation required, much of the cost being met by a single pious benefactor.[35] As so often elsewhere, Catholicism in Cambridge was to prove much less monolithic than its enemies assumed, and the Hills Road church actually played a relatively minor part in the lives of Catholic members of the University.

Leaving aside the point that they were not obviously welcome in an oppressively Anglican culture, the problem that faced Catholic students at Cambridge in the first half of the nineteenth century was characteristic of the challenge that their community had faced ever since the English Reformation. How was it possible to practise a religion that required priestly ministration in places that lacked resident priests? George Petre, a Lancashire Catholic, solved the problem when he arrived in 1803 by bringing his personal confessor with him. When Thomas Redington came over from Galway in 1832, he went one better and was accompanied by his mother as well throughout his entire course. Romilly, who was their guest for dinner, noted in his diary that the priest, Father Prendergast, "crossed himself in saying Grace", clear evidence that Cambridge dons rarely encountered Catholic ceremonial.[36]

A few colleges were relaxed enough to accept Catholics: Magdalene admitted Charles Acton in 1819 and so can claim Cambridge's only post-Reformation Cardinal.[37] St John's was less tolerant. F.A. Paley was driven out in 1846 on suspicion of having encouraged an undergraduate to defect to Rome. Romilly noted that although a "good scholar", Paley was "a weak man" whose own muddled religious views were inclined to Catholicism. "It is a good thing for the University that he is dismissed." The episode may even have been helpful to Paley, since it seems to have made up his mind to be received into the Church of Rome.[38] The fact that the offender was grandson of Archdeacon Paley, whose *Evidences of Christianity* were a compulsory text in the Little-Go, probably added to the pressures to excise his influence from Cambridge. However, no such motive can excuse the Fellows of Jesus for the action they took against one of their own graduates in 1856. The offender, coincidentally named Pope, hailed from Prince Edward Island, and had become a Catholic three years previously. On discovering that he had joined the "Romish mission" to England, his college showed its disapproval by formally expelling him.[39] It should be remembered that 1856 was the year which saw the end of the Anglican monopoly over the University's BA degree. Mentalities changed more slowly in the constituent colleges.

In the era of the Synod of Thurles, which thunderously barred the faithful from attending even Ireland's harmlessly neutral Queen's Colleges, it may seem strange that there should have been any Catholics at all in the heretical environment of an English university. It is no coincidence that the few exceptions were wealthy enough to afford Cambridge, some even enrolling among the privileged minority as Fellow-Commoners. Many came from aristocratic families who could usually find ways of securing the blessing of the Church upon their actions. Yet even fortified by lofty social eminence, they could find their position in Protestant Cambridge irksome. When the Union discussed Maynooth in 1845, the debate record noted that Lord Bernard Howard "spoke with reference to subjects touched upon by one of the Speakers, but not immediately to the subject of the Debate".[40] While we have no record of his comments, it is possible to guess at the nature of a clarification offered by the son of the Duke of Norfolk, England's premier Catholic layman.

On most social and political issues, the responses of a wealthy English Catholic might well be identical to those of his Protestant fellows. Gerald Strickland was the heir of a long-established family of Westmorland landowners. At the age of fifteen, through his Maltese mother, he acquired the title of Count Della Catena. He was educated at Oscott and at Cambridge, where he called himself Count Bologna Strickland and was elected President of the Union in 1887. (In later life, when he served a term as governor of New South Wales, his fondness for titles led him to be nicknamed Count Delicatessen.) [41] He was also President of the University Carlton Club, the student Conservative organisation. His Catholic upbringing in no way qualified his Tory opinions. He proposed a motion declaring trades unions "to be injurious to the interests of this country": Cardinal Manning might support the workers, but Cardinal Manning was not a Westmorland landowner. Strickland even spoke against a motion demanding the disestablishment and disendowment of the Church of England. His Maltese connection probably explains his twin enthusiasms for Imperial Federation and for an interventionist foreign policy. However, although his Union career coincided with intense interest in Home Rule in 1886-87, he never spoke on Irish issues, although he supported a motion that deplored "the growing tendency to place political power exclusively in the hands of the people".[42] Ironically, he eventually became prime minister of Malta and was thus the only Cambridge Union politician ever to operate a Home Rule constitution.

In Strickland's time, the Catholic population of Cambridge University rarely rose above a dozen students, out of a total of around three thousand.[43] From 1867, it had became harder for devout Catholics to enrol at Cambridge. Cardinal Manning persuaded Rome to condemn, although not absolutely to forbid, attendance at the English universities as places dangerous to faith and morals. Manning's motive was probably a back-handed compliment to the gradual opening of Cambridge: with reform in the air, the University might become less oppressively Anglican and so less inherently repulsive to his flock. Although Manning's attempt to create a Catholic University in Kensington quickly failed, the policy of discouraging attendance at the ancient universities survived until his death in 1892.

In 1895, the Duke of Norfolk brokered an arrangement that permitted Catholics to study at Cambridge under appropriate supervision: by 1899, there were at least 45 Catholic students, still less than two percent of the total.[44] The appointment of an ex-Army officer and convert, Monsignor Barnes, as chaplain to the University in 1902 was a further step in helping the Catholic student community to find its feet in Cambridge. Fortunately, his alien title and its equally unfamiliar abbreviation were disguised in his nickname. In the "Mugger" Catholic students had not only a dedicated pastor but their own surrogate for the archetypal Cambridge don. The Church also established St Edmund's House, which acquired the former Ayerst premises, and in 1898 petitioned the University for hostel status, pleading the precedent of Selwyn for its identification with a single denomination. The application caused a minor intellectual crisis for Cambridge liberalism, which was not sure whether or not its principles required toleration of a venture that it regarded as illiberal. As so often in Cambridge, the decision did not lie in the hands of liberals, and St Edmund's House was made to wait for formal recognition until 1965, long after it had become an accepted part of the University scene.[45]

The Union's Laws banned the discussion of theology. However, when a member challenged the intention to debate Papal Aggression in 1851, the President ruled that the ban applied "to *strictly* Theological questions only".[46] Pronouncements on the political aspects of Catholicism were intermittent but sufficient to make disapproval clear. In Praed 's evocation of Union oratory, Bulwer Lytton was portrayed as denouncing "the horrible massacres … of the Bloody Queen Mary" and, by heavy implication, warning against her co-religionists two and a half centuries later. The Jesuits were condemned by 52 to 18 in 1829, and again by 30 votes to 5 in 1844. The temporal power of the Pope was unanimously criticised in 1862 in a house of 35. In 1874, Seyyid Mustafa Ben-Yusuf of Downing proposed a motion disapproving of Gladstone's attack on the Vatican decrees, presumably as a vehicle for preaching religious pluralism. The Union would have none of it, amending the motion to thank Gladstone for having "strengthened the political position of Great Britain, and the cause of Civil and National Independence". It was rare for Cambridge opinion to feel such gratitude towards Gladstone. In 1898, the refusal of official recognition to St Edmund's House was endorsed by 103 votes to 83.[47] Thus in formal terms, at least, the Union occasionally condemned international Catholicism and deplored its English manifestations, but it did not explicitly link Irish problems to the majority faith of the country's people. However, debate reports quoted in Chapters Nine and Ten suggest that the actual discussion of those issues was markedly less high-minded.

It is never pleasant to discuss sectarian animosity, and perhaps the most positive point that can be drawn from the 1898 debate is the size of the minority. Indeed, it was at around that time that it is possible to trace one of the more dramatic shifts in Union opinion on an Irish issue, which produced a growing acceptance of the idea of a Catholic university. This may well be linked to the return of Catholic students to the Cambridge community after 1895, even if still in small numbers. It was probably unfortunate that the period in which the Church discouraged attendance at Cambridge, the years from 1867 to 1895, coincided with the formation of attitudes to the central issue of Home Rule, often equated by Protestants with Rome Rule.

If Catholics of any nationality were scarce in Cambridge, Irish Catholics were rarer still, and very few argued their case in Union debates. The first to make an impact on the Society was Richard Dillon Boylan in 1824-25. Boylan came to Cambridge from Drogheda by way of Oscott. He was an early member of the Apostles, then emerging as Cambridge's self-selected intellectual elite, and in later life became the English translator of Goethe and Schiller. He was also an officer of the Union, serving successively as Secretary and Treasurer in 1825. His acceptance in the University's two elite societies suggests that there was no necessary barrier to a Catholic Irishman provided that he came from a congenial social background. It is unlikely that he owed his election to office in the Union to his administrative genius. Like most Secretaries of the eighteen-twenties, he bemoaned the loss of books from the Society's unsupervised Library but confessed that he was "quite unable to offer any new arrangement for its perfect regularity".[48] Worse still, when it came to handing on his responsibilities as Treasurer, he was alarmingly casual.

In the summer of 1825, Boylan left Cambridge to travel on the continent – no doubt because there was little point in staying on for degree examinations when his religion barred him from graduating. Boylan later denied "a culpable inattention, or a wilful neglect of the Society's affairs". He explained that he had asked a friend to hand over his accounts and papers, along with a bank draft for the balance, to his successor. Unfortunately the friend had fallen ill and did not return to Cambridge for the autumn term.[49] The Union's business methods were clearly chaotic, and one obvious reform was the establishment of its own bank account. However, this did not solve the problem of Boylan's missing surplus, and almost a year later a curt letter was despatched to his home demanding settlement. It is fortunate that the letter reached its destination, since the officers of the Union seem to have lacked a clear idea of the location of Drogheda: "Mr Boylan not being in England, his Brother had opened the letter".[50] Michael Boylan confessed himself "more than astonished at hearing of so strange a transaction" and promised to make good the missing sum himself, since his brother was travelling in France and could not be contacted.[51] This was enough to restrain moves to expel Boylan from the Society altogether, although an earlier vote of thanks for his services was formally rescinded on account of his "culpable negligence".[52]

Perhaps the most revealing incident in the saga was Michael Boylan's anguish at his brother's behaviour: he wrote that the episode had "caused me the greatest distress of mind".[53] A Catholic Irishman had been sent to study among English gentlemen and had failed to live up to their unwritten code. This sensitivity may also be seen in Richard Boylan's choice of subjects on which to speak in Union debates. In 1824, he did venture to criticise British policy towards Ireland, but he was the tenth speaker out of eleven on his side, and as the Union overwhelmingly agreed with his point of view by 94 votes to 17, he was addressing a friendly audience. More significant is his silence in debates on the more specific question of Catholic Emancipation, either in 1824 or the following year when, as Treasurer, he was the Union's second-ranking officer.[54] Even if apparently successful in gaining a foothold among the English elite, an Irish Catholic remained an outsider who needed to tread carefully and, on the most sensitive issues, not to tread at all.

In the following decade, two Irish Catholics championed unpopular Irish causes in the Union. In 1833, Thomas Redington was one of a small minority to argue in favour of outright Repeal. The following year, he was equally outnumbered when he praised the career of Lord Edward Fitzgerald. Redington soon disavowed his youthful fling, and in 1846 was appointed under-secretary at Dublin Castle, making him the highest ranking Catholic in the Irish government since the seventeenth century.[55] He was followed by John Ball who in 1839 argued, without success, that the unpopular Daniel O'Connell was entitled to the gratitude of the Irish people. He was certainly entitled to the gratitude of a young man whose father had become the second Catholic to be appointed to the bench after Emancipation. John Ball pursued a brief career as an Irish Liberal MP in the eighteen-fifties, and may well be one of the models from which Trollope fashioned Phineas Finn.[56]

One device that gives a snapshot of the relative representation of the Irish in Cambridge is an indicative surname sample. If there is one surname that is conventionally regarded as emblematic of the Irish Catholic peasant, it is surely Murphy. It is of course one of the most common surnames in Ireland, in 1997 accounting for sixty columns in both the Dublin and Cork telephone directories. Well over 50,000 students enrolled at Cambridge University during the nineteenth century. Just thirteen of them bore the surname Murphy.[57] By contrast, to take a surname associated with the Irish ascendancy, there were 22 Beresfords (or 23, if we include John Bottom of Caius who changed his name in

1863). Moreover, as a measure of Irishness, the Murphy cohort must be further reduced: one was an English Catholic, three were born overseas, and in two further cases information is inadequate for identification. Of the seven from Ireland, four were almost certainly Protestants and one cannot be classified. Thus the Murphy "sample" at Cambridge was untypical of the surname as a whole. Of the two Irish Catholics, one was probably a member of the prominent local family of distillers in Midleton, County Cork, who came to Cambridge by way of Newman's foundation, the Oratory School at Birmingham. The other was the son of William Martin Murphy, the Dublin entrepreneur, from whom in 1919 he inherited control of the *Irish Independent*. Neither could remotely be described as an Irish peasant.

The nearest to a peasant Murphy at Cambridge was the son of a shoemaker from Mallow in County Cork which, like many Cork towns, contained a Protestant artisan community. Robert Murphy was a prodigy who published his first mathematical proof at the age of eighteen. A public subscription enabled him to go to Caius in 1825. He won a fellowship in 1829 and was ordained in the Church of England. Unfortunately, the pressures on him were too great and he took to drink. In 1832 his fellowship income was impounded to pay his debts and he returned to Ireland. He made a second attempt at an academic career at London University, but died in his mid-thirties.[58]

Only one Cambridge Murphy defended an Irish cause at the Union: John Arthur Murphy argued for Home Rule in 1890. Later that year he supported a motion describing Cambridge University as "a ridiculously overrated institution". He left soon afterwards without taking a degree and returned to his home on the verdant island seared by a tragic history that lay on the fringes of a mighty continent. The island was Tasmania.[59]

Thus Ireland was something essentially external to Cambridge opinion. There was nothing new in this. In 1429, Irish students had been banned from the University after allegations that they were responsible for a campaign of robbery and arson.[60] One "rayny & darke night" in December 1688, as King Billy ousted James II from the throne, Cambridge was swept by panic caused by a report that five hundred Irish soldiers had sacked Bedford and were marching on the town. Some even claimed that the Irish had broken into the town by Magdalene and had started "cutting of throates, soe that ye scare ... was very great & dismall".[61] Individual episodes faded from the memory but contributed to an overall English assumption that the Irish were unaccountably and perversely different. James Stephen, later Professor of History, provided a revealing reminiscence of his education:

> One day I happened to see a map and being then nearly fourteen years old, found out to my extreme surprise, that Ireland was not part of the Island of Great Britain but they were separated by a wide channel of the sea.[62]

Many English attitudes to Ireland derived from the assumption that the sea either did not, or ought not to exist. Even the officers of the Union could slip into the assumption that Drogheda was in "England".

Half a century after the Catholic Emancipation controversy, one Cambridge Union veteran retained a sense of guilt about British rule in Ireland. Charles Merivale, Dean of Ely, confessed himself to be "pro-Turk" in 1876, or at least unhappy at the imposition of reforms by the European Powers upon the Turks. "All that we can say against them the Irish have said, and still say, against us; and I don't want to set a precedent for a European Conference to extort home rule for Ireland, and the occupation of Ulster by the Russians, and Dublin by the Americans." Other Cambridge observers were less sympathetic.[63] William Whewell began his energetic travels across continental Europe in 1819, but did not visit Ireland until the British Association met in Dublin in 1835. He went armed with his own preconceptions. "You have no reason to fear for me," he assured his sister, "for, though they are fond of breaking each others' heads, they never molest strangers." Observation of the poverty of the south of Ireland only increased the tendency of the carpenter's son to dehumanise its people:

> No English pig of the slightest respectability would think for a moment of living in such cabins as you see in long rows in every town and village ... and the dress of the people is so ragged that I never could comprehend the possibility of its being taken off and put on again.

The Irish, he concluded, "do not find any peculiar wretchedness in being in rags". Indeed, they probably "rather prefer them to whole clothes".[64]

For some Cambridge Protestants, Irish ethnicity was interwoven with language and religion. Joseph Romilly had an inexhaustible taste for preaching. He often confided his opinions of pulpit oratory to his diary, but only rarely was he moved to record the actual contents. One exception was an entry for February 1836 when he attended a service intended to raise money for missionary work in Ireland. From the sermon he learnt that "there were 500,000 in Ireland who understood no language but Irish, & that the Irish had such a veneration for their language that they thought nothing heretical could exist in it".[65] George Corrie actually taught himself Irish, although mainly to facilitate his research into Church history. A sabbatarian (as he showed in his denunciation of a Sunday excursion trains to Cambridge), Corrie deplored the fact that "in Ireland nothing is so common as to have your feelings shocked by Sunday dances, and games of all kinds". None the less, his sympathies were with the poor Irish, "in having for a long time before them the example of Sabbath-breaking countenanced if not encouraged by the Priests". Perhaps he attended the sermon that had so interested Romilly, for by July 1836 he felt "a most itching desire" to visit Achill Island, off the Mayo coast, where Protestant missionaries were rolling back the frontier of superstition, "to the no small consternation of the [sic] McHale's Popery".[66] His wish came true in 1839, thanks in part to the hospitality of Stafford O'Brien at Cratloe.

Two themes predominate in Corrie's comments on Ireland, and both of them may be confidently regarded as chosen in advance as organising principles for his observations. One was the evil influence of the priesthood. He carefully noted clerical interference in politics, priestly opposition to popular education, and the physical violence and spiritual intimidation employed to obstruct Protestant missionary work. From Achill, he travelled on to Ventry, the Protestant bridgehead in Kerry. There he encountered an old man who had converted because he could not accept that a priest could absolve him of his burden of guilt. As a young man, he had stolen twenty sheep. The crime was duly confessed to the parish priest, who had promised divine forgiveness so long as he received a sheep and several fleeces of wool every Christmas. It was just the sort of story that Corrie eagerly lapped up: a tormented soul sacrificed to a corrupt and worldly racket. However, two experiences challenged this all-embracing interpretation. One was that Corrie's visit coincided with the brushfire early stages of Father Mathew's Temperance campaign. Corrie first heard of Theobald Mathew from one of Stafford O'Brien's estate workers:

> He told me that there is now a *Friar* in Cork who cures people of a love for whisky, by means of a charmed medal which is worn about the neck, and is purchased for eightpence. The medals are numbered, and it is calculated that not less than ten thousand have already been sold. The effect of the medal is said to be such that whosoever possesses it is seized with a hatred of whisky, and in fact, would be prevented from possibility of drinking any more, since if he were to attempt it, the whisky would become maggots.

Corrie's informant believed that Mathew "had shewed one of those who went to him *the whisky actually changed into maggots*". Another local man had taken his son to Cork "to be miraculously cured of lameness", and insisted that Father Mathew had performed a miracle, "though the contrary was manifestly the case". "The Friar, it seems, made the sign of the cross, uttered some prayer, touched the lame part, and the boy was instantly relieved from pain!" Whether for good or ill, some priests were evidently trading on the ignorance of their people. Yet Corrie related another tale with evident approval. A Protestant minister visited by converts from the Blasket islands off the Kerry coast had "greatly excited their attention" by striking a lucifer match. "On their return to the Island, they had some argument with Romanists respecting the power of the priests", which the Protestants had won by proclaiming that their minister "brought fire out of a *stick!*" Tactics condemned as mummery and superstition in the hands of the enemy evidently became fair game in a good cause.

The other challenge to Corrie's preconceptions took the form of a meeting with a local priest, Father Malone, whom Stafford O'Brien invited to dinner. Corrie does not seem to have made any allowance for the pressures upon a Catholic priest, asked to dinner at the Big House to meet an unusually zealous Protestant clergyman from a famous university. "At first Mr Malone seemed shy and embarrassed, but after some general conversation he became chatty." Presumably Malone decided that it would spoil a pleasant evening to tell the host and his English visitor that they were heretics destined for Hell. Instead, he adopted a workaday attitude to his calling, leaving the disapproving Corrie with the impression that he "seemed to regard his office as a profession by which he had to live". When O'Brien remarked on the good looks of a local girl, Father Malone replied: "I don't know much about her, for she will be no *profit* to me, since she is not in my parish, and *so* if she were to marry, I should be none the better for it." Corrie concluded that "Malone came quite up to my notion of a Popish priest. ... There was not a particle of apparent religion about him, but on the contrary he seemed to be a mere trading ecclesiastic." The sole positive quality detected by Corrie in his fellow dinner guest was a certain scepticism about the Temperance crusade. According to Malone, "the road between Mallow and Cork was covered with people dead drunk ... in consequence of their having drunk very copiously, as a kind of farewell to whisky" before presenting themselves before Father Mathew and abjuring alcohol for ever. When it came to the denigration of a Catholic venture in social reform, the worldly and cynical Father Malone suddenly became a highly credible source.

Corrie's second theme, set in convenient counterpoint, was the inherent goodness of the Irish people themselves. Like Whewell, he was struck by the squalor in which so many of them lived, such as the old woman he met in County Limerick who lived in "a most miserable cabin, not nearly so good as almost every pig-stye in England". Not far away, Corrie was struck by the contrast between two adjoining fields, one neatly cultivated, the other poorly tended. On learning that the tenant of the former was a Protestant, he was moved to comment that "Popery seems like a blight of heaven resting on this land!" It was religion, and not the inherent character of the people, that accounted for their backward condition. "That there is no *ignorance* strictly speaking in the

Papists that makes them less worldly wise, may be seen at once by any who will pay the slightest attention to their ready intelligence." The inherent goodness of the Irish people also shone through "a great gathering of peasantry" organised by Stafford O'Brien as a sort of Merrie Ireland celebration on the Cratloe estate. "They are indeed a light-hearted, social people, their whole demeanour marked by the utter absence of all rudeness," Corrie wrote, before launching into his familiar moral. "One can only marvel at the cruel superstition which habitually converts such beings into relentless savages." [67]

The relentless and uncompromising intellectual framework that shaped Corrie's view of the Irish is one that arouses little sympathy today. However, our own distaste may lead us to miss an important element in his attitudes. Corrie did not simply abominate Catholic Emancipation as the "legislative renunciation of God". He regarded concessions to Catholics, especially in Ireland, not as overdue acts of justice but rather as artificial attempts to reverse the course of history in defiance of that divine will that he would later voice so confidently in his opposition to Sunday excursion trains. "Surely the great general purposes which God has declared toward the human race, are inconsistent with the long continuance of such a system as Irish Popery!" Even so ostensibly secular an issue as reform of the Irish corporations was to Corrie a battleground for religious truth. He rejoiced at the demise of "the Popish Municipal Corporation Bill intended for Ireland" during the parliamentary session of 1836. "May a merciful God grant that this may be the first step towards our deliverance from the spirit of Popery." When the bill was reintroduced the following year, Corrie concluded that the sole aim was that Ireland should be "thrown into the hands of the Papists, as to secure a permanent majority in the House of Commons efficient only for mischief". A modern response might be that such a move would merely recognise Irish reality. To such an argument, Corrie would have responded that present reality could not possibly correspond to divinely ordained destiny: "we may expect a not distant termination to a superstition which is at variance with all those great principles which hold society together". Indeed, only the reluctance of the English "as a nation to turn to God" could delay the victory of Protestantism, and "till then we may well be permitted to suffer the national detriment".[68]

For all its sectarian narrowness, Corrie's analysis had room for a mellow if patronising view of the Irish themselves. They were, in his perception, quaint and inefficient, but essentially they were victims of their faith, from which they must in time escape. While Corrie was hardly a prophet of modernity, there was a sense in which he was right: railways, telegraphs, schools and the English language did undoubtedly change Ireland and its people. Remarkably, however, modernisation did not significantly change Ireland's religion. Indeed, in many respects the Church exploited the forces of change to become a more powerful organisation as the nineteenth century progressed. By the time Charles Kingsley took a break from preparing his inaugural lecture as Professor of History to visit Mayo twenty years later, hopes of a massive conversion to Protestantism were starting to fade. The Catholicism of the Irish increasingly appeared to be their own self-inflicted burden, something accepted not in ignorance of a better way, but wilfully adopted in defiance of the paths of light. The logical corollary was an interpretation of the Irish that elaborated Whewell's pastiche of a quaint peasantry into a full-scale portrait of an inferior race.

Kingsley was moved by the poverty and the physical monuments to famine in "this land of ruins and the dead". "You cannot conceive to English eyes the first shock of ruined cottages; and when it goes on to whole hamlets, the effect is most depressing. ... what an amount of human misery each of these unroofed hamlets stands for!" Like Whewell, Kingsley's solution was implicitly to deny the humanity of the victims and, by 1860, he could call upon Darwin to do so. "I am haunted by the human chimpanzees that I saw along that hundred miles of horrible country. ... to see white chimpanzees is dreadful". With his usual insensitivity, Kingsley extended the metaphor into a full-scale racist comparison: "if they were black, one would not feel it so much, but their skins, except where tanned by exposure, are as white as ours". The emphasis in these reports was upon Kingsley's own anguish at having to witness Irish suffering:

> I don't believe they are our fault. I believe there are not only many more of them than of old, but that they are happier, better, more comfortably fed and lodged under our rule than they ever were.

If Irish degradation was not "our fault", then by default the blame must fall upon the people themselves.[69] One of the few English commentators who managed to escape from the simplistic equation of ethnicity with poverty was George Cornewall Lewis, an Oxford academic, who had conducted a more detailed government enquiry into Irish social conditions in 1833:

> Before I went to Ireland I had very strong opinions as to the influence of *race* on the Irish character. But when I came to look at things more nearly, and to see all the demoralising influences to which they have been and are subjected, I asked myself whether a people of Germanic race would have turned out much better; and I really could not answer in the affirmative.[70]

In most English perceptions, the notion of racial inferiority was carried forward to the later nineteenth century, long after Ireland had become a modernising and even prosperous country: it was Salisbury who casually equated Irish Celts with "Hottentots" as peoples who, in his opinion, were unfit to operate representative institutions.[71]

Undergraduates love paradox, and the racial argument could be stood on its head: Home Rule, Edward Selwyn told the Union in 1907, was necessary because of "the difference between the Anglo-Saxon and the Celt".[72] Outright racism was rare in the Union, but there are clues to suggest that debates were conducted within an intellectual framework that presupposed an ethnic as well as a social hierarchy in which the Irish occupied an ambiguous position, close to that of Cambridge's Indian students, who were regarded with mild amusement. As late as the nineteen-thirties, Geoffrey de Freitas could report for the *Granta* that "the Maharaj Kumar Prafulla Chandra Bhanj Deo of Mayurbhanj and Bastar spoke, but there is no room to say what he said". Forty years earlier, a contribution by an Indian student to the debate on the Parnell commission was reported in equally patronising terms – "obviously doing his best to grapple with a subject of which he knew about as much as most Irishmen do of the Punjab".[73] An even more striking, and indeed offensive, attempt at wit was uttered during a light-hearted debate on the Irish in 1897: "America will only be tolerable when every negro [sic] kills an Irishman and is hanged for it."[74] Remarkably, the perpetrator of this sentiment, which lacked even the doubtful merit of originality, was Charles Masterman, an exponent of the new social liberalism and a member of Asquith's government during the Home Rule crisis of 1912-14.

Overall, ethnic prejudice against the Irish formed a minor element in Cambridge attitudes to Ireland. Even the fact that the University was almost totally devoid of a Celtic, Catholic, peasant voice may be of little moment: the assertive and demanding presence of Irish MPs at Westminster did little to win English hearts and minds. The most consistent quality in Cambridge attitudes was neither racism nor ignorance, but the simple assumption that Ireland was something external, a nuisance and an intrusion. In November 1888, Montague Rhodes James was obsessed by the need to save a valuable collection of medieval manuscripts for the British Museum: "instead of making a fuss about Ireland", the House of Commons should "attend to the best interests of the country". Parliament, of course, was not notable for its enthusiasm in its consideration of the Irish question in 1888, but was forced to do so by nationalist pressure. An exasperated James had "no patience ... with the Home Rulers". England was "the country" and its "best interests" lay in preserving medieval manuscripts.[75] Looking back half a century at the achievement of Catholic Emancipation, A.M. Sullivan had identified as the most dynamic aspect of the County Clare election the fact that the Irish people had seized the political initiative for themselves. "What ought to be done, or might be done, *for* them was constantly debated," but never before had British opinion been obliged to respond to a political agenda of Irish dictation.[76] This was a fair criticism of the political culture at large. For the Cambridge Union, a society operating in a very English university, buttressed by a sense of social and intellectual superiority and dedicated to the art of debating, it could not be other than a necessary limitation.

The University Library (later Squire Law Library) 1896

Part Two

The Cambridge Union

1815-1914

Falcon Yard 1883.

One of the last Cambridge inn-yards recalls the "tavernous" atmosphere of the Union in
the days when it occupied rooms at the Red Lion and Hoop Inns.

5: The Early Years of the Cambridge Union

The inaugural meeting of the Cambridge Union Society took place on 13 February 1815, and the first debate was held one week later.[1] The Union was "formed by the combination of three other Societies, which had previously existed in the University".[2] According to legend, the occasion was the black-balling (vetoing) of an Etonian, Edward Gambier, who was a candidate to join one of the three clubs. "His friends rallied to his behalf, effected the amalgamation of the three Societies under the designation of the Union, and elected him President." The most important of the antecedent societies was the Speculative, which is further discussed below. The second club was "nicknamed the Anticarnalist, in consequence of one of its members having been expelled on account of some flagrant act of immorality".[3] If it was the Anticarnalist to which Gambier had sought entry, it would be easy to understand the furious response of his friends to the implied slur of his rejection. The third society was quickly forgotten. Wright recalled in 1827, that the Union was formed from "two regular 'Spouting Societies'".[4] George Pryme, later Whig MP for the borough, was living in Cambridge in 1815 and about to begin the University's first course of lectures in political science. His recollection was that the Union arose from "the junction of two rival societies".[5] A possible reconstruction might suggest that there was a mass defection from the Anticarnalist to the Speculative in protest against the implied slur upon Gambier's sexuality, and that a small third society threw in its lot with the merged grouping.

So engaging is the legend of the black-balling of Edward Gambier that it is easy to overlook the significance of the founding of an openly constituted university debating society with its own independent premises. The Union hired "a dingy room" in the Red Lion Inn on the south side of Petty Cury, known by ironic pun as the *Comitia Curiata*, the title of the early assembly of the Roman people.[6] Meeting in a local inn did not place the Union beyond the jurisdiction of the University, as was to be underlined when the authorities put a stop to debate two years later, but it ended the inconveniences of meeting in members' rooms in the various colleges. The origins of the Speculative's nickname, the "Fusty", are obscure,[7] but in an age when facilities for personal freshness were severely limited, it is neither difficult nor pleasant to imagine the atmosphere of a college room crammed with young men for a lengthy meeting. Nor was it easy to regulate access or ensure security when meeting in college. In 1805, members of the Speculative, gathered in an undergraduate's room in Trinity, caught a freshman, W.J. Bankes, listening at the door. It is likely that the young Bankes was genuinely interested in politics. Twenty years later, he and Palmerston were rivals for the representation of Cambridge University, divided over the issue of Catholic Emancipation. Regarded by some as the equal of Sydney Smith in wit and conversation, Bankes would have been an excellent recruit for the Speculative. However, its members took a dim view of his eavesdropping and forced him to write out a set of Latin lines as a punishment.[8]

The Speculative seems to have limited its membership to a maximum of about twenty, probably the physical limit imposed by a college room. Members took turns to read an essay on some abstruse topic, which was then discussed by those present. Palmerston contributed five such papers between 1804 and 1806, on subjects as varied as the policy of transfer of the Portuguese government to Brazil and the political character of Cardinal Fleury, whose pacific policies in the reign of Louis XV were no doubt recalled with some nostalgia as Napoleon dominated the mainland of Europe.[9] In 1806 the society dwindled dangerously close to extinction, but in more buoyant times, acceptable candidates for membership might have to be passed over. A small society also had to be exceptionally careful not to elect an interesting but disruptive personality, as the Apostles later discovered in the case of the unstable Thomas Sunderland.[10] By 1814, as the long wars against France came to an end, an increase in the student population could be expected, and it was unlikely that they could all be accommodated within traditional college buildings: in 1818, numbers were rising so steadily that the University formally began to supervise lodging houses.[11] There would thus have been good reason for the three smaller societies "consolidating into one mass of noisy ignorance"[12] even without the affront to Edward Gambier. To put it in modern terminology, there was a niche in the market for a central student clubroom.

The entrepreneurs who masterminded the project were identified by C.J. Shore, the first Secretary of the Union. The three amalgamated societies were "provisionally" administered by Charles Fox Townshend and Charles Fox Maitland, two young aristocrats who shared – as their names indicated – a distinguished Whig godfather. According to Shore's recollection, the Union was "finally constituted, in the spring of 1814", but the rest of his account suggests that this was incorrect, presumably stemming from the fact the initial moves to establish the Society, including the hiring of premises, had begun some months before the first official meeting in February 1815. Early debate records are incomplete but it seems that Townshend and Maitland faded into the background, perhaps because "other officers were substituted" in what may have been a revolt against their dominance.[13] One reason why the two were not better remembered was that they both died, still very young men, in 1817.

Townshend, who spoke in the Union's third debate, was a member of one of the great Whig clans. Moreover, in 1811, he had founded a debating club at Eton, officially called the Eton Society, but generally known in the school's private language as "Pop". Townshend's enthusiasm for his creation survived his transition to university, for when Pop fell on hard times in 1816 he issued a bombastic appeal from Cambridge to rally its schoolboy members to the rescue of the society.[14] One of the strengths of Pop was that it broke down the barriers at Eton between the elite of foundation scholars, the Collegers, and the fee-paying pupils scattered around the town in boarding houses, and known as Oppidans. It is possible that Townshend threw his weight behind the Union project to break down similar, inter-collegiate barriers at Cambridge. There may have been more than octogenarian nostalgia behind Gladstone's description of Pop in 1894 as "the mother and model I believe of all the debating societies of the schools and universities of the kingdom".[15] The response to the black-balling of Edward Gambier points to the existence of an easily manipulated Eton network among Cambridge undergraduates, and three of the first five Presidents of the Union were Etonians.

There was nothing new in the idea of a debating society as such, but there was something challenging in the formation of one so openly constituted in an English university. Eighteenth-century London had been enlivened by a vigorous debating culture, societies being encouraged and even organised by tavern-keepers as a means of generating trade. The Robin Hood Society was established before 1740, and its name became a by-word to be borrowed by imitators in the provinces. In 1764 the Robin Hood even produced its own history, which advanced the doubtful claim that it had originated as far back as 1613. By 1780, at least 35 debating clubs were meeting in London, although the numbers were reduced by the enforcement of Sunday observance laws in the seventeen-eighties, and by wider political repression in the decade that followed. None the less, over two thousand debates have been traced in reports from London newspapers between 1776 and 1799. Similar societies were meeting in Edinburgh by 1764, Liverpool by 1768 and Birmingham in 1774. Most of these societies met in rooms hired from taverns, sometimes shared with other activities, just as the Cambridge Union of the eighteen-twenties often had to change its debate night to make way for the assize dinner. By coincidence, the Birmingham and Wolverhampton societies even met at hostelries called The Red Lion.[16]

Most of these ventures provided for open participation. In London audiences of several hundred were not uncommon, with speakers including both women and men. In an age when the House of Commons barely even pretended to be representative, such gatherings were a potential challenge to authority. A disapproving bishop in 1795 denounced them as "idle and seditious public meetings for the discussion of laws where the people were not competent to decide upon them", adding that "he did not know what the mass of the people in any country in the world had to do with the laws but to obey them". Four years later, William Pitt was even more sweeping in his denunciation of debating societies for "loosening the foundations of morality, religion and social happiness".[17]

Debating was not necessarily harnessed to subversion: there is evidence that Pitt himself had been a member of one of the London societies. Semi-secret select clubs, such as the Speculative Society at Edinburgh, helped young gentlemen aspiring to enter the professions to gain experience in arguing a case before an audience. One indirect precursor of the Cambridge Union was the Academical Society, which was established in London in November 1798, having grown from a discussion group founded at Oxford five years earlier. It was open to members of any university in the United Kingdom as well as to lawyers from the Inns of Court, the Faculty of Advocates in Edinburgh and King's Inns in Dublin. Even more unusual, membership was also open to members of Maynooth, the priestly seminary in Ireland. The Academical Society was devoted to "discussion of philosophical, literary, and historical questions", with an emphasis upon "the general principles of political science, together with the practical illustrations of them which history affords". There were limitations on debate, which probably influenced the Cambridge Union, whose original Laws declared that "controversial theology shall not be introduced", and "no observation shall be made upon any living character of the United Kingdom".[18] George Pryme was a member of both the Academical Society and the Cambridge Speculative, although in 1815 he was probably an inactive senior patron of the latter.[19]

Debating societies were established at Edinburgh by 1800. Indeed, debating was adopted as a form of progressive education by Dugald Stewart as a means of sharpening the brains of adolescents like the sixteen-year-old Palmerston. Even in institutions that were far from progressive, it was a tolerated activity. Eton boys lived their lives with very little official supervision when Townshend founded Pop in 1811, but the ferocious headmaster, Keate, seems to have approved. One of the most sardonic barbs in the Union's protest against the interruption of debates in 1817 was that Cambridge students, many of them graduates, were "now deprived of a privilege which has been uniformly extended by the Masters of the Public Schools to the Boys under their charge".[20]

In Edinburgh, where undergraduates were usually several years younger than their English counterparts, only a few favoured university students became members of the Speculative Society. Some of these went on to Cambridge where the arrival of "an élève of the Speculative" could be hailed as "a real acquisition" for its southern derivative, the Fusty.[21] The Edinburgh Speculative also provided a partial precedent for a free-standing debating club within a university. Founded in 1764, the Speculative Society had secured permission to build its own premises in the university precinct, with right of perpetual occupancy. However, there were important differences between Edinburgh and Cambridge. The Speculative was not merely a student club, but a joint venture of Town and Gown. This in turn reflected a very different relationship between the two. In Cambridge, the university was not only independent of the town, but exercised a measure of supervision over local affairs. In Edinburgh the relationship was the reverse, with the Town Council maintaining a considerable degree of authority over the university. The contrast was well illustrated in 1817 when the programme to rebuild the original College involved the demolition of the Speculative Society's building. While the Vice-Chancellor of Cambridge was closing down the debates of the Union, the Edinburgh Speculative successfully insisted that the agreement of 1769 gave it the right to specially designed chambers in the new buildings – which it retains, independent of any academic control, to this day. Nor was it the only debating society to operate at Edinburgh University. The Dialectic Society, for instance, began life in 1787. [22]

The charming story of the dispute over the character of Edward Gambier obscures the real significance of the establishment of the Union. An openly constituted debating society in Cambridge was something more than a natural development from private essay-reading clubs such as the Speculative. However, Palmerston in 1825 described the Union as "the enlarged Fusty",[23] and some element of transition can be seen in the earliest Laws, published in 1817: members were still formally required to take turns in opening a subject for discussion, even though the Society was already too large to accommodate them all.[24] Much later, in 1878, J.F. Skipper confidently identified nine founders of the Union, including the future judges, Henry Bickersteth, Frederick Pollock and Edward Hall Alderson. This tradition cannot be correct, since most of those named seem to have left Cambridge by 1811, when the outcry against the plan to form a student-led branch of the Bible Society, discussed below, clearly proves that nothing resembling a proto-Union could then have been in existence. Skipper's informant was probably the Lord Chief Justice, Sir Alexander Cockburn, who had been President in 1824. Bickersteth was a formidable debater in his Cambridge days, while Pollock at least was a member of the Speculative and, as distinguished lawyers, both would have been known to Cockburn.[25] It seems likely that, like Palmerston, Cockburn assumed that the Union had inherited the traditions of its predecessor, and simply co-opted an immediately preceding generation of "Fustyarian"[26] notables as its own. When the Union was challenged in 1817, it suited its defenders to emphasise that the Society "was the common successor of several which have existed for a great number of years in the University".[27] This was a sensible strategy adopted by very effective publicists who sought to play down the implications of the Union's very recent origin in a period of political turbulence. Such claims should not obscure the fact that there was a difference between a small essay reading club and an open debating society, albeit one along a common scale of "spouting". Essay clubs rose and fell: Thackeray helped to form one in October 1829, but it survived only briefly.[28] None the less, it may be that by displacing the Speculative, a prestigious intellectual club limited to twenty members, the Cambridge Union left a gap that was to be filled by the rise in the following decade of the Apostles, a prestigious intellectual club limited to twelve.

Among the small debating clubs known to have existed in Cambridge before 1815 was one called the House of Commons, which flourished in the seventeen-nineties, giving the Evangelicals of Magdalene the opportunity to practise their pulpit oratory by discussing such weighty issues as a proposal to tax cats.[29] In 1811, their successors had set a more formidable feline among the donnish pigeons, with a proposal to form a branch of the British and Foreign Bible Society. The consternation that followed demonstrates just how great a breakthrough was the founding of the Union only four years later.[30]

The British and Foreign Bible Society had been founded in 1804. The duality of its title was reflected in its first project, the distribution of a Welsh translation of the Scriptures. This might seem an unexceptional outlet for undergraduate enthusiasms. However, while undoubtedly anglocentric, the Bible Society was not one hundred percent Anglican. Dissenters were guaranteed seats on its management committee, and no attempt was made to link distribution of Holy Writ to any form of liturgy. In this, it differed from the rival Society for the Promotion of Christian Knowledge, which took the much more robust view that Christian knowledge was synonymous with Anglican ritual. Thus the possibility that enthusiastic undergraduates might form a branch of the Bible Society spelt trouble in Cambridge. William Farish, Evangelical Fellow of Magdalene, listened to their ideas with his head in his hands. Academics who believed so fervently in the redemptive power of Scripture could hardly refuse to support a body dedicated to the distribution of Bibles. Yet if a society open to Nonconformists could operate in Cambridge, what reason could be given for continuing to refuse non-Anglicans the right to take Cambridge degrees? Furthermore, once undergraduates began to busy themselves with the circulation of the Bible, they might be tempted to agitate for a system of public education to equip the poor with the literacy skills needed to absorb the Christian message. From this, it might be but a short step to demanding that the bellies of the people be filled so that their minds could concentrate on the saving of their souls. In short, "if the young men assumed the character of a deliberating body, it would be productive of great mischief to the discipline of the University".[31]

As with the attempted suppression of the Union in 1817, the situation was saved by conservative over-reaction. The Professor of Divinity, Herbert Marsh, was obsessed by the threat posed by the Bible Society to Anglican hegemony. Indeed, his "most injudicious" invective seemed to challenge the fundamental Protestant tenet that the Word of God did not require the mediation of priests. His attacks opened the way to a deft manoeuvre by Evangelical senior members. They took control of the project and established a Cambridge branch of the Society in December 1811, taking care to praise the "self-denying zeal" of its original undergraduate promoters in stepping aside.[32]

Since the pace of change of unreformed Cambridge was measured in decades, if not centuries, it is striking that just over three years later, the founders of the Union managed to get away with establishing a deliberative body with such an obvious potential to subvert university discipline. The answer probably lies in the social standing of the initial office-holders. Townshend and Maitland, who formed the original steering committee, were young grandees with formidable connections. Townshend's family had provided the University with two MPs in the previous century and, despite his youth, Charles Fox Townshend himself was soon to become a candidate to follow them. Although the inscription records that he was just twenty years, nine months and five days old when he died in 1817, Townshend's social eminence was sufficient to ensure him a large memorial in the chapel of St John's.[33] Maitland was the son of the Earl of Lauderdale, "a violent-tempered, shrewd, eccentric man, with a fluent tongue, a broad Scottish accent, and a taste for political economy".[34] While a recent historian has noted that by 1815 Lauderdale "was drifting steadily to the right at a rate of knots calculated to carry him out of the Whig haven altogether",[35] none the less he had been a supporter of the quasi-revolutionary Friends of the People in 1792 and had denounced the persecution of the "Scottish Martyrs" two years later. He might well have responded with some asperity to any decision by mere dons to interfere with his son's plans to form a debating club. Indeed, he did protest in the Lords against the general repression of 1817.

Townshend and Maitland were not alone in their social eminence among founders of the Union. The first President was a nephew of Admiral Lord Gambier, who had commanded the Channel Fleet in the last years of the wars against Napoleon. The Admiral suffered from religious scruples that made him question unrestricted warfare, such as the destruction of Copenhagen in 1807 without the formality of declaring war upon Denmark. However, even if he distinctly lacked the Nelson touch, he was still a national hero, if only of the second rank. The first Secretary of the Union, C.J. Shore, was the son and heir of Lord Teignmouth, governor-general of India from 1793 to 1798. Teignmouth, who had also undergone a religious conversion, was President of the Bible Society.

Even if the first President and Secretary of the Cambridge Union were tainted with Evangelicalism, their colleague, the Society's founder-Treasurer, was unimpeachably aristocratic. In later life, Lord Normanby sailed insouciantly through a distinguished political career, even nominating himself (unsuccessfully) for the office of prime minister. As Irish viceroy in the eighteen-thirties, he earned the censure of the Union by befriending Daniel O'Connell. He was still only seventeen years of age when he succeeded Gambier as the Union's second President, and almost certainly its youngest. Freshman though he was, Normanby carried huge prestige in a university that bent over backwards to accommodate aristocrats: as Shore mildly recalled, "his social qualifications were appreciated by the dons".[36] His father, the Earl of Mulgrave, soldier and politician, had sat in the cabinet almost continuously for a decade, holding offices as senior as Foreign Secretary, First Lord of the Admiralty and Master-General of the Ordnance. While his administrative talents were at best moderate, Mulgrave was seen as a key figure in government: when he sought to retire in 1818, the Prince Regent insisted on keeping him in the cabinet even without formal office. He had swung round in 1812 to supporting Catholic Emancipation once it became clear that George III would not recover his health, but otherwise Mulgrave had impressive credentials as a reactionary. He had once confuted Wilberforce's denunciation of slavery by stating he had spent a year in Jamaica without seeing a single act of cruelty. It was implausible to suggest that Lord Mulgrave's son was conspiring against the social order, and unlikely that the University would take steps against any society which he chose to ornament.

The debating club founded in Cambridge in February 1815 added a term to the English language: social centres for students at British universities are more or less automatically called "unions". The most obvious explanation for the adoption of the title is of course the origin of the Cambridge society in a junction of three smaller clubs. However, the name may well have carried other overtones. In eighteenth-century Cambridge, the nobility had patronised a Union Coffee House, which provided a chance to read newspapers and a forum to discuss politics.[37] For Townshend, an Englishman, and Maitland, a Scot, perhaps it evoked the Union of 1707, much celebrated in the contemporary street-names of Edinburgh's New Town. A Union Club was founded in London in 1822, with Peel as one of its early members: its handsome building later became Canada House.[38] An elite reared on the classics would have recognised the principle attributed to Periander of Corinth: union is strength. "Union" was a benign term that carried positive connotations. As the title of a debating society, it offered the reassurance that members might disagree while remaining comrades.

Unfortunately, the very universality of the term could also encourage confusion. Undergraduate humour played upon the parallel with the American Union,[39] while even Erskine Childers perpetrated a punning allusion to the union between Britain and Ireland.[40] In 1838, under the provisions of the New Poor

Law, Cambridge acquired a large workhouse (which subsequently became the local maternity hospital). This quickly became known as "the Union", and comic misunderstandings occasionally ensued.[41] These, however, were minor inconveniences compared to the rapidity with which the term acquired dangerously subversive connotations within a year of the Society's foundation.

In 1811, a hardy group of advanced reformers had formed a Society of the Friends of Parliamentary Reform, the first such openly constituted body since the repression of the seventeen-nineties. In June of the following year, this body was reconstituted with a significant change of name:

> The word "Society" being applicable to a vast variety of associations, it was judged politic to adopt the title of Union; especially as the great object ... is to promote a National Union.[42]

The title, then, was a hint at a long-standing radical policy of challenging the legitimacy of the system through mass extra-parliamentary activity, underlined by the participation of such veteran agitators as Sir Francis Burdett and Major Cartwright. Known familiarly as "the Union", "the Union Club" or "the Union Society", it soon spawned a more popular movement called after the seventeenth-century champion of the people, John Hampden. By 1816, the terms "Hampden Clubs" and "Union societies" were virtually interchangeable.[43] Perhaps the name "Union" appealed to the two young Foxite Whigs, Maitland and Townshend, for that very reason, but there were too many political viewpoints represented in the Society from its inception to make it plausible that the Cambridge Union was deliberately named in sympathy with the London group. It was rather that as post-war social unrest seemed to be erupting out of control, the name adopted in 1814-1815 for its wholesome and virtuous overtones suddenly came to suggest the threat of bloody revolution. On 24 March 1817, the proctors, the University's own police force, headed by the Vice-Chancellor himself, interrupted a debate of the Cambridge Union and ordered members "to disperse, and on no account to resume their discussions".[44]

As with the traditions of the founding of the Union two years previously, so the tale of its suppression in 1817 has become obscured by legend. The President, William Whewell, is said to have responded to the intrusion with the defiant words: "Strangers will please to withdraw, and the house will take the message into consideration". Did this episode really happen? The confrontation makes a poignant story, matching the Vice-Chancellor and Master of St John's, James Wood, son of a Lancashire weaver, against Whewell, son of a Lancashire carpenter who would eventually rise to become Master of Trinity and twice serve as Vice-Chancellor himself. Many legends gathered around the intimidating figure of Whewell who, even as a host on social occasions, was remembered for "radiating repulsion". In later life, he became an inflexible defender of the powers of the Vice-Chancellor, and may have wished to discourage recollections of his own act of defiance. This may explain why the tale of his clash with Wood cannot be traced before 1866, a year after his death. However, Whewell's biographers accepted it as true and one of them related in 1876 that the incident was "still well remembered by one who was present".[45] Whewell may have been making the point that, although the Vice-Chancellor had the power to forbid members of the University to hold debates, he did not necessarily have the right to enter the Society's rooms at the Red Lion Inn to pronounce his edict. The Oxford Union similarly dismissed the proctors a few years later when they sought to interfere on private premises.[46]

A protest deputation was promptly sent to the Vice-Chancellor, "hoping their woe-begone physiognomies might work upon his compassion", as a detractor put it.[47] Whewell was accompanied by Connop Thirlwall, who was to be driven out of Trinity in 1834 for denouncing compulsory chapel, and the Irishman Charles Brinsley Sheridan, son of the dramatist (who affectionately referred to his offspring as "Beastie"). However, Wood stood firm in "his determination not to permit the Society to continue its debates on political, literary, or any other subjects".[48] Not merely was the Vice-Chancellor inflexible, but he played into the hands of his young critics by a dangerous admission, telling the deputation that he was

> in a great measure induced to prohibit their debates from the circumstance of his having received a letter from one of their Members stating that the studies of the writer, and those of several of his friends, had been checked, and their prospects blighted by the attention and attendance which they had been obliged to bestow on the Society....[49]

Authorship of this letter was subsequently half-claimed (in an anonymously written book) by a member of Trinity, J.F.M. Wright. Given the depth of Wright's contempt for "boy-babblers", it is hard to believe that he had wasted much of his own time at the Union, and indeed he recalled that he gave as examples "a few of the victims of delusion ... as samples of the whole lot". It is tempting to agree with an Edwardian historian of Cambridge that Wright was "unquestionably a blackguard" and pleasant to note the belief "that he died in the hulks". Alas, he became a fashionable clergyman and lived to an extreme old age. Wright sneeringly alleged that the hope of "reaching the lofty eminence of a presidency" encouraged "the almost total abandonment of such pursuits as alone could terminate in the substantial rewards and honours of the University".[51]

Wright's slur provoked a devastating rebuttal from the defenders of the Union. They pointed out that debates lasted for only two hours each week and that "the attendance of all Members preparing for their degrees is excused". In addition, they triumphantly listed nineteen members who had won University prizes and laid claim to "many names which ranked high in the Tripos". If other boy-babblers had failed to distinguish themselves academically, it was always possible that without the stimulus of the Union, their lack of native wit might have been even more evident:

> the existence of a large Speaking Club, forming a weekly point of re-union of its Members, has materially tended to diminish the attendance on weekly Clubs or Meetings, whose conduct is likely to be less orderly as their amusements are less intellectual than those of the Union.[52]

Furthermore, even Wright acknowledged "that a club of the kind ... might be a useful institution" for young graduates preparing for the professions,[53] but Wood had put an end to that possibility as well.

Wood's decision to defend his action on academic grounds not only opened the way to impressive refutation, but threw doubt on his good sense and equity. D.A. Winstanley, himself a don of the old school, disapprovingly commented that the Vice-Chancellor had "practically admitted that he had condemned the Union on the unsupported testimony of a single person".[54] The aggrieved deputation pounced upon the tactical error, expressing the indignant hope that "they will not be the victims of the calumnies or the folly of a single Member". Wood's response showed that his instinctive talent for poor public relations had not deserted him. Conscious of the dignity of his office, he stated that it was "neither necessary, nor perhaps proper" for him to reply. To this he added an assurance designed no doubt to silence all doubts: "I had considered the subject fully in my own mind."[55] Naturally, the Union included this gem in its published Remonstrance, and the Masters of Arts and noblemen among its members turned their attention to petitioning the University's Chancellor, the Duke of Gloucester.

It is not surprising that James Wood has received a bad press from historians for his handling of the affair. However, the standard account obscures two important points. The first is that the focus upon the theatrical confrontation between Whewell and the proctors fails to do justice to the wider context of an atmosphere of panic and repression. In effect, Wood faced the choice between being damned on the one hand for over-reaction and on the other for failing to rise to his responsibilities. It is hardly surprising that a Vice-Chancellor should seek to defend an act of University policy on academic grounds, inadequate though they might seem. Indeed, it says something for Wood's fair-mindedness that he agreed to receive a protest deputation at all. Secondly, the dramatic episode of 1817 did not put an end to the Cambridge Union and probably did not even seriously restrict its members' opportunities for debating. The Union continued to occupy its own premises, and this independent existence was protected by divisions among senior members of the University, by no means all of whom sympathised with Wood's actions.

It is not fair to judge Wood's move against the Union without taking account of the fact that it was made in an atmosphere of national crisis. Massive radical meetings, accompanied by sporadic rioting, on London's Spa Fields in November and December 1816, were enough to persuade the government that it faced a major revolutionary conspiracy. In January 1817, the Hampden Clubs met in a potentially revolutionary convention in London and there was an attempt on the life of the Prince Regent.[56] The following month, a committee of the House of Lords warned of "a traitorous conspiracy" aimed at "overthrowing, by means of a general insurrection, the established Government, laws, and Constitution of this kingdom" in order to bring about "a general plunder and division of property".[57] On 4 March, Habeas Corpus was suspended, and immediately afterwards the prominent radical William Cobbett fled to the United States. Legislation to suppress seditious meetings was pushed through parliament in March. Hunger marchers, the "Blanketeers", set out from Lancashire for London on 10 March, but were quickly dispersed.[58]

The House of Lords committee had no doubts of the existence of a revolutionary command structure that had to be eradicated. "It appears that there is a London Union Society, and branch Union Societies corresponding with it, and affiliated to it."[59] The secretary of the London Union Society promptly petitioned the House of Lords, seeking permission to prove that the body was moribund. Despite a rousing speech from Lord Lauderdale, the petition was rejected.[60] The revolutionary conspiracy was almost certainly much less alarming than ministers feared. Some of it was the work of *agents provocateurs* seeking to worm their way into the imagined leadership by the extravagance of their radicalism: it was a government spy who issued the memorable call for the last king to be strangled in the guts of the last priest. Although it was rumoured that there were 150 Union Societies around the country, they were not all especially menacing. The Leeds Union Society collapsed after a life of only ten weeks, its total assets amounting to just over seventeen shillings. As one journalist put it, this was not much of a threat to a government with an annual revenue of sixty million pounds.[62] None the less, it was embarrassing that at the heart of Cambridge, there should be a body calling itself the Union Society and engaging in the discussion of political issues.

It might have been thought that Cambridge would have been isolated from the storm-centres of instability. Even London was over five hours away by the fastest stagecoach. Lancashire (which, as *The Times* uncharitably remarked, "can neither read nor write")[63] might as well have been on another planet, although James Wood, a weaver's son from Bury, probably felt closer than most to the turmoil in the North. Unfortunately, however, the unrest had not been confined to urban and manufacturing districts. For several days in May of 1816, the Isle of Ely had been swept by a labourers' insurrection, with both Littleport and the cathedral town of Ely itself falling to the insurgents. The revolt was crushed, five men were hanged and nine were transported to Australia. Incongruously, one of the judges was Edward Christian, Professor of Law at Cambridge, whose brother had led the mutiny on the *Bounty*. He remarked that the labourers received "great wages" and predicted that any increase would only encourage them to get drunk.[64]

Such attitudes were emphatically shared by the University of Cambridge, that is by the senior dons who spoke on behalf of the institution. In February 1817, Wood headed a deputation to London to present the Prince Regent with an address of congratulation on his escape from assassination. Since such documents were either drafted by the Vice-Chancellor himself or required his active approval, the address gives an insight into James Wood's thinking a few weeks before he moved against the Cambridge Union:

> We witness, with disgust and horror, the numerous artifices employed to seduce and pervert the illiterate and unwary; to inflame their evil passions; and to infuse into their minds principles calculated to overturn every form of civilized society. ... While doctrines of anarchy and misrule are disseminated with such malignant industry, the duty which our station most imperiously requires of us, and which we hope faithfully to discharge, is to instruct those whose education is entrusted to our care in sound principles of religion and loyalty, and to impose forcibly upon their minds the value of that civil constitution which has been productive of so much individual happiness and national glory.[65]

While the university's senior minds were nailing their colours so firmly to the mast of reaction, the younger spirits of the Union seemed more inclined to question policy and institutions. "Even the distress arising from the visitations of Providence has been wickedly ascribed to the misconduct of their rulers," the University's deputation had indignantly assured the Prince Regent. The Union thought this was a matter for debate. "Is the present Distress in the Country owing to the unavoidable pressure of circumstances, or to the bad policy of the British Government?", it had asked in November 1816, before blaming circumstances rather than policy by 30 votes to 13. Similarly, the crisis of 1817 was an interesting subject for theoretical discussion. On 10 March, a house of 87 agreed by just one vote that the suspension of Habeas Corpus was "constitutional". The following week, the "present system of Public Meetings" was deemed not to be "advantageous", but the majority of 33 against 24 was hardly reassuring. Evidently the University of Cambridge contained a stubborn minority unimpressed by the value of the existing constitution. On 24 March the Union embarked upon an even more provocative discussion: "Is the increased attention which has been paid to our Army likely to have a good effect upon Society?"[66] Parliament was in the last stages of passing the Seditious Meetings Act. Cambridge would hardly be living up to the professions of duty it had pledged to the Prince Regent if it allowed revolutionists to plead that a Union Society of young gentlemen was discussing such inflammatory ideas at the heart of one of the ancient bastions of Anglican privilege. Moreover, the Presidency had passed from the young aristocrats to the son of a carpenter whose life history sounded remarkably similar to the Lancashire radicals who appear in the pages of Samuel Bamford's autobiography.[67] In the context of March 1817, Wood had little alternative but to take action.

The deputation to Wood appealed to what Cornford would later term the Principle of Washing Linen:[68] to take decisive action was to admit to the world that the University suffered from serious problems, and therefore it was always better to do nothing:

> The Members of the Union most earnestly request that their Society may not be put down precisely at this period, when the universal suppression of Societies bearing accidentally the same name, may lead those unacquainted with the real state of the University to suppose, that this Club has been put down from political motives, and that it has been guilty of seditious Meetings or treasonable language.[69]

It was a clever ploy to throw at the Vice-Chancellor the implication that his actions and not theirs risked bringing the University into disrepute, but it was disingenuous. Two paragraphs in *The Times*, both apparently inspired by the protesters, were markedly coy about the Society's name. The first long-windedly referred to "the society which existed in the University of Cambridge, comprising a large proportion of the Graduates and Under-graduates of the younger part of the University, who have been in the habit of meeting weekly to discuss literary and political subjects". The second more succinctly called the Union "The University Debating Club".[70] In an indignant allusion to the suppression during a debate in the House of Commons, the Whig orator Henry Brougham also avoided direct reference and spoke of "a society at Cambridge".[71] When the successor to the Anticarnalist dared not speak its name, it was possible to see why James Wood had felt the need to take action.

Another motive probably helps to explain not simply the Vice-

Chancellor's action, but his timing. In 1817, the University attempted to assert its ascendancy over the town of Cambridge by reviving an archaic and objectionable ceremony called the Magna Congregatio. A charter of 1317 had required forty representative townsmen to swear an oath each year in the presence of the Vice-Chancellor as a means of providing a local police force. The imposition was resented and had fallen into disuse around 1800, not least because it had long since ceased to bear any relation to the policing of Cambridge. In July 1817, Wood abruptly invoked his dormant power to enforce the ritual, ostensibly because the Town had failed to clear the streets of vagrants. To drive home his demand, he threatened to cut off the University's contribution to local charities.[72] The following April, his successor as Vice-Chancellor staged a confrontation with the Mayor over the right to preside at the local magistrates' court. The Mayor refused to back down, and received the thanks of the council "for his firm and independent conduct in supporting the rights of his office".[73] (In the University's defence, it should be said that the dispute was no clash between antiquated academic privilege and local democracy. The Town Council was a closed corporation, notable for its spectacular feasting on the proceeds of local charities.[74])

Wood's decision to go to war with the local community has been condemned by historians[75] but, once again, something may be said in defence of his aims, if not of his methods. Student numbers were bursting the bounds of available accommodation: within a few years half of all Cambridge undergraduates would live in lodgings in the town. The fate of the Union was merely the first shot in a potential battle between Town and Gown over the issue of student discipline. One of the provisions of the Seditious Meetings Bill required any group planning to hold a meeting of more than fifty people to apply for permission from the local magistrates. As a condition of issuing a licence, the magistrates could interrupt proceedings at any time on the mere suspicion of insult to the government or the constitution. Since the Union met at the Red Lion, this provision would probably compel its members to ask the Cambridge magistrates to allow them to continue their deliberations, thus raising the spectre of the Town exercising jurisdiction over the young men of the University. Hence, in April 1818, the attempt to oust the Mayor from his presiding role as a magistrate.

Like most contemporary legislation, the Seditious Meetings Act was ineptly drafted. When the Academical Society sought a licence for its meetings, magistrates in the City of London were genuinely unsure whether the legislation was intended to ban all such gatherings, and they thought it safer to refuse.[76] If magistrates in the capital found the provisions difficult to interpret, the local bench in a country town might also decide to play safe. This suggested the nightmare scenario in which the Town could claim credit for suppressing a dangerous nuisance that had flourished under the nose of a somnolent Vice-Chancellor. As James Wood considered the subject fully in his own mind, he presumably came to the conclusion that it was simpler and safer to silence the Union himself.

However, the Union was not eliminated. In Cradock's standard account, the Society "remained merely as a Reading Club for the next four years" until a subsequent Vice-Chancellor, Christopher Wordsworth, allowed it to resume its debates on condition that it kept clear of contemporary controversies.[77] This is not the whole story. In one sense, the Union survived by legislative accident. As the Seditious Meetings Bill passed through parliament, some of its more extreme provisions were dropped, including the threat to outlaw reading clubs. Within Cambridge, the Union clung on to existence partly because Wood lacked support within the University. There was probably an undercurrent of social distaste towards the weaver's son who had dared to put an end to the pursuits of young gentlemen. Everyone referred to Wood as "Jem" or "Jemmy". "I pity the man who is too great for these diminutives", commented J.M.F. Wright, secure in the confidence of possessing three forenames himself. Wright claimed that the "familiar appellation" was a sign of popularity, but Kenneth Bourne has described Palmerston's use of the nickname as "rather condescending".[78] Traditional rivalry between the two largest colleges also played a part. Whewell and Thirlwall intended to make their academic careers in Trinity, and could afford to take a defiant attitude to a mere Master of St John's. Yet most fundamental of all was the realisation that the suppression of the Union could easily be guyed as an over-reaction.

William Whewell probably knew that he was not courting martyrdom but exploiting the divisions within a University establishment which doubted the good sense of Wood's action against the Union. George Pryme was told by one of the proctors "that he did not like it, but felt obliged to obey orders".[79] A whimsical versifier captured Wood's isolation:

> Master of a mighty College,
> Without his robes behold him stand,
> Whom not a Whig will now acknowledge,
> Return his bow, or shake his hand.[80]

In his hostility, Wright missed the point in calling Union orators "as thunderstruck as so many Thistlewoods at the intrusion".[81] Their strategy was to dissociate themselves from the advanced radicals of Spa Fields and locate their cause in the longer-term struggles of English freedom. Hence Whewell's bold pastiche of Mr Speaker Lenthall's dismissal of Charles I when the king invaded the House of Commons in 1642. It was easy to imply that Wood was a throwback to the repressive seventeen-nineties, when government spies had drowned the proceedings of London debating societies with chants of "God save great George our king" and courts had been given power to impose the death penalty if a seditious meeting did not disperse within one hour.[82] Although they took the precaution of formally speaking through graduates who were subject to less intense academic discipline, what is significant is not that the young men worsted the Vice-Chancellor in argument, but that they dared to answer back at all. Their published Remonstrance was couched in terms of impatient insolence which could only have been adopted in the knowledge that they were not alone in their opposition. There was a contemptuous, take-it-or-leave-it, attitude in the statement that members were "willing, *if their meetings can be tolerated on no other condition*, to exclude all political, as they have uniformly all theological, discussion from their debates".[83]

The Wood-Whewell confrontation was thus at best a draw, and increasingly it seemed that the Union had won on points. The Society continued to occupy its premises at the Red Lion. The Vice-Chancellor had the power to "discommune" shopkeepers who cheated undergraduates, or alehouses that offered the temptations of sex and billiards – that is, it could bankrupt the proprietors by declaring the offending premises off limits to members of the University. However, the Red Lion was no backstreet pothouse, but a major coaching inn, part of the Cambridge's lifeline to the outer world. In any case, Wood simply lacked adequate backing within the University to carry out any further action against the Union.

In effect, the Union carried on much as before. The election of officers quickly resumed. Since it was perfectly legal to function as a reading club, it was appropriate for the Union to hold business meetings to determine which newspapers it wished to buy. Before and after the interruption of 1817-1821, a session devoted to Private Business preceded the formal debate. Now Private Business simply filled the whole evening. An apparently innocuous motion to cancel the *Morning Chronicle* provided cover for an attack on the political principles of the Whig opposition that the paper supported. Henry Malden, later to become Professor of Greek at London University, proposed that the Union subscribe to a newspaper from Athens in order to trigger impassioned debate on the rights of the Greeks to resist Turkish rule.[84] In its protest against James Wood, the Union had claimed that "latterly many of the questions debated have been in no degree political".[85] Like most activities that are driven underground, Union debates became entirely unrestrained – especially in being dangerously contemporary. Part of the *quid pro quo* for permission to resume formal debating in 1821 was the adoption of a new and emphatic Law: "*No discussion whatever* shall take place on a motion for the admission or rejection of any newspaper." Members were also obliged to accept a ban on the discussion of "political questions of a date subsequent to the year 1800".[86] The latter condition, as will be shown in Chapter Six, proved to be more formal than real and lasted only until 1830.

Thus Christopher Wordsworth's decision to permit the Union to resume its debates in March 1821 fell somewhat short of a policy of unrestricted free speech but was rather an attempt at control through more subtle means. Wordsworth himself was popular neither with undergraduates nor among senior members,[87] and it was unlikely that he would have made any concession to the Union simply out of the kindness of his heart. By 1821, the threat of revolution seemed to have passed. Popular anger had been channelled into support for George IV's wronged consort, the vulgar Queen Caroline. On this issue, undergraduate opinion, like the rest of the fashionable world, predominantly sided with the king. The collapse of royal divorce proceedings in November 1820 triggered one of the largest ever Town-and-Gown riots, which passed into folklore as the Battle of Peas Hill. The dark fears of Dr Wood, that a university society could be seen as a mouthpiece for popular radicalism, were retreating into the past.

Wordsworth was well placed to take a cool view of his predecessor's action. First, he had only recently returned to Cambridge, and so was unencumbered by any position taken in 1817. Secondly, he was Master of Trinity and as such splendidly equipped to ignore the opinions of any Master of St John's. By 1821, three of the earliest officers of the Union had progressed to Fellowships at Trinity. Gambier and Thirlwall were absentees, using their stipends to finance careers at the Bar. The workaholic Whewell, on the other hand, was already climbing the administrative ladder to become an indispensable academic bureaucrat. If it was indeed Whewell who persuaded Wordsworth to allow the Union to resume, he must have savoured his victory over Jemmy Wood. Wood was still Master of his college, but in 1820 he had acquired the additional post of Dean of Ely, which gave him the consolation of preaching the virtues of obedience to Fenland peasants. When he died in 1839, he left a giant fortune to St John's. In the eighteen-sixties, the college drew upon Wood's bequest to finance the construction of Gilbert Scott's new chapel. In the event, the project proved too expensive even for the massive proceeds of Wood's pluralism, and it was at that time that St John's sold land in nearby Round Church Street as a site for the Union's permanent home. Thus, in a curious way, Wood suffered two defeats in his battle against the Union, one of them posthumous. However, this is not to say that the University had entirely repudiated him when it allowed the resumption of formal debating. Cambridge had certainly moved some distance in the decade since William Farish had sat with his head in his hands as enthusiastic undergraduates explained their plans to form a society dedicated to the distribution of that dangerous book, the Bible.

None the less, in 1821 nobody could be sure that the six-year-old Union Society, still subject to academic control, would survive into the distant future.

Trinity Great Court 1911

6: The Union and its Debates 1821-1914

The Cambridge Union survived its officially enforced four-year silence because it was a well-established club, occupying its own premises. As *The Times* noted in 1886, "the debating business is in the eyes of members only one, perhaps a secondary one, among many attractions of the Union".[1] Even an ex-President could recall that he had joined the Society "for its merits as a club rather than with any thought of incursion into debates".[2] To interpret those debates, it is first necessary to look at the history of that club throughout the nineteenth century.

The Union remained at the Red Lion in Petty Cury until 1831. The accommodation was expensive – rent alone cost £52 a year and heating and lighting could treble the overall cost[3] – and not always convenient. The Society occupied a reading room and had access to an adjoining chamber (in modern hotel jargon, a function room) for its debates, so long as the landlord, William Mitchell, did not need it for other purposes. A description of 1829 confirms that from earliest times, debates were conducted in mimic parliamentary format, with four rows of benches facing each other on opposite sides of the debating chamber.[4] Hence the decision in 1823 that "the President should regulate his conduct as nearly as possible by the Precedents of the House of Commons" in cases where the Union's own laws offered inadequate guidance.[5]

Pressed in 1826 "to provide a more commodious reading room", Mitchell agreed to build one "double the size of the existing room, to be in the constant occupation of the Union Society".[6] However, there were complaints the following year that the landlord had not fulfilled the contract, and there was general dissatisfaction with the accommodation.[7] Monckton Milnes remembered the debating chamber as "a low, ill-ventilated, ill-lit, gallery at the back of the Red Lion", which he described as "cavernous, tavernous – something between a commercial-room and a district-branch-meeting-house".[8] His recollection was probably exaggerated, since the Cambridge Philharmonic Society seems to have taken over the Union's tenancy and even the modest standards of English provincial music presumably demanded decent acoustics. However, there is contemporary evidence that the debating room was poorly lit. In 1826, additional candles were purchased "to enable the President to read Motions &c without stooping".[9]

The intrusion of non-members into the Society's premises was a recurring problem. Gate-crashing debates was regarded as "a *good lark*". In 1822, members seem to have over-reacted in the eviction of the obviously inoffensive Charles Taylor of Christ's. Taylor explained that he was about to leave Cambridge and had wished to observe the proceedings of "a society of whose fame I had heard so much". While acknowledging that he had been misinformed that "the admission of strangers, if not absolutely allow'd" was "customary by courtesy", he refused to apologise in the light of the rough treatment he had received. Taylor was declared "for ever ineligible" for membership.[10] An equally fruitless sanction was invoked in 1826 when the Union resolved that any student committing a similar offence was "guilty of Conduct unbecoming a Gentleman & a Man of Honour".[11] More heinous was the practice of "certain individuals" who secured election to the Society without any intention of paying the subscription. This was dealt with by imposing fines upon those who had proposed them for membership.[12] However, early administrative procedures were so casual that it was possible for an indignant member to claim that he had paid his subscription, but no record could be found.[13]

As the Boylan affair showed, in the early years administrative procedures were unimpressive. Members were reluctant to pay their subscriptions: in October 1826, it was estimated that during the two previous years, the Society had lost over £137 in this way, while in the more efficient days of 1831, subscription arrears still exceeded £134.[14] In 1825, there was something of a financial crisis: a motion for better ventilation of the perennially stuffy debating room prompted Praed to comment that he was "ready to advocate any measure for *'raising the wind'* in the present low state of the Society's finances".[15] A special committee convened by Benjamin Hall Kennedy came to the unexpectedly optimistic conclusion that "if unusual expenditure could be avoided, the funds of the Society are fully adequate".[16] Administrative procedures were gradually established, culminating in the appointment of a chief clerk in 1831 (although originally responsible for "attending to the Library and other affairs connected with the Reading Room".[17]) A regular bank account was established, along with printed membership lists and a proper system of issuing receipts, which could double as membership cards. By October 1827, the Union's finances were "rapidly improving".[18] Contrary no doubt to Kennedy's warning, donations were made to distressed manufacturers in 1826, when Spencer Walpole persuaded the Union to double its proposed contribution to £100, and to Italian and Spanish refugees the following year.[19] Healthier finances encouraged dreams of larger premises. In 1828 members discussed "the possibility of borrowing money ... for the purpose of erecting a structure suitable to the credit & respectability, and sufficient for the purposes of the Union".[20] It would be thirty-six years before they were bold enough to act upon the idea.

Instead, in 1830 a committee was established to search for "more convenient Debating and Reading Rooms, as the present are quite inadequate to the purpose for which they are intended".[21] The committee quickly produced an "earnest Recommendation" in favour of accepting a proposal from Thomas Bird of the Hoop Inn, which stretched from Sidney Street to Park Street, behind the houses on the north side of Jesus Lane. Bird offered to build a room 85 feet long and 29 feet wide, with a ceiling at least 16 feet high, which would presumably improve ventilation. He also undertook to provide an additional room and to allocate a servant for the sole use of members. The rent was to be £150 a year, fixed for three years, with Bird retaining use of the debating room for five nights each week.[22] It is possible that the terms were too generous. Bird defaulted soon afterwards, and his successor as landlord, William Ekin, seems never to have been happy with the arrangements, although the premises were enlarged in the early eighteen-forties.[23]

The entrance to the Union, from Garlic Fair Lane (Park Street) was "not grand or imposing", but a freshman of 1846 was impressed by the club he had joined. "We have a magnificent room, I am afraid to say how long, for Debates and reading-room; also a smaller and snugger room, and ... a smoking-room, and a really excellent Library of all subjects, which is a great resource."[24] By 1850, Union opinion had become less happy with the premises, and the "various inconveniences which greatly diminish their suitability". A further move was masterminded by Homersham Cox, who was approaching his thirtieth birthday and was something of a permanent student. (He also seems to have invented the phrase "British Commonwealth".) Cox argued that the growth of the Library made the accommodation inadequate. Access was "from a small obscure street" and the taproom of the Hoop was "a frequent source of nuisance". Worst of all, the Union was located "at an inconvenient distance from the largest Colleges". This was a tribute to the microscopic world of Cambridge, since Park Street was all of three hundred yards from the Great Gate of Trinity. Cox was no doubt laying it on thick. The truth was that relations with Ekin had deteriorated to the point where the Union's request for a cut in rent was met with a frosty demand for an increase.

Best of all, alternative premises were available which met the "essential condition" of proximity to the larger colleges. For years, the local Methodist congregation had crammed in more and more converts by adding galleries to the old Dissenting chapel in Green Street. Finally, in 1849, the Methodists built themselves a new and larger church on the edge of town, and so were anxious to offload the 38-year lease remaining on the old building. By ripping out most of the galleries, it would be possible "entirely to destroy its present appearance of a Chapel", thus creating a debating chamber that would resemble the House of Commons – and all within easy strolling distance of Trinity, Caius and St John's.[25]

Relocating the Union involved a good deal of disruption, and debates suffered in the autumn term of 1850. One November evening, "in consequence of the very few Members in attendance, and a Concert about to take place at the Town Hall", the planned debate was abandoned.[26] In the event, the Green Street premises were never wholly satisfactory. "All the eloquent speeches delivered within its walls by attached members of the Church, and all the alterations by which it had been adapted for its purpose, failed to purify it thoroughly from its meeting-house flavour."[27] Although Henry Fawcett remembered the "dingy old rooms" with affection,[28] the contrast with the Oxford Union, which built its own premises in 1857, became invidious. That same year, the Cambridge Union established a Building Fund, financed from annual operating profits plus a proportion of subscriptions. It grew slowly and became something of a joke. Supporting the Southern States in the American Civil War, G.O. Trevelyan rhetorically asked: "Can the North restore the Union?". "Never, Sir", a heckler replied; "they have no building fund."[29] As late as 1860, the Union's official aim was simply to rebuild in Green Street "on a scale more commensurate with the wants of its Members". "The present buildings are certainly not ornamental; and it is of the utmost importance that steps should be taken to erect handsome and permanent rooms."[30] In the longer term, it was almost certainly in the best interests of the Union that so little progress was made. By the early eighteen-sixties, the undergraduate population was again rising and it became increasingly clear that the Green Street site was inadequate for development.

In 1864, the Society purchased a larger site in Round Church Street from St John's, probably through the good offices of the Professor of Divinity, William Selwyn. A Union patriarch from the eighteen-twenties, Selwyn was especially keen to see his college complete its expensive new chapel, Gilbert Scott's "sermon in stones", and would have seen the sale as a way of supporting two worthwhile projects simultaneously. The physical and mental bounds of urban Cambridge were still very restricted, and Leslie Stephen complained that the Union had "crept into so retired a corner".[31] Credit for the galvanising of the building project is conventionally given to Charles Dilke, who served two terms as President to see it to completion. It is likely that an important role was also played by another officer, Henry Peto of Trinity, eldest son of the founder of the great construction company of Morton Peto and Betts.[32] Guided by Dilke, members voted in a referendum to choose Alfred Waterhouse as their architect. Unexpectedly, the buildings were ready for occupation in the autumn term of 1866, and an official opening ceremony was hurriedly arranged for a rainy day at the end of October.[33] "The style is thirteenth-century Gothic", reported Leslie Stephen, adding with a touch of irony, "but this has not been strictly adhered to throughout the building."[34]

The new Union was an expensive project, imaginatively conceived and boldly executed. The cost of the site alone swallowed almost all of the Building Fund. A modern-sounding appeal was launched, with circulars sent to four thousand "life" (i.e. former) members. This helped to raise £4,000 towards the total cost of £11,000. The remaining sum was covered by the issue of debentures, which threatened to burden the Society with heavy interest charges.[35] Fortunately, the gamble paid off and twenty years later, at a further cost of £6,000, Waterhouse added a matching north range that would survive even Hitler's bombs. As *The Times* remarked, by 1886 the Cambridge Union provided "many of the conveniences that the Londoner finds at his club".[36] One of these, presumably, was the nine-course banquet that celebrated the extension of 1886.

These club facilities were probably more important to the majority of members than the debates themselves. It was claimed in 1852 that many who joined were "attracted solely by the reading room", while forty years later a Cambridge magazine waspishly insisted that the record intake in the October term "must be more due to the energy of the officers in making the club comfortable and attractive than to the excellence of this term's debates".[37] Even the quasi-official *Student's Guide* listed the Union among Cambridge's "more intellectual recreations" because of its library and reading room.[38] The Library had started to assume a formal shape in the late eighteen-twenties, after repeated complaints about irregular borrowings that amounted to theft. In 1821 the Union had reached the sensible conclusion that "the only effectual mode of preserving a library would be to hire a librarian", but unfortunately it could not afford to do so.[39] In a desperate move in 1829, it was proposed that every member be required "to declare upon his honour" that he was not in possession of any library books.[40]

The reading room was even harder to police. A member was expelled in 1822 for attempting to steal a newspaper.[41] Six years later, J.M. Kemble, who "gave up all his time to newspapers and political essayists", deplored the "scramble" that greeted the delivery of newspapers to the reading room. In 1829 he also denounced "the infamous & felonious practice ... of tearing pages from the reviews & magazines".[42] (Kemble's concern for newspapers tends to confirm the suspicions of Tripos examiners who, that same year, deferred the award of his degree because they were not persuaded that he had read any of the set books.) These pressures increased enormously in time of war or political upheaval. As the Duke of Wellington fell from office in 1830, there were complaints that "the supply of Newspapers" was "quite insufficient ... at the present extraordinary crisis".[43] The problem recurred a quarter of a century later, although the Crimean War was unusual in producing not merely grumbles but a helpful suggestion:

> At the present time a great number of members come into the Union in the morning merely to see what news there is from the seat of War. It

would save these gentlemen a considerable waste of time, if instead of their having to wait until their neighbours have read the leading articles, correspondence & police reports, they had a single copy of the Times suspended in a frame, where several members could see at once all they wanted.[44]

From earliest times, newspapers constituted by far the largest single item of expenditure. The Long Vacation of 1826 was used to define an absolute minimum provision: six London dailies, the local Cambridge papers and (surprisingly) Cobbett's *Weekly Register*.[45] By 1878, the Union was subscribing to over seventy newspapers, "embracing every shade of political and religious faith".[46] The emphasis, however, was heavily metropolitan. In 1884, the list included just one Dublin daily, the *Irish Times*, a paper unlikely to challenge English and Conservative preconceptions, although later the nationalist *Freeman's Journal* was added. Single copies of the most popular newspapers were no longer sufficient. In 1893, it was term-time practice to take in six copies of the *Westminster Gazette* and seven of the *Daily News*. Pressure to widen subscriptions tended towards the frivolous: there was an attempt in 1827 to add the *Racing Calendar*,[47] while in 1912 the Union was criticised for refusing to take "the *Pink 'Un*" (or *Sporting Times*).[48] As technology advanced, there were new opportunities to spend money. The Franco-Prussian war seems to have been the first major crisis that members followed through up-to-the-minute news agency telegrams.[49] By the time of the general election of 1895, "large sums were expended" to provide a results service.[50] Two years later, the Union bought its first typewriter in order to display legible transcriptions of telegrams. The typist had very hazy notions about punctuation and so added entertainment to the immediacy of the news flashes.[51]

A student society generated student politics, complete with rhetoric and techniques redolent of more recent and activist generations. In 1823, Praed denounced as "cowardly & unworthy of a Gentleman" an anonymous notice claiming that Union elections were controlled by an in-group, "the faction". He "most solemnly denied any inference that might be drawn from it, that a Committee sat to exercise illegal influence over the votes of the Society".[52] Praed's over-reaction illustrates why outsiders sometimes dismissed the entire Union as a breeding-ground for precocious self-importance. A lampoon of 1849 poked fun at "the Unionic Undergraduates", experts on "all questions legal, political, poetical, historical, or metaphysical" who could be seen on debate nights to "whisper mysteriously to the President, once in every five minutes".[53] Seventy years later, "leading lights at the Union" could be identified by the pomposity of their expression: even in ordinary speech, they "always said 'and so forth', instead of 'and that sort of thing'".[54] Detractors claimed that "nobody outside a restricted circle of busy-bodies takes the faintest amount of interest" in the proceedings of "a Society which is made up of all the Smugs of the University".[55]

Within the restricted circle of Union politics, a turbulent individual could create a great deal of discord. George Yorke of Christ's was clearly the product of an unusual upbringing. Yorke's father had been imprisoned for his revolutionary views in 1795. From the point of view of a repressive government, the experience produced a salutary effect. Yorke senior married his gaoler's daughter and became an extreme opponent of political change. The father's judgement may be measured from the fact that he named his son George Charilaus Camperdown Redhead Yorke. Yorke junior persuaded himself that the Union's Treasurer, John Simpson of Corpus, should be censured for inefficiency. The President, Henry Luscombe of Clare, ruled the motion out of order. Yorke returned to the attack at the next meeting, provoking Simpson into dramatic resignation in protest against "vexatious accusations, and undeserved attacks".[56] Such disorder prevailed that the evening's debate had to be abandoned, thus giving rise to the pleasant legend that Cambridge undergraduates came to blows over the rival merits of the poetry of Wordsworth and Byron.[57] The term ended with a further meeting at which over two hundred members joined in the factional battle. From the chair, Luscombe rejected one censure motion on suspicion that the names of its seconders had been forged, and another on the grounds that signatures had been cut off another document and "tacked on". The following term, Yorke sought his revenge with a motion censuring Luscombe for "his insufficient & unsatisfactory discharge" of his duties, piously claiming that he wished to record "a salutary example to gentlemen canvassing for offices for which they are utterly incapacitated". The motion was rejected by 84 votes to 52.[58] This was a larger turn-out than for seven of the eight debates on Catholic Emancipation during the eighteen-twenties – and the Catholic question was one of the most prominent political issues of the period.

In the late eighteen-thirties, rival factions again struggled for control. This time the battle lines were drawn between the studious and the sporting. The atmosphere was poisoned by George Smythe, a violent personality who later inherited the title of Viscount Strangford, although he had little connection with Ireland. Smythe was twice threatened with expulsion from Eton and went on to fight the last duel on English soil. In 1847, 782 of the electors of Canterbury returned him to parliament. When he sought re-election five years later, just seven of them stayed loyal. However, in his student days, he was more than a mere hearty. Along with Lord John Manners, he was one of the first Cambridge disciples of the Tractarian principles that were coming out of Newman's Oxford. He called the Cambridge Union "the nursing mother of principles, which, I hope, will knit us together through life".[59] Smythe and Manners were to form the core of the Young England ginger group in Peel's Conservative party. In his novels, Disraeli portrayed Smythe first as Coningsby and then as Waldershare. "He had been the hero of the debating club at Cambridge, and many believed that in consequence he must become Prime Minister."[60]

The macho Smythe seems to have been predestined to clash with the mild C.J. Vaughan, a noted classical scholar, later headmaster of Harrow and later still, after a carefully hushed-up homosexual scandal, ex-headmaster of Harrow. "He left a strict injunction that no life of him should be published," the *Dictionary of National Biography* enigmatically recorded.[61] Spotting a notice signed by Vaughan and his ally, W.J. Butler, another future cleric of an unworldly type, Smythe added the names of five racehorses or, as he explained, five more brutes and then typically quietened protests by threatening to issue challenges to duel.[62] In Union elections, the reading men were usually able to defeat their opponents, "the same industry and ability that aided them in their studies, generally enabling them to triumph in the canvas". However, the sporting faction managed to block Vaughan from the Presidency in 1838 by running against him an undergraduate of St John's who had inherited a baronetcy, "a Johnian nonentity who had *Sir* before his name".[63]

Alliances in the Union's housekeeping politics sometimes crossed party lines. In 1858, "considerable dissatisfaction" at the management of the Society brought together a rising Conservative, Cecil Raikes, who later held office under Lord Salisbury, and G.O. Trevelyan, already a committed Liberal and destined to serve in two of Gladstone's cabinets. As the only "two *speaking* members" of the opposition, they found themselves in the pleasant position of always having "a tumultuous cheering body behind us ... without any rivals aspiring to lead the party". Although triumphant in business meetings, both Raikes and Trevelyan had to wait for electoral success. In 1857, for instance, under the leadership of a future Archbishop of Sydney, the Union elections were won by "the party who combine considerable religious profession with the lowest Radical doctrines and the most overbearing and repulsive vulgarity". So, at any rate, thought Cecil Raikes, who was on the losing side.[64]

The exploitation of procedural details was a hallowed device that made its appearance early in Union history. In 1821, the President, John Punnett of Clare, realised that Dr Wordsworth's compromise solution for the resumption of debating would not be popular with members. Accordingly, he railroaded through the necessary changes in the Laws on his own casting vote. Critics complained that he had not given the one week's notice of the proposals required in Law XXVIII. Punnett dismissed all challenges on the grounds that Law VII declared the President to be sole interpreter of any disputed regulation.[65] Punnett spent most of his later life as rector of a Cornish parish, where he wrote religious tracts. It is hard not to feel that his political talents were wasted.

Another issue of principle proved more durable. In 1833, a sabbatarian party began to press for the closure of the Union on Sundays. In 1847, they succeeded in forcing a motion through a business meeting that closed the premises until three o'clock on the day of rest. The decision was promptly challenged, on the grounds that a quorum of forty members was required to amend the Laws. Since nobody seems to have raised the point at the meeting, it is likely that the necessary quorum had been achieved. However, some of those present must have abstained, since only 37 members voted on the actual motion for Sunday closure.[66] The ensuing row is reminiscent of the famous split between the Mensheviks and Bolsheviks in the history of Russian Communism. The sabbatarians soon lost their transient majority status, but could still muster a twenty-five percent vote against all proposals to open the Union on the sabbath. Since such a motion required a three-quarters majority to become effective, the Union remained closed until mid-afternoon every Sunday.

Among those who resisted Sunday closure was Hugh Childers, who emigrated to Australia soon after he left Cambridge in 1850. There he helped to establish the colony of Victoria, extended its school system and took part in the founding of the University of Melbourne. In due course, he returned to Britain, entered parliament and in 1868 joined Gladstone's cabinet. Meanwhile, at Cambridge, a watchful religious faction kept the Union in its sabbatarian grip. Diverse strategies were attempted to prise open the doors. One was a proposal to give the Society's officers the right to admit personal friends to the building before three o'clock on Sundays. The officers would then discover that they were hugely popular from one end of Cambridge to the other. The ploy was frustrated, and the Union was still closed during the hours of Sunday worship when C.E. Childers followed in his father's footsteps to Trinity in 1868. Bringing with him a parent's recollections of the battles of long ago, the younger Childers finally found a way around the problem of the three-quarters majority. Frustrated in their head-on assaults, repealers adopted a flanking move. In 1873, they persuaded a business meeting to rule that the original vote of 1847 had been inquorate and hence invalid, a decision that could be carried by a simple majority. Thus ended twenty-six years of internecine but no doubt enjoyable controversy. Lesser rows continued to erupt. In 1891, a reporter noted that the Union found "the excitement of personal disputes ... less monotonous than ordinary debates on Home Rule or Vivisection". In 1894, a member was fined for bringing his dog to a debate. His boat club friends packed a business meeting seeking to overturn the penalty, and local urchins were hired to parade the streets with sandwich boards, "Vote for Thompson and the dog." The campaign failed.[67]

If rival activities to debating existed within the Union, there were far more alternatives on offer outside. "There were many clubs in the University", the President of the Union commented in 1886, " – some with strange names, such as the Owls, and the Gravediggers, and some distinguished mainly by the members wearing coats of many colours."[68] Names and functions of Cambridge clubs were not always precisely related: Rupert Brooke and Hugh Dalton were members of a play-reading circle called The Fish and Chimney.[69] Clubs rose and fell: there was even a short-lived Atheist Club around 1815.[70] "Subscriptions to these clubs are often imperfectly collected," warned the *Student's Guide*, "and an unfair burden is thus thrown on those who pay punctually."[71] A society dedicated to the works of Browning collapsed after its Etonian secretary met the poet, concluded that he was middle-class and refused to convene any further meetings.[72] A few student clubs still manage to radiate the comfortable golden haze of Victorian England. The Upware Republic met convivially between 1851 and 1856 at a riverside inn in the Fens, the Five Miles From Anywhere. Its citizens were a group of students messing about in boats to secure "a few hours' escape from the restraints of academic life".[73] They included J.E. Gorst, President of the Union in 1857, and later a member of Lord Randolph Churchill's "Fourth Party", who returned to denounce Home Rule in 1887. Another was James Clerk Maxwell, Edinburgh-born and the University's first Professor of Experimental Physics.

One society, the Majlis, apparently originating in Edwardian times, may have exercised some slight influence on world history. Primarily but not exclusively a meeting place for students from India, it was remembered by Nehru for its "somewhat unreal debates", in which members tried to copy the "style and mannerisms" of the Union. Another member was Hugh Dalton, who knew Nehru "slightly", but confessed that he failed to foresee his future eminence. Nehru himself recalled that "shyness and diffidence" inhibited him from taking an active role. However, other aspects of Indian independence were perhaps foreshadowed in the Majlis. Dalton remembered a Sikh student drawing a knife on a Muslim. In 1933, it was a group of Muslim students at Cambridge who coined the term "Pakistan" for their objective of a separate state. Student politics was not always irrelevant to the real world.[74]

A few clubs were as enduring as the Union, perhaps because they too occupied their own premises and provided members with practical facilities. The aristocratic Pitt Club "defrayed the postal-charges of its members when they wrote their letters there". Late Victorian Cambridge speculated that over a lifetime it would be possible to recoup a subscription several times over through free postage alone, but it is possible that the Pitt Club committee simply had a realistic appreciation of its members' pretensions to literacy.[75] The Amateur Dramatic Club was formed in 1855, and took over the old Union premises at the Hoop Inn. The opportunities created for time-wasting, cross-dressing and disrespectful burlesque aroused donnish suspicions. In 1871, there was a move to ban the ADC, but memories of the failure to suppress the Union fifty years earlier persuaded a wiser generation of academics to prefer loose supervision of a tolerated nuisance.[76]

It is unlikely that any University authority could have suppressed the Athenaeum, an institution which, unlike its London namesake, had "no connection with learning, literature, or the fine arts". Limited to twenty-four members, with rooms in a Georgian house opposite Trinity, it was a haunt of "titled members of the aristocracy who had kindly consented to come up to the University and patronise the ancient institution". Athenaeum members were racing men who gathered for lavish dinners called "Athenaeum Teas" (so-called because the profoundly alcoholic meal was served at a T-shaped dining table), followed by gambling at cards. Condemned by a German princeling in 1851 as "Sodom and Gomorrah", the Athenaeum none the less escaped divine retribution to survive well into the twentieth century. On the eve of the First World War, Oliver Lyttelton was deputed by fellow members to travel to Windsor races and stake their money on a hot tip. The unfancied horse won at 11-2, netting the syndicate around £700. On his return to Cambridge, Lyttelton was met by a brass band playing, "See the Conquering Hero Comes". Athenaeum men ignored the Union, some – such as Lord Cavendish, the future Duke of Devonshire – on parental orders. Most continued their career of decorative uselessness into later life, but there were some exceptions: Lyttelton became Colonial Secretary under Winston Churchill. Cavendish was the Lord Hartington, "Harty-Tarty", of Liberal Unionism. His brother, Lord Frederick Cavendish, went on from the Athenaeum to a violent death in Phoenix Park in 1882.[77]

Clubs were not the only form of student recreational activity. The purposeful afternoon walk was free to everyone: Bertrand Russell "got to know every road and footpath within ten miles of Cambridge" and the poorest of reading men could be seen striding along the Grantchester Grind. On wet days, students paced the sheltered cloisters of Trinity's Nevile's Court. Even if confined to his own room, an undergraduate could engage in a form of exercise that was "a strenuous affair, taxing muscle and ingenuity alike". The game involved "making the circle of your room by climbing over the furniture along the walls without setting foot on the ground".[78] Some more mature and adventurous young men sought other forms of indoor recreation. There was perhaps an element of exaggeration in the disapproving comment of the American, C.A. Bristed, in 1852 that many undergraduates "thought no more of committing fornication than a Southerner would of murdering an Abolitionist".[79] None the less, it is a reminder that there were some recreational facilities that even the Union could not provide.

Organised games provided a rival attraction to participation in Union debates. Alfred Lyttelton consciously excluded the Union from his activities in order to concentrate on sporting excellence.[80] It was not entirely true that the rowing fraternity consisted of "young gentlemen whose muscles were more developed than their brains".[81] Charles Dilke managed to be both oarsman and orator, while a future Lord Chancellor, F.H. Maugham, rowed twice in the Boat Race against Oxford while holding office in the Union. However, to combine the two activities required remarkable time management skills. No sooner had the rowing mania taken hold in the late eighteen-twenties than it became clear that it competed voraciously with other activities in its demands. In May 1828 the Union complained "that much inconvenience is occasioned … by the Racing Day being on Tuesday Evenings", which was also debate night. The secretary of the University Boat Club, William Snow, tersely replied that his committee refused to budge:

> Both Monday and Wednesday are days appointed for Cricket, and as there are many men that both pull in the boats and play at cricket, they were unwilling to give up either – and the hour cannot be changed on account of Chapel.[82]

Snow did not explain what was wrong with racing on a Thursday. Enthusiasm for rowing was a nuisance that often made itself felt in later years. Exasperation surfaced in May 1855. "In consequence of the Boat-races occurring on *every* evening during this week, no meeting was held for Debate."[83] There is some slight consolation in noting that 1855 was the year in which William Snow was convicted of a banking fraud.

As the University became larger, so the range of alternative activities grew. Attendance at Union debates suffered most during the summer term, especially after examinations when energetic relaxation was the order of the day. A debate on Ulster suffered in June 1892 from the "rival attractions of four balls and three concerts", while in May 1914 a poor turn-out on the same topic was explained by the fact that "tennis and the river have seduced all but the faithful".[84] At other times of the year, the Union could usually hold its own. When a recital by the Basque violinist Sarasate clashed with a debate in November 1890, "an unsoothed remnant of considerable size resorted to the Union" to argue over the future of Ireland.[85] Where alternative activities were on offer, members resorted to Union debates presumably because they were interested in the subject to be discussed. This in turn makes it likely that, either through tribal allegiance or intellectual analysis, they already possessed opinions on the issues involved, a point of some importance for the assessment of debates as records of opinion.

It would be misleading to convey the impression that debating was the sole activity or greatest glory of student life. If anything, the evidence would suggest that the reverse was the case, with a considerable falling-off in the quality of debate after the great era of the eighteen-twenties. Ironically, during that golden age, the Union was still fettered by restrictions on subjects for discussion.

Indeed, the Cambridge Union chafed under the "1800" rule imposed upon it in 1821. It was inherently absurd to be forced to discuss, as happened in 1824, the proposition that the Greeks would have been justified in asserting their independence in 1799. In any case, it was difficult to prevent individual members from straying into more recent territory, despite the resolution in 1823 that "any mention of a Political Event of a date subsequent to the year 1800" was "a breach of order".[86] In 1824, a committee was established "to consider the propriety of petitioning the Vice Chancellor for an extension of the period, to which our debates are at present restricted". The office-bearers entrusted with the task quickly decided to take "no further steps" in the matter, explaining that "they had not been influenced by their opinion as to the general expediency of the Measure proposed but by circumstances existing only at the present period".[87] It is possible that these circumstances included the inconvenient fact that the University's senior members were implacable defenders of Anglican ascendancy, while the Union was equally resolute in championing the extension of civil rights to Catholics. The Senate had petitioned against any concessions on the issue five times between 1817 and 1823, on the last occasion "by a considerable majority".[88]

In February 1825, as the Senate was gearing up for yet another blast against the Catholics, the Union quietly amended the restriction to refer to "a floating period of twenty years anterior to the date of discussion".[89] In any case, motions on such issues as the Game Laws were routinely proposed without limitation of time.[90] The dam finally burst with the fall of the Duke of Wellington's ministry in 1830. On 9 November, the twenty-year restriction was set aside, on the motion of a former President, by a vote of 112 to 83. Two days later, a special meeting had to be convened following an objection from the proctors "to discussing politics of the present day".[91]

The special meeting of 11 November 1830 was dominated by a procedural dispute, with "much angry discussion as to the right of the President to bring forward again a question during the same Term in which it had been once decided". Eventually, a motion was carried that "the present discussion be adjourned sine die".[92] The proposer, the Earl of Kerry, was a Fellow Commoner at Trinity. Lord Kerry's grandfather, the Earl of Shelburne, had negotiated the peace treaty with the United States in 1783. His father, the Marquess of Lansdowne, had assured the House of Lords the previous year that there were 250 undergraduates in Trinity alone ready to sign a petition in favour of the Catholic claims, clear evidence of the wider political importance attributed to

Cambridge student opinion on the issue. Lansdowne was about to join the incoming cabinet, and would remain a mainstay of Whig ministries for a quarter of a century, even though he was usually too grand to take an active portfolio. Trollope portrayed him as the Duke of St Bungay, but in real life Lansdowne could not be bothered to accept advancement in the peerage. Once again, the cause of student free speech at Cambridge benefited from the backing of a young grandee unlikely to be challenged by mere dons.[93]

The President, L.S. Orde of Queens', found himself in an awkward position. On 16 November, the Union rejected by 40 votes to 4 the proposition that "the extended Education of the lower Orders" was a threat to good government. Even the supporters of the motion did not take it very seriously: one of the speakers for the proposition had his contribution asterisked in the official report: "Only with regard to Scientific Knowledge."[94] At the formal close of the debate, the real business of the evening began. Orde confessed "his incompetency ... any longer to maintain order in the Society" in consequence of the repeal of the twenty-year rule, and offered his resignation. This was evidently a pre-arranged manoeuvre, since it was a member of his own college who successfully moved that the resignation be refused. Fortified in office, Orde proceeded to activate the new dispensation.[95]

One week later, on 23 November 1830, the Union boldly decided that Wellington's ministry had not merited "the support of the Independent Members of Parliament". No doubt it would have been absurd to have wrapped this motion in some reference to 1810, a year in which everybody knew that the Duke had been otherwise engaged than in politics. Even so there was "angry and disorderly feeling" over the abandonment of the twenty-year rule, and a further attempt was made to censure Orde.[96] The issue continued to divide the reading men from the aristocrats. Two theologians on the verge of distinguished careers in the Church, Charles Merivale and Henry Alford, headed a petition of 97 members warning that the "breach of the contract entered into between the University Authorities and the Society" was likely to cause the "suppression" of the Union. More immediately, they warned that discussion of contemporary events "will render unavoidable much bitter feeling and personal altercation through the necessity which it entails of discussing without any limitation the conduct of Individuals with whom many of the Members of the Union Society must be closely connected".[97]

The issue flared again in November 1831, this time over whether formally to expunge the twenty-year rule from the printed version of the Union's Laws. Once again, the proposal for change was associated with a young aristocrat, W.C. Wentworth Fitzwilliam. A member of a family that was not only hugely wealthy but also benefactors of the University, "little Wentworth" (as Milnes dismissively called him) was unlikely to be a target for proctorial intervention.[98] The Alford-Merivale camp collected 103 names for a further protest against the violation of "an understood compact" with the University, adding that "experience had shewn that such an alteration tends to introduce tumult into the Debates, and to lower the character of the Society". The reading men also asserted their superior claim to experience, disapproving of an attempt to settle the question in the autumn term "when many of the members are from their short residence in the University ignorant of the nature & interests of the Society".[99] The aristocrats won the fight for free speech, but at a cost of division, bitterness and, for a time, the practical secession from the Union of the purists.

"Men came from London to hear us", Bulwer Lytton recalled of the Cambridge Union in the eighteen-twenties.[100] It might be expected that the breaking of the remaining shackles upon free expression would have made the succeeding decades a still greater era in Cambridge debating. In fact, the Union fell into malaise. Interest in politics waned and for a time the Society even gave up publishing its annual reports. One debate in 1839 collapsed because the proposer of the motion failed to turn up. Meetings were "sometimes adjourned in half an hour for want of speakers".[101]

The quality of discussion did not markedly improve when the Society passed from the hands of the fogeys of Young England to the tenants of the old Wesleyan chapel in Green Street. Leslie Stephen was admittedly writing during an uncharacteristically bitter phase of his life when he dismissed the Union of the eighteen-fifties as the training ground for stupendous bores.[102] He was, after all, one of them himself, as he admitted in mellower recollection. "We made orations at the Union Debating Society; but admitted to ourselves, though we did not perhaps state in public, that we were very young and not competent to instruct the nation at large."[103] More telling is the testimony of the first American President of the Union, William Everett, who bluntly dismissed the Society's debates as "death itself" and "beneath contempt". However, even Everett admitted that occasionally "there is an animated discussion, still less often a good speaker, and on very rare occasions a full house". It is however possible that Everett's verdict that Cambridge audiences "are habitually carried off their feet by the most worn-out claptrap" owed something to the fact that he was a supporter of the North in the American Civil War, and held office in 1862 when Cambridge opinion was obstinately pro-Southern.[104]

Perhaps the notion of the eighteen-twenties as an isolated golden age was exaggerated.[105] Even the Union's critics acknowledged that in the decades that followed occasionally "an animated debate would be got up" on a controversial political issue.[106] The Union still attracted passionate defenders. "I love it and reverence it," wrote Lord John Manners, "and would no more think of treating it slightly than I would my best friend".[107] Another member looked back on "brilliant debates and stirring scenes" even in those leaden years of the eighteen-thirties.[108]

One contributing element in the decline of Union debating may be found in a changing intellectual agenda. At precisely the moment when the Union threw off restrictions on the discussion of current events, the nature of British politics changed. Between 1828 and 1832, Protestant Dissenters and Roman Catholics were brought within the system, and a major reform of parliamentary representation achieved. By 1835, Peel had turned the Tories into Conservatives, but it would be a quarter of a century before the Whigs finally metamorphosed into Liberals. The old issues that had divided the social elite in the eighteen-twenties suddenly disappeared, to be replaced by a degree of consensus that lasted for thirty years. Even free trade and the fate of the Corn Laws failed to arouse much excitement among Cambridge students. When pressure for further structural change began to build up again after 1860, it came mostly from outside the political system, and hence from outside Cambridge.

By contrast, attention shifted to wholly new issues. Keble's celebrated Assize Sermon at Oxford in 1833 touched off a movement for liturgical change in the Church of England that focused serious young minds on religion.[109] Theological questions were expressly excluded from Union discussion, while the social implications of the High Church movement did not easily reduce themselves to topics for debate. "We have now virtually pledged ourselves", wrote Lord John Manners in 1838, "to restore what? I hardly know – but still it is a glorious attempt".[110] March 1844 saw the largest attendance at a debate between March 1832, when 181 members had narrowly approved of the poor laws, and October 1862, when 150 would divide heavily in favour of the Southern States in the American Civil War. The 1844 motion asserted that "the suppression of the Monasteries by Henry VIII has proved most injurious to this Country; and the circumstances of the present times imperatively demand the restoration of similar institutions". The fact that it was passed by 88 votes to 60 suggests that Union debates preserved a certain distance from reality throughout the Young England years.[111]

However, the shifting of the intellectual agenda towards questions unsuitable for adversarial discussion is not the only reason for the relative decline of the Union after 1830. The dispute over the abandonment of the twenty-year rule produced an enduring split, with the Apostles sponsoring a rival society "for the purpose of debating in a more gentlemanly manner". Called the Fifty, its membership was limited, in a fine English tradition of eccentricity, to sixty-five. It operated for several years under the leadership of J.W. Blakesley, who had been President of the Union in 1829.[112] Although one undergraduate thought that he "looks like a fog and speaks like an east wind", Blakesley exercised considerable influence over serious young men as a Fellow of Trinity. "He ought to be Lord Chancellor," thought Tennyson, "for he is a subtle and powerful reasoner, and an honest man."[113] When marriage removed him from Cambridge and he became vicar of Ware, Blakesley bombarded *The Times* with letters on social reform, giving national prominence to the by-line of the "Hertfordshire Incumbent".

One of the defectors to the Fifty was Tennyson's friend, Arthur Hallam, son of a distinguished medieval historian:

> And H[allam] spouts from out the pages
> Of his own father's "Middle Ages"[114]

The Fifty was still active in 1835, but had probably lapsed by 1841, when Arthur's younger brother, Henry Hallam, formed the Historical, which had "about forty members" who conducted "tolerably lively debates".[115] Its name was perhaps a tribute to the long-standing debating society at Trinity College Dublin. Members of the Fifty tended to boycott the Union, except for major issues such as the Reform Bill. Fellow Apostles discouraged the younger Hallam from speaking in Union debates, although the *Dictionary of National Biography* recalled his defence of Maynooth. The Historical was not an out-and-out rival, and its members "attended the Union pretty regularly so as to form the nucleus of an audience there".[116] It may have been the Historical that gave Harcourt his first experience of debating. The existence of two successive independent debating societies seems to suggest that there was a swing in support away from the Union as an institution for some time after 1830, rather than a lack of interest in spouting societies as such.

By the end of the nineteenth century, the rise of the junior common rooms created a new in-college focus for undergraduate social life.[117] One by-product was that several colleges either had debating clubs of their own, or formed joint societies – not necessarily with immediate neighbours – as did Emmanuel and Caius in the Edwardian period.[118] Debating was one of the activities that Non-Collegiate students pursued as a means to create their own sense of community. Their first attempt to form a society in 1874 foundered within two years. "This I do not regret", reported the Censor, but its successor in 1886 campaigned for the Non-Colls to be given a distinctive name.[119] By the eighteen-nineties, college debating societies operated mainly as feeders for the Union, even if the training they provided did not always make for an easy transition.[120] With the exception of Trinity's engagingly named Magpie and Stump, surviving reports hardly suggest that they flourished.[121] It seems that the only advantage college societies offered over the Union was that members were permitted to smoke; Trinity, once again, operated in a league of its own by deciding in 1893 to provide members with snuff.[122] In St John's, on the other hand, the most notable feature of the college debating society before 1914 was "its remarkable capacity to survive occasional lean years".[123]

It was fortunate that the Magpie and Stump was an expression of Trinity particularism, since it was the sole society that might have challenged the university-wide supremacy of the Union in the later nineteenth century. Attempts to open membership to King's, probably yet further evidence of the Cambridge Etonian network, were rejected in 1874 and 1877. In choosing to venerate the Magpie, its founders were probably signalling an intention to treat debating as a frivolous activity. However, the original limitation of membership to thirteen was rapidly expanded to 70 in 1873, and all restrictions were abandoned in 1887. Although it expelled Stanley Baldwin for failing to speak, Trinity's debating club made no serious attempt to ensure that loquacity was matched by political education. In January 1888, it was decided to use surplus funds to send an investigating committee to Ireland, but soon afterwards a dissenting faction forced through a qualifying motion declaring that no funds were to be considered as surplus.[124] Indeed, the most notable Irishman in the club's history, Erskine Childers, actively collaborated in its most light-hearted episode.

There is some reason to believe that as Master of Trinity, H.M. Butler hoped to make the college debating society into a serious rival (in both senses of the term) to the Union. In this, he may have been too successful. By 1892, the Magpie and Stump "had got more or less into the hands of the Trinity scholars, and had lost its popularity and interest".[125] To reclaim the society for mainstream frivolity, a dissident faction got up "a Great Rag" in support of George Hamilton-Gordon, who had been expelled for failing to speak. Hamilton-Gordon's friends retaliated by nominating him for the presidency of the Magpie and Stump, in opposition to the official candidate, Childers. The election was a highly successful stunt to revive and publicise the college debating club: the "Gordon Riots" were reported in the national press, and gave E.F. Benson an idea for a novel. Slogans were chalked on walls all over Cambridge, the challengers adopting blue as their colour, in contrast with the red of the "legitimists". Both parties issued manifestos. Hamilton-Gordon offered to convey his supporters to the polls in a sedan chair. With Irish Home Rule once again in the air, Childers declared that he attached "the greatest importance to the maintenance of the Union (to which I have paid my subscription regularly)". Hamilton-Gordon's campaign manager was R.C. Bosanquet, later famous as an archaeologist. Other participants were the emerging historian G.P. Gooch and F.S. Jackson, whose varied career would make him captain of the England cricket team, chairman of the Conservative party and governor of Bengal. In an episode not mentioned in the great philosopher's autobiography, Bertrand Russell "took red chalk and ran round the town in a last-minute attempt to attract the votes of a fickle electorate". However, Trinity voters seem to have been swayed by the slogan "Speech is Childers, but Silence is Golden", for Hamilton-Gordon was elected by 127 votes to 103. The victorious candidate promptly appointed Childers as Vice-President and designated him as his successor.[126] Subsequently, the Magpie and Stump abandoned expulsion for silent members, imposing instead a termly fine upon those who failed to speak. "Often I paid the fine," recalled Nehru.[127]

For a study of student opinion, the most important element at any debate was not the speakers, but the audience. For most debates, "this House" eludes the historian: who were they? Why were they there? One generalisation does seem possible: Union audiences were generally livelier in the earlier period, and as the century wore on they became positively supine – even though, paradoxically, they also grew in size. Major disorders were rare, and confined to the years before 1850. In 1826, the Union briefly expelled a member, Thomas Holt of Trinity, for disorderly conduct during a debate. Holt had "made use of insulting language" when called to order and replied to his expulsion with "a disorderly & abusive speech". (After he had been forcibly evicted, the Society proceeded to private business and agreed to subscribe to a periodical called *The English Gentleman*.) The following week, a grudgingly apologetic letter was received from the offender. Holt could not remember that he "had said or done any thing derogatory to the dignity of the society" but friends had told him that his behaviour had been "quite unjustifiable". He pleaded for the Union to "take into consideration that I was at that time in such a state as not to be accountable for any thing I might have said or done". In the face of the perennial student strategy of regarding a description of the offence (in this case, being offensively drunk) as in some way constituting its own excuse, the Union agreed to Holt's re-admission.[128]   A more mysterious episode occurred in 1830, when "the decency of the Society was violated in a manner too gross to be particularly recorded" by Henry Ward of St Catharine's.[129] Whatever he had done to merit his expulsion, Ward went on to become an Anglican clergyman.

The factional disorder that prevented the Society from debating the respective merits of Wordsworth and Byron in 1828 was untypical. One other notably violent episode took place in 1849 during a debate on a motion declaring that Richard Cobden represented "the rising good sense of the nation". The proposer, Richard Sedgwick of Trinity, was a nephew of the famous geologist, and it was probably his relationship to a Fellow of Trinity that saved him from expulsion when he became embroiled in a scandal over a young woman. A contemporary recalled Sedgwick as "a cleverish, excitable, worthy fellow whose mind was a marvellous mixture of inconsistent opinions which he expounded with a kind of oratory as grotesque as his views". One of his highly-coloured mixed metaphors damned the clergy as "priests sitting upon their golden middens and crunching the bones of the people". His opponent, the coldly conservative and sadistically logical James Fitzjames Stephen, demolished Sedgwick's rhetoric with such devastating sarcasm that the proposer of the motion hurled himself furiously upon his tormenter. A general fist-fight erupted, in which an exceptionally distinguished part was played by a future Clerk of the Calcutta High Court, Charles Piffard. Sedgwick and his supporters were evicted, leaving Cobden to be dismissed by 47 votes to nil. Two future cabinet ministers, Childers and Harcourt, spoke in the debate and presumably also took part in the fight.[130] Although Sedgwick eventually suffered a major mental breakdown, he did manage to overcome his anti-clerical feelings sufficiently to take orders in the Anglican Church and continued a family tradition by serving as perpetual curate in the remote Yorkshire village of Dent. The most venomous of radicals would have been hard put to portray Dent as a golden midden. The clash between the Sedgwickians and the Stephenites was an isolated incident. In 1891, the Union's long-serving chief clerk recalled that "no member had been expelled by force since 1849".[131]

Debates seem to have been livelier in the earlier period. Perhaps this was because the generally smaller attendance encouraged a more informal atmosphere. It may also be related to the probability that the average age of the audience was higher in the first half of the nineteenth century. The American, C. A. Bristed, who was active in the Union in the eighteen-forties, noted that the

> English style of speaking and *of hearing* is very different from ours. Expressions of approbation and disapprobation on the part of the audience being frequent, the speaker aims more at points than with us, and when he has said a good thing or what he means to be such, looks out for the *Hear! Hear!* as a matter of course.[132]

One of the peculiarities of the Fifty was a rule banning its members from responding to speeches in any way.[133] Interjections were not necessarily witty or profound. A speech in 1826 attacking the character of Swift was interrupted by "loud & repeated cries of No, No". Eventually, the chair ruled that "No! No!" was not necessarily objectionable, "but that the repetition in this case made it disorderly".[134] Tedious speakers might face shouts of "adjourn, adjourn". In 1831, there was an unsuccessful move to give the President "a discretionary power" to terminate speakers whose "tiresome prolixity" provoked members "to such a pitch of obstreperousness" as to threaten order.[135]

All this seems to have disappeared by the end of the nineteenth century. An observer in 1899 suggested that an "electric-shock machine" was needed "to persuade the audience to indicate its existence as an audience".[136] One regular speaker "always felt inclined to stop and beseech his hearers to hoot, revile, or even proceed to physical violence, anything rather than continue to regard him with contemptuous indifference".[137] Whereas in the eighteen-forties, Union offices frequently "went a-begging" for lack of candidates,[138] half a century later, Union audiences were well aware of "the power vested in them" as they "exercised a continual domination in silent and profitless self-complacency" over the aspirants who performed to win their favours.[139] It was those same members, whether assertive or silently supine, whose votes determined whether motions passed or failed. A study of Union debates as evidence of opinion must seek to understand how and why they voted as they did.

7: Oratory and Opinion

The Cambridge Union was a debating society, "little pifflers spouting big piffle", as a later detractor put it.[1] Consequently, the historian cannot simply take for granted that the results of its sometimes juvenile proceedings constitute a serious record of opinion. Did votes in Union debates simply represent the verdict of a studio audience on a weekly oratorical beauty contest? The argument offered in this chapter is that the Cambridge Union existed primarily as a training ground for public speaking, in which inspiring oratory was unusual and persuasive debating rare. Consistent patterns of voting on major issues can be identified throughout long periods, usually well beyond the average span that any individual student spent at Cambridge. Accordingly, debate records can be treated as evidence of opinion.

There was no single style of speaking that could be identified with the Cambridge Union, and fashions varied throughout the century. Indeed, the turn-over of personnel in a student community meant that the quality of debates could change very quickly. Many of the participants in the first inter-varsity debate in 1828 had been at Eton together, yet the delivery of the Cambridge delegation astonished their Oxford hosts. Standards could drop very suddenly: in 1891, the Vice-President's report complained that debates had suffered from "a considerable falling off in interest, and the speaking has not been of so high an order as is usual in this Society".[2] The following year, a reporter lamented that "with one or two exceptions, there is really nobody at all at our Union now who has the smallest idea of even making an indifferent speech". In 1899, "contempt for style" was said to be endemic.[3]

Style included not only speech but also body language, which could range from the violent to the languid. Praed sarcastically claimed to "be somewhat afraid of the knock-down arguments" of an opponent "when I see how much the table of the house has suffered from the fist of the honourable gentleman". Yet he was equally capable of lampooning Macaulay for speaking "with his arms and his metaphors crossed", while Leslie Stephen archly suggested that practice at debating could "enable the orator to attain that last pitch of perfection at which he knows what to do with his hands".[4] A reporter in 1902 regretted "the increasing tendency" of Union speakers to solve that particular problem by speaking "with their hands in their pockets, a practice never becoming, and in a young speaker savouring somewhat of arrogance".[5]

Even among shifting fashions, individuals had their own mode of delivery. Recalling the Union of the eighteen-twenties, Benjamin Hall Kennedy distinguished between the styles of Cockburn, the lawyer, and Praed, the poet. Cockburn engaged in minute preparation, rehearsing his contributions in detail, and could sometimes be seen "in the most retired part of the Trinity grounds, slowly pacing and moving his lips, as if reciting to himself". The end product would be a speech of "great fluency, power, and precision". Praed, on the other hand, although sufficiently well-informed "to escape any semblance of shallowness or incoherence" managed to give the impression that he was simply speaking with discursive wit on the spur of the moment, in a display of "instinctive readiness".   Merivale also recalled distinct styles. Kemble was notable "for his stores of information". Sunderland unleashed a "copious flow of rhetoric, enlivened by much incisive wit and by well-wrought bits of flowery declamation". Another lost talent was the heir to a radical family, William Tooke, who died on his twenty-fourth birthday. His contributions to debates were "precise and logical deductions of the utilitarian school".[6]

Although there was no single "Union" style, the required posture of shallow omniscience perhaps encouraged the less positive quality of a Cambridge Union attitude. A practised speaker might adopt different approaches at different times. A speech by Keynes in support of Home Rule was judged to be "one of the best examples of the undemonstrative school; quiet, fluent and logical", but Wilson Harris recalled a peroration in which Keynes roused the Union to fever pitch with a witty appeal "to all right-thinking persons, when the division came, to 'go streaming through the noes'". Unfortunately, a style that amused "right-thinking persons" within the confined world of Cambridge might be experienced in a very different way by outsiders. A.F.W. Plumtre, a Canadian who studied under Keynes, doubted whether the Union's influence upon his mentor was "for the best". "I have seen the Union debating style, with its fluency, its flippancy, its intentional controversy, and its unintentional condescension, used in international arguments with people accustomed to more suave and courteous ways of talking – and with very bad effects." As a Union orator, Keynes "was devastatingly successful and obviously enjoyed it" but when he used the same techniques in other contexts, "he probably hurt more people than he knew or meant to". Like Keynes, Plumtre was both a civil servant and a scholar. Keynes was a product of Eton; Plumtre of its transatlantic equivalent, Upper Canada College. It is noteworthy that this thoughtful Canadian assessment should have so firmly singled out the Cambridge Union, rather then privileged education or superior intellect, as the source of a flaw in an English genius.[7]

Some speakers probably never overcame their natural disadvantages, however compelling their arguments. Perhaps G.H.R. Barton of Clare was related to the Wicklow gentry family of that name, for he spoke like an Irish unionist when he opposed Home Rule in 1892. His warnings fell on deaf ears, a reporter noting only that he "talked prettily of demons of rapine and murder, but was otherwise dull".[8] Despite repeated attempts, the soporific delivery of George Epps of Emmanuel never won the ear of the Union. He suffered from the additional disadvantage of sharing his surname with a well-known brand of cocoa, advertised with the slogan "grateful and comforting". The phrase was too great a temptation for Union scribblers to pass over, and his speech in support of Home Rule in 1906 was soon dismissed. "Mr Epps talks sound common sense, but the temptation to listen to him is easily resisted."[9] It was in character that Epps crowned a worthy career by rising to the post of Government Actuary.

Union speeches are best analysed under three headings: oratory, public speaking and debating. Oratory dazzles and may be suspected of disguising flawed arguments to bamboozle the unwary into endorsing illogical propositions. At the other end of the spectrum, debating is the art of dissecting an opponent's argument in order to demonstrate its fallacies, a process that seeks to persuade rather than to overwhelm. There is plenty of evidence that the Cambridge Union was disappointing on both these headings. Rather, it operated principally as a forum for the encouragement of cogent public speaking. Most debates were nothing like a continuous logical engagement with the proposition under discussion but were rather a series of individual performances in which participants concentrated on the articulation of their own views. In short, the more the deficiencies of the Cambridge Union are recognised, the more plausible it becomes to regard its votes as evidence of opinion rather than the outcome of gladiatorial oratory.

A persistent criticism of the Union was that it tended "to encourage volubility of speech where there is abundance neither of knowledge nor of ideas".[10] Praed poked fun at one speaker of the eighteen-twenties for "panting and blowing like a courier", riding his personal hobby horse. "Off he goes! Mounts at Magna Carta, breakfasts with the Long Parliament, dines with William and Anne, and finds himself comfortably at home in the state of the nation." To his embarrassment, Charles Merivale found himself confusing basic facts about the life of Mary Queen of Scots when he denounced her execution in his maiden speech in 1827. He was equally surprised that "their fallacy was not discovered. Indeed, I believe one might practise very considerably on the credulity of the house, if one chose." Inaccurate information was almost certainly matched by erroneous logic. As a fin-de-siècle critic put it, "if skilfully delivered, a fallacious argument has much more effect than the most weighty utterance monstrously mumbled".[11] *The Times* had taken a more indulgent view in 1886. It was true that some speeches were "all flashiness" and that "a Union audience likes fluency, smart hits, and well-rounded periods". However, many undergraduates were "fairly proficient students of politics" and so were "neither likely to talk nonsense nor to be moved by it". The second part of the statement was perhaps more plausible than the first. "A shallow rhetorician may be applauded, but a large part of his youthful audience is quite capable of taking his measure."[12] Hugh Dalton immodestly claimed that the Union made him "almost too fluent", but many of his contemporaries distrusted him and he failed to become President.[13]

Monckton Milnes was disappointed to hear "a great deal more declamation than argument" when he attended his first debate, on Catholic Emancipation, in 1827. By contrast, Thackeray reported "some excellent speaking" on the same issue in 1829.[14] Yet, as Chapter Eight shows, the division of opinion on the Catholic question remained remarkably stable in Union debates throughout the eighteen-twenties. We must assume either identical levels of declamation and excellence in all eight debates between 1822 and 1829, or conclude that most speeches bounced off minds that were already made up. Dilke was unimpressed by G.O. Trevelyan when he attended his first debate, on the American Civil War: his verdict of "mere flash, but very witty" had much to do with the fact that Trevelyan supported the South while Dilke was a fervent partisan of the North.[15] Trevelyan carried the day, or rather the Confederate cause triumphed, by 117 votes to 33. A year later, with entirely different speakers, the Union again voted in favour of the South, this time by 66 votes to 18. In two debates, the result was statistically identical: 78 percent of a Cambridge audience supported the Southern states.[16] It seems unlikely that the flash or wit of any single speech was sufficient to upset opinions already formed. Undergraduates who were sufficiently interested in the American Civil War to attend a Union debate on the issue had probably already determined which side they supported. Certainly Trevelyan did not always sway the Union. As a freshman, he had delivered "a most eloquent speech" demanding "condign punishment of the Indian mutineers", but the motion was rejected by almost two to one (70 votes to 36), a result which even its proposer generously conceded gave "a very high, and at the same time just, idea of the sense and manliness of the Cambridge Union".[17]

If oratory had swayed Union audiences, we should expect to encounter violent swings in voting and inconsistency in motions passed or rejected. In fact, there seems to be only one example of a dramatic see-saw, over State payment of Catholic priests in 1846-47. This may have been the result of the debating skills of young Henry Hallam, but probably it cannot be entirely dissociated from the crisis of the Irish Famine.[18] Moreover, if students were capable of being swayed by the bulk or the cogency or the passion of the speeches delivered, we should expect to find progressive causes in general triumphing far more often than was the case. "A great majority of Union orators are almost invariably desperate Radicals", wrote Leslie Stephen, whereas most undergraduates were "Conservatives of the most orthodox type". One hallmark of English conservatism, at least until the Thatcher era, was its marked distrust of the theoretical, sometimes verging upon complete repudiation of all forms of logical argument. Hence, at Cambridge, "against this solid Tory phalanx all the rhetoric of fiery Radicals and premature Republicans spends itself in perfect harmlessness".[19]

The collision between radical rhetoric and conservative resistance can be seen in debates relating to Ireland, especially in the late nineteenth century. In 1890, the "main object" of one advocate of Home Rule "seemed to be the wearing down of his opponents by a system of oratorical blockade".[20] None the less, he failed to make any impact upon an ingrained unionist majority. Another example can be found in a debate of 1903 on the trial of Colonel Arthur Lynch. The Australian-born Lynch had fought for the Boers in the small but politically significant Irish Brigade, where he had also clashed with the gigantic ego of John MacBride. Lynch's gesture had secured him a by-election victory at Galway in 1901, quickly followed by prosecution for high treason and sentence of death. His cause was passionately championed by the Union's Secretary, J.C. Arnold of St John's. "We felt, as we seldom feel in the Union, that we had a born orator in our midst." However, "all his persuasiveness could not prevail against the settled conviction of the House". The Union consigned Lynch to his fate by 118 votes to 30, a very large majority in the teeth of Arnold's undoubted tour-de-force.[21]

After the First World War, the programme of the Cambridge Union began to be dominated by "big-name" visiting speakers who provided "less a debate than an exposition of a thesis by an outstanding master of it".[22] Were pre-1914 undergraduates swept off their feet by the seductive arts of the veteran public figures? In fact, the practice of regularly inviting outsiders to speak at debates was a late-Victorian innovation and, as outlined in Chapter Nine, mainly a controversial by-product of the Irish Home Rule crisis of 1886. On one occasion in 1874, special arrangements had been made "to enable a non-member of the Society to take part in the Debate", so that an old Bengal hand could warn against the principle of competition for admission to the Indian Civil Service.[23] The first set-piece visitor debate occurred in February 1884, when H.M. Hyndman and William Morris urged the adoption of "an ordered socialistic system in every department under the control of a completely democratic State". However, Hyndman was a life member of the Union, and valued his standing as a Cambridge man, while Morris equally was eligible to speak at the Union as a member of the sister society at Oxford: one of his first works of art had been the frescoes with which he decorated the original Oxford Union debating chamber in 1857. Hyndman was pleasantly surprised to find that as many as 58 Cambridge students were prepared to back his cause. More to the point, six times as many Cambridge students resisted the pleas of the distinguished visitors, and the motion was heavily defeated.[24]

Opinions varied on the desirability of introducing "set speeches" by prominent visitors to an undergraduate forum. *The Times* disapproved when the Oxford Union copied the Cambridge experiment in 1888 and invited Lord Randolph Churchill and John Morley to duel on Home Rule. Both had been members of the Oxford society, but the start of the debate was delayed by a skirmish as anti-Randolphites alleged that the Tory Democrat had been struck off for failing to pay his subscription.[25] However, when the rising Liberal MP Frank Lockwood came to Cambridge to denounce Lord Salisbury's Irish policy the following year, a university journalist commented that "the cultivated oratory of veteran politicians serves the useful purpose of communicating vitality to debates which run the risk otherwise of degenerating into a reiteration of trite commonplaces and stale conventionalism".[26] The fact that it was Home Rule that encouraged both the Cambridge and Oxford Unions to experiment with outside speakers is itself testimony to the extent to which Irish issues were seen to be external to the student world.

At the core of the explosion of anger by C.V. Stanford, Cambridge's Dublin-born Professor of Music, in 1887 was the allegation that the Union was being turned into a platform for Irish nationalists.[27] Once the practice of inviting guest speakers began, both sides insisted on representation by external champions. In fact, anti-Home Rulers were never able to muster their biggest guns, although in fairness it should be said that they were hardly needed. In contrast to later decades, it was not easy to lure leading politicians to address a student audience. John Redmond cancelled at the last moment in 1894, although he made amends with a tremendous performance the following year. Dillon spoke in 1886 and again in 1909, while Swift MacNeill made a personal pilgrimage in 1913 for a repeat performance of a motion on Home Rule similar to the one he had proposed in 1873. In addition, Sir Horace Plunkett spoke in favour of the establishment of a Catholic university in Ireland in 1903. Prior to 1914, the most prominent public men evidently concluded that the risks of addressing a mercurial audience of young men outweighed any possible advantages.

What was the impact of visiting speakers? "Judging from the comparative closeness of the division," wrote the *Granta* of the Home Rule debate of 1895, John Redmond "must have made converts." Home Rule had been defeated by 237 votes to 180, whereas there was usually "a two-to-one Unionist majority in a large House".[28] Perhaps: Redmond was to register an even greater triumph at Oxford in 1907, when his "thrilling" speech was thought to have been responsible for a Home Rule triumph, a majority of 133 votes in a division of 585. "It is doubtful if the Union has ever heard or will ever hear again a speech that will have such an influence on its hearers," wrote an Oxford reporter.[29] However, examined more closely, Redmond's impact on Cambridge opinion was probably not overwhelming. Out of 417 votes registered under his spell at Cambridge in 1895, 43 percent were for Home Rule. In the two previous debates in February 1893 and March 1894, the proportions had been 31 percent in a house of 389, and 34 percent in a division of 394. Dillon's visit in 1886 had caused a similar blip, a "swing" to Home Rule of about ten percent.[30] When the Congress leader G.K. Gokhale spoke in 1906, he seems to have increased the vote in favour of Indian nationalism by about 13 percent.[31] It was probably true at Cambridge, as has been claimed of Oxford prior to 1914, that some students thought it discourteous to vote against a visitor.[32] Indeed, as late as 1933, one of the contributing elements to the Oxford vote in the "King and Country" debate was that the pacifist C.E.M. Joad was the sole guest speaker.[33] In some cases, the "swing" to the unpopular cause might be explained simply by the increased attendance attracted by a distinguished visitor.

Prior to 1914, visiting speakers remained the exception at Cambridge, not least because the Union was primarily seen as a forum for undergraduate debate. One President from Edwardian times complained half a century later that the subsequent practice of inviting "every star in the contemporary firmament seems better calculated to produce a good stage-show than to provide a training ground for native talent".[34] The Union grudgingly approved the principle of inviting outsiders in 1887, "provided that the necessary arrangements are submitted to the House for approval". An ambitious short-list was compiled, consisting of the Irish Nationalists, Thomas Sexton, T.P. O'Connor, Justin McCarthy, and their opponents, Colonel Saunderson, T.W. Russell and Leonard Courtney.[35] (It is revealing that even the young optimists of Cambridge did not expect to secure Parnell.) It quickly became clear that public figures were not consumed with enthusiasm to address the Cambridge Union, so permission was granted to consider other names "provided they be men to whom the Committee feels sure the House could not personally object".[36] The issue arose again in 1901 over an unauthorised approach to Lloyd George, then deeply unpopular because of his opposition to the Boer War. Critics called it "unfair and extraordinary" to extend an invitation "before the permission of the House has been obtained".[37] When Lloyd George did appear in 1904, he proved more acceptable, sweeping the Union into one of its few recorded votes of no-confidence in a Conservative government, albeit at a moment when it was difficult for all but the most fervent of Tories to feel much loyalty to the Balfour ministry. "I must have heard him, and helped to swell his majority", Wilson Harris wrote half a century later, "but of the great occasion I remember precisely nothing at all".[38] Another Edwardian recalled that "we did not attach overmuch importance to Visitors' Debates".[39]

However, even if the prominent politicians exercised only a relatively slight influence, deference towards authority could take more subtle forms.[40] The pre-1914 world was characterised by respect towards even marginally calibrated seniority. When the freshman Bertrand Russell received a social call from J.E. McTaggart, he was so overwhelmed by the presence of a former President of the Union that he could not summon up the courage to invite McTaggart into his rooms.[41] Wilson Harris recalled "the reverential haze through which a freshman views the achievements of his seniors": during his first term, he was awe-struck by the President of the Union, the "majestic" Edwin Montagu (an adjective that Montagu himself would have endorsed).[42] Norman Birkett found himself "under a kind of spell" in 1908 on encountering F.D. Livingstone, who "had the prestige that belonged to ex-Presidents".[43] In this case, the hero-worship is especially noteworthy. Birkett was a mature student, twenty-four years of age when he came to Cambridge, not a star-struck adolescent. Moreover, he was not the product of a public school and so had escaped the prefect culture that undoubtedly underlay much of the hierarchy of undergraduate life.[44]

Cambridge Union memoirs occasionally recall examples of outstanding oratory from across the years, such as Charles Merivale's confession that John Sterling's "vehement oratory carried our youthful judgments away with it". These do not always bear close scrutiny. Sometimes it appears that the impact of the dazzling speaker was confined to the writer of the memoir. On other occasions, the motion that occasioned the tour-de-force resulted in a division that reflected votes in more humdrum debates on the same question. Edward Bulwer Lytton recalled of the eighteen-twenties that "the greatest display of eloquence" came from "the renowned Macaulay", who was "some years our senior". A speech by Macaulay on the French revolution was etched in his memory "as the most heart-stirring effort of that true oratory which seizes hold of the passions, transports you from yourself, and identifies you with the very life of the orator, that it has ever been my lot to hear". The only contribution by Macaulay that squares with Lytton's reminiscence was delivered in February 1823 in a debate on the political conduct of Mirabeau. There were only three speakers, all for Mirabeau, and one of them was W.M. Praed, an equally formidable performer. None the less, the vote was tied at 33 votes on each side: half of those present were unmoved by the oratorical torrent, and voted for a point of view that nobody had bothered to expound.[45] Oddly enough, Lytton recalled one other speech by Macaulay, on the liberty of the press, as "a failure". This was delivered in December 1824, after Macaulay had become a Fellow of Trinity, and on that occasion his side won by a margin of almost three-to-one, 71 votes against 24.[46]

Similarly, two brilliant speeches by young ex-Presidents from the Edwardian era were recalled with delight but probably made relatively little impact on the actual vote. Birkett remembered a speech on tariffs by A.C. Pigou, President in 1900, which "annihilated" the opposition and "ended with a peroration ... which roused the House to the wildest enthusiasm". Pigou spoke twice against Tariff Reform while Birkett was at Cambridge, in May 1908, the year he succeeded Marshall in the Chair of Economics, and in February 1910. Free trade was victorious in both, carrying the day by 131 votes to 115 on the first occasion, and by 182 votes to 153 on the second.. A contemporary report confirmed that he was a dazzling speaker, even suggesting that it was cruel to match him against mere undergraduates.[47] But Tariff Reform was a "swing" issue: free trade carried the day five times in the seven debates on the issue between 1908 and 1913, and even Pigou could only achieve majorities of 52 and 54 percent in 1908 and 1910. True, he did better than another ex-President, J.M. Keynes, who helped free trade to a narrow three-vote victory in a house of 301 in November 1910 (with Hugh Dalton and Philip Noel-Baker in support). However, it had not always been so. In 1903, in company with two other formidable ex-Presidents, J.E. McTaggart and E.S. Montagu, Pigou had been unable to stem the flood of support for Joseph Chamberlain's recently launched protectionist campaign, going down on that occasion to defeat by 255 votes to 195.[48] There is no doubt that Pigou was a devastating speaker as well as a brilliant economist. Yet this did not alter the fundamental fact that those who attended debates on the tariff question because they supported protection regarded him as brilliant but also wrong.

F.D. Livingstone continued to speak at the Union after his Presidency in 1907. His father was a Canon of Liverpool Cathedral, a background that probably explains both his Toryism and his explosive opposition to Irish Home Rule. Livingstone was a formidable speaker. "His very grocer's bill becomes a matter of immense importance to all his hearers", commented the *Cambridge Review* after he had denounced Liberal policy towards Ireland in 1908.[49] The following year, he went head-to-head with John Dillon. Arnold McNair, who spoke alongside Dillon, recalled that Livingstone "was so effective that I had the sensation that he was actually 'punishing' our guest physically". A contemporary reporter doubted whether any summary could do justice to Livingstone's speech: "the reply he made to the arguments of the other side must have won back the votes of many waverers". However, the division at the end of the debate produced a tie: 184 votes on each side. Perhaps Dillon and Livingstone had cancelled each other out?[50] However, when the Union returned to Home Rule one year later, the audience was one-third the size, the speakers were all undergraduates and nobody produced any fireworks – but the result was another dead-heat, this time 56 votes against 56. The *Granta* thought it "a strange coincidence" that two consecutive debates should have produced exactly the same result.[51] The precise balance may indeed have been accidental, but the medium-term trend of student opinion was evidently towards Home Rule, and 1909-1910 seems to have been the cross-over point. Three debates between 1906 and 1908 produced majorities against Home Rule between 51 and 54 percent, with attendances varying between 142 and 280. Two debates in 1912 saw opposition to Home Rule drop to 43 percent in a House of 427, and 48 percent when the attendance was just 73.[52] Oratory entertained and sometimes entranced, but it does not appear to have made dramatic conversions.

During his first year at Cambridge, Charles Dilke defined the ideal Union style as:

> common-sense discussion in well-worded speeches with connected argument, the whole to be spoken loud enough to be heard, and with sufficient liveliness to convince the hearers of the speaker's interest in what he is saying.

"So far as this is oratory," he added, "it is cultivated (with very moderate success) at the Union."[53] This, it might be said, was not oratory but rather public speaking, and it was the mere act of addressing an audience that was often cited as the chief value of the Union. Debating was "the very best school in the world for teaching a man to speak in public", pronounced the *Granta* in 1895.[54] "The training in speaking which the Union has provided generation after generation has been of incalculable value to thousands of its members", wrote one ex-President.[55] It is significant that in 1866, at the time of the inauguration of the premises in Round Church Street, celebrations of the value of the Union concentrated not upon the cut-and-thrust of debate but on the simple mechanics of "the powers of utterance". Speaking in the Union, Milnes told his successors, "will give you that faculty of prompt and precise diction which is indispensable for political success, and advantageous in every profession".[56]

Henry Fawcett took the argument a step further: the Union helped undergraduates "to think while you are speaking and to frame your ideas in suitable language".[57] Bulwer Lytton recalled that when he first spoke in debates, he "was hurried away into imperfect articulation" by the "tumultuous impetuosity" of his thoughts.[58] "The groundwork of many speeches is a rumble of inarticulate sounds", wrote Leslie Stephen, "from which a few half-finished sentences detach themselves at intervals." Mastering "the art of putting together tolerable connected sentences in public is worth something on its own account; but indirectly it leads to a good deal more." Cogent expression of ideas was a long step towards comprehending their meaning.[59]

All this helped to prepare young men for social and political leadership. The *Pall Mall Gazette* hailed the Union as "a very useful introductory discipline for men who are to engage in public life".[60] As Lord Powis put it, Englishmen lived in "a country in which not only all the national, but all the local business is conducted by representative assemblies .... whom, to influence, you must persuade by discussion".[61] Lord John Manners looked back on the Union as the educational highlight of two and a half years at Cambridge. "If ... I have gained no distinctions, and have squandered away, as I fear I have, a very large sum of money, I have still the consolation of thinking that I have acquired confidence and a certain knack of speaking in public which may be useful to me in after life." For Manners, an additional benefit was that public speaking helped him to curb a stammer.[62] A decade later, Lord Aberdeen's son, Arthur Gordon, found that speaking in the Union helped him to overcome his shyness.[63]

The career of every Union debater began with the ordeal of a maiden speech. Officially, in keeping with parliamentary custom, maiden speeches were treated with indulgence and sympathy, but "if you can't think of a word, everybody begins to stamp".[64] Even in a supportive atmosphere, maiden speakers were often forced to recognise that they were not born orators. Bulwer Lytton spoke first in a business session. "My speech was short, but it was manly and simple, spoken in earnest, and at once successful." Since his intervention had been in defence of a maligned officer, Lytton found himself immediately welcome among "the leading men of the Union. ... I had emerged from obscurity into that kind of fame which resembles success in the House of Commons." Over-confident in his sudden popularity, Lytton decided to speak in a regular debate, but "I fairly broke down in the midst of my second speech". This he regarded as a blessing in disguise. "I set myself to work in good earnest, and never broke down again".[65] Monckton Milnes reported that his maiden speech "was nearly a failure". He was so "dreadfully nervous" that he felt ill. "I was applauded & complimented, but it was ill-delivered – another attempt may be more propitious."[66] By contrast, Thackeray, two years later, resolved never to repeat the experiment. "I have made a fool of myself! ... I spouted at the Union." Some "malignant daemon" impelled him to speak on the character of Napoleon. "I got up & stuck in the mud at the first footstep then in endeavouring to extract myself ... I went in deeper and deeper still .... & blustered & blundered, & retracted, & stuttered".[67]

Harcourt's description of his maiden speech probably refers to a meeting of the Historical, but the experience seems typical enough:

> I am sensible enough that I broke down, though my friends were very good-natured and said "a successful first attempt" and all that. The truth was that ... not having the least idea I should lose my wits I went down

without my notes, and found all at once as soon as I got on my legs that my heart was ... in my stomach. However I was determined not to sit down and worked off as well as I could.[68]

A notable failure was that of Henry Labouchere, later the conspiratorial "Labby" of late Victorian politics, whose self-appointed role as intermediary between Parnell and the Liberals was not always entirely helpful to either. At the start of his academic career, such as it was, Labouchere arrogantly believed that he could take Cambridge by storm and without effort. He was quickly disabused. He sat down to write a prize poem, only to find that his muse did not flow. In his second term, a Union debate on the English Civil War seemed to provide an opportunity for him to shine. "I went to the Debating Society and commenced a speech in favour of the regicides," he recalled, "but, to my astonishment, entirely broke down."[69] The truth was that Labby had to come to terms with a great deal of personal baggage, and Cambridge was not the place for him to sort out his problems. Despite bringing humiliation upon himself in the Cambridge Union, he went on to become an effective performer in the House of Commons.

Given the attrition rate, the Union needed a steady flow of maiden speakers to ensure its own renewal. Thomas McDonnell had a personal mission to defend all things Irish, but as an officer of the Union he was also conscious of his responsibility to encourage new recruits. Noting that the "one regrettable feature" of the October term of 1897 was "the almost total absence of promising maiden speeches", he issued a general appeal to members, reminding

those gentlemen who are thinking of postponing their debut at the Union till a late period in their first year, that for the Society's benefit as well as their own, they should beware lest other interests and pursuits may compel them to lose sight of so honourable an ambition.[70]

Happily, the following year, it was reported that "several very promising maiden speeches have been made".[71] The *Granta's* "Union Jingles" of 1892 suggested that maiden speeches were not always promising. "Freshman rose / Chairman bowed / Out there goes / Such a crowd...". The ordeal is dragged out in staccato verse: "Till at last / Sounds of feet / Thick and fast / In retreat – Foes and friends / All and each / Fly – thus ends / Maiden speech."[72] A steady infusion of maiden speakers was necessary for the health of the Society, but they did little for the cut-and-thrust of its debates.

Bulwer Lytton made steady progress after his embarrassing debut but "it was long before I could be called a good speaker."[73] The next stage in public speaking, and for most Union speakers probably the highest level of perfection, was to learn how to present a point of view in a manner that made it acceptable to "an assembly every member of which is intellectually and by cultivation on a level with the speaker, before which he cannot presume, and which he dare not attempt to cajole, misinform, or despise".[74] As the *Granta* emphasised in 1895, a speaker could not adopt "the easy and almost contemptuous familiarity that he might use before a small gathering with all the members of which he was intimately acquainted." Not only was it necessary for speeches to be carefully prepared, but the speaker "must clothe his thoughts in language appropriate both to the subject in hand and to the mixed and critical audience he has to address".[75] In the opinion of a hostile reporter, a speaker who got the tone of the house wrong was responsible in 1902 for an uncharacteristic if narrow vote against landlordism in Ireland. Opposing the motion, the Etonian A.B. Geary of King's, flatly stated that Irish tenant farmers had no grievances deserving of sympathy. Advanced to a select circle of fellow reactionaries, Geary's sentiments would no doubt have produced grunted agreement. Unleashed as an *ex cathedra* pronouncement to 150 members of the Cambridge Union, Geary's attitude aroused more resentment than assent.[76] As Leslie Stephen had put it: "It is odd how different a speech sounds when it is made in public and when it is made to your private chairs and tables."[77]

If the first target of successful public speaking was to advance opinions in a manner that made them attractive to others, then the highest stage of Union achievement was to proceed to actual debating. *The Times* in 1886 insisted that the "real triumph, in a Union debate" was won by the speaker who might lack "external graces of speech ... but who can take his opponent's argument to pieces and quietly demolish it".[78] Unfortunately, the evidence suggests that such speakers were rare. Norman Birkett remembered the Scot, H.D. Henderson, "as the best pure debater that I heard in my time". "[R]elentless, pugnacious, inexorable," Henderson seemed to latch on to an opponent "and certainly would never let him go until he had reduced him to the equivalent of pulp" – and "all done with consummate grace and ease" coupled with "a most radiant and indulgent smile".[79] Henderson, who was President in 1912, was a person of no ordinary talents. He later became Professor of Economics at Oxford and was elected Warden of All Souls shortly before his death in 1951. In much the same way, in the nineteen-twenties R.A. Butler stood out because "he *debated* – a none too common occurrence in Union 'debates'".[80] "There is probably very little real debate in the Union," Dilke conceded in 1898, adding there had been "little in my time". He did however offer the consoling thought that the House of Commons was just as disappointing.[81]

We may therefore dismiss any assumption that the term "debate" referred to the continuous engagement of two integrated lines of argument for and against a proposition. It was rare for speakers on either side to be precisely balanced, and in the earlier decades some members liked to indulge in explanations of their refusal to back either point of view. The Cambridge Union was a good training ground to learn one of the great truths of politics, that allies can prove a greater threat than opponents. A dull speaker could be sufficient to destroy a good case: Hort assured himself that he lost his motion on Macaulay's *History* in 1849 because another member had "cleared the house by speaking".[82] Student debaters could be remarkably discursive, using "the avowed subject" as "a pretext for something else – when the orator says, for example, that to appreciate the character of Charles I, it is necessary to form a distinct opinion as to the merits of Mr. Bright's present agitation".[83] The *Cambridge Review* was glad when J.M. Keynes spoke on Home Rule in 1903, since Ireland gave him "fewer opportunities than usual of discussing the Education Act or the Disestablishment of the English Church", obsessional topics to a committed Nonconformist.[84]

An account by Monckton Milnes of a debate in 1829 indicates the extent to which discussion fell short of a true meeting of minds. The motion asked "Will Mr. Coleridge's Poems [sic] of the Ancient Mariner, or Mr. Martin's act tend most to prevent cruelty to animals?" and it had passed into Union folklore by 1866 as an example of the precious style of the Society's early years. This was unfair. Coleridge's poem, with its dramatic warning of the dire consequences of killing wildlife, had been published in 1798, and was on its way to making the albatross a symbolic image in common speech. Richard Martin, "Humanity Dick", was a Galway landowner with half a century of legislative experience on College Green and at Westminster. A founder of the Royal Society for the Prevention of Cruelty to Animals, he had succeeded in 1822 in carrying the first parliamentary enactment for animal rights, banning "the cruel and improper treatment of cattle". Thus, at its core, the motion embodied a key issue, whether human behaviour was best modified through education or by compulsion.

The debate began well, "with some very deep poetical criticism by a friend of Coleridge's", but this was followed by the attempt of "a great unpoetical Kingsman ... to turn the poem into ridicule". Milnes then spoke, in defence of Coleridge, but without taking sides on the motion. He was followed by the thunderous and unstable Thomas Sunderland, who denounced both camps "in a most absurd strain of hyperbolic radicalism". The people, he concluded, could only appreciate poetry if they were properly educated, and this would be impossible without the overthrow of aristocratic government. Then J.C. Symons of Corpus tried to shift the focus of discussion to Humanity Dick, whose political career had crashed. After losing his Galway seat at the general election of 1826, he had been forced into bankruptcy and fled to the cheaper pastures of Boulogne. Symons assured the Union that "he knew Mr. Martin very well" and that he "had been much hurt by the aspersions cast upon him in that Society". It was "absurd to compare his senatorial abilities" with Coleridge's "silly production". This was followed by a "clever Utilitarian speech" from Joseph Carne, also in defence of Martin and the principle of legislation. The debate was concluded by "a very superior man", J.W. Blakesley, who gave "a most eloquent commentary upon the poem itself", which "so won the hearts of the House, that when he read the last verse the cheering was tremendous". Coleridge won by two votes in a division of 92. Alas, however, for the cause of poetry, it was an Irish issue, one not even mentioned in the debate, that determined the outcome. Humanity Dick had lost his Galway seat partly because he had championed Catholic Emancipation. Late in the evening, members of the Tory Brunswick club "arrived in full orange badges to vote against Martin". The Coleridge-versus-Martin motion generated a memorable evening, but it could hardly be called a true debate.[85]

If debating had formed the predominant element in the proceedings of the Cambridge Union, we might expect to find evidence that some members changed their minds as a result of exposure to argument, even on an issue as contentious as Irish Home Rule. Such evidence is remarkable for its absence: dramatic conversions may have taken place on the road to Damascus, but they did not often occur in the vicinity of Round Church Street. While debating is ostensibly a logical activity, it is also adversarial. "Very few men are made wiser by being publicly convicted of having reasoned ill," warned James Stephen,[86] a maxim that his son Fitzjames might well have pondered. Fewer still were prepared to admit that they had been so convicted. Palmerston noted that a debate on the existence of ghosts during his Edinburgh years "ended exactly as all our debates have as yet and I fancy always will". The combatants "exhausted all our arguments on each side of the Question ... & we each retired more strongly than ever confirmed in his own opinion, and more convinced that the other was wrong."[87] The Nationalist MP for Galway, Stephen Gwynn, formed part of a formidable Home Rule team when he visited the Union in 1911, although he might have made an even bigger impact had he mentioned that his grandfather, Smith O'Brien, was the only President of the Cambridge Union ever to have been sentenced to death for treason. "Rumour has it that not a few members changed their opinions ... as a result of the speeches for the motion," wrote one student journalist. "We are loth to credit this report, which would signify a severe breach of the highest Union traditions."[88] Remarkably, there seems to be only one traceable case of a student admitting that he had changed his mind about Ireland under any circumstances. C.V. Barrington of Trinity announced in January 1887 that he "had been a Home Ruler but the Plan of Campaign had brought about his conversion to the Unionist ranks".[89] Since his father was a land agent in Tipperary, this was hardly surprising. The real mystery would lie in the motives – perhaps of youthful idealism or rebellion – that had seduced the young Barrington into the Parnellite camp in the first place.

Overall, the striking degree of consistency in Cambridge Union votes on most Irish issues suggests that they were not audience evaluation of "the art of logical fencing" but records of opinion. Since the evidence can easily be reduced to percentages for and against a particular proposition, it is useful at this point to confront the implied similarities with modern opinion polls.[90] In contemporary Britain, pollsters rarely work with fewer than one thousand respondents, and would generally frown upon reducing to percentages any sample below eighty. Where five percent of the population (or "universe") to be sampled constitutes an identifiable minority, for instance by ethnic origin, pollsters are not content with simply interviewing fifty people from that community, since those respondents might not be typical. Rather, they seek to identify a larger and more representative cross-section, whose overall responses are mathematically reduced to equal fifty people out of the thousand total. Pollsters must also face the challenge of dealing with don't-knows, non-respondents and those who choose, for whatever reason, to disguise their true allegiance. Even with the most sophisticated forms of sampling, one poll in every twenty will produce a "rogue" result, a distortion of more than three percent.

Since divisions in the Cambridge Union rarely counted more than two hundred members, it would seem that the "sample" fell far below a safe minimum. Furthermore, it is necessary to distinguish between a "random" sample and one that is merely haphazard. Random sampling by pollsters does not involve simply picking people with a pin, but rather selecting respondents from within social or occupational or regional categories according to a consistent method – knocking at every fifth house, or calling every hundredth person in the telephone directory. By contrast, attendance at Union debates must be regarded not so much as random as accidental. An undergraduate might be persuaded by a friend to attend a debate at the last minute or decide to remain in college because an essay had to be written. Thus, if two dedicated foes of Home Rule were prevented from joining one hundred other students for a debate, there would be a one percent "swing" towards the nationalist cause in the final division. A Union audience was a genuinely random gathering, in the colloquial sense of the word, too small and too casually assembled to inspire the trust of a pollster.

None the less, the consistency of Union voting is remarkable. Thus the fact that four of the six Home Rule debates within an eighteen-month period of 1886-1887 produced hostile majorities of between 56 and 60 percent suggests a remarkable consistency in houses that varied from 108 to 271. The remaining two debates rejected Irish devolution by majorities of 66 and 67 percent. One advantage of voting in the Cambridge Union was that it effectively eliminated don't-knows. There were some experiments during the Edwardian period in the way that votes were registered, but for most of the century the division was taken at the very end of the debate, by which time those undecided had presumably departed. However, the major difference between Union votes and modern opinion polls must lie in the nature of the "sample". Pollsters prefer a carefully selected minimum of two thousand respondents to capture an accurate snapshot of public opinion across the whole of modern Britain simply to take account of class, ethnic and regional diversity. Vastly smaller numbers of Cambridge students produced consistent responses. The most obvious explanation for this is that they constituted a remarkably homogeneous group.

Cambridge students constituted a statistically consistent "universe" for the simple reason that they were in no way typical of the community at large. For precisely that reason, "it would be unwise, to say the least, to assume that the Junior Intelligence of England, or even of Cambridge, is to be accurately adjudged from the debates of the Union Society".[91] R.A. Butler recalled of the nineteen-twenties that "we were not representative of University undergraduate opinion", adding, "we were not intended to be".[92] One of the few comparisons that can be made between Union opinion and the sentiments of Cambridge students at large comes from the division at the mass meeting on women's degrees in 1897, as discussed in Chapter Three. This suggests that active debaters were marginally less reactionary than the undergraduate population as a whole. More broadly, there would seem to be no intrinsic reason to suggest that Cambridge opinion represented anything more than the prejudices of a privileged and very small minority. How, then, can their debates be studied to throw light upon British attitudes to Ireland?

The fact that Irish questions were debated at all – or, conversely, ignored – itself constitutes historical evidence of some value. Because the nineteenth-century Union was not dominated by big-name visiting speakers, it was unnecessary to organise the programme of debates far in advance. Members suggested motions for debate and where more than one topic was on offer, the house itself selected the subject for discussion at the next meeting, although this practice appeared "to have fallen into disuse" by 1860.[93] Notice of debate was given simply by displaying the motion on the Society's notice-board six days in advance. Occasionally, there was a broad range of choice, as on one occasion in 1883 when thirteen rival motions were on offer.[94] Sometimes, a bee would escape from somebody's bonnet for lack of alternatives: in 1891, David Dodge from Minnesota failed to persuade the Union that a recent lynching in New Orleans had been "perfectly justifiable".[95] At other times, apathy ruled. "It seems hard that the duty of providing for the weekly Debate, should always fall upon the Officers", they complained in 1860, warning that "the Debates must materially suffer, if a more general interest be not taken in them, than has of late prevailed".[96] This was one of the reasons for William Everett's irritation with the Union. "Anyone is at liberty to propose a subject; but there is so little eagerness to assume this post, that it generally falls to the officers to bell the cat, or else do it themselves."[97] In 1864, as the Society was about to build its own premises, the Vice-President could still regret "that so few Members are found ready to propose subjects for discussion".[98] Eventually in 1902, when the President assumed control of the organisation of debates, the programme came under the more formal control of the officers – and there were, in any case, by then more debates. Either way, for the purpose of assessing topicality, it does not much matter whether subjects for debate were chosen by members because they wished to discuss Ireland, or arranged for them in the belief that Ireland would attract an audience. Appendix One gives a general overview of the most controversial issues in the half century before 1914 when politics had come to dominate the Union agenda. Table Eight calculates the largest division on an Irish question in each academic year as a percentage of those voting in the most numerously attended non-Irish debate. Not surprisingly, there were peaks of interest in 1880-82, during the decade of the first two Home Rule crises, and again in 1912-14.

There are some limitations in assessing the selection of motions. For much of the century, Union debates occupied less than half the year: in an age of slow travel, student activities tended to commence not at the start of term, but towards the end of the months of October and January when the latecomers had arrived. From 1880, some debates were also held in the Long Vacation, but these were poorly attended and notably frivolous. The choice of motions was subject to two other restrictions. One was laid down in the Laws of the Society: topics "of a theological nature" were expressly excluded. Since it was possible to debate the political implications of a religious issue, perhaps it was simply good taste that ensured that the Cambridge Union never confronted the underlying English assumption that Irish social problems were somehow caused by adherence to the Catholic Church. Another limitation was that many public events did not easily lend themselves to adversarial discussion. The Cambridge Union barely discussed the Irish Famine, but this does not necessarily prove that members were indifferent to suffering (although the Oxford Union memorably declined to vote money for famine relief).[99] More telling was the relative lack of interest aroused by the political issues arising out of the effectiveness of government response to the catastrophe. Nor was there much sense in debating questions on which there was obviously an overwhelming consensus. The Union debated the existence, role and composition of the House of Lords thirty times between 1860 and 1914, because a hereditary upper house aroused strong feelings, for and against. It would be misleading to conclude that Cambridge

students did not care about the monarchy simply because the same period saw
only five motions in favour of the republican principle, one of which carried the
saving clause "England, of course, excepted".[100] Members of the Union voted
overwhelmingly in favour of a State dowry for Princess Louise in 1871, and
rearranged debate night to avoid a clash with her wedding day. In 1886, they
prevailed upon the vacuous Prince Albert Victor to perform the opening
ceremony for their new building. If debates on the monarchy were rare, it was
because critics of the institution were scarce. Thus although Cambridge Union
attitudes to Irish questions may irritate modern observers, some credit should be
given for the fact that enough interest was aroused and opinion was sufficiently
divided to permit their discussion at all.

   One device that may make it possible to relate Cambridge Union votes
to wider public attitudes is to relate divisions on Irish issues to those on
mainstream party-political questions. This form of "triangulation" needs to be
approached with some caution, since it assumes the existence of a detailed set of
attitudes uniformly shared across the membership. That this may not always
have been true can be seen from two debates from 1852. In the first, Leslie
Stephen proposed a motion that baldly demanded the abandonment of "the
British Possessions at the Cape of Good Hope". (Half a century later, he
commented acerbically that there would have been no Boer War had his policy
been adopted.) In this case, straightforward rejection was not enough for the
Cambridge Union, and by 28 votes to 11, members insisted upon an amendment
demanding "that more energetic measures for subjugating the Kaffirs should be
immediately adopted". Two weeks later, the Union resolved, this time by 30
votes to 16, that "a speedy emancipation of their slaves by the Americans would
be right, practicable, and politic". This was an equally uncompromising
sentiment, since on this occasion members rejected a milder amendment stating
that immediate emancipation "though just, is not politic". Thus within a
fortnight, the Union had resolved by almost identical majorities to subjugate one
black community in South Africa, while liberating another in the United States,
both policies to take effect immediately. Of course, mid-Victorians did not
equate colonialism and slavery, and some might have argued that the
substitution of imperial conquest for the rule of chiefs and witch doctors would
prove as great a boon to the average Xhosa as the abolition of slavery would be
to the ordinary Southern black. However, it is impossible to know how many of
the 39 members who butchered Stephen's motion were among the 46 who
recorded their views on American slavery. Only two members spoke in both
debates: one wanted to keep the Cape but free the slaves, while the other
opposed both motions.[101]

   Thus it would not be safe to assume identical profiles of opinion across
what were essentially secondary issues. More revealing is the relationship

between attitudes to Ireland and positions on major issues. Cambridge undergraduates cared far more about the Church than they did about the colonies, and so it is of some importance to note that during the eighteen-sixties, many of them came to feel that upholding a Protestant Established Church in England did not require them to impose its counterpart in Ireland. A more consistent comparison may be found in the forerunners of the later ritual of debating "No Confidence" in the government, which demonstrated the truth of W.S. Gilbert's dictum that every child born into the world alive was either a little Liberal or else a little Conserva*tive*. From the death of Palmerston in 1865 through to the outbreak of the First World War, the Cambridge Union held 75 debates in which divisions can be tabulated into pro- and anti-Tory columns, as shown in Tables Three to Seven. Of these, 64 registered Conservative majorities, and with remarkably consistent patterns. In 41 out of the 58 endorsements between 1865 and 1903, Conservative support was over 60 percent, rising above 70 percent on four occasions. Thereafter, their share of the House only once touched 59 percent. Liberal successes were transient: they carried the day in four out of nine debates between 1881 and 1884, but never pushed the Tory share of the division below 46 percent. Liberals managed a narrow win in a small house in 1902, and a more comfortable margin thanks to Lloyd George's visit in 1904. There were five Liberal victories out of eleven debates between 1907 and 1911 but, generally speaking, the Union remained steadily though not overwhelmingly Conservative until 1914.

In this, it was obviously out of step with the electorate at large, although it is worth noting that the Cambridge student community adapted in rough parallel to the expansion of the political nation. A provincial shopkeeper's son like Norman Birkett, President in 1910, would probably not have reached the chair half a century earlier, but no more would David Lloyd George, a Criccieth solicitor, have become Chancellor of the Exchequer. By relating votes on Irish issues to the overall Liberal/Conservative divide, it is possible to supply some sort of benchmark to Union debates.

The debates of the Cambridge Union can be subjected to endless theoretical analysis, but in the last resort the proof of this particular pudding must lie in its own consumption, in an examination of the debates themselves. It is time to travel back into the past, to the large, low, gloomy, airless room at the back of the Red Lion Inn. It is early evening as members gather, their faces indistinct in the candle-light as they take their seats on the opposing rows of benches. From the chair, the President makes his announcements and moves motions for formal business before calling upon the honourable opener to open the evening's discussion:

'Tis pleasant to snore at a quarter before,
When the chairman does nothing in state,
But 'tis heaven! 'tis heaven to waken at seven,
And pray for a noisy debate.[102]

It was such on an evening, in March 1816, that the Cambridge Union first turned its attention to Ireland.

Girton College 1897
The threat to Cambridge masculinity

Part Three

The Irish Debates

1816-1914

A Debate at the Union 1859

8: The Irish Debates 1816-1885

On 18 March 1816, the Cambridge Union resolved by 33 votes to 25 that "the present conduct of Government towards Ireland" accorded with the dictates of "Justice and Policy".[1] In the absence of any account, the debate is hard to interpret. The result squares neither with the condemnations of British policy towards Ireland registered after 1821 nor with the equally firm endorsements of the union of 1801. The motion probably meant what it said in referring to "present conduct". The Irish executive was cracking down on dissent. The Catholic Committee had been forced out of existence in 1812. Following the Tipperary assizes in January 1816, the Chief Secretary, Robert Peel, insisted on "making a terrible but necessary example", hanging all those found guilty of capital offences. "We find convictions attended with so many difficulties that we are obliged to be very sparing in the extension of mercy."[2] In one respect, the first Cambridge debate on Ireland was characteristic of the many that would follow: there was at least one speaker from Ireland, and he was on the losing side. Presumably Charles Brinsley Sheridan had inherited some of his playwright father's skill in the use of language: he was thought sufficiently persuasive to be included in the deputation to the Vice-Chancellor that protested against suppression of debates the following year. Not for the last time, first-hand testimony was insufficient to carry the day.

Young Cambridge was massively in favour of the union between Britain and Ireland. No vote was recorded in the debate of November 1816, on a motion that the union of 1801 had proved "advantageous" to Ireland, but the balance of speakers (four against two) suggests that the motion was carried. John Beresford, son of the bishop of Kilmore and Ardagh, spoke against the motion: once again, an Irish voice was in the minority.[3] It was nine years before the question arose again, and by December 1825 it was almost certainly entangled with the controversial question of Catholic Emancipation. This time only one speaker argued that Ireland had "been benefited by its Union with this Country", while five spoke against, including the Dublin-born Richard Chenevix Trench. The motion was rejected by 45 votes to 20.[4] That this did not imply support for "a complete separation" between the two countries can be seen in the massive rejection of a motion to that effect in December 1828 by 95 votes to 23. Outright Repeal was dismissed even more brusquely in 1833 by 90 votes to 4. On that occasion, the majority may have been distorted: the debate had been adjourned to a second night, and it is likely that by the close of the proceedings, even the six speakers for Repeal had lost heart.[5] One of them was Thomas

Redington, who quickly abandoned his Repeal sympathies to become, in 1846, Lord John Russell's under-secretary for Ireland. Even during its retreat into otiose historical issues during the eighteen-thirties, the Cambridge Union remained firm in its belief that it was part of the natural order that Ireland should be subordinate to England. "Had William of Nassau any just claim to [the] Sovereignty of Ireland before the surrender of Limerick?", the Union asked itself in 1837. Predictably it decided that he did, although only by eight votes to three.[6]

However, Cambridge debaters were less sure about the effectiveness of the union of 1801. This can be seen in the vote on the composite motion of March 1830: "Was the Union with Ireland in 1800, a justifiable measure, or conducive to the welfare of that Country?" The margin of rejection, by 39 votes to 31, suggests that emphasis was placed on the second part of the motion.[7] This interpretation of the vote would certainly be in line with a series of condemnations throughout the eighteen-twenties of British policy in Ireland, although as they were carefully wrapped within the rules forbidding discussion of current issues, interpretation is not always straightforward. For instance, in December 1821, a sizeable majority of 37 votes to 16 decided that "the conduct of the English Government with respect to Ireland, in the three years previous to the Rebellion in 1798" had been inconsistent with "sound policy". Presumably one element in the criticism was that the government had failed to prevent the uprisings of 1798, but the focus on the preceding three years may have been intended as an allusion to the founding of Maynooth in 1795. The motion may also have been intended to avoid the issue of Emancipation by excluding from the debate the decision of 1793 to admit Catholics to the Irish franchise.[8] Majorities for Catholic Emancipation between 1822 and 1829 were consistent in a band between 54 and 61 percent. The 70 percent affirmative vote in the debate on 1798 suggested that it was easier to condemn past errors than to accept current reforms.

At the height of the controversy over Catholic Emancipation, there was a hardening of the conviction that the relationship with Ireland had not been a success. In February 1823, a debate on "the conduct of England towards Ireland (up to the year 1800)" resulted in all fifty members present withholding their "approbation". Macaulay was one of a battery of Union luminaries who denounced the record, but oratory alone does not seem to have been the sole determinant. It was just one week later that Macaulay delivered the speech that entranced Bulwer Lytton but failed to persuade members to endorse the political character of Mirabeau. Similarly, in November 1824, one of the best attended debates of the year saw the Union vote by 94 votes to 17 that "the conduct of England towards Ireland, up to the year 1800" could not be "considered conducive to the happiness of the Inhabitants of the latter kingdom". It was notable, too, in that Richard Boylan, who spoke tenth out of eleven against the motion, became the first Irish Catholic to address the Union on an Irish issue. Still carefully treading within the twenty-year rule, in May 1827 the Union condemned England's conduct towards Ireland prior to 1807 by 35 votes to 23.[9] Among those critical of England was Richard Chenevix Trench, who as Archbishop of Dublin forty years later failed to prevent the disestablishment of the State Church which figured so largely among Irish grievances.

Catholic Emancipation "was of course the burning question of this period", Charles Merivale recalled of the Cambridge Union of the eighteen-twenties. It was debated eight times between May 1822 and March 1829. The first seven motions spoke of "the Catholic claims" (or "the claims of the Roman Catholics"). Not until March 1829 was the more controversial term "emancipation" introduced. On five occasions, the issue produced the best attended debate of the term, and on three, the debate had to be adjourned to a second night (in 1825, even spanning two terms) to accommodate the numbers who wished to speak. The division of March 1829, in which 257 members voted, remained the largest in the Union's history until 1866. In accordance with the restrictions imposed by Vice-Chancellor Wordsworth, the motions debated in 1822 and 1824 referred to the failure of both the British and Irish parliaments to admit Catholics before 1800. Four of the remaining six debates used a formula "previous to" a date twenty years earlier. The exceptions were the debate of 1827, which specified "in 1807", and that of March 1829 which set the moment of decision "in 1808". It is possible that the first of these was intended to focus on George III's ousting of the Ministry of All the Talents by demanding an undertaking that they would never press him to allow Catholics to sit in parliament. The second may have been designed to refer to Henry Grattan's attempt in 1808 to trade the admission of Catholics to parliament against a government veto on Rome's appointment of bishops. If so, this was the only hint of qualified emancipation or safeguards, while such reports as survive suggest that some of the pro-Emancipation oratory was revolutionary in tone. Overall, it is unlikely that the date restrictions were taken seriously. "We might not speak directly of any event nearer to us than a floating period of twenty years back," Merivale recalled, "but it required no great ingenuity to evade this restriction, by resolving, for instance, that Catholic Emacipation should or should not have been carried so many years before the current year." If Emancipation was a matter of principle, then the timing of the concession was irrelevant. Merivale recalled "Kemble, being called to order by the President for thus dodging the law of our institution, eliciting thunders of applause by vociferating, I take my stand in the year '6'."[10]

Table One demonstrates a remarkable degree of consistency in the division of opinion. Support for Catholic Emancipation across the eight debates fell consistently within a very narrow band, from 54 to 61 percent. The pattern is all the more remarkable, given a fourfold range in the "turn-out", from a low of 62 in 1822 to a high of 257 in 1829. Nine speakers feature in more than one debate – Benjamin Hall Kennedy spoke four times between 1824 and 1827 – but the turnover of student generations means that few of those who voted in 1822 were still attending Union debates seven years later. The evidence points to the existence of a modest but firm majority for Catholic Emancipation among a privileged and Protestant social group throughout the eighteen-twenties. Those who sympathised with the Catholic cause presumably saw it primarily as a matter in which civil rights overrode sectarian identities. Thus in the immediate aftermath of Emancipation, in May 1829, the Union rejected by 52 to 18 the notion that the Jesuits had been "beneficial to mankind", while in February 1831 and December 1832, over eighty percent voted against the separation of Church and State.[11]

The eight Cambridge Union debates on Catholic Emancipation also underline the disparity between oratory and argument on the one hand, and preconceived opinions on the other. The Catholic cause was supported by 51 speakers who delivered a total of 65 speeches. By contrast, there were only 22 speakers and 24 speeches against. Across the eight divisions, there were 8.4 votes cast for every speech in favour of Emancipation, but 17.4 for every speech against. It is highly unlikely that the speeches against Emancipation were individually twice as cogent and convincing as those in favour. Rather, a collective portrait indicates that the case for change virtually monopolised both the talent and the potential of young Cambridge.

Of the 51 supporters of the Catholic claims, 18 became officers of the Union, 13 of them elected to the Presidency. This was the golden age of the Cambridge Union, and no fewer than 21 gained entries in the *Dictionary of National Biography*. Those who went on to make their mark in public life included Edmond Beales, President of the Reform League in 1866, Alexander Cockburn, who became Lord Chief Justice and Edward Strutt, the first heir to a manufacturing fortune to enter the House of Lords. Careers in parliament also beckoned for Edward Ellice the younger, who was taken prisoner by Canadian rebels in 1838, while Charles Buller and William Hutt both supported colonisation projects and had rivers in New Zealand named in their honour. J.W. Blakesley, Charles Merivale, and R.C. Trench became influential figures in the Church. Benjamin Hall Kennedy and Henry Malden made their mark as classical scholars and J.M. Kemble, "energetic & fluent"[12] on the issue in 1827, was a pioneer in archaeology. The list would probably be all the more impressive but for the early deaths of lively figures such as Buller, along with the poets William Mackworth Praed, Thomas Hankinson and John Sterling, the last of them commemorated in a celebrated biography by Carlyle.

By contrast, only four of the 22 opponents of Catholic Emancipation were elected to Union office, and just one got into the *Dictionary of National Biography*. He was Peter Borthwick, briefly editor of the *Morning Post*, and indisputably a second-rank figure in public life. Few of those who spoke on either side seem to have close connections with Ireland. L.S. Orde of Queens', one of the few opponents of the Catholics to become President, was a nephew of the Orange champion, Lord Roden – but it is possible that there were others who had family links with Irish factions which cannot now be easily discovered. Overall, there can be little doubt that the balance of ability, as well as brute force of verbosity, favoured Catholic Emancipation, and it is unlikely that there was sufficient countervailing personal testimony on behalf of the Irish Ascendancy. Therefore, it must be concluded that if two members in every five managed to resist the torrent of argument in favour of admitting Catholics to parliament, it can only be because they had already made up their minds to do so.

Unusually for this early period, some reports survive that make it possible to recover something of the atmosphere of Union debates on the Catholic question. Richard Monckton Milnes included accounts in letters to his family. On the first occasion that he attended the Union, in November 1827, Milnes was not impressed by the level of argument. One speech was delivered in such a "strain of sarcasm & irony" that it provoked a demand to know which way the honourable member intended to vote. Some speakers not only ignored the notional limitation of the twenty-year rule, but widened the Catholic issue to a general onslaught on the status quo. Thus "a Mr. Sterling told us we were going to have a revolution", adding that he "didn't care if his hand should be the first to lead the way".[13]

Milnes may have been the author of a report of a Union debate on Catholic Emancipation discovered in a contemporary periodical by Peter Allen when studying the Cambridge Apostles. This account not only disguises the names of speakers, but seems to have conflated the debates of 1828 and 1829. The proposer of a motion in favour of the Catholics, "my friend Williams", was probably William Merywether, who opened the debate in 1829. A member of the same college as Milnes, Merywether was an early Cambridge cricket Blue but – it would seem – a radical none the less. "Williams" was reported as saying that the Catholic question was not "commonly discussed elsewhere on the proper grounds". He defined the real issue as "a contest between the people and the aristocratic monopolies" and proceeded to flay the latter for half an hour. Ireland, it seems, was not the chief element at issue.

The motion was opposed by "Mr Billingsgate, a soft-voiced young gentleman of large fortune ... a fool" but "a favourite with the society". Billingsgate was probably based upon Lord Norreys, son of the Earl of Abingdon, whose family name of Bertie perhaps suggested the nickname by alliteration. At Eton, Norreys had pulled off the highly dangerous stunt of impersonating the headmaster, Keate, and taking a roll-call in front of the whole school. Perhaps surprisingly, he subsequently overcame some of his prejudices and followed Sir Robert Peel when the Conservatives split over free trade in 1846. Faithful to his nickname, "Billingsgate" denounced the "decidedly unconstitutional" speech of the proposer in an equally wide-ranging diatribe. The House of Commons, he insisted, "does fully and fairly represent the people", although his definition excluded "the rabble" and was confined to "persons of birth, influence, fashion, and fortune". Britain's "glorious constitution" was "composed of three powers, all exactly equal to each other, and yet no two of them superior to the third". We cannot know whether this intriguing calculation was inspired by Cambridge's teaching of advanced mathematics or its commitment to higher theology, but it was enough for "Billingsgate" to denounce all thought of concessions to "the bloody papists".

These were real issues treated in mock-serious manner. "An evening of this kind seldom terminates without a supper party."[14] None the less, the debates were regarded by outsiders as evidence of the march of opinion. Palmerston, canvassing for the University seat in 1825, took comfort from the fact that "the Catholic Question has always been carried at the Union".[15] The last debate in the series, that of 1829, was seen by both sides as an event of more than mere local importance. Ostensibly, a squabble in the Cambridge Union on the politics of 1808 might seem more than usually irrelevant. The debate began on 3 March when the bill for Catholic Relief was in its last stages at Westminster, and was adjourned to 10 March, by which time Emancipation had become law. However, the Cambridge debate took on a larger significance because it followed Peel's defeat in a by-election at Oxford. Peel had resigned as MP for Oxford University by way of apology to his high Anglican supporters for abandoning pledges to resist the admission of Catholics to parliament. In doing so, he not only endorsed the revolutionary principle that an MP was merely a delegate subject to recall by his constituents, but he made the tactical mistake of failing to foresee the practical implications of his decision. It quickly became apparent that there was considerable support for Emancipation at Oxford, and that Peel could not refuse to fight the by-election he had brought about without seriously damaging his own cause.

The composition of the constituency made Oxford University an unpromising battle-ground for progress. As at Cambridge, the right to vote was conferred upon Masters of Arts, most of them resistant to novelty in all its forms. On 27 February 1829, Peel was forced to acknowledge defeat. The Oxford by-election was so unprecedented that it was followed by a frenzy of speculation about its significance. Upholders of the Catholic cause took comfort from the fact that the margin of defeat had been relatively narrow: 755 votes to

609. They argued that although Peel had been defeated in quantity, he had been easily victorious in the quality of support he had received. Analysis of the poll showed that he had received the support of the majority of resident members of the University but had been defeated by the non-resident backwoodsmen. In particular, Peel had been overwhelmingly backed by the ablest of Oxford's minds, whether measured by professors, graduates with First Class Honours, or the solid support of the most intellectually vigorous colleges. In the context of an argument over the meaning of the vote at Oxford, the debate among the young men of Cambridge took on a wider significance.

Milnes had planned to speak in the adjourned debate on 10 March, "but the tumult grew so great about 10 o'clock – that it was impossible to make a word heard". The long, low debating room was so crowded that the division had to be taken outside, "a most noisy proceeding" punctuated by cheers and groans. On one side of the inn yard, Lord Norreys was "screaming out, 'three cheers for the Church & State'", while others urged three cheers for the highest of high Tories, Lord Eldon. On the other side, "little Wentworth" urged "3 for Ireland", and Augustus FitzRoy, cousin of the Duke of Grafton, was sufficiently carried away to urge three cheers for the Pope. "The tellers at last appeared at the windows & announced that the votes were, a majority of 10 against the Catholics". The rejoicing of Protestant zealots was short-lived, for "one of the tellers came forward & said that owing to the confusion, a mistake had been made & the votes were 46 in favour of the Catholics". The episode was hardly a tribute to the mathematical training provided by Cambridge University. Conscious, no doubt, of the difficulty of persuading some *soi-disant* members to disgorge their subscriptions, the officers decided upon a detailed scrutiny of the division. Some days later they announced a definitive vote of 143 against 114 in favour of Catholic Emancipation.[16]

Milnes hastily sent the news of victory to the *Globe*, a liberal evening paper in London, claiming that the margin of victory "marks the feeling of the rising generation" and so morally outweighed Peel's defeat at Oxford. Privately, he was disappointed that the majority was "so small". (Thackeray, who was also present at the debate and who opposed Emancipation, drew some comfort from the "very small majority".) According to Milnes, the Tories "had exerted all their influence in 'packing' members, and bandied about all the cant phrases of their faction as vigorously as their Seniors in the other place [Oxford]". The "late hour" of the division was also a factor: at least fifty supporters of Emancipation had departed "in full conviction of the success of their cause". Milnes insisted that the small majority should be set against the fact "that this question has uniformly passed in favour of the Catholics on all previous occasions". Thus the "Cambridge Union Debating Society" had demonstrated that "the feeling of all the intellectual men at Cambridge and at Oxford is the same". Milnes, at least, was in no doubt that Union debates were registers of opinion, although he was in fact wrong in assuming that the 1829 majority was proportionately smaller than in earlier years.[17] However, the Union's Secretary promptly assured readers of the *Globe* that it "was by no means the case" that members had been discussing the bill before parliament: "such a proceeding would not only have been contrary to the laws of the Society, but to those of the University".[18] No doubt he was right to keep the proctors in mind, for the question of Cambridge student attitudes continued to have political repercussions.

Two weeks after the debate, in an attempt to dispel the "stigma" of the allegation that "the young men of education in the country were in favour of concessions to the Catholics", the Bishop of Bath and Wells, George Law, presented a petition to the House of Lords signed by "between six and seven hundred" Cambridge undergraduates opposed to Catholic Emancipation. The bishop had been a Fellow of Queens' in the early seventeen-eighties and deplored the slight moves towards liberalisation of the University since his time. He "was opposed to the introduction of political parties and clubs in the universities, and he was sorry to learn that such clubs were not only tolerated but allowed". This drew a rebuke from John Kaye, the Bishop of Lincoln, an impressive pluralist who doubled as Master of Christ's, and had served as Vice-Chancellor immediately before James Wood. Kaye accused his brother prelate of criticising the University of Cambridge "for not putting down a certain debating club" and roundly told him that he "should have taken more pains to acquaint himself with the reasons which had induced the heads of the university to tolerate its existence". Charles Lloyd, the Bishop of Oxford, could not resist turning the knife in the Cambridge wound by claiming that "no toleration was given ... to debating clubs" in his university. Given the open existence of the Oxford Union and the strong support it received in his own college, Christ Church, this was a foolhardy statement. Lloyd, who was Peel's former tutor, was one of the few bishops who accepted the need for concessions to O'Connell. He added the reminiscence that "twenty years ago, he belonged to a debating club in Oxford University; and that club had continued to exist, because, like the Catholic Association, it had been found impossible to put it down". The Marquess of Lansdowne, who had earlier claimed that Cambridge opinion was in favour of Emancipation, now turned to discrediting the credentials of the petitioners. "He could not perceive any thing in the course of study pursued by these young men, which particularly fitted them for judging of the tenets of the Romish church". In any case, they represented only a minority of the student population of Cambridge, since there were 250 undergraduates at Trinity alone ready to sign a counter-petition. The Vice-Chancellor promptly banned any such demonstration.[19]

It was unusual for the Union to have second thoughts on an issue that had been resolved, but several attempts were made in subsequent years to revive the Catholic question. While these generally attracted small houses, they undoubtedly reflect a continuing strength of feeling. In May 1829, the Union narrowly decided by 25 votes to 21, that it had been "just and expedient" to deprive Irish forty-shilling freeholders of their right to vote. Their disenfranchisement had been part of the price for the admission of Catholics to parliament, and the vote contrasted with the previous series of apparently unqualified support for Catholic political rights. However, overall interest had clearly waned. Whereas a year earlier, a third-term debate on the political character of Henry Grattan had drawn the largest attendance of the academic year, an Irish issue now drew barely one fifth of the number who had voted in the turbulent debate on the principle of Emancipation two months earlier.[20]

Six years later, in December 1835, the Union decided by 22 votes to 17 that "the benefits which were expected from the Roman Catholic Emancipation" had not been realised. Since the Whigs had just clambered back into office thanks to the support of Daniel O'Connell and the Lichfield House Compact, the division seems a muted condemnation from a predominantly Conservative body. In 1840, during the Society's High Tory doldrums, a motion declaring Catholic Emancipation to have been "a measure of wisdom, justice, and expediency" was actually rejected by 18 votes to 9.[21] It is likely that the motion claimed too much. That same year, William Whewell's friend Archdeacon Hare noted that "one hears perpetually among the country clergy" the charge that in carrying Emancipation, the Duke of Wellington "sacrificed principle to expediency". Although a long-time supporter of Catholic Emancipation himself, Whewell agreed in condemning the Duke's "*manner* of passing the Catholic Relief Bill" on the grounds that "the governors of a state are not to acknowledge that they act from *fear* of those who threaten to violate the laws".[22] The attitude of the country clergy was no doubt shared among students many of whom were training to follow the same calling. In their defence, it should be noted that the following year the Union rejected by 15 votes to 3 the claim that "the Penal Laws passed against the Papists" were "beneficial".[23]

Proceedings seem to have been more animated in 1842, when the Union considered a motion which condemned the penal laws as "in the highest degree unjustifiable", praised Emancipation as "a wise and expedient measure" and regretted that it had not been passed earlier. An amendment limiting the motion to the reference to Emancipation was rejected by 27 votes to 24, and the main motion carried by 25 votes to 24. The issue was again debated in November 1852, perhaps as a means of ventilating Protestant feelings aroused by the "Papal Aggression" dispute of 1851 and by perceived clerical interference in the 1852 general election. The concession of 1829 was again endorsed, by 28 votes to 23, almost identical to the division of opinion in 1842.[24]

The century after 1815 saw four major British concessions to Irish demands: Catholic Emancipation in 1829, the disestablishment of the Protestant Church in 1869, the recognition of tenant right under Gladstone and the funding of land purchase in the Salisbury years. In each case, a substantial section of Cambridge opinion concluded that accounts had been settled with Ireland, while others battled to prove that grievances remained. Thus, in November 1833, the Union agreed that "the conduct of the English Government towards Ireland" had not been "consistent with sound policy or justice", but only by 32 votes to 24. The vote was very similar to the 35-23 division on a comparable motion six years earlier, but in 1824 a similar debate had resulted in an emphatic condemnation by 94 votes to 17.[25]

In the aftermath of Catholic Emancipation, Irish issues still attracted controversy. Repeal was massively rejected in March 1833. Three debates in 1833-34 were adjourned to a second night to accommodate the members who wished to speak, although the interest could be fickle. In March 1834, the Union asked itself whether Ireland had been treated with "sound policy or justice ... from the time of the first invasion of the English on [sic] the latter country". The debate was adjourned not simply to a second night, but to the following term, when participation collapsed. Seven centuries of English policy in Ireland were condemned by just 8 votes to 3.[26]

Two new issues appeared in November 1835. Lord John Russell's Irish Church resolutions were dismissed by 32 votes to 18 while the Union declined to condemn "the formation of Tory Political Unions commonly called Orange Lodges" in an unusually large division of 49 votes to 14.[27] It may seem curious that, in a decade fascinated by ecclesiastical questions, the Protestant Established Church in Ireland should not have been the subject of debate until Russell's proposals for surgery put it on to the agenda. Perhaps the liberals of the eighteen-twenties had preferred to imply that Catholics could be admitted to full political rights without challenging the Protestant ascendancy. If so, by the following decade their opponents were alive to the threat of reform by instalments. By November 1836, a poorly attended debate could vote by 12 votes to 8 that "the past conduct of the Roman Catholics of Ireland" made it unlikely that "further concessions on the part of the Protestants of England will be productive of any beneficial result".[28]

Technically, of course, the Act of Union had put an end to any such entity as a separate Irish Church. Like the parliament on College Green, the religious establishment had been merged with its English counterpart. "Does the existence of the Established Church of England and Ireland conduce to the moral happiness of the people?", the Union asked itself in February 1837, determining by 30 votes to 15 that it did. It was still possible in the eighteen-thirties to sustain such a paternalist opinion with reference to much of rural England. "Nobody could deprive us of the Church [even] if they would", wrote Whewell in 1835, "for it has the affections of the people in its favour".[29] To entertain such a sentiment in relation to Ireland involved an effort of will.

In April 1837, the Union confronted the issue more specifically: "Is the maintenance of the Established Church in Ireland in its present condition, consistent with justice and good policy?" The debate was twice adjourned, suggesting that more students were interested in the topic than the final vote indicated. Unusually, the speakers who assailed Church establishment in Ireland included two Catholics, both of whom would go on to make a mark in British politics. Lord Edward Howard, son of the Duke of Norfolk, held minor office under Lord John Russell and later, as Lord Howard of Glossop, became a major figure in Catholic educational charities. John Ball was launched into a brief but promising parliamentary career by the Tenant Right League in 1852. Despite their pleas, the motion was eventually passed, although a majority of 13 votes to 11 fell short of a full-hearted endorsement.[30] However, given the "present condition" of the Irish Church, the outcome was remarkable enough.

"Does England really owe a great debt of justice to Ireland?", was the slightly testy wording of a motion debated in February 1839. In the best attended debate of the term, the Union was persuaded, by 31 votes to 12, that the debt of justice still remained. The proposer was the Welshman Rowland Williams, described by the *Dictionary of National Biography* as bold and uncompromising in controversy. Like other notable Cambridge minds of the century, he could read German and was influenced by new currents of thought from the continent. In his contribution to *Essays and Reviews* in 1860, Williams identified himself with the new Biblical criticism of the Prussian intellectuals. Perhaps this was a case where Cambridge Union experience could be counterproductive: Williams was censured for applying sarcasm to the study of Scripture, and had great difficulty in fending off a condemnation for heresy. Whatever grounds he adduced to persuade his contemporaries that Ireland was owed a debt of justice, it is unlikely that this Welsh Anglican laid much emphasis on the scandal of an endowed Church that failed to inspire the confidence of the people it was supposed to serve. Williams made his first excursion into the public sphere in 1843 as an opponent of a scheme to amalgamate the miniature Welsh bishoprics of Bangor and St Asaph.[31]

When the American Charles Bristed was thrown into gloom by the Democratic victory in the Presidential election of 1844, one of his Cambridge friends commented: "I am sure I wouldn't annoy myself if O'Connell were premier tomorrow".[32] It was a back-handed compliment. The Cambridge Union was obsessed by Daniel O'Connell. From 1836 until the ogre was outfaced at

Clontarf seven years later, it debated his political character on four occasions, and we can be reasonably confident that the spirit of the Liberator hovered over at least four more debates on Ireland in those years.

The measure of hostility may be gauged from the terms of the motion debated in February 1836, which asked whether "the character and actions of Daniel O'Connell up to the year 1835 bear any resemblance to those of Maximillian [sic] Robespierre up to 1789?" This was taking a mere Irish agitator too seriously, and he was acquitted of revolutionary intentions by 25 votes to 17. In December 1836, the Union unsurprisingly denied, by 62 votes to 18, that O'Connell was a benefactor to his country, a view underlined in March 1839 by 21 votes to 9 with the verdict that he did not deserve "the gratitude of the Irish people". O'Connell was unsuccessfully championed by John Ball, whose father was one of the first Catholics to be appointed to the bench after Emancipation. This persistent hostility to O'Connell was in sharp contrast to the overwhelming vote of 1828 in favour of Henry Grattan. However, this was not simply an example of the English view that in Ireland, a statesman is a dead politician. In 1834 Thomas Redington failed to persuade the Union that the character of Lord Edward Fitzgerald was "entitled to approbation". The aristocratic rebel was condemned by 18 votes to 3.[33]

The extent of the Union's phobia about O'Connell was demonstrated in April 1838, in an episode which even the diarist Charles Greville, no woolly progressive, thought unequalled for the "quantity of folly crammed into a short space of time". Speaking at a public meeting, O'Connell had accused Conservatives of perjuring themselves before committees investigating disputed elections. "To recommend moderate language to O'Connell would ... be about as reasonable as to advise him to drop his brogue", Greville thought. O'Connell's defiant rejection of complaints about his language provoked an opposition motion of censure in the House of Commons, culminating in a parliamentary uproar which "appears to have been something like that which a meeting of Bedlam or Billingsgate might produce". No less than five weeks later, when cooler counsels might have wished to forget the episode, the Cambridge Union pronounced by 36 votes to 10 that the parliamentary reprimand had been both "justifiable" and "expedient". This followed hard on the heels of the passage of a motion approving of "the political conduct of the king of Hanover since his accession" by a similar margin of 41 votes to 8.[34] The Duke of Cumberland, now metamorphosed into King Ernest, had shown considerably less respect for parliamentary institutions than Daniel O'Connell. The first act of his reign had been to suspend them altogether.

Government policy towards Ireland came to be measured according to the degree of resistance offered to O'Connell. A motion describing Whig policy to Ireland as "beneficial" was rejected by 28 votes to 10 in March 1838, and the

Melbourne ministry's handling of Irish affairs condemned as "unworthy of our confidence" in November 1840 by 39 votes to 11. The appointment of Lord Normanby as Home Secretary was pronounced "unwise and mischievous" by 60 votes to 22 in December 1839.[35] This hostility to a nobleman who had, after all, been the President of the Union back in 1816, is probably to be explained by Normanby's identification with O'Connell during his term as lord-lieutenant from 1835 to the beginning of 1839.

Not surprisingly, the Cambridge Union preferred the firm hand of Sir Robert Peel's Conservative government, which took office in 1841. In May 1843, Peel stated that he would prefer civil war to Repeal, and in October the government not only forced O'Connell to abandon the planned Repeal meeting at Clontarf but followed up its success by prosecuting him for conspiracy.[36] A month after the cancellation of Clontarf, a hardy minority argued that "the proceedings of the present Government towards Ireland, are disgraceful to it as an executive, and absurd in policy". The debate ran into a second evening, and attempts were made to extend it to a third. On this occasion, the Union was not satisfied with mere rejection of an unpopular proposition, but rather decided to amend it by inserting the word "not" in front of the two provocative adjectives. This was done by 120 votes to 10, a very large turn-out indeed for a third-term debate.[37]

In contrast to its obsession with O'Connell, the Cambridge Union responded in relatively muted fashion to the political and social crisis of the eighteen-forties. In April 1845, the Maynooth grant drew a house of 133 – the third largest of the decade. The debate was adjourned to a second night, when members rejected by 92 votes to 41 a claim that "the plan of the Government for the Endowment of Maynooth is unconstitutional and dangerous to the Country". Loyalty to Peel's government may have been a factor in the vote, and the motion could no doubt be faulted for overlooking the inconvenient fact that Maynooth had been founded by the British government and in receipt of a State grant for fifty years. Perhaps this was a rare case where oratory made a difference: the *Dictionary of National Biography* recorded that Henry Hallam the younger "especially distinguished himself in defence of the Maynooth grant".[38] If "the Country" referred to was England, to have endorsed the motion would have implied a lack of confidence in the ability of the Anglican Church to resist an Irish priesthood. It is probably worth noting that Maynooth split the Young England party at Westminster, and it is not surprising that it should have divided their successors at Cambridge.

None the less, overall, it is noteworthy that Maynooth, so explosive an episode in national politics, does not appear to have been an inflammatory issue in the Cambridge Union. This may have been deliberate policy, since Maynooth involved controversial theological issues: it was probably in defence of his faith that the young Catholic aristocrat, Lord Bernard Howard, addressed the Union when he spoke in the debate, while avoiding direct reference to the motion. When Maynooth was discussed again, six years later in November 1851, a small house of 27 voted to adjourn to a second night, where hardy survivors voted by 6 to 4 that the grant was "neither wise nor conciliatory". In the backwash of the row over "Papal Aggression", this was close to apathy.[39]

By contrast, there seems to have been an element of flexibility in the mood of 1845. In May – just three weeks after the Maynooth debate – a much smaller house resolved by 17 votes to 11 that "a suitable provision for the Irish Roman Catholic Priesthood ought to be made by the State". The topic had been put forward by a Scots aristocrat, William Campbell, who would enjoy the unusual distinction of inheriting peerages from both his parents, eventually becoming Lord Strathedent and Campbell. Campbell's connection with Ireland was slight and hardly one to boast about. His father had been appointed Lord Chancellor of Ireland six weeks before the fall of the Whig ministry in 1841, a blatant piece of jobbery which caused "the greatest disgust". Campbell senior was obliged to forego the £4,000-a-year pension to which his brief tenure of office entitled him, and no subsequent attempts were made to impose an outsider in the post. In the circumstances, his son's opposition to the idea of State funding for the Catholic priesthood stood in embarrassing contrast to the attempt by the Campbell clan to secure their own private endowment at the expense of the Irish taxpayer. However, although William Campbell was on his way to becoming President of the Union and MP for the borough of Cambridge, he was unable to attend his own debate, and it seems that his motion was hijacked by the persuasive Hallam. Campbell had his revenge in November 1846, when he lectured the house for the whole evening on the theme that "our present knowledge of Ireland would not justify the Endowment ... of the Roman Catholic Religion in that Country". The debate was adjourned to a second evening, and his motion was passed by 48 to 10.[40]

The abrupt change of opinion is something of a mystery, and it is a rare example of two closely consecutive Union votes registering very different attitudes to an issue. The wording of the 1846 motion is puzzling if it implied some link between the priesthood and the unfolding catastrophe of the Famine, for even the most zealous Protestant could hardly deny that the Catholic Church was proving itself to be close to the Irish people. Perhaps Hallam was indeed unusually persuasive. The vote against a State-endowed Catholic priesthood in Ireland was in any case repeated in November 1848, when William Harcourt and Fitzjames Stephen argued unavailingly that "it is alike our duty and interest to pay the Roman Catholic Clergy of Ireland". The debate was adjourned and was unusual in attracting a larger attendance on the second night: 71 had voted on the adjournment, but the motion was eventually thrown out by 72 votes to 24 – roughly the same balance of opinion as two years earlier.[41]

There was little debate on the circumstances of the Famine. Hunger as such did not lend itself to adversarial discussion, but it is striking that there was so little controversy over relief policy. The sole motion which came before the Union related as much to domestic party politics. Early in 1847, the Protectionist leader, Lord George Bentinck, put forward a plan for state aid, in the form of subsidised loans for the construction of railways in Ireland. This was resisted by Russell's ministry, partly because Bentinck's proposal was moved as a vote of censure, but also because a major banking crisis had created an unfavourable financial situation. In any case, the scheme was unlikely to provide direct help to people who were starving, since railway construction required able-bodied skilled labour, which was usually provided by gangs of navvies who moved from project to project. In its sole discussion of a scheme for Famine relief, the Union decided by 28 votes to 14 that the government had been right.[42]

The winter of 1847-48 was one of the most terrible in Ireland's history. "Never in my life could I have imagined such distress could exist in a Christian country", reported an army officer from Leitrim. On the streets of Galway, children were "mere animated skeletons ... screaming for food".[43] As a former President, Smith O'Brien, was planning a national uprising, well-nourished young gentlemen at Cambridge gathered in March 1848 to consider the Protestant Established Church in Ireland. By 34 votes to 18, they dismissed the claim that its status was "unjust and impolitic; and requires immediate and extensive alterations". It is not surprising that the defenders of the Irish Church establishment should have included a future Anglican bishop. More surprising is that among those speaking against the motion was Hugh Childers, who twenty years later would be a member of the cabinet that carried disestablishment.[44] Perhaps most remarkable of all was the fact that the Cambridge Union, which had strongly endorsed Orangeism in 1835, should in April 1850 have expressed support for the dismissal of Lord Roden from the magistracy after the Dolly's Brae riots in County Down. However, the division, of 10 votes to 8, does not suggest that Ireland was in the forefront of the Cambridge mind.[45]

Sixteen years elapsed between the debate on the Irish Church in March 1848 and the re-emergence of the issue in the different atmosphere of the eighteen-sixties. During that time, the Cambridge Union turned its attention to Ireland on just four occasions. Three of these debates, on Dolly's Brae, Emancipation and Maynooth, took place between 1850 and 1852 and, as already noted, registered minuscule divisions. There followed seven years in which Ireland was ignored altogether, the longest blank period in the record. The Union was moving away from its earlier practice of leavening politics with historical and literary subjects.

Yet the attention of the young men of Cambridge turned to an Irish issue only when it was forced upon them. The fourth debate to punctuate these years of indifference took place in February 1859 in response to the Phoenix trials in County Cork, which marked the first stirrings of Fenianism. The Phoenix Society of Skibbereen bore a curious resemblance to the early Cambridge Union – a group of young men disguising a dangerous interest in politics behind the façade of a literary club. None the less, the Union voted by 34 votes to 5 to approve "the stringent measures adopted by Government with reference to the Seditious Societies lately discovered in Ireland".[46] The motion was proposed by a recent ex-President, Cecil Raikes, "a clever and ingenious debater",[47] whose political career culminated in minor office under Lord Salisbury. Another supporter of the motion was a young Trinity graduate, Sir George Young, who had inherited a baronetcy in childhood. Young was on his way to the Bar by way of the Presidency of the Union and a college fellowship. In 1880, he served as secretary to the Bessborough Commission and became an authority on Irish land questions. Two years later, when Lord Frederick Cavendish was appointed Chief Secretary, he asked Young to become his private secretary, with the prospect of succeeding T.H. Burke as permanent under-secretary. It was said that Young's telegram of acceptance was found in Cavendish's pocket on the day of his murder. In 1859, the Cambridge Union reflected a familiar British pattern: Irish problems were only noticed under threat of revolution, at which time suppression was put before reform. The inexorable road that led from the Phoenix trials to Phoenix Park suggested that repression was not enough.

The long silence on matters Irish was broken by nine debates in the six years between 1864 and 1870, although it was only for a brief period early in 1868 that divisions on Irish issues attracted as many members of the Union as Church or party questions. In the eighteen-sixties, the University was growing in size, and the Union becoming more secular and political in its interests, so that it becomes much simpler to assess comparative levels of interest in specific issues. In March 1864, members rejected by 50 votes to 24 the claim "that the English Church, as established in Ireland, is an injustice to the Irish people".[48] On the face of it, the 68 percent support suggested that opinions had barely changed since the 77 percent endorsement of 1848. However, there are indications that a shift in attitudes to the Irish Church was taking place. When the issue recurred in March 1865, opinion was more closely divided. In a debate adjourned to a second week, two future Liberal ministers, Dilke and Lord Edmond Fitzmaurice, were among those who opposed the motion that "the Established Church in Ireland ought to be maintained as an endowed establishment". An unsuccessful amendment argued that "it is the duty of our Government to show strict impartiality towards *all* religious communities within its jurisdiction; and especially in Ireland". The hint of a wider attack on the Church of England was too much for the Union to swallow, but the main motion scraped home by just a single vote in a division of 109.[49] Since the seconder of the motion was Henry Lowry-Corry, son of the Earl of Belmore and future Conservative MP for Tyrone, it is unlikely that the case for the Establishment went by default.[50] The Irish Church, it would seem, was already losing support before the Fenian campaign of the mid-sixties.

This steady movement of opinion was further illustrated in February 1867 when, in an almost identical house of 106, a motion that "the maintenance of the Irish Established Church on its present footing, is an injustice to the people of that country" actually passed by six votes.[51] The slight shift since the debate of 1865 might be explained by the moderate terms of the motion, which implied reform rather than disestablishment, but opinion had moved a long way since 1864, when two-thirds of the house had dismissed the notion that a privileged Protestant Church was an injustice to the Irish.

It is just possible that personalities played a part in tipping the outcome of the 1867 debate. The first speaker in defence of the Irish Church was R.E. Verdon of St John's, an exception to the general pattern that the most brilliant Union minds argued for reform. Verdon had already taken an outstanding degree in Mathematics, and was heading for a First in Moral Sciences. However, his communication skills may not have matched his intellect. Soon afterwards, he "became very odd", and took to announcing "that certain mental processes could not be described in words, and that he was writing a book on them".[52] Perhaps, by 1867, this was the only kind of mindset that could detect any merit in the Irish Church. It is noticeable that in 1869, as the Establishment met its doom, even its Cambridge defenders declined to fight the battle head-on. A sudden subterranean change had taken place in educated opinion: after all, as late as the summer of 1865, Gladstone had privately commented that the prospect of disestablishment in Ireland was "remote and apparently out of all bearing on the practical politics of the day".[53] Moreover, the debate of February 1867, the first indication that the Cambridge Union was prepared to ditch the Irish Church, came four weeks before the attempted Fenian rising, and so cannot be written off as a concession to crisis.

It is unlikely that an explanation for the changing balance of opinion is to be found in the arrival of Nonconformists at Cambridge. The Anglican grip on the BA degree had been broken in 1856, but remained in place for most other degrees and for college fellowships until 1872. Thus Cambridge had not become entirely open to Nonconformists, although they probably formed one element in the rising admissions of the eighteen-sixties. So far as Union debates are concerned, the evidence points less to modification of the overall constituency as to changes in the opinions of individuals. If Nonconformists had been responsible for the decreasing popularity of the Irish Church, then we should expect to see an equally large dent appearing in support for Anglican supremacy. In fact, the shift in opinion regarding the Irish Church may be compared with two debates on the issue of disestablishment in England, in 1865 and 1869, in which the link between Church and State was upheld by majorities of 78 and 74 percent – a level of support which remained characteristic of such debates until the eighteen-eighties. In December 1865, a motion condemning the link between Church and State as "wrong in point of morality and public policy" stung Anglican partisans into imposing an intemperate amendment, professing "horror and aversion" at the thought of robbing the established Church "of one jot or tittle of its property, privileges, or prerogatives". In 1869, a more neutrally worded motion for the disestablishment of the Church of England was defeated by 101 votes to 35.[54] A handful of speakers defended the privileges of both churches, but it seems that in this case, the Union's silent majority drew two distinctions between England and Ireland. Attendance figures in Table Two suggest that they found the latter cause less interesting, while division records show that they also found it less compelling.

Doubts about the validity of Church Establishment in Ireland were accompanied by a measure of ambivalence about the causes of the country's problems. In October 1865, the Union rejected by 74 votes to 26 a motion which stated that "while this House condemns the recent Fenian Conspiracy, it nevertheless considers that the disaffection in Ireland has been produced by English mis-government". Lord Edmond Fitzmaurice, son of one of the largest Kerry landowners, was among those denouncing the proposition. It might have been expected that when the Fenians actually struck, in March 1867, opinion would have hardened. In fact, the reverse was the case, despite the bold claim of the motion that "the present Irish Rebellion, though ill-considered, is by no means dishonourable to the Irish people". Two attempts were made to amend the motion. One stated that "every loyal subject of this Realm must consider any attempt to subvert the existing Government of this Kingdom as dishonourable; and deserving the utmost rigour of the Law". The other condemned the insurrection as "utterly mistaken in its objects" but described it as "the result of past misgovernment, and of substantial grievances which ought to be redressed". This more moderate amendment was put forward by N.E. Hartog, who had arrived in Cambridge after a career of unprecedented brilliance at London University. Hartog was on his way to become the first Jew to head the Mathematics Tripos, yet another example of the relationship between intellect and reform causes in Ireland that was one of the hallmarks of the nineteenth-century Cambridge Union. Remarkably, members rejected the conventional demand for law-and-order and carried Hartog's amendment instead. Then, by 36 votes to 30, members perversely rejected the motion that they had just amended. Perhaps the procedural squabble accounts for the relatively small number of members who stayed to vote. The previous month, more than twice as many had expressed a view on the question of repression in Jamaica following the Morant Bay disturbances of 1865.[55] None the less, in just eighteen months, the proportion of a Cambridge Union audience prepared to blame English misgovernment for Irish insurrection had risen from a quarter to almost one half.

While the spirit of conciliation was gaining ground, the process was by no means one-way. In December 1867, three Fenians were hanged for shooting a policeman on the streets of an English city. The Union resoundingly approved the execution of the "Manchester Martyrs" by 110 votes to 18 in February 1868. The strength of feeling was remarkable, since the debate came ten weeks after the hangings, when passions might have cooled. Even more remarkable, just three weeks later the Union rejected a general motion in favour of the abolition of capital punishment by a much smaller margin of two to one (78 votes to 39). This is one of the episodes that challenge the idea of rational, integrated opinion among Cambridge students: if precisely the same people attended both debates, we should be forced to conclude that more than half of those who opposed the death penalty on principle managed to support the hanging of Allen, Larkin and O'Brien.[56] The most that can be said by way of explanation is that the mid-Victorians were mercifully less accustomed to political murder than their twentieth-century descendants, and that there was genuine horror at what had happened in Manchester. This was probably mixed with a less elevated sentiment, also detectable in the more recent Ulster Troubles, that was prepared to romanticise Irish violence so long as it was confined to Irish soil, but which drew the line at its intrusion upon the streets of English cities.

However, the mood of revenge was short-lived. Six weeks later, a two-night debate beginning on St Patrick's Day 1868, showed that the view that discontent stemmed from injustice, which had attracted almost one half of a moderately attended debate a year earlier, was now endorsed by two-thirds of a very large house in one of the best-attended debates of the decade. By 115 votes to 57, the Union agreed that "the state of Ireland justifies the use of extra-ordinary conciliatory measures". In addition to the shift in opinion and the clearly implied link between revolt and reform, the debate has two other interesting features. One was an unsuccessful amendment arguing that "the state of Ireland shows that the only permanent measure of conciliation would be her establishment as an independent country".[57] It seems unlikely that the amendment was put forward as a wrecking tactic, since its proposer had the previous year moved the motion denying that the Fenian uprising was dishonourable to the Irish people. It may also have been easier to vote for "extra-ordinary measures of conciliation" (which implied generosity) rather than for motions blaming previous misgovernment (which implied guilt).

Unfortunately, it proved easier to support conciliatory measures in principle than to define them in practice. In May 1869, a well-attended third-term debate went into a second night to end with a vote of 56 to 19 that "the settlement of the Land Question in Ireland is of far greater importance than any measure in connexion with the Church". In the absence of any report of the debate, it is difficult to determine whether supporters of the motion genuinely sought to shift the focus of policy towards the land question, or simply wished to divert attention from the Church. The proposer, Arthur Coote, had been reared in England and schooled at Eton, but he was in line to succeed as premier baronet of Ireland, and inherit an estate in Queen's County (Laois). While waiting for his inheritance, he worked as secretary to the British and Foreign Bible Society. It seems that the Union found his views on this world more persuasive than his beliefs about the next: the previous month, he had failed to secure majority support for the claim that "the increase in convents in this Country requires some immediate check".[58]

The debate of May 1869 was unusual in the number of speakers who seem to have had connections with Ireland. J.D. Fitzgerald of Christ's, who had defended the Manchester martyrs, now tried the equally unpromising ploy of amending the motion into an anodyne endorsement of Gladstone's Irish policy. Also critical of the motion was Arthur O'Neill, who was about to leave Cambridge without a degree and head for the Irish Bar. There was even a visiting undergraduate from Trinity College Dublin, who spoke for the motion.[59] The debate was also remarkable in constituting the sole attempt at a defence of the Irish Church in the year of its disestablishment. The three-quarters majority in favour of Coote's motion was probably the result of a junction between social radicals and diehard defenders of ecclesiastical privilege. It is noteworthy that by 1869 the latter were unwilling to argue their case on its own terms.

The coalition did not translate into support for specific action. In February 1870, just one week before Gladstone unveiled his Irish Land Bill, a Union vote of 52 to 16 strongly condemned any measure "which in the least degree violated the rights of existing proprietors". An unsuccessful amendment called for "a Royal Commission empowered to deal with large Irish estate proprietors for the purchase of land".[60] How the land question could be settled without either affecting the rights of landlords or attempting to buy them out was left unexplained: fortunately, undergraduate debaters were not expected to be consistent. There was nothing amazing about the Cambridge Union supporting private ownership of land. What is surprising is that so few bothered to vote.

In November 1873, a debating team from Oxford introduced the Cambridge Union to a new issue, one which it would continue to discuss for forty years. The Oxford visitors were led by an Irishman, the 24 year-old J.G.S. MacNeill from that most fashionable of all colleges, Christ Church. On the verge of a distinguished career at the Bar, Swift MacNeill urged the Cambridge Union to resolve that "'Home Rule' is absolutely necessary for the welfare of Ireland". MacNeill remembered an "animated" debate with "brilliant contributions" from two rising Cambridge lawyers, C.S. Kenny and Perceval Laurence. Indeed, proceedings had to be adjourned to a second night, by which time MacNeill had departed. In due course, "the news came to me in Ireland, to my great gratification and somewhat I must confess to my surprise, that the Home Rule motion had been carried". MacNeill was right to be surprised. In reality, nine of the ten speakers from Cambridge had opposed the motion. The tenth, Kenny, had moved an amendment to replace the phrase "Home Rule" with "some measure for securing local legislation on local affairs". It was this inoffensive proposition that was carried, in a very small house, by 36 votes to 17.

It is tempting to see this episode as a repetition of the tentative response to the question of State payment of the Irish priesthood thirty years earlier: a proposal which seemed meritorious as a relatively abstract issue soon became anathema as practical politics. However, even this would probably be reading too much into a stray vote that may have been simply a forced courtesy to the odd notions of the Oxford visitors. The propounder of the compromise certainly exaggerated its significance. In 1885, Kenny began a brief career as a Liberal MP. Two years later, MacNeill followed him into the Commons as MP for South Donegal. By 1887, the outlook for the Liberal-Parnellite alliance was bleak, and any straw of encouragement was eagerly embraced. The two men reminisced about the half-remembered debate in their student days, and Kenny assured MacNeill "that so far as he was aware this was the first Home Rule motion ever carried at any meeting at which the vast majority of those present were not Irish but British".[61] Oddly enough, the misunderstanding (if not outright distortion) became self-fulfilling, since MacNeill decided to celebrate the fortieth anniversary in 1913 by re-enacting the debate – at a time when Cambridge opinion had eventually if only marginally swung into the Home Rule column. One can only hope that Gladstonian strategy after 1886 was not founded upon Kenny's amnesiac enthusiasm.

Any notion that MacNeill had planted a new cult of Irish devolution on the banks of the Cam is further undermined by the fact that more than three years elapsed before Home Rule was discussed again. Indeed, no other Irish issues appeared on the Union's order paper. Ireland, it seems, had once again dropped below the English horizon, and it took Parnell's campaign of obstruction to drag it back into view. However, once Ireland returned to the agenda, it asserted its priority. In six years from February 1877, no fewer than seven debates took place in which Home Rule was massively and consistently rejected. True, the overwhelming majorities of 85 and 90 percent registered in

1877 fell back to the 72 to 75 percent band between 1880 and 1882, the years when debates on Irish issues were among the best attended topics. In October 1882, when there was heady talk of granting Ireland some measure of local autonomy, opposition even dipped below 68 percent. However, by May 1883, the proportion opposed to Home Rule had bounced back above eighty percent. Moreover, at that point, the series came to a halt, underlining the extent to which the Home Rule crisis of 1886 was something that was forced upon the British political agenda from without.

Comparison with the now regular party political debates also suggests that hostility was not confined to Conservatives. Indeed, Gladstone's second ministry seems to have enjoyed something close to a "honeymoon period" in the early eighteen-eighties, at a time when opposition to Home Rule remained strong. Assuming a high degree of overlap between those voting on Home Rule and those taking part in debates on the Conservative party, it would seem that at least one-third of Cambridge Liberals were opposed to Irish devolution in the first half of the eighteen-eighties. Table Three demonstrates that in the decade before the first Home Rule Bill, opposition considerably exceeded support for the Conservative Party.

No attempt to massage the wording of a motion seems to have made much difference to the vehemence of opposition. In February 1877, the Union was invited to agree that "a system of government, which, reserving for the Imperial Parliament the consideration of affairs of Imperial importance, should give local self-government to the Irish nation, would be beneficial both to Ireland and the Empire". The motion, debated on the very evening that Parnell and Biggar launched their campaign of systematic obstruction in the House of Commons, was defeated by 90 votes to 16 – more sweeping even than the rejection the previous week of the disendowment and disestablishment of the Church of England.[62] There was a certain John Bull-ish pomposity about the claim in December 1877 that Home Rule would be "detrimental to the interests" of Ireland "and of the English Empire", a phrase that perhaps suggests the influence of J.R. Seeley in the Chair of Modern History. Absurd or not, the motion passed by 69 votes to 8.[63] In February 1880, the Union refused – by 125 votes to 42 – to accept that Home Rule "would not be incompatible with the integrity of the United Kingdom". Two weeks earlier the Union had shown more sympathy for the Afghans, who were resisting (successfully, as it turned out) their forcible incorporation into the British empire.[64]

Attractive packaging made no difference. A motion in March 1881, arguing that "the present condition of Ireland" would justify "granting self-government to that country, similar to that enjoyed by the Canadians" was rejected almost as decisively, by 241 votes to 94.[65] In February 1882, proponents tried again, arguing that "the provisions of the Land Act, are not likely to prove the means of restoring prosperity to Ireland" and proposing instead "a scheme of compensation for Irish landowners, and the establishment of self-government for the Irish people in all but Imperial affairs". The Union did not like the 1881 Land Act, but refused by 99 votes to 36 to accept its condemnation as a Trojan horse for Home Rule.[66] In October 1882, it dismissed by 98 votes to 47 the notion that "no permanent satisfactory settlement of Ireland can be hoped for without the re-establishment of an Irish Parliament".[67] In May 1883, there was even less sympathy for the bald claim that "Ireland ought to be governed by the Irish", which was rejected by 94 votes to 19.[68] The only faint hint of flexibility came in March 1884, when a relatively small house voted by 37 to 27 to "welcome the formation of a close federal union between Great Britain, Ireland and the English Colonies".[69] Although proposed by the same member who had moved the Home Rule motion of May 1883, its modest acceptability owed more to the popularity of Imperial Federation than to any swing of opinion towards Irish Home Rule.

As C.S. Kenny had noted of the 1873 debate, these were discussions dominated by young Englishmen. A few surnames suggest an echo of Ireland, but it cannot always be proved that their owners saw themselves as Irishmen. Since these were the years in which the Catholic Church placed the greatest obstacles to study at Cambridge, Irish voices were likely to be Protestant – and it was already evident that the Parnells and the MacNeills were atypical in their nationalism. One exception was J.H. Monahan, the son of a Dublin lawyer who had come to Cambridge by way of an English Catholic School, the Oratory at Birmingham. He spoke twice on the Home Rule side, but left the University after his freshman year. Others were evidently Irish Protestants, even if they bore surnames of Gaelic origin. Robert Donovan of Trinity, who opposed Home Rule, had come to Cambridge from Ferns in County Wexford by way of an English public school, and went on to a career at the Irish Bar. In two other cases, the links with Ireland were tenuous. The example of Henry Lynch, who moved the composite motion of February 1882, was cited in Chapter Five. His father was from Ireland, his uncle retained the family estate in Mayo, but young Lynch had been reared in London and sent to school at Eton. Another opponent of Home Rule was A.H. Leahy of Pembroke. Leahy's father, born in Killarney, was part of the Irish professional diaspora that sustained the British empire. An officer in the Royal Engineers, he had a distinguished record in the Crimean War and died a victim of the appalling conditions in the garrison at Gibraltar. The son came to Cambridge from Trinity College Dublin but, unlike Donovan, he did not return. Exile, however, may not have affected his self-identification, since he combined the Chair of Mathematics at the University of Sheffield with authorship of a book on *Heroic Romances of Ireland*. Irish identity was a complex quantity which did not always generate predictable responses to political issues.

It is worth noting that one young Englishman did not pronounce upon Home Rule. Austen Chamberlain threw himself into Union debates soon after his arrival in Cambridge in October 1882. Twice he denounced the cabinet in which his father was a member for imposing Coercion upon Ireland. In the Political Society, founded by Oscar Browning in emulation of the Apostles, Austen Chamberlain supported the proposition that "an Irish Parliament would be a rebel Parliament". But the Political Society was limited to twelve members, each of whom was obliged to record an opinion on the subjects discussed. Young Chamberlain's silence on Home Rule in the more public forum of the Union tends to compound the enigma of "Joe's" attitude to Irish devolution.[70]

It might be easier to accept the implacability of opposition to Home Rule had Cambridge opinion shown any accompanying willingness to solve Irish problems within the existing framework of the United Kingdom. A measure of the extent to which the University itself was becoming more serious-minded could be found in the increasing numbers of undergraduates in residence during the summer, and from 1880 Long Vacation debates became a regular part of the Union calendar. In August of that year, an attempt was made to deplore as "impolitic and unjust" the rejection by the House of Lords of the Compensation for Disturbance Bill, the first attempt by the incoming Liberal ministry to appease agrarian discontent in Ireland. The motion was rejected by 39 votes to 27.[71] However, an element of ambivalence was suggested in November of that year when the Union voted by 58 votes to 53 "that the present state of Ireland is due to the misguided policy of English Statesmen in the past".[72] The motion was so broad as to be almost without meaning, and admission of past misgovernment did not translate into practical support for conciliation. In February 1881, a motion condemning Coercion and urging that "such a measure ought to be preceded by Remedial Legislation" was rejected by a massive margin of 291 votes to 27.[73] In contrast to the more open response to the Fenian challenge a dozen years earlier, agrarian outrage brought Irish problems to English attention, but ruled out their solution. In May 1881, the Union disapproved of the Land Bill "both with regard to its principle and probable effect" by 86 votes to 72, the historian J.R. Tanner forming part of a surprisingly large minority.[74] However, a Long Vacation debate in August refused by 43 to 26 to regard Lords interference in the legislation as an argument for abolition of the upper house.[75] In October, the first debate of the new academic year returned to the question, with a motion that the Land Bill was "utterly inadequate to settle Irish grievances" and favouring "the establishment of peasant proprietorship in Ireland, with a view to the permanent pacification of that Country".[76] Land purchase had been mentioned in the unsuccessful amendment proposed during the 1870 debate. It remained a radical proposition in 1881, although one which would become orthodox Conservative policy within a decade. The motion was rejected by 194 votes to 80.[77] In February 1882, the Union once again refused to condemn the House of Lords, this time by 151 votes to 101. Their Lordships' alleged offence lay in planning to establish a committee to investigate the operation of the Land Act, a move which the motion described as "injurious to the interests of Ireland, and deserving of the strongest censure".[78]

All concessions to the Irish seemed equally objectionable. Thus when in February 1882, the Union was invited to support a land purchase scheme coupled with Home Rule, the vote of 73 percent against (99 votes to 36) was only slightly higher than the 71 percent rejecting land purchase alone four months earlier.[79] However, the debates of May 1881 and February 1882 specifically on Gladstone's land legislation saw the opposition to reform falling to 54 and 60 percent.[80] Support for Coercion ran at roughly the same levels as opposition to Home Rule. The Union rejected a motion expressing "indignation" at "the administration of the Crimes Act in Ireland" by 113 votes to 48 in January 1883, and the proportions remained the same when in May 1885, the Union supported the renewal of the Crimes Act by 43 votes to 20 – 32 percent opposing on both occasions.[81] A debate in February 1884 on a motion of "no confidence in the Irish administration of Her Majesty's Government" was complicated by the party issue involved. The motion was passed by 124 votes to 83. The 60 percent level of support was higher than the 51 percent who had voted "no confidence" in the government as a whole in October 1883, but almost identical to the vote of 135 to 90 that rejected Austen Chamberlain's claim that "the Tory Party does not in any way possess the confidence of the Country" in March 1884.[82]

On the other hand, two debates on the eve of the Home Rule crisis suggest an intriguing element of ambivalence. By 1885, the Union had lost interest in the Irish land question, as shown by the small numbers voting on Coercion in May 1885. However, it decided by 70 votes to 54 that "the condition of the Scotch Crofters calls for instant and radical reform of the rights possessed by landed proprietors"[83] – an interesting contrast to its "no concessions" approach to Irish tenants in 1880-82. While the Union did not specifically debate the Third Reform Act, it did reject two motions condemning the House of Lords for interfering in its passage. It was thus the more remarkable that a motion in June 1884 disapproving of "the extension of the Franchise Bill to Ireland" should have been rejected by 94 votes to 79.[84] Politically, at least, the Cambridge Union was prepared to admit the Irish masses to the benefits of full citizenship within the United Kingdom. Presumably they did not foresee that the newly enfranchised voters would enable Parnell to sweep

Ireland at the general election of 1885 and force the hated concept of Home Rule to the centre of the political agenda.

St John's College Chapel from Thompsons Lane 1897

9:   Gladstonian Home Rule 1886-1898

Gladstone's conversion to Home Rule meant that the idea of a parliament on College Green was no longer a mere debating society mirage. Between January 1886 and October 1887, Ireland was undoubtedly the dominant political question at the Cambridge Union, with seven debates in less than two years, two of them adjourned to a second night. In five of the six terms in which it was discussed, Home Rule drew the largest attendance. The exception was the January term of 1886, when it was probably the fact that the debate was adjourned to a second night that pushed it into second place. The Union chose to discuss Home Rule before Gladstone's plan had been fully revealed, and members presumably decided that in doing so, they had closed the issue for the term. None the less, it is bizarre to find that young Cambridge was arguing over the existence of ghosts while the United Kingdom trembled in the balance. Overall, however, six of the seven best-attended debates in 1886-87 were on Home Rule, while the seventh endorsed Coercion. The sudden centrality of Ireland was typical of Britain as a whole: in London, Leslie Stephen in May 1886 commented that he had "never found any subject so all-pervading".[1]

Although there is some evidence of boredom, Home Rule continued to draw large attendances until the time of the Second Home Rule bill in 1893, but there was an increasing sense that it was once again a debating society issue rather than a real threat to the unity of the United Kingdom. Indeed, the Gladstonian phase of the question whimpered to a conclusion by 1898. After 1886, as before, majorities against any form of devolution in Ireland were remarkably consistent.

Given the disastrous split in the Liberal party at national level, it is perhaps surprising to find that once Home Rule became a practical issue in 1886, it gained slightly in acceptability. Between 1877 and 1883, opposition to Home Rule had not only been overwhelming – peaking on one occasion at almost ninety percent – but had even exceeded the general level of support for the Conservative party. During the period of the first Home Rule crisis itself, the level of opposition actually fell, varying between 56 and 69 percent. At national level, Cambridge graduates included such prominent Liberal Unionists as Hartington, Leonard Courtney and Austen Chamberlain, the last of them a former Vice-President of the Union who had left Cambridge as recently as 1885. Yet no indication can be found in the division records of the Union of the existence of a substantial body of Liberal Unionist opinion in the undergraduate population. Among dons, Henry Sidgwick was a fervent Liberal Unionist. An attempt was made to start a "Women's Liberal Unionist League" in 1889. Although disapproving on gender grounds, the *Granta* accepted it as "a dull thing enough in all conscience".[2] There is no evidence of young men in Cambridge yearning for Mr Gladstone to abandon his flirtation with Ireland and return to office at the head of a reunited Liberal party. Nor did the Union ever debate Joseph Chamberlain's proposal – if his various hints may be so termed – to restructure the United Kingdom as a federation. By contrast, if Wilfrid Blunt is to be believed, the Cambridge undergraduate population even included a handful of Conservative Home Rulers.

From the late eighteen-eighties, reports in the *Cambridge Review* and the *Granta* provide some evidence of the flavour and content of debates. The completion of an extension to the Union building in 1886, itself a response to the growing student population, attracted more members, most of them silent participants who attended debates as consumers rather than as participants. Home Rule spawned a new practice, of inviting politicians to address the Union, and occasionally even to dent entrenched prejudices. Indeed, by the early twentieth century, debates would demonstrate a slow but steady shift in opinion towards more liberal attitudes on Irish issues. However, down to 1898, majority opinion in the Cambridge Union continued to be not only hostile to Home Rule but unsympathetic towards Ireland in general and nationalist concerns in particular. By the middle of the eighteen-nineties, Ireland had once again ceased to be a threat. Indeed, during a final, unpleasant phase in 1897-98 before the Union mercifully lost interest altogether, Ireland became a joke.

The Cambridge Union turned its attention to Ireland on 26 January 1886, the evening on which Lord Salisbury's minority administration faced defeat at Westminster. The motion for debate strongly condemned "any scheme of Home Rule which would lead to the establishment of an Irish Parliament in Dublin" although a sub-clause approved "concessions to Ireland in the way of local self-government". The proposer insisted that Home Rule was not a step towards Repeal. "Of course the precise manner in which local self-government would be submitted would depend upon the events of the next few days." Two of the five speakers were Protestant Irishmen, one on each side. Arthur Cane, Dublin-born, resident of Westmeath and a member of the Apostles, attacked Home Rule, which was defended by C.V. Barrington, from Cashel in Tipperary. Shortly after ten o'clock, the debate was adjourned for one week, even though there was still plenty of time to accommodate other speakers. Three hours later, Salisbury's government was defeated on an amendment to the address proposed by Jesse Collings, the advocate of "three acres and a cow". It suited politicians at Westminster to avoid immediate confrontation over Ireland. Like the student debaters at Cambridge, they wanted to know what Gladstone intended to propose.

When the debate resumed on 2 February, the picture remained opaque but, none the less, a week had proved to be a long time in politics. Gladstone was now in the process of forming a ministry, and the lack of enthusiasm for Home Rule among some of his leading party associates was increasingly obvious. Twelve years earlier, in November 1873, C.S. Kenny had saved a Home Rule motion by substituting an anodyne reference to local self-government for the dangerous phrase itself. This time, the process was reversed. The harmless sub-clause was deleted by 70 votes to 57 and the main motion, now unambiguous in its rejection of constitutional change, endorsed by 65 votes to 43. It is unlikely that there was any significance in the fact that 55 percent opposed any form of local self-government as against 60 percent who disapproved of Home Rule: it was more likely that some of those who had failed to sustain the more moderate part of the motion had not bothered to stay to be defeated on the main issue. The Union evidently agreed with the speaker who had insisted that "they could not separate the two questions of local self-government and home rule".[3] None the less, opposition to Home Rule was less pronounced than it had been in 1882, when 68 percent had rejected the idea of an Irish parliament, and much reduced from the level of 1877, when 85 percent had voted against any form of local self-government.

Opposition had hardened slightly by May 1886, when the Union pronounced its "severest condemnation" upon Home Rule, by 96 votes to 49, 66 percent voting against. Gladstone had unveiled his scheme for Ireland almost a month earlier, and it is not altogether surprising that its various novelties and inconsistencies had failed to inspire. More to the point, on the day of the Union debate, 4 May, English newspapers published the prime minister's fiery manifesto to his Midlothian constituents. In this, he had denounced the opponents of Home Rule as a "formidable enemy", consisting of "class and the dependants of class", who at every great political crisis in the previous sixty years had "fought uniformily on the wrong side, and have uniformily been defeated ... by the upright sense of the nation".[4] In the circumstances, a lukewarm response was to be expected from the young men of Cambridge University. The Union, of course, had not fought "on the wrong side" in the two great issues of Catholic Emancipation and the Irish Church. Fundamentally, its members simply did not share Gladstone's interpretation of the nature of the Home Rule crisis. Recent historical writing has stressed the integral relationship between Home Rule and land purchase, as Gladstone himself had made clear in April 1886, but none of the seven debates of 1886-87 appeared to link the two issues. Indeed, in January 1887, a life member of the Union, B.R. Balfour, asserted that "the land question had really no connection with Home Rule".[5] Balfour owned an estate near Drogheda but apparently practised as a barrister in London. Eleven years later he turned up in the Union again, offering his own unnecessary touch of immoderation in the suggestion that male undergraduates should refuse to graduate if degrees were conceded to women.

On 7 June 1886, the Home Rule bill was rejected in the House of Commons by 341 votes to 311, and the United Kingdom embarked on its second general election within eight months. Since the Commons vote cut across party lines, and the election was in large measure a referendum on Home Rule, it is possible to make some comparison between Cambridge Union opinion and the attitudes of politicians and voters. At first sight, anti-Home Rule margins in the Union were larger than the 52 percent opposition registered in the lobbies of the House of Commons on 7 June. However, for comparative purposes, we should subtract the Parnellites, who represented an element almost totally absent from Cambridge, if not Irish MPs of all shades. Among members of parliament representing constituencies in Great Britain, the proportion against the bill was about 58 percent. If we further bear in mind that Scotland was heavily Gladstonian, and recall that Scots were not especially numerous in Cambridge, then the division of opinion in the Cambridge Union looks remarkably close to that among MPs from England.

However, since MPs were the product of a less-than-perfect electoral system, it is not safe to conclude that they represented a cross-section of public opinion either. Analysis of the popular vote in nineteenth-century general elections is complicated by the vagaries of two-member constituencies, in which voters sometimes crossed party lines or for tactical reasons used only one of their votes. Voting statistics cited by John Morley, who was a Liberal campaign manager, point to a popular vote in Great Britain of about 52 percent against Home Rule. A modern calculation gives 53.9 percent in Great Britain, rising to 54.9 percent in England alone.[6] However, the 1886 election saw an unusually large number of unopposed returns: in England, 21 of the Liberal seats contested in 1885 produced unopposed returns in 1886, while in 101 constituencies, Conservative or Liberal Unionist candidates were returned without opposition. How these constituencies might have polled is a matter for guesswork. Liberals secured a clear run mainly in industrial areas in Yorkshire and the north-east, where it may be assumed that there were local Irish communities who had heeded Parnell's call to vote Conservative in 1885 but would have switched sides in 1886. Across wide areas of suburban and rural southern England, Liberal organisers evidently assumed that their support had collapsed: about one-third of all English Conservative and Liberal Unionist MPs were returned unopposed. Thus the fact that there were five times as many uncontested Conservative as Liberal seats in England strongly suggests that the "real" level of voter resistance to Home Rule was above sixty percent, an estimate that makes the division of opinion in the Cambridge Union look relatively typical. Yet even that may not give the full picture. The mass electorate as extended by the Reform Act of 1884 contained two notable elements favourable to the Liberals. One was the agricultural labour force, and the other consisted of Irish migrant communities in the English towns and cities. Neither element was well represented among Cambridge undergraduates, and both were almost certainly invisible among members of the Union. Therefore, remarkable though it may seem, members of the Cambridge Union may have been more favourable towards Home Rule than the generality of the social group from which they came.

It was unusual for the Cambridge Union to discuss the same issue twice in a single term, and it was perennially difficult to arouse enthusiasm for debates of any kind in May and June. Confirmation that the Home Rule crisis of 1886 was an abnormal episode may be found in the fact that the Irish debate that began on 8 June attracted a massive attendance at a time when Cambridge was normally throwing itself into party mode. Interest was high because the Home Rule bill had been thrown out by the House of Commons the previous day. The debate was ground-breaking in another respect. For the first time, the Union became the platform for a public figure unconnected with Cambridge. The debating chamber was packed, "extra accommodation being provided for members on the floor of the House, and the gallery thoroughly occupied by ladies and their friends".[7] The attraction was a defence of Home Rule by John Dillon, recently elected to parliament for East Mayo but well-known for his part in the Land War. Dillon was supported by Wilfrid Scawen Blunt, a renegade English gentleman noted for his heretical view that the British had no right to rule over Egyptians and Indians. There was, too, a visiting speaker on the unionist side, but subsequent controversy suggests that George Dames Burtchaell was a straw man invited to create a bogus pretence of balance. Burtchaell was a Dublin barrister and enthusiastic genealogist. He was not in the same league as John Dillon.

The invitation to Dillon appears to have come about almost by accident, as a by-product of an intrigue between Blunt and a couple of undergraduate politicians. Indeed, if the Union had formally decided to adopt a policy of inviting distinguished public figures to its debates, it is unlikely that it would have started with an Irish nationalist. In 1886, no fewer than five former Presidents were prominent in Westminster politics, while another cabinet minister, the Home Secretary, Hugh Childers, had been an active participant. It is probable that the Chancellor of the Exchequer, Harcourt, would have felt it beneath his massive dignity to have accepted invitations to speak, while G.O. Trevelyan, who had resigned from Gladstone's cabinet along with Chamberlain, would no doubt have preferred to state his position to a more predictable audience of his Edinburgh constituents. However, one former Union luminary might have been approachable: Charles Dilke had been obliged to withdraw to the political sidelines after being named in a divorce case the previous year, and was believed to be using the Home Rule crisis as a means of working his passage back into acceptable society.[8] On the Conservative side, Richard Cross was already too much of an elder statesman, but an approach might have been made to Cecil Raikes, while Sir John Gorst did indeed deliver an assault on Home Rule at the Union in 1887. Other Cambridge men at the heart of the Home Rule crisis included Hartington, Labouchere, Lord John Manners and Parnell himself, although of these, only Manners had affectionate memories of the Union. How, then, was it that the unlikely duo of Dillon and Blunt came to initiate the tradition of "big-name" visiting speakers?

Blunt visited Cambridge early in March 1886 to have lunch at Trinity with Herbert Vivian, secretary of the Cambridge University Carlton Club, the student Conservative association.[9] During his confrontation with the party's "Old Guard" in 1884-85, Lord Randolph Churchill had flourished his connections with the Cambridge Carlton as a symbol of his claim to speak for youth.[10] In the fluid and speculative atmosphere of 1885, it appears that Randolph had converted "half a dozen or so" young Cambridge Tories to the cause of Home Rule: Vivian himself assailed Gladstone in the Union, but was conspicuously silent on the Irish issue. Since Blunt had contested the 1885 general election as a Conservative Home Ruler, Vivian had been keen to include him among the speakers at a forthcoming party rally in the Cambridge Guildhall. Unfortunately, this was vetoed by the guest of honour, Ellis Ashmead Bartlett: Tory Home Rulers were being read out of the party, and the idealism of Randolph Churchill's young followers had become a distinct embarrassment. Hence the presence at lunch of Vivian's friend, Leopold Maxse, a Liberal who was on the verge of election to the Presidency of the Union.

Blunt left Cambridge with the assurance that "these young fellows will arrange a separate meeting for me", but he does not seem to have been aware of the plan forming in Maxse's mind.[11] Leo Maxse made a point of defying conventions.[12] He passed his final examinations in 1886, but did not bother to take his degree. He claimed to be incapable of understanding why people wished to have letters after their names or titles before them. Of course, it helped to be rich, and in 1893 his father purchased the *National Review* so that Maxse would have his own political mouthpiece. Maxse had been elected President for the summer term, traditionally the quietest time of the Union year. It was in keeping with his personality to make a splash by inviting the controversial Blunt. Moreover, just a fortnight before the lunch at Trinity, the Union had inaugurated its extended premises. Initiatives to shake up debates could be justified if they attracted the new members needed to pay for the building programme.

It seems to have been through Blunt that the Cambridge Union acquired John Dillon as a visiting speaker. Blunt's typically bombastic verdict that "it was a most fortunate idea bringing him with me"[13] conveys an unduly casual impression of events, but it seems likely that the invitation resulted from the joint effort of two unconventional personalities, Maxse and Blunt. One of the implications of the election campaign into which they were abruptly plunged after the defeat of the Bill on 7 June was that Irish Nationalists suddenly had to reverse a decade's defiance of British opinion and start arguing their case to English voters. This was something that does not seem to have been foreseen: Parnell himself began a tour of southern England on 25 June, only a fortnight before the start of polling.[14] It was no doubt in this context that John Dillon agreed to accompany Blunt to Cambridge on 10 June. (Blunt may have held heretical views about the British imperial mission, but he was amazed to discover that Dillon insisted on travelling second class.) Since few Cambridge undergraduates were old enough to vote, even if they possessed property in their own right, the excursion was not an obviously efficient use of Dillon's time.

Opening the debate on 8 June, W.H. Wilkins of Clare proposed a motion strongly condemning "Mr. Gladstone's scheme of Home Rule for Ireland". Although Blunt characteristically dismissed him as "a fluent speaker but shallow enough", Wilkins evidently cared strongly about the subject. This was not the first time that he had attacked Home Rule in the Union, and after graduating in 1887, he worked for a time as private secretary to the Earl of Dunraven, a prominent Irish unionist. The son of a Dorset farmer, Wilkins had come to Cambridge with the intention of taking orders in the Church of England, but emerged instead to become a pioneer of modern royal biography. Like many Union stars of the nineteenth century, he died young, at the age of 44, but not before he had revealed the full story of George IV's secret marriage in 1785 to his Catholic mistress, Mrs Fitzherbert. His strong opposition to Home Rule is a reminder that 1886 was not simply an Irish dispute.

Naturally, Blunt believed that his personal account of the Irish land question attracted "attention and sympathy", but there was no doubt that it was Dillon who "created a wonderful impression" on the undergraduate audience. Although "quite two-thirds" of those present were instinctively opposed to Home Rule, Dillon's speech "carried all opposition before it".[15] The *Cambridge Review* caught the combination of liberalism and reassurance in Dillon's peroration:

> Let them trust the Irish people for once in their history, for England was strong enough not to be afraid if they then abused that privilege.[16]

Afterwards, Dillon confessed that "he had meant to deal in argument, but instead he narrated facts ... this was not at all what he had intended to say, and therein doubtless lay its merit". Blunt felt that it was the finest speech he had ever heard on Irish affairs, and he wished that Dillon had delivered it in the House of Commons. "It was not the speech of a rhetorician, but of a man profoundly convinced, and perfect master of his subject". Several undergraduates told Blunt that they were "converted". "The debate at the Union was an immense success for us." Indeed, the nationalist triumph later created a unionist backlash against visiting speakers.

The debate was adjourned to a second week, when a visiting team from the Oxford Union sought to redress the balance by attacking Home Rule. Even then, the motion was defeated by the relatively narrow margin of 150 votes to 118. A week after Dillon's speech, the impact still lingered, with the percentage against Home Rule falling a shade below 56 percent, a whole ten points below the debate of the previous month. Blunt had believed that "the feeling of the House was wholly with us".[17] Was this simply the courteous response of Victorian young gentlemen, or might a division on the first night of the debate have produced a sensational endorsement of Home Rule? Blunt was a poor judge of other people's opinions, but it was a theme of Dillon's speeches throughout the 1886 election campaign, on both sides of the Irish Sea, that for once there was a reservoir of English goodwill towards the sister island.[18]

"The defeat is a smash," Gladstone had commented as the results of the 1886 election started to flow in.[19] Lord Salisbury was returned to office at the head of a Conservative ministry but, smash or no smash, his was still a minority government. In the depths of the Long Vacation, Maxse moved an unsuccessful motion declaring the return of Salisbury to be "a public calamity" but drawing "one crumb of comfort from Lord Hartington's refusal to join him".[20] There was still a faint possibility that the shattered Liberals might reunite and find some other basis of alliance with the Parnellites that would return them to office. Thus, for a year or so, Home Rule could still be portrayed as a live issue, albeit with declining plausibility.

The terms of the various motions debated suggested very small differences in the level of hostility to concession in Ireland. Invited in October 1886 to accept a mildly worded motion describing Home Rule as "the only hope of a permanent settlement in Ireland" and looking forward "to its extension in a thorough and liberal form", the Union demurred by 106 votes to 74, opposition still running just below sixty percent.[21] In January 1887, the proposition that "the condition of Ireland demands the concession of Home Rule" was rejected by 102 votes to 50. The increase in the level of opposition to 67 percent suggests that there was no inclination to knuckle under to renewed agrarian disturbance. It was in this debate that C.V. Barrington announced that the Plan of Campaign had driven him out of the Home Rule camp.[22] Two future cabinet ministers also took part in this debate, one on either side: Reginald McKenna served under Asquith at the time of the Third Home Rule Bill, while F.H. Maugham became

Lord Chancellor under Neville Chamberlain. In June 1887, in the face of a motion advocated by Alfred Mond that merely described Home Rule as "desirable", opposition fell slightly to 58 percent (158 votes to 113). The debate was adjourned to a second week to enable an ex-President and Conservative MP, Sir John Gorst, to respond to Mond, but his contribution evidently made little difference to the division.[23] Challenged, however, to agree in October 1887 that Home Rule had become "absolutely essential", opposition jumped to 69 percent, in a vote of 124 against 55.[24] Reluctance to bow to constraint is also suggested by the rejection of a motion in May 1887 calling for the "severest censure" on Salisbury's ministry for the introduction of what opponents had called "perpetual" Coercion. After a one-week adjournment, the Union rejected the motion by 118 votes to 56.[25] The 68 percent majority for Coercion was almost identical to the opposition registered against the two anti-Home Rule motions implying concession under constraint.

Whether individually or collectively, undergraduates have a limited attention span. As the proposer of the motion for a Dublin parliament admitted in January 1887, "they had Home Rule dinned in their ears for a long time, and a great many hon. members no doubt thought it a rather worn out subject".[26] To F.E. (Edmund) Garrett, the obvious answer was to repeat the triumph of the John Dillon debate by inviting more Parnellites, a solution he presumably found all the more attractive since he was already Vice-President of the Union and could expect shortly to succeed to its highest office. On 31 January, he persuaded a business meeting that "when questions of great interest are under debate, it is desirable that strangers distinguished as orators or politicians, who are entitled to speak with authority on such questions, should be invited to take part in debates". The initiative was not universally welcome, and members insisted on advance consultation. After "prolonged discussion", Garrett managed to secure a decision that "should a suitable occasion occur during the next few months" to debate the Irish question, invitations should be sent to "a distinguished Unionist and Home Ruler".[27] There the matter rested until Garrett, now President, raised it again with the Union Committee in May of 1887.

Edmund Garrett is another of the brilliant young men of the Cambridge Union whose lives were cut short by ill health. A struggle with tuberculosis drove him to the warm, dry climate of South Africa, but even so, he died at the age of 41. Yet, stripped of the aura of the lost imperial hero, Garrett does not come across as a pleasant personality. In 1895, despite persistent ill-health, he took over the editorship of the *Cape Times*, the most influential newspaper in South Africa, and used it to fan the flames of conflict with the Afrikaner republics. An ally of Rhodes, an apologist for the Jameson raid and a confidant of Milner, Garrett had some share in the responsibility for the Boer War. The prominent Cape liberal, J.X. Merriman, a shrewd if rarely a charitable judge of character, called him "a *beastly* fellow".[28]

Perhaps all this could have been forgiven on the plea that the British empire was a mighty cause, a noble end that justified promotion by sordid means. However, as he headed for his Third in Classics, the undergraduate Garrett projected a much more flexible attitude to issues of principle. On 15 June 1886, he spoke in support of the Union motion strongly condemning Home Rule. Almost immediately, he threw himself into Oscar Browning's hopeless campaign to persuade a south London "villa constituency" to elect him as their Liberal MP, with impassioned street-corner harangues that prompted delighted crowds to hail him as a future prime minister. Untrammelled by consistency, Garrett returned to Cambridge ready to urge the Union in October 1886 to accept Home Rule as the miracle solution to Irish difficulties. In the whole sweep of Cambridge Union debates on Irish issues, Garrett comes across as the sole example of an undergraduate orator for whom self-advancement seems to have taken precedence over intellectual consistency.

Oscar Browning had come to know Garrett because the "O.B." was one of the senior members of the University who served on the Union Committee. Their presence was valuable in providing continuity and support for its young officers: even the olympian M.R. James briefly held the office of Librarian. "We were at that time intimate friends," Browning wrote of Garrett, "having been brought together by the Cambridge Union."[29] (Browning's frequent use of the term "intimate" was intentionally provocative as well as faintly salacious.) Another senior member of the Committee was evidently less impressed by Edmund Garrett. Charles Villiers Stanford had been organist at Trinity since 1873, and was about to become Professor of Music. Stanford was a notable figure in English music, not least in his own estimation. He helped popularise Brahms – the first British performance of a Brahms symphony was at Cambridge in 1877 – and, until the unexpected rise of Edward Elgar from provincial obscurity a decade later, he was the main rival to Arthur Sullivan as Britain's leading composer. More to the point, Stanford was an Irish Protestant who kept in touch with his roots, and worried about the threat of terrorism to his friends in Dublin. "During the troublous years of the early eighties which came to a climax in the Phoenix Park murders, I paid a few visits to Ireland," he later recalled. "The developments which followed that crime came very near home to me".[30] Young Edmund Garrett might regard Home Rule as a convenient lever for self-advancement, but to Stanford it was literally a life-and-death issue.

On 5 May 1887, the Union Committee agreed to invite Penrose Fitzgerald, the Conservative MP for the borough of Cambridge who was also a prominent Cork unionist and active in resisting the Plan of Campaign. From the point of view of Home Rule supporters, the notion of inviting Fitzgerald may have seemed the line of least resistance; perhaps their opponents fastened upon such a readily available politician to test the sincerity behind the arguments for inviting outside speakers. In the event, Penrose Fitzgerald continued to sit for Cambridge until 1906, but he never addressed the Union. The Committee also agreed that visitor debates on Home Rule should be adjourned to a second week so that guest speakers could be heard on both sides of the issue, the implication being that a direct clash of opinions should be avoided. Stanford was present at the meeting and succeeded in carrying a further proviso: invitations should only be extended to members of the Cambridge Union or its affiliated societies.[31] Since the chief affiliated societies were the Oxford Union and the Literary and Historical Society at Trinity College Dublin, Stanford's amendment effectively closed the door on the Parnellites, most of whom hailed from very different educational and religious backgrounds.

When the Union Committee next met, on 30 May 1887, Stanford was absent, probably in London, where he also taught at the Royal College of Music. Pressed by two active Liberals, the Committee decided that to set aside his ban on outside speakers in order to invite Thomas Sexton, a noted Nationalist orator whose formal education had terminated when he had escaped from the mercies of the Christian Brothers. The rest of the story sounds like a cross between Tammany Hall and Byzantium. The proposed invitation was referred to a hastily convened business meeting two days later, where it narrowly failed to secure the required three-quarters majority. Garrett then successfully demanded a poll, a referendum of all members of the Union, on a motion to invite Sexton along with Edward Saunderson, the Ulster scourge of the Home Rulers. On grounds of simple efficiency, it made sense for the poll to take place at the same time as the termly elections for new officers and Committee. The poll was duly called to coincide with the elections – which were scheduled for the very next day. This effectively gave Garrett the advantage of surprise over his opponents.[32] Furthermore, canvassing to encourage members to turn out for the poll was a discreet cover for mobilising support behind favoured candidates for the Committee. Stanford returned to Cambridge a day or so later to find that not only had his safeguards been swept aside, but the Union's gentlemanly electoral traditions had been set at naught.

There ensued an angry exchange of letters from which neither Stanford nor Garrett emerges with much credit. The *Dictionary of National Biography* neutrally observes that the composer "was easily led by his fiery temperament into indiscretions of utterance".[33] Perhaps he counteracted the Victorian tendency to equate the cultural with the effeminate by playing up the rival stereotype of the combative Irishman. However, there was nothing contrived about his anger on this occasion. A little reflection might have persuaded Stanford that it was unwise to embark on a thunderous denunciation of a young man of 21, and all the more so if the target of his wrath affected contemptuous indifference.

Stanford opened with the portentous announcement that if he had been in Cambridge on the night of the change-of-officers debate, he would have opposed the customary vote of thanks to the retiring President. In a deftly contemptuous choice of words, Garrett managed to imply that plain cowardice accounted for his opponent's failure to argue his case in person. Stanford laid much emphasis on alleged manipulation of the referendum, alleging that the fact that he had not received an official notification of the poll was evidence of "an underhand proceeding". The core of his charge was that "the whole arrangement was made in order to provide a political platform for one of the Irish party" and the invitation to Saunderson had been tacked on merely "to lend an air of apparent fairness". Garrett barely troubled to rebut the allegations and implied that he could not even be bothered to brand Stanford as a liar. His allegations, he contemptuously remarked, could be dismissed "very briefly in a monosyllable".[34] In the exchange of unpleasantness, the angry professor had undoubtedly come off second best but, in a broader sense, it was Stanford who carried the day. The Conservative Sir John Gorst was the star turn at the adjourned Home Rule debate on 14 June 1887. Sexton never did speak at the Cambridge Union, and it was to be eight years before another member of the Irish party appeared at the despatch box.

After seven passionate debates on Home Rule in 22 months, a year passed before the Union made a more mechanical return to the issue in October 1888. "No session of the Union would be complete without a discussion of the Irish question," remarked the proposer of the motion. Adopting a new style of informal reporting, the *Cambridge Review* observed that "there were hon. members enough prepared to assist in the discharge of this sacred task". Enough, no doubt, but the attendance was well below the audiences that Home Rule had drawn the previous year, and barely a quarter of the numbers who voted at the following debate on disestablishment. Home Rule itself was moving out of focus, being replaced by an omnibus motion that urged the Salisbury government to couple the "extension of Local Self-Government" with the expenditure of "a large sum of money" on public works and land purchase. "Local Self-Government" may have seemed a less threatening formula in the light of the establishment of county councils in England and Wales, but it did not win universal approval. An Ulster member claimed from "personal observation" that Local Boards in Ireland were incapable "of transacting any business .... They usually began with whiskey and ended with fighting." The motion was defeated by 46 votes to 19. The previous week, in an almost identical division of 43 votes to 17, the Union had refused to support the reintroduction of the stocks for minor offences.[35] Once again, Ireland was ceasing to be a serious concern.

To restore interest, in March 1889 the Union once again resorted to a set-piece debate featuring visiting speakers. The motion condemned "the policy and conduct" of the Salisbury government "in the administration of Irish affairs", a further shift away from a specific focus upon Home Rule. Liberals and Parnellites were moving into closer alliance. A Special Commission had been established to investigate allegations made by *The Times* of Parnell's complicity in agrarian violence in Ireland. Under pressure of cross-examination, which included proof that he could not spell, Richard Pigott had confessed to the forgery of documents upon which this hapless and incompetent piece of journalism had been based. In a wave of English fair play, Parnell was suddenly hailed as the victim of a conspiracy while Pigott fled to Madrid and shot himself. It seems that there was no problem in securing two high-profile Liberal speakers, R.C. Lehmann and Frank Lockwood. However, despite his "strenuous efforts" to secure "a counter-blast to the Gladstonian visitors", the President, F.H. Maugham, was forced to take on the role of main opposition speaker himself.

Lehmann was a former President of the Union, who had in fact spoken against Home Rule in 1877. He was now an aspiring Liberal activist, and had recently founded the *Granta* at Cambridge. He did finally get into parliament in 1906, and his name is included among that lost legion of Liberals whom Asquith would have sent to the House of Lords in 1911 had the peers continued to resist the Parliament Act. However, his real enthusiasm was always for the river, and perhaps it is because he retired to a house by the Thames and continued to mess about with boats that Lehmann seems eternally to belong to the world of the *Wind in the Willows* rather than the era of the Plan of Campaign. Indeed, on that March evening Lehmann was not the chief attraction.

Frank Lockwood had come up to Cambridge in 1865 intending to take orders in the Church of England, but he was a product of a decade that saw a marked swing towards the secular, and he opted for a career in the Law instead. A witty and confident court-room performer, who became a national figure as defence counsel in the sensational murder trial of the burglar Charlie Peace, Lockwood was bitten late by the bug of politics. He had never taken part in Union debates as an undergraduate but, after two failed attempts, he was elected to parliament as a Liberal in 1885. Later he endured the frustrating experience of representing Katharine O'Shea in the Parnell divorce case, and in 1894 Lord Rosebery made him Solicitor-General. Like so many others, he died young, at the age of 51 in 1897. In 1889, he was the star attraction who drew a packed house.

"Every seat was occupied, a crowd of members stood at the entrance, and the gallery was crammed." The evening was less a debate than a series of brilliant lectures. Lehmann spoke for fifty minutes, Lockwood for "close upon an hour". Although Lockwood courteously congratulated Maugham upon his "able debating speech", it was clear that the Liberals had outgunned their opponents. Lack of time limited the numbers who could speak, but Maugham was unlucky in being supported only by the two rising Ulstermen, Malcolm MacNaghten, the future judge and the ebullient (and, on this occasion, absurd) E.W. MacBride.

Maugham dealt with the Pigott forgeries with what the *Granta* not unreasonably called a "somewhat remarkable" argument. Parnell, he argued, "ought to consider himself the most fortunate of men for having had the authorship of the forged letters imputed to him by *The Times*, since otherwise he would never have been able to clear himself of the charge". The anti-Home Rule case was reduced to scoring points at the expense of Dr Tanner, the Parnellite member for Mid-Cork, who was widely believed (not least by his own party colleagues) to be mad. Lehmann had excused Tanner's overwrought public utterances by explaining that "his occasional deviations from moderation in conduct and language were due rather to the warmth of his heart and the ardour of his patriotism than to any other cause". Maugham retorted that "it was almost impossible to say which was the deviation, and which was the ordinary course of that gentleman".

The debate was adjourned to a second week to redress the balance and, unusually, there was no decline in the size of the audience. The house was treated to another hour-long address, this time from W.F. Maclean, who was a lawyer, a Liberal Unionist MP and a Cambridge graduate. Alfred Mond was among the student speakers who sought to neutralise his impact, but without success. The motion was defeated by 310 votes to 115. "The most pessimistic Unionist will find satisfaction in these figures," commented the *Granta*. "Settled convictions cannot be lightly uprooted," said the *Cambridge Review*, adding that "so far as the main issue is concerned ... the position is very much the same as it used to be".[36] The point was underlined by the fact that that this was only the second time in the Union's history that over four hundred members had taken part in a division.

The "main issue", of course, was Home Rule, which the Union once again discussed a year later, in February 1890, "as the only final settlement" for Ireland. "The Irish Question may be a well-worn subject," remarked the *Cambridge Review*, "but it is still capable of producing a very good debate." More to the point, it was well attended even though there were no prominent visitors. The debate began on a high note, with a "magnificent display of rhetoric" from the proposer, F.R. Keightley of Corpus. For three-quarters of an hour, the "crowded house listened entranced", although there was some puzzlement when he claimed that there were only 113 paupers in the whole of Ireland. Once again, the main opposition case was shouldered by the two Ulstermen, MacNaghten and MacBride. MacNaghten poured "much scorn on the words 'final' and 'settlement'". MacBride spoke at a "tremendous speed ... which made it extremely difficult to follow him". The *Granta*, not always vocal in admiration of MacBride, praised his "sound and logical defence" of the union between Ireland and Britain, during which he called the Irish peasantry a "lazy dissolute race" and dismissed the Parnellite party as "eighty-six bog-trotting ruffians". In the circumstances, it is best to draw a veil over the report that in its later stages, the debate "fell off appreciably". The motion was rejected by 133 votes to 47. Opposition to Home Rule, at 74 percent, was at its highest since the tense days of 1882-83. "Once again the Union has proved itself Unionist to the core by the decisive rejection of a Home Rule motion," commented the *Granta*.[37]

A year after the unmasking of Pigott, the Special Commission finally published a balanced report on the charges against Parnell and his party. Naturally, the more extreme allegations were dismissed, but individual Nationalists were found to have behaved irresponsibly during the Plan of Campaign. "I think it is just about what I should have said myself", was Parnell's private comment.[38] Conservatives made a brief attempt to keep the issue alive but, by and large, it suited all sides to claim a victory and move on. Not so at Cambridge. The Special Commission's timing had been inconvenient, the publication of its report following hard on the heels of the Home Rule debate of February 1890. Yet there did seem to be an obsessive tenacity in re-opening the subject at the start of the third term, late in April 1890. MacNaghten, now President, was no doubt determined to have his pound of Parnellite flesh. (In his later career he would become an Ulster Unionist MP and later a judge.)

The debate was not a success. "The perennial Irish question failed to attract a large House" and many speeches were "rendered somewhat dull by the frequency of quotations" from the report. The proposer, A.C. Deane of Clare, had the good sense to deliver a speech "judiciously cut shorter than usual". Deane claimed to be "heartily glad" that Parnell had been "excused from the worst charges that had been made against him" but insisted that "because a man is absolved of greater crimes", he was not necessarily acquitted of lesser offences. MacBride "electrified the assembly" by claiming to be descended from the leader of an Irish insurrection (presumably in 1798) and proclaiming that his ancestors "would turn in their graves could they see the modern patriot". Once again, "the debate fell off rapidly" later in the evening. Despite the advocacy of C.P. Trevelyan, who would serve in Britain's first two Labour cabinets, the

Union agreed by 61 votes to 33 that "the Irish Party stands condemned by the report of the Special Commission". [39]

By contrast, there was a "full house" on 4 November 1890 for a motion censuring "the late conduct of the Irish executive". The wording was ungracious, given Balfour's increasing willingness to smother Ireland with kindness, and the large attendance was explained partly by a rumour that there would be a clash between two popular ex-Presidents, MacNaghten and the Eton schoolboy hero, J.K. Stephen. In the event, neither of them spoke, but MacBride rumbled forth as usual. "Unintelligible at first, his remarks gradually assumed the form of a speech." Typically, he declared that Ulster was the "only respectable part of Ireland", and that in the rest of the country the people spent their time "lying around or shooting or batoning the police". The *Cambridge Review* found him "amusing and eloquent", but did not venture to claim that he was informative. Another speaker claimed to possess "a knock-down argument for Home Rule" but nobody seemed to know what it was. The audience melted away. By half past ten, there were barely fifty members present and proceedings were adjourned. [40]

Unexpectedly, the resumed debate on 11 November was "fertile in good speeches" and "a distinct success", with well over two hundred members staying for the vote. One possible explanation lies in rising speculation about the Parnell divorce case, which began to be reported a few days later. Deane had referred to the running joke in *Punch*, which characterised the Leader of the House of Commons, W.H. Smith, as "Old Morality", adding that Smith was to be preferred to "the 'young immorality' which so characterized the Gladstonian ranks". This was guilt by association with a vengeance. The *Granta* felt that the failings of the two principal speakers cancelled each other out. The proposer, T.A. Bertram of Caius, had done well enough but "if the latter half of his speech had not so seriously contradicted the first half, the effect perhaps would have been more marked". MacNaghten, who spoke against, was criticised for including a fifteen-minute peroration in a twenty-five minute speech, although he made an impact with his warning that Gladstone in office would mean Parnell in power. The motion was defeated by 153 votes to 64, the 70 percent majority consistent with the general division of opinion against Home Rule. [41]

In 1891, the year of Parnell's death, the Union did not turn its attention to Ireland at all. This was the first blank in the record since 1876, and the following year was not much more fruitful. In June 1892, two months before Gladstone returned to office, an attempt was made to inject some novelty into the Irish question by a motion approving "of an armed rising in Ulster in the event of a Home Rule Bill becoming law". The debate was a failure. It clashed with too many May Week events, producing "a very small House and a large gallery". Worse still, the proposer arrived fifteen minutes late, "in rather a bad temper" and tried to make up for his unpunctuality by speaking at "an incredible speed". A majority of 41 votes to 18 against the motion suggests that the Union agreed with the opposing speaker who "denied that Ulster can be called a nationality". (The proposer and seconder were to register a similar defeat, by 38 votes to 15, two months later when they invited a Long Vacation audience to regret "the prevalence of the habit of Smoking in this University".) [42]

However, in May 1893, the Union took a more benevolent view of the concerns of Ireland's most northerly province, a small house dismissing by 53 votes to 25 the motion that "popular demonstrations – especially those in Ulster – are either dangerous or useless, and ought to be abolished". (There was, of course, some difference between popular demonstrations and an armed rising, even in Ulster.) "The chief fault of the debate", pronounced the *Cambridge Review*, "... was its discursiveness." The *Granta* agreed, criticising the chair for allowing speakers "to roam at their own sweet will over the whole range of Irish history, of Irish politics and other questions still more remotely connected with the announced subjects". However, with Ulster as the theme and MacBride as its champion, the evening was not dull:

> Beginning with the ancient kings of Ireland, he panted down the ages, now wildly abusing the Roman Catholic Hierarchy, now denouncing the universal ignorance which prevails outside Ulster, and now arrogating civilisation to Ulstermen alone, that solid body of Anglo-Saxon settlers imported into the middle of Celtic barbarism.

His eloquent and fiery speech was "evidently inspired by a genuine feeling that saved it from being mere rant". It is unlikely that MacBride's tirade helped those present to any real understanding of Ulster Protestant mentalities. Indeed, the speeches from the opposition were generally condemned for being "violently ulsteric". One speaker conceded that "a revolution that was a spontaneous eruption was justifiable, and even exalted, but one that was incited was deplorable". Another disagreed, pointing to the safety-valve argument. "If we force Ulster to be silent we shall have a revolution."[43]

If there had indeed been a shift in sympathy towards Ulster between the two debates, it was to be attributed to the re-emergence of Home Rule as a practical issue. As MacNaghten had warned, the general election of 1892 had produced a minority Liberal government dependent upon Irish Nationalist support. Table Five indicates that in the early nineties, Home Rule remained a straight party issue.

Gladstone unveiled his Second Home Rule Bill on 13 February 1893; eight days later the Union addressed the motion that it would prove to be "no settlement of the Irish Question" and "beneficial neither to England nor Ireland".

The *Granta* proudly observed that Cambridge undergraduates "certainly cannot be accused of want of interest in politics": it was estimated that almost six hundred of them packed the chamber, drawn by a rumour that Edward Saunderson was to speak. Instead, they heard a little-known Liberal MP, William Allen, who "spoke in hexameters", offering a "stormy defence of Home Rule without saying much on the Bill". Indeed, throughout the evening, it was "no Bill, and anything but the Bill that was debated upon". In "a speech that would seem better read than heard", the student proposer briefly condemned its terms, criticising the dual system which would subject Ireland to the control of Tim Healy at one moment and to a Tory government in London the next, and predicting that no Dublin cabinet would survive more than six months. MacBride took up his familiar position in the last ditch, ready to pulverise anyone who challenged him. In retrospect, probably the most notable feature of the debate was a thoughtful rejection of the idea of a federal relationship between Britain and Ireland from Erskine Childers. The motion was carried by 267 votes to 122, a wholly predictable 69 percent majority against, in the largest division since Frank Lockwood's visit four years earlier.[44]

While opposition to the Second Home Rule Bill ran at levels identical to the First, the controversy of 1893 failed to sustain the intensity of the crisis of 1886. Gladstone's measure dragged its way through the House of Commons but, apart from the moderately attended debate in May on the tangential issue of Ulster demonstrations, the Cambridge Union left the question alone. Home Rule was massively rejected in the Lords on 8 September, but the ensuing autumn term saw no attempt to discuss either the Bill itself or the controversial question of the powers of the upper house, as had happened when the peers had sought to interfere with the Land Act in 1881-82. The Liberal retreat from the incubus of its Irish commitment was as evident among Cambridge students as it was among Gladstone's cabinet colleagues. The Cambridge Union fell back upon the strategy of inviting a front-rank politician to bring in a crowd. The MP for Waterford, John Redmond, agreed to speak on 6 March 1894.

It might have been a memorable evening, had Redmond not withdrawn "at the last minute". On 3 March, Gladstone retired, and within forty-eight hours, Rosebery had succeeded him in office. The political world waited to learn whether the new prime minister intended to make another attempt to secure Home Rule. The issue of co-operation with the Liberals was especially acute for John Redmond, leader of the Parnellite wing of the shattered Irish Party and thus inheritor of the dead Chief's Gladstonian alliance. On 11 March, Rosebery defined his position; Home Rule was only feasible if accepted by "England as the pre-dominant member of the Three Kingdoms".[45] The admission represented both a political blunder and a political truism: 465 of the 670 members of parliament were returned from English constituencies, and England remained unenthusiastic towards Irish Home Rule. It was no doubt true that the change of prime minister rendered it necessary for Redmond to return "to Ireland on most urgent business".[46] Equally, on 6 March 1894, Redmond had little to gain and much to lose from a confrontation with the entrenched unionist sentiments of England's future ruling caste.

At short notice, the Union arranged a set-piece debate that pitted two dons who argued that "justice and expediency" required Home Rule against two ex-Presidents. They held the full house to the end, but it was tacitly agreed that the debate would be confined to the four gladiators. As the *Cambridge Review* put it, "it was virtually impossible to say anything new on such a painfully worked out theme ... one of which everybody is notoriously weary". Not surprisingly, the evening resulted in "the usual overwhelming majority against Home Rule for Ireland". Indeed, both the attendance and the result virtually duplicated the debate of the previous year. The motion was dismissed by 261 votes to 133.[47] Slightly under 69 percent of the 389 students who had taken part in the 1893 division had voted against Home Rule. In 1894, that percentage had slipped to just over 66 percent in a house of 394. In effect, nine young men out of almost four hundred had shifted towards the Irish cause. Given the accidental nature of the "sample", the difference is hardly significant.

By the time Redmond made good his promise to speak, at the end of February 1895, even the terms of the motion reflected the bolting of the stable door: "the abandonment of Home Rule by the Government" was hailed as "the best solution of the Irish Question". MacBride was felled by influenza and unable to confront the visitor. In his absence, the motion was proposed by the incoming President, Montagu Butler (father of R.A. Butler), but not surprisingly Redmond massively outshone the handful of student speakers. As the *Granta* put it, "the most graceful of our academic speakers may be excused if he seemed to fail" by comparison. Redmond delivered "a magnificent speech, strong in its moderation, and convincing in its earnestness". He appealed to the example of Canada, self-governing and prosperous notwithstanding its mixture of peoples and creeds, adding:

> "I am", he said, impressively, amid an expectant hush, "a Catholic, and if I thought that Home Rule would interfere with the rights of my Protestant fellow-countrymen, I would cease to be a Home Ruler."

Redmond failed to defeat the motion, but the *Granta* noted that the margin of defeat was narrower than usual, 237 votes to 180. Since opposition to Home Rule fell by about ten points, to 57 percent, Redmond's impact seems to have been similar to that of Dillon nine years earlier. "He seemed to present the old question in a new light; and caused many opponents to consider how far

their opposition was based on conviction, and how far on prejudice." The
Cambridge Review was more noncommittal. It was "always interesting to hear a
man on the subject which forms his life-work" and especially so "when he is so
eloquent and earnest a speaker". None the less, "we were discussing a question
which at the moment had lost its pressing importance".[48]   Perhaps most
significant of all was the fact that Redmond's tour-de-force on a dormant issue
had still proved insufficient to win over a majority among the young elite of the
United Kingdom's predominant member state.

Four set-piece debates on Ireland in six years had attracted consistently
massive attendances, with the numbers voting ranging from a low of 389 to a
high of 425. The only issue that was remotely comparable as a source of
controversy was the decision of the London County Council to close a popular
music hall, which drew 331 members to a protest vote in November 1894. Yet
the *Cambridge Review* was right. Redmond's visit marked more of a requiem
than a revival in the consideration of Home Rule in Cambridge. Two years were
to pass before the Union turned its attention to Ireland again. It was the report of
the Financial Commission in 1897 that broke the silence with a motion viewing
"with disfavour any attempt to break up the existing Union between England
and Ireland" or – as the *Granta* put it, "our old friend Home Rule". The link
between Irish finance and Irish devolution was by no means straightforward.
Gladstone had indeed promised the Commission as a step towards untangling
the funding of a Home Rule settlement, and Rosebery had gone on with it as a
way out of the devolution imbroglio. The Commission's findings, which began
to leak out during 1896, were at least an embarrassment, if not a bombshell. Its
first chairman had been the former President of the Cambridge Union, Hugh
Childers, who had died while the enquiry was in progress, but not before he had
become persuaded that Ireland was substantially overtaxed. To argue from this,
as did John Morley, that the solution lay in Home Rule was essentially to return
to the opening problem that Gladstone had hoped to solve: what share of the
common revenue of the United Kingdom ought to be handed to an autonomous
Dublin executive? Yet the principal lines of argument open to those seeking to
rebut the implications of the Financial Commission's report literally made a
mockery of the United Kingdom that they sought to defend. One was that the
United Kingdom was a single state in which it was impossible to apportion
either burdens or advantages by kingdom or county or parish. The other was that
if the Irish drank less whiskey, they would not contribute so much to the
Treasury through indirect taxation.

Such arguments made light of the genuine anger that swept Ireland in
the aftermath of the Commission's report. By the time of the Cambridge debate a
shared sense of injustice threatened to create a cross-community political
alliance. Edward Saunderson was as outraged as Tim Healy, and Lord

Castletown, a former Conservative MP, warned that the American colonies had been lost because of a dispute over taxation. In the Cambridge Union, even the Honourable Henry Prittie, son of the Tipperary landlord Lord Dunally, weighed in to defend the Commission. So did Cecil de Burgh Persse, "an indignant Irishman" from Glenarde in County Galway, who "condemned the gross ignorance of Englishmen" and "urged the claim of Ireland to be considered an independent nation". Persse continued to be both proud of his identity and indignant in the defence of small nations: he was nearly forty when the First World War broke out, but he joined the Irish Guards and was killed in 1915. The debate attracted the "largest House of the term", but this was not saying much since debates were temporarily in the doldrums and few topics attracted more than one hundred members. More surprising to observers was the fact that Newnham and Girton packed the gallery. The motion was carried by 57 votes to 37, the 61 percent majority suggesting a conventional vote against Home Rule, irrespective of the validity of Irish grievances, but in a notably smaller house than had been seen in earlier years.[49]

In November 1897, the Union degenerated into an episode of apparent bad taste. Indeed, even the proposer of the motion regretting "the existence of the Irish Nation" was sufficiently embarrassed to explain that he had agreed to take part in order to enable the Vice-President, Thomas McDonnell, to attack stereotypes "which he had opposed from childhood upwards with great success". The elder of two brothers from St Paul's School in London, both of whom rose to the Presidency of the Union, McDonnell was a dedicated champion of all things Irish, so long as they were Nationalist and Catholic: "anyone standing up for Ireland was always in difficulty, as he had to contend against prejudice". He had taken his pet motion on the circuit of college debating societies, but its frivolity did not translate well to the larger stage of the Union. Inclined to the histrionic, McDonnell delivered his "clever speech" with dramatic effect, although the audience was "astonished when he portrayed the Irish members as a solid brotherhood of patriots". Although by the eighteen-nineties, it was a "rare event" to challenge the terms of a motion, members responded to an unsatisfactory situation with "the unusual proceeding of an amendment directed essentially against Irish political methods". By 82 votes to 64, they resolved to regret "the continued existence of certain Members of the Irish Nation". The qualification was directed against Tammany Hall and the Irish parliamentary party, and the adjective "continued" carried the specific meaning that "we do not mind their existence if only we can get rid of them when we want to". After the passage of the amendment, the debate simply disintegrated. As a result of a "peculiar lack of members at the end", no final vote was recorded.[50] One can only hope that they had all slunk away in embarrassment at having participated in such an absurd discussion.

The last Union debate of the Gladstonian era took place in February 1898 and, like the first discussion of Home Rule twenty-five years earlier, it drew a distinction between "approving of the granting of a system of Local Government to Ireland" and opposition to "any legislation tending towards Home Rule". Salisbury's government had announced legislation to extend the system of county councils to Ireland, an example of a contradiction within unionist thinking, which at one moment justified separate treatment for Ireland as the price of its inclusion within the United Kingdom, while at the next insisting on identical institutions as the theoretical corollary of integration. With Thomas McDonnell as the principal speaker against the motion, the debate focused upon Home Rule. The fact that the motion was defeated, if only by a single vote in a division of 91 members, is not easy to interpret. Possibly some members objected to any form of local democracy for the Irish and felt it safe to vote against a motion condemning Home Rule simply because the larger issue seemed safely dead. Overall, however, the most striking feature of the debate was its triviality. Ireland had often aroused strong feelings in the Cambridge Union. Now the contemptuous attitudes triggered by McDonnell's ill-judged motion surfaced again: Ireland was little more than a target for derision.

The debate drew "a languid House", reported the *Cambridge Review*. "The cause lies no doubt in the sound knowledge of the subject which the majority of us imagine we possess and the profound boredom thereby induced." "The Debate was about as dull as the subject", agreed the *Granta*. "In all the speeches argument was the last consideration." Even by its own account, this was not wholly true. The proposer of the motion, William Finlay, was the son of R.B. Finlay, a prominent Liberal Unionist who had replaced Frank Lockwood as Solicitor-General when Salisbury had returned to office in 1895. Taking advantage of the fact that Gladstone was now safely in retirement, he risked lauding the Grand Old Man: "two Cabinets and the greatest political genius of the century had been unable to set forth a really adequate scheme". Another speaker "laid great stress on the danger that Ireland, if autonomous, would threaten in time of war". An Indian student was criticised for levity but contributed the bright thought that the "only maxim for the Irish that England could give was the Maxim gun".

Home Rule, the *Granta* pronounced bluntly, was "defunct". More than twice as many members had turned out a fortnight earlier to hear a young History graduate from Trinity, G.M. Trevelyan, denounce the injustice of the Dreyfus case. Yet perhaps the single most depressing feature of the Home Rule debate of February 1898 "was the Irish brogue, real or feigned, which so many speakers affected".[51] The Cambridge Union had often shown itself indifferent and even insensitive to Ireland and its needs. Yet this seems to have been the sole debate in the hundred years under review that sank to the level of merely treating the sister island as a subject for juvenile mirth. Five years would pass before the Union once again debated Home Rule. Somewhere in that interval there are the first signs of a sea-change in attitudes that at least ensured that Edwardian Cambridge treated Ireland with the dignity that it deserved.

King's Parade 1896

10: Ireland in the New Century

If the debates of 1897-98 represented a low point in the Cambridge Union's consideration of Irish issues, they were at least followed by a decade characterised by shifts in opinion towards more liberal attitudes. To some extent, moderating views may be attributable to revulsion against the jingo high tide of the Boer War. They are probably also related to continuing gradual broadening in the social composition of the undergraduate population. However, neither social change nor the extent to which opinions changed should be exaggerated. Debates on Ireland rarely drew large audiences throughout the Edwardian period. Yet in some respects, the movement of opinion was remarkable. Between May 1899 and January 1902 – almost exactly the span of the Boer War – the Union shifted from condemnation to endorsement of the idea of a Catholic university in Ireland. A recent scholar has suggested that "the university problem appeared to trouble British consciences more than it aroused nationalist feeling"[1] but, even so, Protestant and traditional Cambridge is perhaps not the most obvious place to find those consciences stirring. One possibility is that the greater, although still slight, presence of Catholic students at Cambridge after the removal of the Church ban in 1895 helped dissipate prejudice against their faith, the more so since the cost of attending the University ensured that they were drawn from the same social groups as their Protestant contemporaries.

Back in October 1889, the Union had unsurprisingly disapproved "of any Government aid being given to Sectarian Education in Ireland", with E.W. MacBride from Belfast and Lord Corry from Fermanagh helping the motion to victory by 55 votes to 37. Although the *Cambridge Review* thought that "the subject was one which suited the society very well for debating purposes, since the usual party divisions were broken up", the 60 percent vote in favour was consistent with the majorities regularly registered in the late eighteen-eighties against concession in Ireland.[2] Ten years later, in May 1899, the Union considered a proposal to "establish a University in Ireland to meet the special needs of Roman Catholics". The issue drew "an average May Term house" (summer term attendances were usually thin) and generated "a little better than average debate". The dedicated but histrionic Thomas McDonnell supported the motion, but he was opposed by, among others, by Cecil Persse. The "indignant Irishman" of the Financial Commission debate two years earlier did not on this occasion see any need to meet the requirements of the majority of the country's people. One reporter condemned the audience for being unusually supine, but a

58 percent vote against the motion (42 votes to 30) suggested that the opposition of the silent majority of Cambridge students to sectarian education in Ireland had barely moved in ten years.[3]

The consistency of attitudes shown in 1889 and 1899 makes all the more remarkable the debate of January 1902, when a motion sympathising "with the claims of the Irish Roman Catholics to a University" was passed after "a very long and interesting debate" which "created considerable interest". The speakers, who included a "strong Irish element", were congratulated on managing "to keep controversial theology at a distance", and one attack on the Catholic priesthood was condemned by the *Granta* as "in very bad taste" – although, it acknowledged, probably true. The usual negative stereotypes were aired. One young orator announced that "when the Irish had nothing to grumble at they would grumble at it purely for the love of grumbling". Another claimed that "the only business concerns which prospered in Ireland" were Guinness's brewery, Jameson's distillery and the priesthood. There is nothing surprising about such attitudes. What is remarkable is that, for once, they were rejected. Thomas McDonnell had graduated, but his younger brother, Michael, had succeeded him as champion of Irish causes. "Even if Ireland were priest-ridden, which he did not grant, it was better that the priesthood should be educated." The campaign for a Catholic university was endorsed by 66 votes to 48.[4] It is true that a sympathetic Royal Commission was preparing the way for public recognition of Catholic claims in higher education. However, Union opinion had managed to resist the implications of the Financial Commission report five years earlier.

This shift in attitudes was confirmed the following year, when a motion arguing that "the establishment of a University for Roman Catholics in Ireland would be for the best interests of that country" was passed even more emphatically, by 100 votes to 51. Opposition to the idea had fallen from 58 to 34 percent in four years, although the margin was probably partly to be explained by the presence of a popular guest speaker, Sir Horace Plunkett. The motion was proposed by the outgoing President, J.C. Arnold, an Irishman and a Liberal, who insisted on a continuing debt of honour. "The mere granting of a measure of land reform was not enough to make England even with Ireland." Plunkett, who received a magnificent ovation, made "a deep impression" with "the speech of the evening". The *Granta* commented that he was "not perhaps an eloquent speaker, but he has a great gift of earnestness and speaks from practical experience".[5]

The Catholic University was not the only issue to produce more open attitudes. In May 1902, Hugh Law, MP for West Donegal, found himself in the unprecedented position for a Nationalist visitor of being on the winning side. After "a memorable debate", the Union decided by 64 votes to 53 that it regretted "the action of the Government in returning to a system of coercion in Ireland". The motion was a touch overblown: Balfour's Chief Secretary, George Wyndham, was hardly engaged in a full-scale campaign of repression. However, the claim by opponents of the motion that his policy was "not true Coercion" provoked a histrionic response from J.C. Arnold. "'I tremble,' said Mr Arnold with tears in his voice, 'to think what true coercion would be!'" The strategy of the proposition was to make light of rural discontent in Ireland, stressing that "the peasantry had not resorted to crime". Michael McDonnell argued that boycotting was "precisely the system employed by lawyers and doctors" within their own professions. As for victims of social exclusion, a "pro-Boer was worse off in Birmingham!" (The pro-Boer David Lloyd George had narrowly escaped lynching at an anti-war meeting in Joseph Chamberlain's home city a few months earlier.) In any case, McDonnell claimed, only seven people in the whole of Ireland had been targeted by boycotters. Arnold scornfully rammed the point home. "If seven people out of five million got their groceries from the Royal Irish Constabulary, that was no reason for suspending the British Constitution."

The nature of Irish identity was a running theme throughout the debate. In "an admirable speech", Hugh Law rebutted the case for Coercion and cited examples of the injustices that it created. "To elegance, clearness, and evident sincerity, he added a charm of manner which contributed much to the great effect of his words." Law was a product of Oxford, someone who could present Irish nationalism in a manner that made it acceptable to a gathering of young English gentlemen. By contrast, when William Dobbs of Trinity "spoke as an Irishman opposed to the aims of the Nationalists", an attempt was made to deny his own self-definition. A supporter of the motion "called attention to the origin of Irishmen on the other side, and declared that the North could hardly be called Ireland". This was unfair on Dobbs who, despite the Ulster antecedence of his surname, hailed from Castlecomer in County Kilkenny. It was one of several indications in the Edwardian years that the Ascendancy, for so long regarded in Cambridge as the legitimate voice of the sister island, was becoming tarred with an Ulster brush and so marginalised, its claim to be Irish denied, and its demand to be simultaneously considered British increasingly dismissed. It was presumably Ulster particularism to which Edwin Montagu referred, in a "pleasant speech" in which he offered a "solution for the Irish question, in which a canal and a bridge played leading parts". Ulster Protestantism and by extension, unionism in general were in the process of being excluded from the Irish scene.

It is a measure of the change in the focus of Irish issues since 1893 that the 1902 debate on Coercion was not a surrogate discussion of Home Rule. Montagu, who opposed both Home Rule and Coercion, seems to have been one of the few speakers even to mention the issue. Even with a partial separation of the two issues, the condemnation of Coercion was in sharp contrast to the unwavering desire to crush Irish discontent manifested until the end of the Gladstonian years. Nor was it an accidental vote. "The number of members who remained in the House until nearly midnight, awaiting the division, is proof of the manner in which the interest was sustained." For the first time, the Cambridge Union had rejected Coercion as a response to agrarian unrest in Ireland.[6]

Even more remarkable was the vote in November 1902 in favour of a motion proclaiming that "the Abolition of Landlordism is the only remedy for agrarian discontent in Ireland", albeit by the narrow margin of 77 to 72. The *Granta* attributed the outcome in part to the "real typical eighteenth century Tory point of view" contributed by A.B. Geary, who insisted that there was "no real discontent which calls for sympathy". Yet it is unlikely that a single speech, however ill-judged, could have exercised so much influence on the outcome. Geary was the first opposition speaker in a debate of "record length", and the division did not take place until 11.45. The *Granta* thought the repetition of arguments made the debate "dull ... though illuminated by not infrequent flashes of interest", including "a masterly exhibition of debating skill" from Michael McDonnell. The *Cambridge Review* was more impressed by the quality of "reality" in the Union's Irish debates that was lacking in other topics:

> When Irishmen talk of Ireland they do so with a knowledge of their subject which they have slowly been acquiring from childhood, and with a depth of interest and conviction which it is hard for those who speak on more academical subjects to reach.

We may smile at the thought of young men bringing to bear their life-experience of two whole decades on the insoluble Irish question, but the fact that so large a house remained to the very end (many of them must have been obliged to climb into college after midnight) suggests that they were captured by the issue. Geary's pastiche of Marie Antoinette can hardly have provided the sole reason for their tenacity.[7]

These signs of more open attitudes towards Catholic higher education and Irish land ownership seem to reflect, at least in part, shifts of opinion among a student body that was still predominantly Conservative in its politics. Even so, flexibility had its limits. An attempt in February 1903 to condemn the trial of Arthur Lynch, charged with treason for fighting on the side of the Boers, was thrown out by 118 votes to 30, an outcome that the *Cambridge Review* described as "rather a foregone conclusion". Indeed, the margin suggests that many Liberals joined the majority, despite J.C. Arnold's inspirational appeal.[8] Overall, the Cambridge Union retained a Tory majority right down to the debacle of the 1906 election. A small house did take the unusual step in preferring the Liberals to the Conservative government in May 1902, by just 48 votes to 46, but the rejection of a no-confidence motion six months later by 116 votes to 77 more accurately reflected a continuing Tory tinge of the Cambridge Union. Between November 1902 and March 1906, Conservatives triumphed in eight of the nine divisions on straight party lines, winning the support of between 52 and 65 percent of those voting in houses ranging from 113 to 279, although with signs of declining support after March 1903, when Balfour's government was weakened by divisions over tariffs. At the remaining debate, in November 1904, 443 members turned out to hear Lloyd George – but even then, as Balfour's government staggered towards its fall, 44 percent of them resisted the charms of the Welsh Wizard to remain loyal to the Conservatives.[9]

For the brief period of the disintegration of the Balfour ministry, Irish issues perhaps ceased to be the touchstone of division between the parties. In the debate on Coercion in 1902, Edwin Montagu "spoke as a Liberal, but an opponent of Home Rule". It was another rising Liberal, Maynard Keynes, who in May 1903 moved a motion that hoping "that Home Rule for Ireland is beyond the sphere of practical politics". Omitting to point out that it was five years since the last debate on the issue, the *Cambridge Review* described Home Rule as "a much discussed but ever interesting subject". The *Granta* rated the evening "the best we have had this term". (However, it was only the third meeting of the term, and the previous week had been devoted to the solemn subject of Temperance.) Keynes adopted a "well defined and uncompromising attitude" and a "quiet, fluent, logical" manner, warning that Ireland wanted not devolution but "to be given the status of Canada", a proposition no more attractive in 1903 than it had been when the Union had rejected it back in 1881. Although the prospect of "a display of first class Irish oratory" drew a large attendance for a summer term debate, Michael McDonnell proved a disappointment as the principal opposition speaker. "There is no other member who can crush an illogical or ineffective speaker with such concentrated scorn as Mr McDonnell, but unless he has some such opportunity he is not at his best". Keynes carried his motion, but only by the narrow margin of 57 votes to 51.[10] In 1903, Liberal disenchantment confirmed that Home Rule was indeed beyond the sphere of practical politics, but it had ceased to be the bugbear of the previous decade.

In June 1904, Michael McDonnell marked his retirement from the Presidency with a visitor debate on the uncompromising motion that "the only solution of the Irish Question is to be found in the grant of self-government". Four years later he would publish a book on the subject, which John Redmond in an obliging preface would praise for its sober summary of the case for an Irish parliament. Now he argued his case with unaccustomed moderation, which "rendered it the more powerful", emphasising not so much the wrongs of Ireland as the advantages of Home Rule to England – "even from the lowest point of view – that of accelerating business at Westminster". McDonnell appealed to the successful introduction of elected local councils under the Act of 1898, challenging opponents of Home Rule to cite "a single instance where powers of local government had been abused" – an argument that was to become more controversial in the years ahead. However, the star of the night was his guest speaker, Hilaire Belloc, a former President of the Oxford Union in the process of establishing a reputation as a writer and Liberal party activist. "It is impossible to reproduce on paper the impression Mr Belloc left with the House." The motion was carried, by 68 votes to 49. For the first time, the Cambridge Union had accepted a motion that explicitly called for self-government in Ireland.[11]

The shift in attitudes towards Ireland went hand-in-hand with its demotion as a political priority. Between 1902 and 1905, the numbers voting at debates on Ireland were generally low. Irish issues attracted fewer members than Tariff Reform (which drew an unusually large house of 450 in November 1904), and issues such as the future of the public schools, compulsory Greek and the admission of women to degrees, all of them immediate to Cambridge undergraduates. By contrast, Ireland was remote. The debate on landlordism in November 1902 seems to have exhausted interest in the agrarian question: there was no debate on Wyndham's Land Act, perhaps the single most important piece of British legislation for Ireland since the recognition of tenant right in 1881. In May 1905, the Balfour government's handling of the controversy over Sir Antony MacDonnell's involvement in a devolution scheme was hailed as evidence that "our present system of Governing Ireland is radically unsound", but only by 41 votes to 37. The motion was proposed by C.R. Reddy, the first Indian to be elected an officer of the Union, who claimed that it "was not a Home Rule debate". Indeed, it was not obvious what issue was at stake, and the *Granta* reported that "at some times our representative was almost soothed to sleep". The motion lacked a clear focus, leaving it open to the principal opposing speaker to plead that MacDonnell's only shortcoming was that "he was not extreme enough for Nationalists or Orangemen". Consequently, it was easy to wander off the point: one speaker was congratulated by the *Granta* for his "brilliant remarks" but advised that "it might be a good thing if he studied relevancy a little more". There was a light touch from A.M. Faulkner of Caius, who admitted being an Orangeman but insisted that he "was neither a convict nor a lunatic". Predictably, Faulkner denied that there was anything wrong with the system of government in Ireland, a view contradicted by an avowed nationalist, J.C. Shannon of St John's.[12]

Its sweeping victory at the polls in January 1906 not only confirmed the new Liberal government in power, but seemed to promise a long period in office. The size of the majority meant that the Liberals did not have to rely upon Irish support in the House of Commons, and so – unlike Gladstone's minority administration in 1892 – they could postpone confronting the question of Home Rule. In the event, the new government spent much of its first two years in office attempting to design a moderate form of devolution for Ireland that satisfied nobody. None the less, a Dublin parliament was a good deal closer to the sphere of practical politics than it had been when denounced by Keynes four years earlier.

In October 1906, a motion favouring "the creation of an Irish Representative Assembly with full powers of Self Government" was rejected by 106 votes to 81, the 57 percent vote against Home Rule suggesting a swing back to levels of opposition during the Gladstone years. The *Cambridge Review* regarded it as "an excellent debate all through". To the *Granta*, the outcome was an assertion of normality: "For the nth time Home Rule was discussed, and the champions of the Emerald Isle retreated before the stubborn phalanx of Cambridge Toryism." The motion was proposed by E.G. Selwyn of King's, a brilliant Etonian whose "political creed is Tory Home Rule".[13] Selwyn argued his case with the enthusiasm of a convert. "We must not lay too much stress on the Fenian outrages", he insisted. "If Ireland really desired separation we had no right to stand in their way." He was opposed by F.D. Livingstone, the committed anti-Home Ruler who would verbally pulverise John Dillon in 1909. "The ignorance of the people, fostered and encouraged by priestcraft, had long been the curse of Ireland" he claimed, insisting that the only way forward was to treat the country "as a unit in the Imperial scheme". The *Granta* thought him "unnecessarily bitter", although the *Cambridge Review* credited him with "a lucid sketch of the barbarous state of the Irish people".[14]

Attitudes to Home Rule remained fluid and fairly evenly balanced during the Campbell-Bannerman years. Like Michael McDonnell, whom he invited to speak, Selwyn chose Ireland as the subject for his retirement debate from the Presidency in March 1907, making a "brilliant speech" in support of "the early introduction of a measure giving Home Rule to Ireland". Selwyn argued that Home Rule was necessary because of "the difference between the Anglo-Saxon and the Celt", a line of argument that had more often been employed to support the claim that the former should rule the latter. Given the racial basis of his analysis, there was an element of ambiguity in his confidence that Ulster Protestants "could rely upon their fellow Irishmen for justice". Selwyn's Toryism shone through in his assertion that "the granting of Home Rule would not lead to the dismemberment of the Empire". Presumably he had in mind the recent concession of responsible government to the Transvaal when he insisted that "self-government was the essence of Imperialism".

Selwyn's speech was countered by a display of oratorical fireworks from another ex-President, J.G. Gordon, who somewhat unsportingly claimed that Grattan's parliament had passed 54 Coercion acts in its eighteen-year history. The guest speakers were Stephen Gwynn, an Oxford graduate and Nationalist MP for Galway, who delivered "a most interesting speech", and Viscount Castlereagh, an Irish Conservative who represented the English constituency of Maidstone. In 1915, Castlereagh became seventh Marquess of Londonderry. He served in the first cabinet of Northern Ireland, but is mainly remembered for his alleged partiality to the Nazis. "Lord Castlereagh made a most vigorous and emphatic speech from the Ulster standpoint", arguing that its people "contributed one third of the revenue in Ireland, and ought not to be handed over to the mercies of their foes the Nationalists". He denied Selwyn's implication that Ireland was a colony and rejected imperial analogies as irrelevant to an integral part of the United Kingdom. The debate was top-heavy with set-piece speeches and, as the evening wore on, members were "too tired" to appreciate the final contribution to the debate, a "convincing speech" from Michael McDonnell. Evidently, it was not convincing enough, for Home Rule was narrowly rejected, by 142 votes to 138.[15] By comparison, as Table Six demonstrates, seven straight party divisions between November 1905 and December 1909 recording Conservative support at between 51 and 54 percent. The occasional maverick might break ranks, but overall Home Rule once again triggered divisions on party lines. Although Liberals at Westminster were not rushing to create an Irish parliament, their grass-roots undergraduate supporters seem to have swallowed their doubts and once again accepted Home Rule as an article of faith.

Indeed, when the subject was next discussed in October 1908, a certain sense of fatalism can be detected. "We have heard Home Rule discussed before this," commented the *Granta* in tones of desperation, "and until it is finally given it will be discussed again and again; but never have we been so completely and unutterably bored." It seems that the topic itself was not wholly to blame. G.S. Shaw of Trinity proposed the motion that "Home Rule would be no solution of the Irish problem" in a speech "crammed full of rather disconnected arguments which we have heard before". Worse still, he spoke "with the rise and fall of a parish priest who has lived in the same parish for forty years and … cannot be ejected". The principal opposing speaker, "Comrade Hugh" Dalton, was also dull. In a small enough attendance for the October term, the motion was carried by 77 votes to 65.[16] The 54 percent who voted against Home Rule in the tedious debate of 1908 hardly varied from the 51 percent opposition vote registered in the livelier exchanges of the previous year.

By contrast, the return of John Dillon in June 1909 produced "the largest house that had been seen for some years". The Irish veteran "was given a magnificent reception", itself perhaps a measure of the extent to which Nationalist politicians were no longer regarded as a threat. Dillon dismissed claims that Home Rule had been killed by British kindness: remedial legislation "had been extorted by the Nationalists literally at sword's point". He scorned the argument that devolution was unnecessary because improvements in communications were bringing the two islands steadily closer. "On that analogy we might justify the rule of London over Berlin." The demand for Home Rule "had not yielded to coercion or repression because it was based on a people's will". Young Cambridge was impressed. "Mr Dillon was all that we expected; his eloquence and sincerity made a deep impression".

How far that impression translated into votes cannot be easily measured. As a rough rule of thumb, a distinguished visitor could expect a "swing" of about ten percent to his cause. In this case, the baseline was uncertain, since attitudes to Home Rule had been fluid since the issue had reappeared on the Union agenda in 1903. If hostile majorities of 53 percent and 57 percent registered in 1906 and 1908 represented the starting point, then the impact of Dillon should have been sufficient to carry the motion that "the only effective remedy for the Irish difficulty" was the creation of "a Legislature, with an Executive responsible to it, for the management of purely Irish Affairs". But Dillon did not have the field to himself. He was followed by Hugh Barrie, an Ulster MP born in Scotland, who was one of a group of Irish unionists engaged in putting their case on English platforms. "It was a difficult task to follow Mr Dillon; and Mr Barrie discharged it admirably by his clear and logical speech." However, the performance of the evening came from F.D. Livingstone, the young ex-President who was fervent in his opposition to Home Rule. "An abstract does no justice to Mr Livingstone," reported the *Cambridge Review*, while Dillon himself called it "the best anti-Home Rule speech he had heard since the early Nineties". No fewer than 368 members took part in a massive division, producing the unusual outcome of a tie, with 184 votes on each side. "The voting was sensational".[17]

The inconclusive general elections of 1910 brought Ireland back into practical politics, but does not seem to have altered attitudes. A debate in May 1910 on a motion welcoming "a recent improvement in the outlook of the Irish Home Rule Party" was "unusually brisk and enlivening; there was much real humour and a good deal of cogent argument". The motion was proposed by J.F. Roxburgh who, at the age of 34, would not only become a headmaster but be entrusted with the task of turning one of England's greatest mansions, Stowe, into its last major public school. "Urbane, overflowing with knowledge, possessing the most exquisite sense of humour, he delighted the house whenever he spoke." It was in keeping with the subsequent legend of an autumnal golden age that, years later, Roxburgh should have looked back on his Home Rule debate as "a perfectly gorgeous evening". A contemporary felt that he "never made a wittier speech" than on this May evening, as he objected to the Conservative stereotype of an Irishman as "a cross between a criminal and a lunatic, with violet eyes, and a desire to kill landlords". One by one, Roxburgh denounced a "sturdy brood of Home Rule bogeys", terming them the priest-bogey, the wedge bogey and "the biggest, best-fed, and stupidest bogey" of them all, the claim that Home Rule would lead to separation. A decade of elected local government in Ireland was beginning to produce ammunition for those who doubted Irish capacities to manage their own affairs: "some people won't have Home Rule because the Irish County Councils were broken up by the throwing of ink-pots". Roxburgh brilliantly satirised these doubts under the heading of the ink-pot bogey. "Ink-pots with some races lubricated self-government." The audience was entranced. "One never gets tired of Mr. Roxburgh". But members were not necessarily persuaded by him.

The motion was bleakly opposed by Humphrey Burton, who was on his way to a comfortable career in a Lincolnshire vicarage. Burton insisted that "the outcome of Home Rule must be independence" and argued that in any case a Dublin parliament "was impossible owing to the religious, racial and traditional divisions between the two sections of the Irish people". He did not get much effective support. One young orator "dogmatised benevolently" as he demanded that the Irish be "drilled into loyalty" by firm government. Another demanded a royal commission for some unrecorded purpose "and split four infinitives". Only one speaker "confessed himself an Irishman". He was Ronald Ross of Trinity, who had followed Hugh Dalton in the 1908 debate on Home Rule. Ross replied to a denunciation of Dublin Castle as "the most corrupt and useless bureaucracy in Europe" delivered in a "good fighting speech" by W.A.C. Brooke who, like his elder brother, the legendary poet Rupert, was destined to die in the War. Ross "charmed every one" with his defence of Castle rule, blaming Dublin's Nationalist council for constantly digging up the streets of Ireland's capital and forcing up the local rates. As already noted, the motives of Ulster opponents of Home Rule were increasingly denigrated: in 1906 they had been denounced as "Grand Dukes of Repression and Coercion". Ross, at least, could claim that his loyalty was genuine. He served in the North Irish Horse in the First World War and commanded the regiment on active service in the Second. In 1929 he was elected as Westminster MP for Londonderry, holding his seat until 1951, when he was appointed official representative of the Northern Ireland government in London. He retired in 1957 – a career that began in Edwardian times and stretched to within a decade of the Northern Ireland Troubles.[18]

The result of the May 1910 debate exactly mirrored that of the previous year: the division resulted in a tie, with 56 votes on each side. One reporter regarded this as a coincidence[19] and no doubt there was an element of chance in the exact dead-heat. None the less, the fact of identical divisions among 368 young men in 1909 and 112 of them in 1910 (not to mention the very similar split registered in a house of 280 in 1907) confirms that Cambridge Union debates constitute records of elite opinion and do not simply reflect impulsive gusts in response to clever orations.

It is tempting to attribute the shift of opinion towards the Home Rule cause between 1911 and 1913 to the polarisation of attitudes caused by the second general election over the Lloyd George budget and the issue of the powers of the upper house at the end of 1910. However, this would conflict with the attitudes expressed in two well-attended debates during the election campaign, in which the Union refused by 105 votes to 100 "to identify itself with the cause of Democracy as against the claims of the House of Peers" and then hoped for a Conservative victory by 190 votes to 153.[20] Contemporary accounts imply that persuasive speeches by visiting notables helped Home Rule to victory in the years that followed. All that can be said is that the Union had been relatively unmoved by the oratory of such distinguished outsiders at the time of the First and Second Home Rule Bills. As Table Seven shows, for a brief moment between June 1911 and June 1912, the Conservatives lost their seemingly eternal majority in the Union, falling back to the bedrock of the support of between 42 and 46 percent of its members. This drop in Conservative support might in turn be accounted for by the combination of extremism and ineptitude shown by the party's leadership during the latter stages of the Parliament Act crisis. However, it is striking that this temporary revolt seems to have translated itself into increased enthusiasm for the Liberal policy of Home Rule. Indeed, it appeared within two months of the declarations of support for Balfour and the peers during the election campaign.

In January 1911, Stephen Gwynn returned to argue for "the immediate granting to Ireland of the control of Irish affairs". A Dublin Protestant with an Oxford education, Gwynn represented the acceptable face of nationalism, a rare instance of an Irish MP representing a rational contrast with the extremism of English Tories. Unusually, too, he was the sole visiting speaker, and clearly outgunned all opposition. In "a full and attentive House", he was thought to have made many converts. Since the debate also registered the Union's lowest-ever level of opposition to Home Rule, at 41 percent, it merits detailed consideration.

The motion was proposed by an undergraduate Liberal, P.J. Baker of King's, who later metamorphosed himself into a Labour politician with the more impressive surname of Noel-Baker. He accepted that the question of Home Rule was complicated by Ireland's "geographical position" but argued that the notion that devolution would lead to complete independence was "a Tory bogey". Complete separation was not desired by the Nationalists and in any case could easily be prevented by a written constitution. He claimed that the working of the Irish Local Government Act of 1898 was "evidence of the capacity of Irishmen to govern themselves". The problem of sectarian divisions he dealt with by simple denial, insisting that Liberals had a duty "to disarm religious bigotry by aiding Ireland to achieve her national destiny".

Opening for the opposition, L.P. Napier made a "plucky" speech, contrasting "prosperous loyal Ulster" with "the poor disloyal Catholics". "The only real grievance" had been tackled by the 1903 Land Act, and when land purchase took full effect, "imaginary political grievances could disappear". Napier attempted to neutralise Gwynn, alternately warning against his delusive eloquence, and courteously portraying him as a moderate under whose eventual leadership of the Nationalists, Home Rule might become a risk worth taking.

Gwynn cleverly turned the compliment. If he was a respectable figure in his own country, it was largely because his grandfather had been sentenced to death for leading a rebellion. (He did not mention that that same grandfather, Smith O'Brien, had been President of the Cambridge Union.) "In Ireland if you wished the law to be changed you had first to break it". Supporters of the union "boasted" about the legislation that Westminster had passed to tackle Irish problems, but reforms "had been conceded only in response to violence, and not as a result of argument". Gwynn boldly took his case into the camp of the "Imperialists", the people who regarded Canada as the great success story of self-government in a troublesome dependency. In a clever allusion to Ulster, he called the Dominion "a three-hundred-year-old plantation", inhabited by a mixed population. "Ireland is a nation, and would be welded together by Home Rule like Canada." Indeed, Ireland was "a national civilisation many times as old ... a nationality as distinct as that of the Jewish race." He also confronted the claim that Nationalist agitation in Ireland was an artificial creation funded by "American dollars". "They had only appealed to America when it was clear that their opponents' money would be raised in England." Again, he turned a negative argument inside out. "Home Rule would make Ireland a link instead of a barrier between England and America."

A Conservative politician of equal seniority might well have dented Gwynn's impact, but he was followed by a twenty-year-old undergraduate, whom one reporter found "pleasant and fluent" but another reproved for engaging in "platform oratory". Like Roxburgh, Humfrey Grose-Hodge was destined to become headmaster of a major independent school, although in his case by way of a brief career in the Indian Civil Service. Unlike Roxburgh, he had not emancipated himself from negative stereotypes, and not just those relating to Ireland:

> Three classes wanted Home Rule – the priests, the women, and agitators. The women did not know what they wanted, the agitators did not wish to lose their pay, and the priests were the tools of Rome.

Another opponent of the motion launched into a defence of Irish landlords during the Famine, hardly a relevant consideration in a debate on Home Rule two-thirds of a century later.

Overall, Home Rule seemed to have the better of the argument. One speaker took the ethical high ground, condemning Britain's treatment of Ireland as "a blot on our national morality", in stark contradiction to an honourable tradition of support for "aspiring races" in Greece and Hungary and Finland. "England would long ago have rebelled at the treatment she has meted out to a sister people." Another managed the unusual achievement of making "a refreshingly original contribution" to a Union debate, arguing that it was Ireland's union with Britain that "was retarding the natural rise of the people against the priests". This was an "interesting point of view" – although arguably it would take a good half-century of independence before the prophecy began to bear fruit. The motion was passed by an unusually large majority, 137 votes to 97. A contemporary reporter drew the obvious conclusion that Gwynn's speech had "rather weighted the scale".[21] However, the Home Rule debate the following year suggests that the vote was part of a continuing trend.

In March 1912, no fewer than four MPs took part in the discussion of Home Rule, two on each side. Despite the balance of oratory on this occasion, the percentage of a very large house of 427 agreeing that they were "strongly opposed to the prospective passing of a Home Rule Bill", at 43 percent, was very close to the 41 percent who had resisted Gwynn's sweetly reasoned presentation fourteen months earlier. At that stage, there was no Bill to debate. The King's speech four weeks earlier had baldly referred to "a measure for the better Government of Ireland". Thus it was Home Rule in principle not Home Rule in detail that was supported by J.P. Boland, Nationalist MP for South Kerry, and a young Liberal MP, W.G.C. Gladstone. Grandson of the Grand Old Man and, like him, a former President of the Oxford Union, young Gladstone delivered a "thoughtful and eloquent" speech that suggested a dazzling career in prospect. This would be cut short on the Western Front just two years later. Boland seems to have been a last-minute substitute: only a week earlier, the *Granta* had confidently announced that the guest speaker would be Joe Devlin, "the Ulster Nationalist". None the less, Boland "made a sincere and most effective appeal", denying any wish for outright separation between the two countries. The Irish were not "foolish enough to think they could afford to organise a national defence strong enough to repel an English invader". He pointed to an inconsistency in the case against Home Rule:

> Thirty years ago Unionists said that Home Rule could not be granted because Ireland was seething with crime and disorder: today they say that Ireland is so happy and prosperous that Home Rule is unnecessary. They cannot have it both ways.

The case against Home Rule was argued by two Conservative MPs, Hayes Fisher and Captain George Sandys. Fisher was a workaday politician who had regained his London suburban seat in January 1910 after defeat at the 1906 election had seemingly put an end to a moderately distinguished twenty-year career. The wartime coalition later gave him a belated chance of office, and he even managed to get into the cabinet in 1917. His Cambridge speech "was amusing and convincing at the same time, and argued with breadth and cogency". On the other hand, Captain Sandys, father of a later Conservative cabinet minister, was "very charming, but he managed to stir up some very genuine hostility on the other side".[22]

At first sight, it is difficult to square this emphatic majority, of 243 votes against 184, with the fact that a motion expressing "approval of Mr. Asquith's Home Rule Bill" was narrowly defeated in May 1912, just two months later. One explanation may lie in the relative turn-outs. "We have rarely seen the House so comfortably empty", said the *Granta* of the second debate: perhaps at the hardcore of undergraduate politics, fervent critics of Home Rule outnumbered its convinced supporters. A more likely explanation may be found in the difference between a debate on the principle of Home Rule and one on the detail of Asquith's Bill, especially after the proposed legislation had undergone several weeks of parliamentary battering. Alan O'Day has identified "ten significant flaws" in the machinery designed by the Home Rule Bill of 1912. The opening speaker for the opposition, Gordon Butler, baldly summarised its shortcomings. "There was something to be said for Colonial Home Rule; and there was something to be said for Federal Home Rule" but "Mr Asquith's absurd attempt to compromise between them was bound to prove unworkable". Butler's categories suggest that he had read Erskine Childers, who used the same terminology in *The Framework of Home Rule*. Moreover, there was the emerging and massive issue of the fate of the Protestant North, which enabled the opposition to argue for the seductive diversion of "a wide system of Home Rule all round, with self-government for Ulster". Others invoked once again the broader arguments, of enlightened liberalism against *realpolitik*, "the success of the experiment in the Transvaal" against the blunt truth that "self-preservation had compelled Britain to bring about the Union; and self-preservation required its continuance".[23] The motion was defeated by 38 votes to 35, by far the smallest attendance during any of the three Home Rule Bill controversies.

However, political controversy was about to crackle into flame. Speaking at Blenheim Palace, in July 1912, Bonar Law dramatically announced that there was "no length of resistance to which Ulster can go in which I should not be prepared to support them". Home Rule, for so long a revolutionary challenge, was now subsumed within the larger issue of constitutional government. In October, a "crowded and truculent" Union condemned Bonar Law's "unconditional support" for "the seditious character of the recent proceedings in Ulster" by 138 votes to 109. Four months later, a motion supporting the Conservative leader's call for a revival of the use of the royal veto was rejected by 85 votes to 47.[24] It seems that some Conservatives felt distaste for their party's tack towards extremism.

In March 1913, Home Rule was the subject of another visitor debate. The motion, specifically endorsing the Bill "passed by the House of Commons last Session", was a direct challenge to the previous summer's vote against the details of Asquith's scheme. The guest speaker on the Home Rule side was Jeremiah MacVeagh, MP for the Nationalist area of County Down. For the first time in almost a century of debates on Ireland, the Cambridge Union heard from a spokesman for the Catholics of Ulster. MacVeagh was on the winning side but, in a social sense, his visit to Cambridge was not wholly successful. Stephen Gwynn, Hugh Law and Swift MacNeill were Oxford men who slipped naturally into the Cambridge environment. Although Dillon and Redmond were Catholics and Nationalists, they came from the higher professional classes and were instinctively recognised as gentlemen, even by the snobbish Monty Rhodes James.[25] MacVeagh's education had terminated at St Malachy's College in Belfast, and he began his speech by drawing attention to the fact "that he had not had a University career". Reporters were too well-mannered to complain that the guest managed to miss the gentlemanly wavelength of the Cambridge Union, but it seems that his speech was ill-judged. MacVeagh's allegations that a Jewish financier was backing the Ulster campaign against Home Rule produced outraged protests from speakers on the other side, more reminiscent of the House of Commons in an angry mood than of the student society that had been charmed and persuaded by Roxburgh's wit two years earlier. Emerging from this "fierce battle of persiflage and repartee", he thundered ahead in platform manner. "Ireland's soul is being starved. ... The whole civilised world was clamouring for Home Rule." The *Cambridge Review* patronised MacVeagh with very faint praise. "Whatever fault might be found with his logic, no one could resist the power and sincerity of his appeal."

MacVeagh was countered by an Irish loyalist and ex-President of the Oxford Union, Richard Dawson, in a "fine fighting speech, whose genuine arguments were embellished by a well-chosen vocabulary and a true Irish humour". Hugh Dalton, now reading for the Bar in London, also contributed "an extremely good and well-phrased speech" in support of Home Rule although, as he was "sometimes inaudible", its effectiveness must be doubted.

It was symbolic of the tragedy of a dividing Ireland that both guest speakers soon found themselves on the losing side of its politics. The following year, it fell to MacVeagh to persuade the Nationalists of Ulster to accept that their corner of Ireland was to be excluded from the jurisdiction of a Dublin parliament. During the Troubles, Dawson ran the London office of the Irish Unionist Alliance, energetically organising alliances against Lloyd George, but with little success. In March 1913, MacVeagh's sincerity seemed to triumph over Dawson's cogent humour, by 125 votes to 110, with opposition to Asquith's form of Home Rule running at 47 percent.[26]

In the decade since Keynes had broken five years of silence to revive the issue, the Union had undoubtedly see-sawed in its attitude to Home Rule. Overall, the trend had been towards a narrow margin of acceptance, punctuated by occasional expressions of doubt. Opinion was still almost evenly divided, but there had been a long-term shift away from the overwhelming levels of opposition recorded in the late eighteen-seventies and early eighties: it is perhaps surprising, but the prospect of Home Rule seems to have aroused less opposition, and, at times, less interest, decade by decade. Familiarity had bred a degree of resigned acceptance. However, the underlying trend was barely detectable at the time. Nobody seems to have thought of analysing the votes of the Cambridge Union in terms of percentages and turn-outs; the coining of the term "psephology" lay four decades in the future, and even then it was "intended as no more than an academic jest".[27] Hence Swift MacNeill continued to cherish the belief that he had successfully argued the Cambridge Union into accepting a Home Rule motion back in 1873. Forty years later, he was "inspired by a sentimental desire" to repeat his imagined triumph.

The terms of the motion debated on 4 November 1913 were alone enough to indicate just how far the issue had developed since the days of Isaac Butt. The motion welcomed the prospect of "an Irish Parliament with an Irish Executive responsible thereto" and dismissed as "unjustifiable the present attitude of Ulster Unionists". The Oxford-educated MacNeill was treated with greater reverence than the thinly patronised MacVeagh. "The remarkable coincidence of his two appearances in the Cambridge Union lent a special interest and charm to the occasion." Naturally, the veteran fully exploited this sentiment, opening his speech by recounting "that on that same spot forty years ago, on the same date – the fourth of November – at exactly the same hour", he had spoken on the very same subject. This long-term perspective enabled him to emphasise "the remarkable progress and improvement" which had taken place in Ireland in the interval.

Disguised within the reverie of nostalgia, Swift MacNeill unleashed a fierce attack on Ulster unionism. Pointing out that he was the longest-serving MP from the province, and a Protestant representing "the most Catholic constituency in the Empire", MacNeill "very much objected to Ulster having the name of rebel". The proposer of the motion had already described Ulster opponents of Home Rule as "spoilt children". MacNeill threw an elder statesman's gravitas behind a similar burst of abuse:

> The loyalty of the Orangeman was one of the greatest myths in history. With them it was purely a matter of £.s.d. It was various nice fat jobs they were after.

Although MacNeill insisted that "he had not made a speech, but given a historical lecture from the heart", the *Cambridge Review* congratulated him on "one of the finest perorations in recent memory".

As a further compliment to MacNeill, the young men of Cambridge had invited a delegation from the Oxford Union, including its President who, like MacNeill himself, was a Christ Church man. Gilbert Talbot was the son of the bishop of Winchester, a glamorous Etonian with a ferocious interest in politics and "the air of being a coming leader of the Tories". A little over a year later, Talbot was killed leading his men on the Western Front. He was commemorated in the establishment of a rest centre for troops as they came out of the trenches. Talbot House was quickly translated through signallers' shorthand to become Toc H, the soldiers' religious and welfare movement. Talbot's death was one of the casualties of the First World War that left survivors feeling permanently overshadowed by the unfulfilled potential of those who had been lost.

Ironically, on that evening in November 1913, the Cambridge Union was indeed listening to a future leader of the Conservative Party. Cambridge could be forgiven its prophetic myopia. The young Etonian from Balliol who was about to be elected Secretary of the Oxford Union acknowledged that his politics at the time were "confused", describing himself as "a Liberal-Radical, a Tory-Democrat, and a Fabian Socialist". In a poorly crafted (and slightly absurd) sentence, the *Granta* reported that he "combined both the Oxford charm with the logicality of Cambridge". The *Cambridge Review* felt that the visitor's "philosophic calm and dulcet tones in no way distracted from, though at first they almost seemed to conceal, the subtle and telling attacks he delivered upon his opponents". In this case, the undergraduate was father to the statesman. M.H.

Macmillan of Balliol went on to become the "Supermac" of post-Second World War British politics.

In a curious sense, representatives of two very different worlds sat side-by-side on the front bench of the Cambridge Union that night. MacNeill was "an old fashioned Victorian gentleman", revelling in the nostalgia of forty years earlier. Alongside him, Macmillan was embarking on a career in which he would act the part of the last of the Edwardians, and which would end with his resignation as prime minister in October 1963, almost exactly half a century later. In one respect, their careers were artistically linked. It had been Parnell, whom he repudiated during the divorce case in 1891, who had put MacNeill into parliament, and it would be the Profumo sex scandal that effectively tipped Macmillan out of office. As a Conservative, Macmillan was capable of drawing upon some elements of the radical beliefs of his youth, accepting the welfare state and hurrying Britain's African empire to its downfall. In 1913, he described the Home Rule crisis as "the critical hour when it was for England to decide whether or not a small Protestant ascendancy should rule over the whole of Ireland". His six years as prime minister coincided with the sterile violence of the IRA Border Campaign, but in retrospect his failure to force Northern Ireland to confront its underlying problems looks like an opportunity complacently squandered. He had been clear enough in 1913 in his definition of what was wrong in the Ulster Protestant psychology:

> The attitude of the Unionists is, that disorder is only disorder when directed against Toryism, and religious indignation only righteous when based upon anti-Popery.

As prime minister, Macmillan unleashed the Winds of Change in tropical Africa, but no breeze of reform touched the outlying ramparts of the United Kingdom during his term of office.

"I am glad to be able to say," MacNeill recorded of his visit to Cambridge in 1913, "that this Home Rule motion, like its predecessor of that day forty years before, was carried." He did not add that it passed by just three votes out of 389, the largest division of the academic year. If he had been better briefed about the outcome of his visit in 1873, he might have drawn some encouragement from the long-term direction of Cambridge opinion. In the last debate on Home Rule before the outbreak of war, the Union had pronounced in its favour, by a very narrow margin that echoed the shifting attitudes of the previous decades.[28]

There was to be just one other Irish debate before the war: in April 1914, the Union refused by 60 votes to 52 to condemn the "provocative action of the Government" during the Curragh crisis. As so often when the Union turned its attention from the general to the specific, the debate did not take fire. The proposition denounced the "military plot to coerce Ulster" as the latest ministerial crime, while the opposition cried treason and condemned Bonar Law as an "agent provocateur". To the *Cambridge Review*, the evening was just another episode in the eternal discussion of familiar issues. "Next Tuesday, the Welsh Church Bill."[29]

"The War of 1914-18 brought an abrupt ending to this Age of Gold," wrote a Cambridge don in 1926.[30] Three-quarters of a century later, it is still tempting to look back on Cambridge in the summer of 1914 as Paradise about to be plunged into Hell. Emerging from examination halls where "for six clammy hours a days, for six loathesome days of the week", they had "spoilt foolscap with scrawlings", undergraduates threw themselves into the annual round of boat races and garden parties.[31] With typical English perversity, "May Week" always fell at the beginning of June. At the far end of Europe, Austrian officials in the little-known Balkan town of Sarajevo were preparing for the visit of an Archduke. In Cambridge, an influx of relatives took the opportunity to sample student life: "so many sisters and cousins and aunts, to say nothing of mothers and occasional fathers, can hardly have been seen in Cambridge in any one previous May Week". For the young men, these end-of-term celebrations cloaked a gilded mating ritual. "It is by no means an ungrateful task to dance with other people's sisters", especially when to the pleasure of female society was added the music of a German band. For those about to graduate, the atmosphere was heavy was nostalgia. "Many of us have had our last May Week", wrote the correspondent of the *Cambridge Review*.[32] It was a comment that could be made every year, but in 1914 it was to prove brutally accurate in a way that nobody could guess.

An ephemeral May Week magazine, *Mandragora*, satirised prominent Union luminaries by reporting an imaginary debate. Percival Smith of Caius, President the previous year, was on his way to becoming the identikit schoolmaster: under "recreations", his *Who's Who* entry would list "any outdoor games". Smith was portrayed defending his prosaic surname. "Hundreds of Britishers at the present day were arming to the sound of that name." Of course, the humour lay in the inversion of reality, the absurdity of the notion of British people arming for any purpose at all. *Mandragora* also lampooned the serious manner of the outgoing President, Gordon Butler, who confessed himself "assailed by grave fears as to the future".[33] In real life, Butler had been encouraged by the number of "excellent speeches ... by some of the younger members of the Society", and concluded that "the future is bright with hope".[34] Two years later, he was dead.

The Cambridge Union neither expected nor wished for a European war. A motion condemning Sir Edward Grey's pacific foreign policy as "unworthy of British traditions and contrary to the interests of the Nation" had been defeated by 113 votes to 56 in October 1909. There was a similar outcome, by 86 votes to 47, in November 1913. While the *entente* with France was backed in February 1910 by a massive margin of 110 votes to 20, two-to-one majorities steadily and earnestly desired to remain on good terms with Germany. Although a small house had expressed its "apprehension" of German foreign policy in May 1906, by 28 votes to 20, five other debates in the decade before the War show a constant desire to keep the peace. The anti-German attitude of the British press had been condemned by 79 votes to 39 in November 1905. In February 1909, a motion branding the Kaiser a "constant source of danger to the peace of Europe" was rejected by 105 votes to 55. Norman Birkett, who opposed the motion, recalled his argument that "the days were past when any one man could affect the peace of Europe", ruefully adding that he "paid for that particular folly" by serving as a judge at the Nuremberg trials. In fact, the Union regarded the mercurial Winston Churchill as a greater threat to peace, in 1911 expressing by 88 votes to 75 the "utmost concern" at his appointment to the Admiralty "in view of the serious nature of Anglo-German Relations". In February 1913, a motion arguing that "a complete rapprochement with Germany is impractical in view of her Anti-British policy of the last fifteen years" was rejected by 104 votes to 47. Finally, on 26 May 1914, ten weeks before the outbreak of war, the Union voted by 66 votes to 21 to dismiss a motion that "the German Empire is a menace to the peace of Europe". More presciently, the previous week a thin house had disagreed by 27 votes to 13 with the proposition that "Western civilisation is likely to destroy itself through excessive humanitarianism".[35] Prominent among the apologists for Germany on the eve of the War was W.A.J. von Lubtow of Christ's: the *Cambridge Review* urged him to "continue to promote friendly feelings between the two nations in his own inimitable way". He survived the War, to re-emerge in 1920 as plain "Mr Lubtow".[36]

Others were not so lucky. In the summer term, twenty-five candidates contested the Union's three offices and six committee places. Within months, twenty of them would be in uniform, most of them on active service. Their youth and social background marked them out as officer material, and it was as lieutenants and captains that they led their troops into battle. Nine of them were killed. W.B.W. Durrant of Magdalene had been accused of a tendency "to cultivate fluency at the expense of thought" when he denounced Asquith's handling of the Curragh crisis. He served in the Rifle Brigade and was killed in 1915. He was followed a year later by H.B. Barnard of Jesus, who had supported him on that April evening in 1914. H.U. Scrutton of King's, who had taken the other side, was to die of wounds in far-off Bulgaria. A.V. Hobbs of St John's, a die-hard defender of the Welsh Church, joined the Royal Flying Corps. His plane fell out of the sky over Valenciennes in December 1915. W.G. Woodroffe of Pembroke had warned unavailingly against the menace of the German Empire. He won the French Croix de Guerre, before being killed in 1916. Among the survivors, the incoming President, J.H.B. Nihill of Emmanuel, a Home Ruler who served with the Royal Munster Fusiliers, was one of four of those 1914 candidates to win the Military Cross.[37]

We should not forget that one of the features of Victorian Cambridge was the frequency with which promising young men had been cut off in their prime. Even so, there had never been anything like the death toll of the First World War. Over two thousand members of the University of Cambridge were killed, the equivalent of two whole undergraduate years. The carnage was greatest among the younger men: one estimate claimed that one fifth of all undergraduates who had entered the University in the five years previous to 1914 were killed.[38] But they were not the only casualties. It had been his personal qualities that had carried "Honest John" Allen to the Presidency in 1911. He had never been a great speaker, and when he returned to oppose votes for women in the set-piece May Week debate of 1914, the *Granta* had judged him "not very convincing".[39] Allen's was the last peacetime speech in the Cambridge Union. Just over a year later, he was killed at Gallipoli. F.D. Livingstone, the terrifying scourge of John Dillon, was killed in France. So too was Cecil Persse, the "indignant Irishman" whose anger had been aroused by the findings of the Financial Commission back in 1897.

Cambridge had managed to radiate the impression of being untouched by so many of the changes of the previous hundred years, but it could not escape the impact of the War. In the autumn of 1913, 3,200 undergraduates had been in residence. The number halved the following year, and by the summer of 1916 dropped below 600. The sword replaced the pen; khaki uniforms ousted academic gowns. Colleges were excellent locations for training courses, cricket grounds could easily be turned into field hospitals. The first casualties, from the Marne, were actually accommodated in the open air under the cloisters of Trinity's Nevile's Court.

At first, the Union opted for "business as usual", but it became steadily harder to sustain the requisite atmosphere of gilded irresponsibility as attendances fell and debate after debate (none of them on Ireland) had to be prefaced with motions of condolence marking the deaths of members on active service. Plans to celebrate the Society's centenary in 1915 were abandoned. Deprived of membership income, the Union had to be kept afloat by a special subscription, but even supporters among senior members of the University criticised the policy of "continuing to hold debates and elections" through a time of national crisis. Eventually, in June 1916, normal activities were abandoned, and the management of the Union entrusted to a caretaker committee of dons. The final debate was abandoned at the last minute when news arrived of the death of Kitchener. It was "a sad event", wrote the *Cambridge Review* that "the activities of the Union should be interrupted after a life of over a hundred years". The premises became a club for officers: even at a time of world crisis, elitism remained the order of the day.[40] Back in the carefree summer of 1913, undergraduates had rejected a jovial proposal to turn the debating chamber into a swimming bath. In November 1916, it was found to be the ideal venue for a boxing match. "Now that the capabilities of the Debating Hall have been discovered," remarked the *Cambridge Review*, "it is to be hoped that this room will continue to be utilised for a purpose for which it is so well adapted." [41]

Among the support services organised for wounded soldiers was the Cambridge Tipperary Club.[42] Its title had nothing to do with Ireland, but was an echo of the song for ever associated with the rush to the colours at the outbreak of War. Just as the Union had slipped ninety years earlier into the subconscious assumption that Drogheda was in "England", so a popular lyric in 1914 could take for granted that a young Englishman might find the love of his life deep in rural Ireland. In August 1914, it had been a long way to Tipperary. By January 1919, when two policemen were killed at Soloheadbeg in the first act of Ireland's Troubles, the distance between the two countries had become unbridgeable by nineteenth-century solutions.

11 : Conclusion

This study confirms that voting patterns in the Cambridge Union reflected a section of student opinion and were largely unaffected by the content of debates. The relationship of these opinions to wider public opinion is almost impossible to establish. Indeed, the evidence is not even strong enough to permit generalisations about the views of "junior Cambridge". In the one case that provided a statistical comparison, that of attitudes towards women's degrees in 1897, Union activists seem to have been more progressive than Cambridge undergraduates at large: 37 percent and 35 percent voted in favour in 1891 and 1896, but when the chamber was thrown open to non-members in 1897, support fell to 11 percent. On the other hand, Tables Nine and Ten suggest that the Cambridge Union was more resistant to granting women the vote even than Conservative members of the House of Commons. In a wider sense, however, it seems reasonable to assume *some* wider relevance, even to the proceedings of a "spouting society". The social composition of Cambridge students corresponded closely to the profile of the political elite that governed Britain. Cambridge debates were generally reactive: Ireland was discussed most avidly at those times when it was perceived to be a "problem", and in this there was little difference between the Cambridge Union and the British cabinet. Moreover, the content of student oratory was almost invariably derivative. Occasionally, a standard package of arguments might be enlivened by an imaginative touch, as in the claim by a speaker in 1911 that Home Rule would undermine the power of the priests in Catholic Ireland, but such originality was evidently rare. In recycling stale ideas, young Cambridge orators were drawing upon a wider discourse even if, as in the case of one young man who spoke in 1914, this consisted of little more than the opinions, and probably the prejudices of Irish relatives.

The fact that issues were debated at the Cambridge Union provides at least rough-and-ready evidence of the nature and duration of British concern about Ireland. Even if the wider relevance of the balance of opinion recorded in the divisions must be treated with some reservation, the numbers voting at debates gives some clues to the relative intensity of interest. As Appendix One and Table Eight confirm, interest in Irish issues was usually at a peak when Ireland was newsworthy and hence, by definition, "a problem", and it was rarely sustained for long. Thus it is worth noting that in the eighteen-sixties, the fate of the Irish Church drew smaller attendances than did debates on the future of the

Church of England. Considerably more excitement was experienced in 1880-82 over the empowerment of Irish tenants than was generated by land questions in subsequent decades. Home Rule was a central issue in 1886-87, although even then one that was surprisingly muted. The two subsequent Home Rule episodes drew very large attendances but there is a distinct sense that the bugbear had faded. However, the Cambridge Union cannot be a comprehensive source for topicality. For much of the year, debating fell silent. Only rarely did the Union turn back to discuss an event that had happened in the vacation, as in 1868 when it approved the execution of the Manchester martyrs weeks after they had been hanged, or in 1889 when it picked over the bones of the report of the Special Commission. The exclusion of theological questions did not totally rule out discussion of the political ramifications of religious issues but, combined with the demands of good taste, it was probably enough to blunt any tendency among prosperous young Protestants to condemn Ireland to its fate as a punishment for the faith of the majority of its people. It is important, too, to remember that a debating society thrives upon adversarial division. Where there is consensus, there is little to debate. The historian might wish to find evidence that the Famine triggered youthful outrage, and it may seem depressing to report that the only response to the great social crisis of the eighteen-forties was just one debate, on State-funding of Irish railways. Yet this is not to say that Cambridge students were indifferent to the Famine, but rather that only on a single question of State investment in economic infrastructure did they find themselves divided.

The responses of posterity form a part of the equation of assessment that must be confronted. It is beyond the scope of this study to determine whether the Cambridge of the Victorian *ancien régime* was swept away by the 1914-18 war, but it is undoubtedly the case that, so far as the British political agenda was concerned, the Irish question had entirely changed by 1919. Yet this is not to say that historians can look back on the controversies of the earlier period in an entirely dispassionate manner. At the core of Catholic Emancipation in the early nineteenth century lay the same issue that bedevilled Northern Ireland in the late twentieth, the challenge of creating an equality of citizenship that transcends religious belief. The disestablishment of the Protestant Church in Ireland in 1869 embodied the same principle of State neutrality in matters of conscience that Irish voters endorsed 103 years later when they deleted the "special relationship" of the Catholic Church from their constitution. All too often, historians profess scholarly neutrality in their reconstructions of the past while quietly cheering for the progressive side; this study is no exception. Of course it was wrong to deny the right to vote by compelling people to swear an oath that abused their deepest beliefs. Of course it was right to put an end to the privileges of a Church that was spurned by the vast majority of its own people. It is better for historians to cheer openly than to pretend to a detachment that denies their involvement in the politics of their own times.

Facing up to our continuing involvement in some nineteenth-century issues is an important step towards disengaging ourselves from others. Merely because the progressives were "right", in our terms, about the inclusion of Catholics in parliament or the exclusion of bishops does not mean that historians must support them in every campaign that they fought. No doubt it is tempting to sympathise with the legislative cap on Irish rents effectively imposed by 1882. Faced with Irish turbulence, the Cambridge Union did not see the matter in that light, although a more sympathetic view was taken of the problems facing Highland crofters three years later. There could be no difficulty in discerning the side of the righteous in the question of protecting peasants from the rapacity of lazy and luxuriant landlords. But is this the whole story? In an era when even radical politicians espouse privatisation and laud the profit margin, should we at least consider the possibility that in limiting the income of the landlords, the British parliament destroyed the only element capable of generating the capital necessary for large-scale modernisation of Irish agriculture? The objection may be countered by citing the fact that the emasculation of landlords as a *rentier* class was promptly followed by State-assisted land purchase, a reform carried this time not by the progressive side in politics but by the Conservatives under Lord Salisbury. By any standard of historical and political ethics, the transfer of the land of Ireland to the people of Ireland must surely be a Good Thing. Yet the slightest acquaintance with the Irish countryside is enough to remind us that what happened was the transfer of land ownership not to the people of Ireland but to a minority among them. That minority was larger and no doubt – for what it matters – morally worthier than the landlord class that it ousted, but no less determined to protect its own interests. Even to laud the new peasant proprietors as more integrally Irish involves modern historians in elevating nativism into a positive virtue for Ireland at a time when it is regarded as a retrograde quality almost everywhere else in a globalised world. In the long run, land purchase failed even in its fundamental aim of saving the union. Rather, it turned the often distant British State into a mortgage-holder, a surrogate landlord, enabling de Valera in the nineteen-thirties to re-enact the Land War by refusing to continue payment on outstanding annuities.

The dangers of filtering opinion on Irish issues before 1914 through our retrospective ideas of righteous normality are particularly delusive when applied to Home Rule. There may be no such thing as lessons from history, but the experience of the twentieth century seems to suggest that there is no ideal political framework that can accommodate the necessary relationship between Britain and Ireland – or, as we have to accept as that century closes, between the different nations and regions of Britain and the two communities of Ireland. In superficial retrospect, Home Rule may appear an attractive answer to that conundrum.

Arguments voiced in the Cambridge Union come through to us in doubly simplified form: they were probably crude in their original formulation and whatever subtlety they aspired to convey is lost in staccato reporting. None the less, there is enough to suggest that, whether they grasped it or not, undergraduate Home Rulers were often advancing arguments that logically pointed to total separation between the two islands. This was emphatically not how Home Rule was presented by its more sophisticated exponents, including the Nationalist politicians who visited the Cambridge Union. John Dillon in 1886 offered the reassurance that England was "strong enough" to intervene if Home Rule produced injustice. J.P. Boland in 1912 protested that the Irish were not "foolish enough" to believe they could repel an English invasion. On the face of it, Home Rule was simply a scheme for devolution within a continuing United Kingdom. Thus it was that John Redmond rallied to the Allied cause in 1914. Thus it was that the pre-War Nationalist party had virtually vanished from the Irish political scene altogether a decade later. Ireland was part of the British empire, a context that was overwhelmingly omnipresent a century ago but almost impossible empathetically to re-create now. John Ball, one of the first Irish Catholics to speak in the Union, held just one political appointment, as under-secretary at the Colonial Office from 1855 to 1858. Forty years later, it fell to Thomas McDonnell to propose the motion that conferred honorary membership of the Cambridge Union upon Kitchener after his triumphant massacre of the Madhi's army at Omdurman in 1898. "I only wish I had had some of you with me in the Sudan", the distinguished guest told cheering students.[1] Michael McDonnell came close to fulfilling the Sirdar's wishes. After publishing his tract on Irish Home Rule, he embarked upon a colonial career as a judge in West Africa, Palestine and Egypt. The empire also formed part of the career of the fervent Ulster unionist, E.W. MacBride, who took his first academic post at a Canadian university, McGill, before returning to his native Belfast. Nor should these examples be seen as some undignified form of parasitism. "The truth is that Ireland has taken her full share in winning and populating the Empire," wrote Erskine Childers in 1911. "The result is hers as much as Britain's."[2]

On the face of it, Home Rule was very different from the national and republican independence of Ireland's twenty-six counties today. Even its chrysalis version, Dominion status, had seemed a huge step forward in 1921. "Was ever such lunacy proposed by anybody?", Lloyd George had scoffed as late as October of 1920.[3] From this, it seems easy to conclude that the failure to concede Home Rule was not just Ireland's lost opportunity, but England's too. Michael McDonnell pointed to "an unjust dilemma" that had consistently faced

Ireland's demands for its own parliament. In times of disturbance, "the reply has been that until quiet is restored nothing can be done"; when the country was peaceful, "the absence of agitation" had produced "the retort that the request is not widespread, and can, in consequence, be ignored".[4] The Nationalist MP J.P. Boland had used precisely that argument at the Union debate of 1912, telling anti-Home Rulers that "[t]hey cannot have it both ways".[5]

Not surprisingly, some in Britain came to regret that they had missed the chance of a moderate Irish settlement within the United Kingdom. "What fools we were not to have accepted Gladstone's Home Rule Bill," George V remarked of a troublesome Free State in 1930.[6] Unfortunately, the king's sentiment rested upon the assumptions that Home Rule would have worked in practice and so solved the centuries-old Irish question once and for all. Neither assumption can be taken for granted. William Finlay was probably a trifle disingenuous when he praised the departing Gladstone as a political genius in a Union debate in 1898, but he was on firm ground in arguing that neither of the GOM's attempts to design a devolved constitution had been satisfactory. Overall, the three Home Rule bills were uninspiring concoctions of untested and probably unstable machinery. Even in 1912, when much of the passion had gone out of the issue, the Union could approve the principle in March but narrowly reject the actual Bill in May. At the heart of the problem lay the fundamental question of the relationship between Ireland and Britain. The solution of 1886, the removal of Irish members from Westminster altogether, had been grudgingly regarded by critics as one of the few benefits of the scheme, as Michael McDonnell shrewdly recognised when he stressed this aspect of Home Rule in a Union debate in 1904. However, in 1893 Gladstone performed one of his about-faces and proposed to retain an Irish delegation in the House of Commons with reduced voting powers. Sooner or later, this ramshackle arrangement would have resulted in a ministry equipped with a small majority to govern one island but outvoted when it tried to discharge the business of both. The insoluble problem lay not in the fact that Home Rule was a compromise, for compromise is the stuff of politics in a liberal society. Rather, the obstacle was that the trumped-up compromises of successive Home Rule Bills were unlikely to succeed in permanently papering over the cracks between two very different countries. Parnell had said in 1885 that "no man has the right to fix the boundary to the march of a nation".[7] Although no doubt useful as a coded reassurance to the wilder spirits on the violent margins of his coalition, these words represented neither threat nor bargaining position, but simple prediction. In 1893, a young unionist called Childers explained to his fellow Cambridge students that "the Federal system is not applicable to Ireland". In 1911, Childers similarly dismissed "the 'Federal' solution as totally impracticable", but by now he came at the question from the opposite angle. "Compulsory Federation would not last a year."[8] To Childers, once the impracticability of any continuing Irish representation at Westminster was accepted, the only answer was self-government on the Canadian model. "You are letting the cat out of the bag after all the mice have been killed," an opponent had complained of the re-opening of Home Rule in 1893.[9] Each failure to grasp the central conundrum of Irish devolution ensured that, with cat-like tread, the Irish nation was on the march to an eventual rupture of the United Kingdom.

The first step, then, in any assessment of nineteenth-century Cambridge Union attitudes to Ireland is the disentangling of the involvement of posterity. There is no reason for historians to pretend to neutrality in reviewing issues relating to citizenship and conscience that remain central to a liberal society. There is every reason for caution in handling questions, such as land ownership, that are ethically neutral but still stimulate an emotional response. Most of all, we ought to be put on our guard by the simple recollection that aspects of the political relationship between the islands remain problematic a century later. The fact that many who took the "right" side on other issues also predominantly championed Home Rule is insufficient to prove that a devolved parliament in Dublin would have been effective either in solving nineteenth-century friction or preventing twentieth-century confrontation.

Rather, we should seek to interpret Cambridge student opinion on its own terms. Which issues were discussed, and when? Instead of imposing retrospective moral judgement, we should ask whether the balance of opinion represented anything more than the expected outcome of economic interests and social conditioning. Above all, votes for and against each motion reveal both the intensity of interest in Irish issues and the balance between viewpoints. It seems reasonable to assume that both reflected the wider attitudes of an informed minority of English opinion.

In the 98 years between March 1816 and April 1914, the Cambridge Union debated Irish issues on 124 occasions. Excluding the four years between 1817 and 1821 when discussion was driven underground, the average is 1.3 debates on Ireland for each calendar year. At face value, this statistic suggests a steady degree of interest in the affairs of the sister island. However, there are problems both of classification by topic and of clustering in time. An example of the problem of definition was the debate in 1903, at which the Union considered the fate of Colonel Lynch, who had been born in Australia and had fought for the Boers. In some senses an argument about this single individual was much less than a debate on Ireland, but in others it was very much more, a challenge to the morality of British conquest in South Africa. At the other extreme, an apparently esoteric debate on Coleridge's poetic contribution to animal welfare could prove to contain an Irish dimension in the minds of those who refused to bestow even the smallest praise upon Humanity Dick Martin. These are marginal examples – the first has been included, the second excluded – but they are reminders that the Irish question cannot be isolated in a self-contained category.

Similarly, this study has treated Catholic Emancipation as an Irish issue, but of course the question had English dimensions. Cambridge students of the eighteen-twenties certainly regarded Catholicism as an alien religion, but many of them would have been aware of families of nobility and gentry, neighbours in the English shires, who were deprived of civil rights because of their adherence to the old faith. Indeed, the slight accounts that survive of the debates on Catholic Emancipation suggest that neither English recusants nor their Irish co-religionists were the central focus of a controversy that challenged the legitimacy of the entire unreformed constitution. Similarly, to regard Home Rule as a purely Irish issue would be to fall into the blinkered perspective that draws a box around everything perceived by the historian to be Irish and then proceeds to condemn those contemporary participants who failed to conform to the atavistic interpretation imposed. Irish Home Rule was a United Kingdom issue, and it is no surprise that debates on the subject were the best-attended in nine of the 28 academic years between 1886-87 and 1913-14. Nor was this attitude simply a charter to deny Irish participation in the determination of Irish destinies, as was shown by the 54 percent vote in 1884 refused to exclude Ireland from the extended franchise provided by the Third Reform Act.

At the most basic level, the debate records of the Cambridge Union indicate which Irish issues were discussed, and when. The evidence is less helpful during the first half century of the Society's existence since meetings were relatively infrequent and many debates were non-political in character. Even so, there was a striking lack of interest in Ireland between the Maynooth controversy in 1845-46 and the revival of the Church issue after 1864, with no motions on Irish affairs at all between November 1852 and February 1859. The early eighteen-seventies constitute another fallow period, with only one debate on Ireland in the seven years following February 1870. Home Rule aroused interest between 1880 and 1883, but had slipped away from the Cambridge Union order paper in the two years before Gladstone put it on the Westminster agenda. Within two years of its defeat in 1886, Home Rule had come to be regarded as a stale topic. Interest had waned altogether by 1891, a calendar year in which Ireland was not discussed at all, but was kick-started by the Second Home Rule Bill. However, the massive attendance to hear John Redmond in 1895 had something of the air of a requiem for the Home Rule cause, and it was not until 1902 that debates on Ireland were again well attended. Perhaps curiously, Irish issues were ignored throughout the academic years 1904-06, even though it was obvious that Balfour's Conservative government was tottering towards collapse and thus likely that a Liberal-Nationalist alliance would make a third attempt to create a parliament in Dublin. If the Cambridge Union was largely reactive in its consideration of Irish issues, it was even more the case that it failed to be predictive.

The numbers voting at debates offer an indication of the relative importance of Irish questions in the overall political spectrum. Appendix One identifies the issues that attracted the largest houses by academic years from 1863-64 to 1913-14. Table Eight shows the numbers expressing an opinion each year through the same period on Ireland as a percentage of those voting at the most popular non-Irish debate. By the middle of the eighteen-sixties, the Cambridge Union had become primarily interested in a secular world of politics that was dominated by a two-party system. However, special circumstances could still distort turn-out, and general impressions of the comparative significance are more reliable than precise deductions. In October 1866, for instance, a "no-confidence" debate on the merits of the recently installed Conservative government registered an unusually large attendance because it coincided with the inauguration of the Union's permanent premises. In an average late-Victorian year, it would hardly have occurred to the Union to discuss whether Bacon wrote Shakespeare, but in June 1888 a large audience turned out to hear the American visitor, Ignatius Donnelly, argue his controversial thesis, and over two hundred of them stayed to vote. The most wayward statistic comes from the academic year 1896-97, where it appears that an Irish issue drew only an audience equal to just eight percent of the attendance at the most controversial meeting of the session. This was caused by the decision to throw open the debate on the admission of women to Cambridge degrees to all undergraduates, regardless of membership of the Society, resulting in an unprecedented vote of over twelve hundred. Matched against the small but earnest group that discussed the report of the Financial Commission, the comparison produces something of a distortion. As already noted, generally speaking, debates in the October term were better attended than those later in the year. The development from 1886 of the practice of inviting distinguished visitors to address the Union also distorted attendance figures. It is, of course, important to bear in mind that the Union was a debating society and not a deliberative body. Sometimes it responded to contemporary events but, on other occasions, an issue might draw a bumper crowd simply for its intellectual challenge. On the one hand, it is no surprise that South Africa was the subject of the best-attended debates during the Boer War, but it does not follow that socialism was the dominant question in British politics when it headed the list either in 1883-84 or again in 1888-89.

Hence the 51 academic years from 1863 show patterns of peaks and troughs in the consideration of Irish questions. In ten of those sessions, Ireland was not discussed at all; in a further nine, it provided the most controversial debate of the year. In 18 of the 51 years, party political debates drew the largest audiences. Many of these took the form of motions of no confidence in the government of the day, but some were spiced with specific condemnation of the opposition. The fact that these supplanted the Church as the most controversial subject of each year from about 1877 may be taken as a further measure of the secularisation of the Cambridge mind; Church issues, mainly disestablishment, had headed the list five times in the preceding decade. Two related issues, Tariff Reform in 1903-04 and the House of Lords in 1906-07, may be grouped under the party-political heading. The eight years in which Ireland triggered the largest debate constitute the second largest subject category. In some respects, it is surprising that Irish issues should outrank women's rights, which headed the list three times, since in years when both subjects were discussed, the feminist challenge generally drew larger houses. The explanation for the discrepancy probably lies in the development of visitor debates. The Union could just about overcome its social and national antipathies to invite those strange creatures called Irish Nationalists. There was no way that young Cambridge males would overcome their gender prejudices and allow themselves to be harangued by suffragettes. As late as 1933, "it was something of a revolution" when Lady Cynthia Mosley was allowed to accompany her husband to drinks in the sacred male shrine of the Committee Room.[10]

Not surprisingly, general questions relating to Ireland aroused more interest than specific issues. Headline subjects such as Catholic Emancipation and Home Rule grabbed the imagination more effectively than plans for State-funded railway investment in 1848 or the role of Sir Anthony MacDonnell in planning a scheme for devolution in 1905. From this, it would be easy to conclude that opinion in Cambridge – and, by extension, in England at large – was both simplistic and reactive in its attitudes to Ireland. Such a conclusion, however, would not tell the whole story. It is certainly the case that the Cambridge Union debated Ireland most energetically when Irish discontent was at its most intrusive. Yet this is not to say that student opinion invariably reacted against an alien challenge from Catholic nationalism. O'Connell's election for County Clare in 1828 made no difference of any kind to the already firm divisions for and against Catholic Emancipation, although his Repeal campaign produced a confrontational response in 1843. At first, attitudes to the Fenians were remarkably relaxed, although outrage erupted when Sergeant Brett was killed on the streets of Manchester. Although there was a general stance of resistance to Irish demands at the time of the Land War of the early eighteen-eighties, in March 1882 the Union only narrowly approved the reforms in parliamentary procedure designed to outwit obstruction, by 101 votes to 97.[11] If we make the leap of faith and assume that the students who voted in that relatively large division represented the cross-section of opinion reflected in debates on Home Rule, we must conclude that up to half of those refusing to countenance the creation of a parliament for Ireland in Dublin were ready to allow the Irish free rein to advance their case at Westminster. Perhaps most notable of all is the fact that Union opinion swung *towards* Home Rule in 1886, in contrast to the mayhem that Gladstone's conversion caused to his own party at national level. The minority in favour of Irish devolution remained remarkably firm throughout the discouraging decade that followed. Of all the agrarian agitations in Ireland, the Plan of Campaign probably carried the greatest threat of social revolution and was the least clearly thought through. The Plan drove one Cambridge Home Ruler, a Protestant from Tipperary, to abjure his Nationalist heresies, but it does not seem to have frightened anyone else into the unionist camp.

Four main themes can be discerned in the 124 Cambridge Union motions on Ireland. Devolution and separation accounted for 43 of them, under three distinct sub-headings spread through the century. The early decades saw five debates on Repeal and five more on motions condemning O'Connell himself. In the forty years between 1873 and 1913, the Union debated Home Rule on 33 occasions. The second largest grouping concerns sectarian issues, which accounted for 32 debates. Catholic Emancipation was debated eight times before it was conceded and, remarkably, on six further occasions retrospectively. The mid-century decades saw nine debates on the Irish Church and five on the related questions of the Maynooth grant and State payment of the Catholic priesthood. A *fin-de-siècle* tailpiece added four debates on sectarian education. Third came discussions of agrarian issues, coupled with the enforcement of law and order. Irish land was discussed on eight occasions, while Fenianism and Coercion each featured five times. The smallest cluster concerned Ulster, the subject of seven debates, although this classification elides the northern province with the controversial question of Orangeism.

As argued above, we should assess the significance of attitudes registered in these debates not by measuring them against our own notions of enlightenment, but rather by asking whether opinion was more or less progressive than we might expect. The overall conclusion is perhaps unexpected: voting in the Cambridge Union was often in advance of mainstream political opinion, although it should be noted that on most issues there remained a substantial unpersuaded minority. The first clear evidence of consistent opinion can be seen in consideration of Catholic Emancipation in the eighteen-twenties, when votes of between 54 and 60 percent in favour of change were registered in eight debates. Since consideration of the Catholic question was spread across seven years, and the Cambridge student community virtually renewed itself in four-year cycles, it seems likely that these votes reflect something more than accidental popularity polls swayed by youthful harangues.

Rather, a case can be made that they reflect the division of opinion among the social and political elite from whom Cambridge students were drawn.

Catholic Emancipation was unusual in generating no fewer than six retrospective debates on the wisdom of the measure. By comparison, there were only two later attempts to pick over the 1832 Reform Act, neither motion daring to call for a return to the discredited system of rotten boroughs. However, none of the attempts to re-open the concession of 1829 drew a large attendance. Three took place between 1840 and 1842 and were perhaps surrogates for criticism of the hated O'Connell, while the last, in November 1852, was probably sparked by the controversy over clerical intervention in the general election of that year. Lingering attachment to the ideal of Protestant ascendancy did not prevent the Union from supporting the increased Maynooth grant by more than two-to-one in 1845, although a brief expression of sympathy for the idea of State payment of Catholic priests quickly turned into an equally firm rejection.

On the two other sectarian questions, Cambridge Union opinion underwent dramatic and rapid change. As late as 1864, the Irish Church received a two-to-one endorsement. A year later, in a well-attended debate, it scraped home by a single vote. By February 1867, a narrow majority pronounced its existence as a State Church to be an injustice to the Irish people. As the Church faced its doom in 1869, its defenders could do no more than argue that the land question was more important. A similar shift in attitudes can be seen over the question of a Catholic university in Ireland between 1899 and 1903. In both cases, the shift can be traced through several debates, thus dismissing the possibility of an oratorical equivalent of the "rogue poll" in the measurement of public opinion. Since the content of Union debates was usually derivative, and often dismally so, it seems likely that in each case, the evidence reflects wider movement in English attitudes.

As already noted, the Cambridge Union seemed remarkably unconcerned by Fenianism, except when it manifested itself on the streets of Manchester. Perhaps the American origins of the Fenians meant that they were too easily seen as an external nuisance, making it possible for English opinion to regard Ireland as *Punch's* "fair Hibernia", a maiden in distress who merited chivalrous support. Perhaps, too, the availability of the Irish Church as an easy sacrifice made concession attractive, the more so as the Protestant Establishment on the sister island seemed to have lost crucial English support before it became necessary to respond to the threat of armed uprising.

If so, the concession probably reflected an English assumption of a trade-off, a closing of accounts, that was not shared in Ireland. In this, the disestablishment of the Church resembled the aftermath of Catholic Emancipation. "Does England really owe a great debt of justice to Ireland?", the Union had asked itself in 1839. When the question was posed in that form, a majority felt obliged to conclude that grievances persisted, but the impatient tone of the motion is revealing. The abandonment of the Church in 1869 was followed by an eight-year period in which Irish issues were hardly discussed at all. When the next campaign for redress targeted the landlords, young Cambridge was notably resistant to concession. Pacifying the Irish as Catholics was one thing; surrendering to them as tenants was another. Motions in 1881 and 1888 made subsidiary reference to land purchase and peasant proprietorship, but to the Cambridge Union, the central question was the relationship between landlord and tenant. There could be only one alternative to concession. Coercion was upheld by a massive ten-to-one majority at the height of the Land War in February 1881, and was endorsed again by two-to-one votes on three occasions between 1883 and 1887. It was not until 1902 that the Union recorded narrow majorities against both landlordism and Coercion, a measure of change both in English attitudes and Irish circumstances.

The 43 debates on the constitutional relationship between Britain and Ireland can be simply summarised. There were large majorities against outright Repeal in 1828 and 1833, followed by an almost compulsive demonisation of Daniel O'Connell. An unsuccessful amendment to a motion on conciliation in 1868 argued that the only effective answer was the establishment of Ireland as "an independent country", but otherwise the central question dropped from sight. Isaac Butt formed his Home Government Association in May 1870. It was three-and-a-half years before Swift MacNeill prodded the Cambridge Union into discussing its aim, with much less success than he believed. Majorities against Home Rule between 1877 and 1883 ran at levels reminiscent of opposition to Repeal half a century earlier, suggesting an inability to grasp, or perhaps to accept, the subtlety of Butt's quasi-federalist and devolutionist notions. Gladstone's decision to re-open the larger question of Reform in 1884 may have been partly intended as a step towards confronting the intensity of separatist feeling among the Irish masses.[12] In practice, it helped to take Irish devolution off the Cambridge Union agenda, with the probable result that the re-appearance of Home Rule in January 1886 took student opinion by surprise.

None the less, the most striking aspect of the division of opinion in the Union was the swing *towards* the Home Rule cause. Perhaps this was because young men in their late teens and early twenties were approaching the issue *de novo*. While those who had observed Gladstone's political career over many years might regard his conversion to the dangerous idea of Home Rule as confirmation of long-suspected insanity, younger minds might reverse the equation. Those who started from the assumption that Mr Gladstone was a great statesman were more likely to assume that any plan that he endorsed must fall within the bounds of good sense. It is possible, too, that the crisis of 1886 had the educational effect of distinguishing for the first time between devolution and separation. Perhaps the confrontational party-political atmosphere of the Cambridge Union simply ensured that the doubting Liberals who had presumably contributed to the hostile majorities of the early eighteen-eighties preferred to fall into line rather than cross the floor and join their Conservative opponents. All that we can say is that for the next decade, Home Rule was rejected by a consistent three-to-two majority – almost a mirror image of the division of opinion sixty years earlier over Catholic Emancipation.

Opposition to Home Rule declined after 1900 in parallel with changing attitudes to agrarian and sectarian questions in Ireland, and probably for the same fundamental reason: Ireland was ceasing to seem a threat. There were some minor zigzags in the march of opinion. In 1903, a small majority agreed with Keynes in hoping that Home Rule was out of the question, but in 1904 the Union endorsed Belloc's claim that it was the only possible solution. The early years of the Liberal government saw three further close rejections of Home Rule, but opinion switched in 1909-10 as was shown by the artistic coincidence of two deadheats in Union votes. Even so, 33 debates on Home Rule between 1873 and 1913 produced only four majorities in its favour. Three of these occurred between 1911 and 1913, the last of them by just three votes in a division of 389 students. Even these muted triumphs were interspersed in May 1912 by a small majority in the other direction, significantly directed not against the principle of Home Rule but in condemnation of the terms of Asquith's Bill.

The debate records of the Cambridge Union prompt three more general reflections, about political leadership, political biography and the nature of Ireland itself.

For a historian who is the product of a more modern and social democratic Britain, the debate records of the nineteenth-century Cambridge Union often project an irritating mixture of overweening self-confidence and obtuse short-sightedness. The irritation may be forgiven, but the target is misplaced. If Union debates were usually derivative and sometimes immature, then the ultimate responsibility for their shortcomings must lie elsewhere, with political leadership or in the nature of public discourse. If, as the Vice-President's report cheerfully remarked in 1908, the Cambridge Union had solved the problems that perplexed the country's rulers, why was it that governments themselves left so many nettles ungrasped? The question takes us deep into the inter-relationship of political initiative, opinion formation and majority rule.

In retrospect, it may appear that one of the great missed opportunities in the politics of the island group was the failure of Westminster to confront the question of elected local government in the decade and a half after 1870. It is possible to imagine a root-and-branch restructuring on both sides of the Irish Sea that would have created a network of county councils grouped into provincial or central boards capable of harnessing all national and regional pressures within a reinvigorated United Kingdom structure: Canada's prime minister recommended such a structure in 1871, but no British government had the energy or the will to tackle the issue. Gladstone's first ministry self-immolated in its own hyperactivity before the voters dismissed it in 1874. Disraeli's government that followed would not contemplate an open challenge to landlord influence in the localities, even if it simultaneously followed a centralising policy of social reform. Returning to office in 1880, Gladstone inherited a confrontation with Irish nationalism that had overtones of social revolution that are too easily filtered out of historical narratives. It may be tempting to regret the fact that for fifteen years after 1870, the Cambridge Union first ignored and then denied Irish grievances, and we may blame its myopia on the failure of political leadership to confront the underlying issues. Even so, it does not necessarily follow that either Gladstone or Disraeli should be condemned for dereliction of ministerial duty merely because they did not see the need at the time for radical surgery that might have bequeathed a more harmoniously organised island group to posterity.

In the Cambridge Union, Gladstone's leadership seems to have been responsible for a swing towards Home Rule in and after 1886. Even so, it took a further twenty-five years before the Union began to register cautious majorities in its favour. Nineteenth-century statesmen did not believe that duty required them to act in advance of obvious necessity, and even then they preferred to proceed only with clear evidence of public consensus. Charles Merivale thought Lord Liverpool was "the last minister who really governed us .... Since his time all ministers, Wellington and Grey, Peel and Russell, have simply made it their business to ascertain what was the popular will, and to follow it". Peel's downfall in 1846 remained a stark warning against responding to a public opinion that was still divided, while Randolph Churchill's most wounding jibe against Gladstone was that he was "an old man in a hurry".[13]

Even where the existence of majorities could be demonstrated, what was their true significance? Cambridge Union evidence points to a steady majority in favour of Catholic Emancipation for seven years before 1829. Nor was junior Cambridge necessarily in advance of the march of opinion in the wider community. The evangelical George Stephen later concluded that as early as 1820, the Catholic cause was "more advanced than even the most sanguine could have expected, and it was no longer a question of concession, but of extent".[14] Does this mean that Peel and Wellington were dilatory in their handling of the issue? The charge is hardly fair, for the Cambridge evidence equally points to an irreconcilable minority of between 40 and 46 percent who no doubt consoled themselves, as did Thackeray, with the thought that they had only just been beaten. There are both practical and theoretical objections to the assumption that any majority constitutes a valid mandate for change. At a practical level, small majorities may be insufficiently stable to carry through major legislation. In 1831, the passage of the second reading of the Reform Bill by 302 votes to 301 was a major moral triumph, but it was an equally clear indication of the practical need for concessions, simply because the coalition in its favour could not conceivably remain united through a lengthy parliamentary contest. Nor, arguably, would it have been right for so small a majority (especially produced by an electoral system that it proposed to purge) to force through such fundamental change. Countries as theoretically democratic as the United States and Australia have written constitutions which take for granted that amendments to the system of government require endorsement by something more than a simple majority. There is, after all, something to be said for the argument advanced by Erskine Childers in 1893, that the "weight of responsibility" lies with those proposing change, not with those who resist. We need not grudge Swift MacNeill his pleasure at winning a three-vote majority for Home Rule in 1913 forty years after he had introduced the issue to the Cambridge Union. However, we may doubt whether such a vote would have been enough to constitute a mandate for fundamental change, even if it had been won in a more responsible forum.

Cambridge Union debates are valuable in demonstrating the division of opinion, especially if they remind us that minorities may have rights. Yet they do not help us much in tackling the far more impenetrable question of the source of changing ideas. Until the disaster of 1886, Gladstone was superbly effective at detecting the movement of public opinion, as it swung towards Reform after 1864, or away from the Irish Church in 1868-69, just as he sensed the political potential of the Bulgarian horrors a decade later. But what caused these sudden and sometimes seismic shifts in opinion? Historians may offer bread-and-butter explanations, narratives implying that articles in *this* newspaper or speeches from *that* politician somehow touched off a brushfire in public attitudes. In much the same way, correspondents of the *Granta* and the *Cambridge Review* often assured their readers of a cause-and-effect relationship between a spectacular speech and the outcome of a debate, even when comparative evidence shows that the division of opinion on the general issue remained stable from year to year. The truth is that we simply cannot identify the influences that powered changes in attitudes. Victorian Britain was deluged with newspapers and reviews, harangued by political leaders and preached at by clerics. There seems neither rhyme nor reason to explain why a rare essay or editorial, an occasional speech or sermon, managed to strike home when so many hundreds of others bounced harmlessly off the public mind.

Sometimes, the origin of interest in an issue can be identified with some precision and confidence. In November 1866, the Cambridge Union held the first of what would be 31 debates by 1914 on the question of admitting women to the franchise. The debate was probably triggered by the launching of a national women's franchise campaign that same month.[15] If so, it represented a rapid response to a new idea, for the Union was debating votes for women six months before John Stuart Mill invited the House of Commons to substitute the word "person" for "man" in the Second Reform Bill. It is tempting to associate the appearance of female suffrage on the Cambridge Union agenda with the apparently sudden shift in attitudes towards the Irish Church as two aspects of the modernising mentality of the eighteen-sixties. Unfortunately, the two issues did not march in step. Except in 1873 and 1885, when motions specified single women of independent means, suffragists rarely managed to poll even a quarter of the vote. However, as with Home Rule, attitudes moved from overall opposition to indecisive approval after 1905. It is possible to describe these shifts of opinion, but impossible to identify the mechanisms of change, let alone point to any plausible inter-relationship that may link them.

The enigma of opinion-formation may be linked to the art form of biography. As a genre, political biography is uneasy in its handling of early life. Such evidence as survives for childhood consists mainly of the embarrassing reminiscences of nursemaids and proud parents. If the subject is worthy of biographical study, there is usually more than enough material for the reconstruction of a public career. Hence the inclination of most biographers is to put aside the childish things of formative years and hurry the subject into parliament. One biographer of Lord Salisbury has him elected on page 4, although the record was probably achieved by G.M. Young's biography of Baldwin, in which the subject passes his fiftieth birthday after just eight pages.[16]

Of course, it does not follow that the causes espoused in a student debating society necessarily determine any subsequent political career. Hugh Childers changed his mind about the Church of Ireland. More spectacularly, Erskine Childers changed his opinions about Ireland's union with Britain, although it is possible to detect a unifying thread in his consistent rejection of the half-way house of federalism. At the very least, political biography could be more rigorous in fitting products of Oxbridge into one of three categories. Some later politicians cut their teeth in the two Unions. A second group had their interest in public events aroused while at university – Parnell is a case in point – but steered clear of formal debating. A third appear to have caught the bug subsequent to graduation – including, as it happens, the three Cambridge prime ministers, Balfour, Campbell-Bannerman and Baldwin. "Undergraduates should eschew Politics" – but many refused to do so, and the Union threw out that particular motion in 1887. It may help to understand the subsequent role of those "Unionic" undergraduates by appreciating that their political starting point may lie much earlier than standard biographical narratives usually accommodate.

It is hardly controversial to claim that in British social and political life, the eighteen-sixties was a very different decade from the eighteen-twenties. Looking at the eighteen-sixties as a historical "period" to be "explained", it becomes easy to forget that the principal participants did not fully "belong" to the moment under examination, but owed their own formation to an earlier time. In 1866, Russell's Liberal ministry faltered in the face of opposition to the extension of the right to vote. One of the most effective House of Commons skirmishers was Spencer Walpole, who had entered parliament in 1846. Thus Walpole served his apprenticeship during the years in which even his fellow-Conservatives came to doubt the "finality" of 1832. Somehow his own failure to deduce this obvious truth from the world around him renders him inexplicable, a historical dinosaur who even resigned from the cabinet in 1859 rather than back his colleagues in an attempt to settle the Reform issue on moderate terms. But Walpole becomes more intelligible when we trace him in the Cambridge Union, opposing manhood suffrage and the ballot as far back as 1826. Spencer Walpole's political starting point was not his election to parliament at a time when the settlement of 1832 was starting to crack. Rather, his ideas had formed when even the Reform Act itself was still unthinkable. Charles Merivale, who recalled Walpole presiding over the Union "with imposing dignity", added: "Reform was still in the background. I don't think our liberal debaters ever once mentioned it."[17]

Dating Walpole's first engagement with politics is not to insist that he was thereafter programmed to resist all innovation. His near-contemporary at Oxford, W.E. Gladstone, started with very similar beliefs but steadily shed them in the process of responding to modernity. However, there may be one overall benefit in extending the dimension of individual political engagement back into late adolescence and early manhood. The passage of time perhaps eroded the certainties of youth, but it did little to dissolve the intractability of Britain's relationship with Ireland. There was an urgency in the motion of 1887 that "the condition of Ireland demands the concession of Home Rule". Reginald McKenna, who spoke in its favour, would no doubt have been surprised could he have known that twenty-five years later he would be a member of a government still trying to push the measure through. Equally, by the time they reached middle age, even those worthy young men who had argued that firm government would drill the wayward Irish into cheerful obedience may have questioned their own solution. Austen Chamberlain had doubted the panacea when as a young man he attacked Coercion in the Union debates of the early eighteen-eighties. Forty years later, he reverted to the gamble of trust by signing the Treaty, and probably thereby sacrificed his chance to become prime minister. F.H. Maugham crossed swords with McKenna in that debate of 1887. Half a century later, he joined a Conservative cabinet that withdrew the British navy from the south and west coasts of Ireland. At 20, he was violently distrustful of Parnell; at 70 he found himself relying upon the goodwill of de Valera. The earlier we realise that English politicians formed their views on Ireland, the more easily we can appreciate that some of them came to recognise that there was no simple answer to the Irish question.

"Ireland was only demanding to be itself," J.F. Roxburgh assured the Union in 1911.[18] But what was Ireland "itself"? The country contained rival identities, each of them claiming to speak for the whole. On the rare occasions when those disparate Irish voices shared a single sense of grievance, as happened in the aftermath of the Financial Commission report of 1897, they did not necessarily agree on the answer. In any case, solutions preferred in Ireland did not always square with English notions of the fundamental nature of the United Kingdom. Even if we adopt a simplistic and retrospective series of value judgements, we ought to marvel that the Cambridge Union so often got its answers "right".

For most of the century between 1815 and 1914, the Cambridge Union regarded landlord, professional and above all Protestant Ireland as possessing at least an equal legitimacy in its claims to speak for the sister island. It is doubly difficult for us to get hold of this fundamental point, partly because we see the Ascendancy as a colonial-style minority, but even more because they seemed to vanish altogether from independent Ireland and so challenge our powers of imaginative reconstruction. Our tendency to discount them as a minority should not discredit their claims to be taken seriously in their own time. Britain and Ireland did not arrive at the stage of mass (but still not universal) male franchise until 1884. Property and education carried proportionately greater weight in the nineteenth century. Nor did assumptions change overnight: throughout the first half of the twentieth century, the white minority was overwhelmingly accepted as the legitimate voice of South Africa, despite a recent history of spoliation and political exclusion that far exceeded the inherited sins of Protestant Ireland.

None the less, the Cambridge Union did recognise the existence of another Ireland whose grievances were to be met and whose rights had to be acknowledged. Majorities favoured the removal of the disabilities that prevented Catholics from entering parliament, accepted that Maynooth should receive public funding and that the Protestant Church should lose its privileges. If there is a single common thread throughout a century of discussing Irish issues, it is a desire that they should be resolved within the framework of the United Kingdom. Hindsight may regard that strategy as doomed, but it can hardly be condemned as selfish or even necessarily mistaken.

There are signs that, gradually, Catholic and nationalist Ireland was perceived to have ousted the Protestant and unionist identity as the country's legitimate voice. In 1841, a Fellow of Trinity had described a visiting Anglican preacher as "an Irishman of a vehement order; a more violent cushion-thumper I never heard". In this comment, Irish identity was certainly not equated with Catholicism; rather, the preacher's Irishness implicitly explained the ferocity of his Protestantism. Yet in a Union debate in 1902, a critic of Coercion sought to deny his opponents' Irish credentials by pointing to their Ulster origins: Protestantism was coming to be seen as something that undermined the right to speak as an Irishman. In 1835, the Union had upheld the Orange Order's right to exist, although even Lord Roden was too great an absurdity for them to swallow in 1850. By 1905, an undergraduate who acknowledged that he was an Orangeman thought it useful to laugh off his confession by denying that he was a convict or a lunatic. Ulster drew only small houses and less sympathy in 1892-93 and again in 1912-14.

Perhaps it was for the best that so few Ulster voices were heard in the Cambridge Union. E.W. MacBride's description of the Parnellites in 1890 as "eighty-six bog-trotting ruffians" was not especially illuminating. Worse still, it probably tended to convert the Home Rule debate in English eyes from a contest of civilisation against barbarism to a quarrel between two equally incomprehensible and irresponsible factions. If Ireland was really "demanding to be itself", the logical conclusion in the English mind might well be to let the Irish get on with the task. "Aren't they a remarkable people?" wrote Asquith in 1914 after an emotional exchange between the Nationalist John Dillon and his Ulster counterpart James Craig in 1914. "And the folly of thinking that we can ever understand them, let alone govern them!" [19]

By the early twentieth century, the overall tone of the Cambridge debates suggests that the Ascendancy were on their way to becoming the long-term losers. Just as land purchase was removing them from the social scene, so the increasing definition of Home Rule as a confrontation between two Irish tribes marginalised the old elite out of the political equation. Edmund Burke had used the term "Anglo-Irish", but the term was rarely employed in the nineteenth century, and then mainly to describe the political relationship of the two islands rather than any section of its people. T.P. O'Connor and F.H. O'Donnell agreed that Parnell was in many respects more English than Irish, but neither branded him as "Anglo-Irish" and it is easy to imagine their leader's scorn had anyone sought so to qualify his national identity. Modern historians sometimes apply the label retrospectively,[20] but the origins of the process of denial can be seen in the gradual acceptance of the prospect of Home Rule prior to 1914.

Chapter Four argues that neither the Irish identity nor the Catholic faith were prominent in nineteenth-century Cambridge. No doubt it is striking that a major British university should have attracted so few Irish Catholic students. At just the point in the eighteen-sixties when Cambridge began to retreat from its oppressive Protestantism, the Catholic Church erected its own obstacles to access. By the time the ban was removed in 1895, the range of choice (and price) in higher education was becoming wider, making Cambridge correspondingly less attractive. But did all of this matter? Appendix One provides a glimpse of the very broad selection of subjects that the Union discussed through the half century prior to 1914 when its agenda had become primarily political. We simply have to accept the historical fact of life that the participants in those debates were principally members of an English social elite. They discussed the North-West Frontier of India without the participation of speakers from Afghanistan just as they held forth about trades unions without seeking the opinions of manual workers. Every Irish issue but one could be solved within the existing framework of the United Kingdom by dispassionate debate that required no special pleading. The exception, Home Rule as the derived form of Repeal, was probably more effectively argued in the Cambridge Union by English well-wishers than demanded by Irish advocates. True, the Union voted its largest-ever majority in favour of Home Rule at the debate of 1912 on the sole occasion when it listened to the views of an Ulster Catholic, but Jeremiah MacVeagh was clearly uneasy in an alien environment and we may doubt any close relationship of cause and effect.

And so we return to the conundrum of Ireland "itself". As the votes were counted at the debate on Catholic Emancipation in 1829, enthusiasts gave three cheers "for Ireland". In later decades, the Union asked whether this or that reform was in the interests of Ireland or of the "Irish people", even if we may suspect that the strangely worded motion of 1877 was not the sole occasion on which they also had an eye to the claims of the "English" empire. They did at least discuss Ireland. More often than we might have expected, they showed themselves flexible in the face of changes that were shocking to inherited mindsets. If they failed to answer the Irish question and did not always focus clearly on Irish reality, they were not alone. "Nobody knows what Ireland really is, and of what she is capable," wrote Erskine Childers in 1911. "Nobody can know until she has responsibility for her own fate."[21] The Cambridge Union cannot be blamed for failing to solve the enigma, nor should it be condemned if it was sometimes reluctant to gamble on the answer.

APPENDIX I

THE TROUBLES 1919-21

"The life of new Cambridge should differ but little from the old", insisted a university journalist in January 1919.[1] Of course it could not be so. Within a few months, the undergraduate population had swollen to three times its pre-war numbers. Even after the backlog had passed through, Cambridge permanently doubled in size. Compulsory Greek was quickly sacrificed titular degrees, conceded to women and the PhD cautiously adopted. The social composition of the university did not change overnight but the political atmosphere was utterly different from that of 1914. In October 1919, with the Union chamber packed like "a Crystal Palace Cup-Tie", a motion condemning the League of Nations as "a radically unsound and dangerous project" was rejected by a massive 723 votes to 280.[2] A century earlier, Bulwer Lytton had seen the funny side of a debating club where "striplings settled questions spoilt by men". For a brief period, the striplings had a particular claim to set the world to rights. J.H.B. Nihill had won the Military Cross while serving with the Royal Munster Fusiliers and "had seen countless Irishmen make the supreme sacrifice in the hope that they would gain freedom for others". His denunciation in March 1919 of "government by courts-martial" in Ireland was something more than youthful bravado.[3]

The Union burst back into life, quickly clearing its wartime overdraft. Some continuity was provided by activists from the immediate pre-war years, such as Geoffrey Shakespeare, while ex-Presidents like J.R.M. Butler, now well-established as a Fellow of Trinity, made a point of participating to guide the new generation into the traditions of the Society. With far more aspiring speakers, there was an ever-greater danger of repetition and exaggeration, which makes all the more remarkable the evident demand for compromise in discussions of the Irish issue. "Why *will* people talk late for the sake of talking?", asked the exasperated correspondent of the *Granta* reporting the debate on Ireland in May 1919.[4] Five debates between May 1919 and November 1921 demonstrate that "Ireland ... always provides fitting meat for a discussion".[5] Although T.P. O'Connor came as guest speaker in May 1921, the debates predominantly reflected student interest. Indeed, when the debate of November 1921 was organised at short notice after the flamboyant Horatio Bottomley had withdrawn from a commitment to speak on another subject, members outraged traditionalists by passing notes to the chair asking to be called to speak.

The motions and outcomes of the five debates may be summarised. In May 1919 the Union condemned, by 94 votes to 58, "the inaction of the Government with regard to Ireland". Both the motion and its discussion were unhelpfully vague. The proposer, C.D.B. Ellis, later to become historian of the Quorn Hunt, "confessed to a complete ignorance of Ireland" and, thus equipped, denied that he had any "duty to outline a constructive policy".[6] However, in December 1919 Lloyd George made a series of "proposals for the solution of the Irish Question", and the Union voted its approval a month later by 197 votes to 131.[7] The government's scheme, which combined Partition with a proposed Council of Ireland, eventually limped on to the statute book as the Government of Ireland Act. Meanwhile, the situation on the ground deteriorated. In October 1920, the Union decided by 264 votes to 166 that it viewed "with indignation the policy of reprisals" and urged "that Parliament should declare Ireland a Dominion and authorise an Irish Constituent Assembly to frame a Constitution within the Empire". The motion could be faulted, as a Nationalist partisan put it a year later, for saying in effect: "We are prepared to offer you a good place in the British Empire, but if you refuse we will force you to accept our terms".[8] None the less, the debate was an indication of a trend of opinion towards some form of compromise. In May 1921, spurred no doubt by the honeyed words of T.P. O'Connor, the "coercive policy of the Government in Ireland" was again condemned, this time emphatically by 249 votes to 59.[9] Finally, in November 1921, the Union rejected, by 162 votes to 140, a belligerent motion arguing that "in the event of a breakdown of the present negotiations with the Irish Leaders, the only course open would be a return to force".[10] An uncharacteristic contribution to this debate was a maiden speech in favour of the motion from the young R.A. Butler, who managed to speak immediately after a plea for peace from his cousin J.R.M. Butler, to whom he delivered "an admirable retort". "Rab", so often modest in his later career, seems to have engaged in a rare piece of self-promotion, using the debate to proclaim that there was a new Butler on the block. "I leapt up just after Jim", he reported to his family, adding that "I got several people to realise who I was".[11]

The contrast with pre-war debates on Ireland was marked. The opposition to the repression in Ireland was far stronger than the muted rejected by 64 votes to 53 of George Wyndham's mild form of Coercion back in 1902. The open endorsement of some dominion status also went far beyond the narrow and fluctuating acceptance of Home Rule in the last years before the War. "The speeches were very moderate in temper", commented the *Cambridge Review* of the debate on the bloodcurdling motion of November 1921, "and if they are indicative of the country as a whole, a settlement of the Irish question will undoubtedly be obtained in the near future."[12] Four weeks later, the Treaty was signed in Downing Street.

One sign of changing attitudes was the virtual disappearance by 1921 of pejorative caricatures of Ireland. "The Irish objection was not that they governed well or ill but that they were governed at all," one young man announced in May 1919, adding that "Ireland can't be given her independence, because she hasn't got any money."[13] Another complained in January 1920 that "[t]he most obvious characteristic of the Irish was their inability to think in political terms".[14] But by October of that year, a rising Union star called Ian Macpherson offered a far more sober case against concession, even invoking Abraham Lincoln's resistance to Southern secession in the American Civil War. "They could not treat Ireland as dominion because geography would not allow them. Ireland was too near England's back door."[15] The debate took place two days after the death of Terence MacSwiney at the close of a prolonged and harrowing hunger strike, a sacrifice to which Macpherson made an honourable acknowledgement. Watching from the gallery was the correspondent of the *Granta* (whose editor unctuously rubbed home the point that the magazine had actually commissioned a reporter from one of the women's colleges). She was outraged that some of Macpherson's supporters did not "share his reasonable opinion of the Lord Mayor of Cork". In a trenchant rebuke, she told them that they should "at least refrain from making their opinions audible in an objectionable manner. It simply isn't done."[16] Overall, ethnic stereotypes told more about the personalities of their perpetrators. "Nicely outspoken!" exclaimed the *Cambridge Review* in January 1920 when Victor Raikes "called the Irish lazy pro-German assassins". In a long career in Conservative politics, Raikes later supported Winston Churchill's Die-Hard campaign against concessions to Indian nationalism in the nineteen-thirties and became President of the Monday Club in 1975, the year that Margaret Thatcher was elected leader of the party.[17]

The Irish national cause was vocally upheld by two popular speakers, both of whom were elected to the Presidency, L.A. Abraham in October 1920 and W.D. Johnston in January 1922. Abraham's father had sat as an Irish MP at Westminster for thirty years, but he is best remembered for proposing the motion to depose Parnell from the party leadership during the fraught confrontation in Committee Room Fifteen in 1891. There is reason to suspect that it fell to William Abraham to wield the knife because he was "a Protestant member of the Party".[18] Louis Abraham objected to being considered a species of savage simply because he was an Irish nationalist. "The only way to treat Ireland", he told the Union, "was to trust her and regard her as a country with her own ideals and traditions."[19] His view of Ireland as a single entity naturally led him to play down the existence of a separate Ulster identity, something which he insisted was "confined to two counties and a borough and a half".[20] The *Granta* condemned him in January 1920 for a "rather hysterical defence of Signor [sic] de Valera", but none the less he was a popular speaker. "Never have we listened to such absurd, illogical, bigoted and unbalanced rubbish", remarked the *Granta* of his speech in May 1919, "and, very never [sic] have we enjoyed a speech so much."[21] Like John Redmond and Erskine Childers, Abraham later became a clerk of the House of Commons. Unlike them, he did not return to Irish politics.

The son of a Dublin judge, Denis Johnston burst upon the Union in October 1920 with a "brilliant" speech in favour of justice and understanding. In hailing this young Protestant who had been at school in Scotland, the *Cambridge Review* drew deep upon ethnic stereotype. "With his combination of Irish wit and eloquence the hon. Member should go far."[22] In November 1921, on the verge of the Presidency, he delivered "a great speech", in which he "proclaimed Ireland a nation amongst thunderous applause".[23] After graduation, Johnston returned to Dublin where, for some years, he was Director of the Gate Theatre. In 1936 he joined the BBC and, after distinguished service as a war correspondent, he went on to make an academic career in the United States.

Yet effective advocacy of the Irish case is hardly enough to explain the muted attitudes of the Cambridge Union. Throughout the previous hundred years, debates on Irish issues had assumed complete freedom of action. Catholic emancipation, disestablishment, Home Rule, land reform – all of these might or might not be conceded, according to the free and unconstrained decision of the "pre-dominant partner", the English elite. Even the apparent exception, O'Connell's election in the County Clare by-election of 1828, had done little to shift the balance of attitudes towards the Catholic claims, although in 1867 the Union had shown itself perhaps surprisingly flexible in the face of Fenianism. In 1919-21, for the first time, English opinion had to confront an Ireland that it could no longer control. "The choice was between Dominion Home Rule and the re-conquest of Ireland," Granville Sharp told the Union in October 1920, "between chaos and peace".[24] Six times in the next thirty years Sharp would fight without success for a seat in Parliament, one of the gallant band who kept the Liberal Party faintly alive through its darkest decades. But if his party faltered, its spirit surely spoke for an important thread of English opinion.

For many ways, the debates of 1920 and 1921 were not so much about Ireland as fundamental confrontations with the nature of Englishness. Sharp insisted that reprisals by Crown forces in Ireland "were not acts of legitimate self-defence but premeditated, and inflicted on the innocent rather than the guilty". Kingsley Martin, future editor of the *New Statesman*, attacked apologists for the policy of reprisals: "they could not conceive of an Englishman doing wrong". Another speaker likened Lloyd George's government to a "fourth rate cricket team. Hit the batsman if you can't get the wicket."[25] That wise old performer, T.P. O'Connor, took up the theme, insisting that he "did not come to speak for Ireland, but came to speak primarily in the interest of the British Empire". The dominions, he said, had rallied to the cause in 1914 because the Empire was "based upon law, liberty, love, order and honour". Insisting that the

Crown forces in Ireland "were miserable caricatures of the true English soldier", he warned that "England would find it hard to recover her old name for honour and love of order and speaking the truth".[26] Ian Macpherson had urged members to pause before condemning the reprisals: "let them think of the provocation".[27] For the majority, provocation was not a sufficient excuse. Three times in eighteen months, the Cambridge Union voted against the use of force in Ireland.

It has been called "the most melodramatic moment in modern Anglo-Irish relations".[28] At Downing Street late on the evening of 5 December 1921, as the Irish delegates hesitated to sign the terms hammered out in exhausting negotiations, Lloyd George dramatically produced two letters, announcing that one of them must be sent by special messenger to the prime minister of Northern Ireland, Sir James Craig, that very night. One letter announced that there would be peace, the other the resumption of terrible war. "Whichever letter you choose travels by special train to Holyhead, and by destroyer to Belfast. The train is waiting with steam up at Euston." The delegates opted for peace and signed the agreement for a Treaty.[29]

The messenger was one of Lloyd George's private secretaries, Geoffrey Shakespeare, who was just down from Cambridge. Shakespeare had first been elected to the Union Committee in 1914. War service had taken him to Gallipoli, where mystified Australian troops hailed him as "a perishing Bard", before scarlet fever had invalided him back home.[30] He had been President of the Union when it had first endorsed Lloyd George's scheme to pacify Ireland in January 1920, but had only once spoken in an Irish debate himself, before or after the war, and then from the cross-benches on the inconclusive motion of May 1919. "The office of President is a useful passport into political life," he would later write. "I was to find that true in my own career." In fact it is a great deal more likely that he was taken on to the Downing Street staff because his father, a prominent Baptist minister, was one of Lloyd George's closest allies, part of the inner circle that had planned the Coalition Liberal campaign for the general election of 1918.[31]

Shakespeare never could understand why the Irish delegates failed to call Lloyd George's bluff. As Pakenham pointed out, whatever the nature of the undertaking to inform Sir James Craig of the outcome, he had already been kept waiting for months. In any case, a British obligation to Craig "could hardly be set against the whole future of both parts of Ireland".[32] The Irish delegates might well have stood on their formal position that Craig was the creature of an alien government, and added the more prosaic objection that since he had hardly gone out of his way to advance the chances of an all-Ireland settlement, the Northern Ireland premier could be left to read the newspapers like everybody else.

It is possible that Lloyd George's theatrical gesture represented a manoeuvre at a much more fundamental level. Not merely did the Irish delegates accept the threatened mission "like a law of nature".[33] They conspicuously failed to demand similar facilities – at least the special train to Holyhead if not the connecting warship – to enable them to refer the terms of the Treaty back to Dublin. It would seem that the British negotiators realised that their Irish counterparts had implicitly resolved to reach their own decision. If so, then the elaborate charade of sending news to Craig can be seen as a device to force the Irish to come to terms with the implications of their own decision not to refer the terms on offer to Dublin. To consult Dublin – which, in effect, would be to place the decision in the hands of the inflexible de Valera – would be tantamount to a rejection of the proposed agreement. By demonstrating how easily a messenger could be rushed to Belfast, Lloyd George obliged the Irish delegates to confront the corollary of their own strategy: once they had resolved to decide for themselves, they had in effect determined upon acceptance. It was not, as Pakenham put it, that Lloyd George "had conjured Dublin off the map" and thereby "obsessed each Delegate with an inescapable sense of personal responsibility".[34] It was rather that he had compelled them to recognise the consequences of that personal responsibility by reminding them of the proximity of Belfast.

The little comedy had to be played out to its end. At twenty minutes to three, the jovial prime minister promised young Shakespeare a state funeral in Westminster Abbey should his mission fail and bundled him out into the December darkness. At once it became clear that the dramatic elements of the dash to Belfast, the special train and the waiting destroyer, had been emphasised at the expense of the necessary supporting detail. Downing Street had made no arrangements to get its envoy to Euston: indeed, it was one of Shakespeare's own informal responsibilities to act as the prime minister's chauffeur. Clutching a copy of the document that was to bring peace to Ireland, he headed into Whitehall to look for a cab. The first taxi that he hailed refused to stop, its driver perhaps mindful of the fact that a delegation of Irish terrorists was at Downing Street. By the time he reached Euston, Shakespeare was in a state of high excitement about his mission. Earlier that night, he had passed the time grilling Erskine Childers about the plot of *The Riddle of the Sands*. Ushered into a sleeping compartment on the special train, his first thought was to thrust the precious Treaty under the pillow, resolving to guard it throughout the night in full wakefulness. In fact, the next thing he knew was the steward rousing him with the news that the train would reach Holyhead in five minutes. He was whisked aboard the warship and rushed to Belfast. There he encountered a further reminder that melodrama had been emphasised over practicality. No arrangements had been made for him to be met on arrival. The herald of peace went to a public telephone box to call Craig's office, only to find that he did not have the pennies needed for the coin-box. In desperation, he dialled the operator and pleaded the urgency of his need to speak to the prime minister of Northern Ireland. Fortunately, the Belfast telephone exchange had orders to put "the English envoy" through without charge. Using a code of spectacular naivety, Shakespeare was soon able to telegraph to London an assurance that the customer was prepared to do business on the quoted terms.[35] It had been seven and a half centuries since Strongbow had sailed from the shores of Lloyd George's native land. In that time, governments in London had rained down upon Ireland armies of conquest, laws of repression and projects of improvement. It fell to the Welsh Wizard to achieve a settlement of the Irish question through the bizarre device of threatening to unleash a young private secretary just down from Cambridge.

APPENDIX II

NUMBERS VOTING AT DEBATES

1863-1914

Column A gives the month and year of the debate. The information is grouped into academic years, running from October to the following June. Attendances varied from year to year.

Column B briefly indicates the topic. Frequently discussed topics are grouped under the headings "Church", "Drink", "Party politics", "Votes for women" and "Women at Cambridge". Church debates usually focused on disestablishment. The most common "Party politics" debates were those on motions of "no confidence" in the government of the day, but these were occasionally varied with attacks on the official opposition. Motions relating to Ireland are *italicised*.

Column C gives the numbers voting. Votes were taken at the close of debates, making it likely that only the most committed members remained to register their opinions. On some occasions, procedural motions were taken earlier in the evening, and where votes are recorded, they often indicate that the attendance was larger than the final division. The best-attended debate for each year is asterisked. *Note*: only well-attended debates on non-Irish issues are included.

A	B	C
Oct 63	American Civil War	84
Nov 63	Laird rams (American Civil War)	97
Nov 63	Poland	71
Dec 63	Women at Cambridge	78
Feb 64	*Palmerston's foreign policy (Denmark)	102
Mar 64	*Irish Church*	74
Nov 64	Nonconformists at Cambridge	159
Nov 64	"Brother Ignatius" (Church)	134
Nov 64	Character of Oliver Cromwell	139
Dec 64	*Compulsory chapel at Cambridge	191
Feb 65	American Civil War	105
Feb 65	Capital punishment	94
Mar 65	*Irish Church*	107
Oct 65	Party politics	131

Oct 65	*Fenians*	100
Nov 65	Franchise reform	124
Nov 65	Gladstone's defeat at Oxford	135
Dec 65	*Church	163
Feb 66	Cambridge American Lectureship	160
Oct 66	*Party politics	312
Nov 66	Act of Uniformity of 1662	128
Nov 66	Votes for women	178
Jan 67	*Irish Church*	106
Feb 67	Parliamentary Reform	140
Feb 67	Governor Eyre	156
Mar 66	*Fenian rising*	66
Mar 67	Toleration of Mormons	100
May 67	Women at Cambridge	88
Oct 67	Parliamentary Reform/Disraeli	162
Nov 67	Sunday opening of museums	160
Nov 67	Religious tests at Cambridge	148
Nov 67	Legislation against Ritualists	138
Jan 68	*Manchester executions*	128
Feb 68	*Votes for women	184
Feb 68	Capital punishment	117
Mar 68	Disraeli	120
Mar 68	Compulsory chapel at Cambridge	134
Mar 68	*Conciliation in Ireland*	172
May 68	Party politics	108
Oct 68	Anonymous journalism	144
Nov 68	*College kitchen system at Cambridge	240
Nov 68	Admission of non-collegiate students	131
Dec 68	Party politics	124
Feb 69	Abandonment of Gibraltar	144
Feb 69	Party politics	124
Mar 69	Sunday opening of museums	103
May 69	*Irish Land and Church*	75
Nov 69	National education	95
Nov 69	Religious tests at Cambridge	132
Nov 69	Church	136
Dec 69	Women at Cambridge	104
Feb 70	*Irish Land Bill*	68
Feb 70	National education	117
Feb 70	Votes for women	115
Mar 70	*Compulsory chapel at Cambridge	143

Oct 70	*Franco-Prussian War	146
Nov 70	Boating regulations on the Cam	116
Nov 70	French republic	127
Nov 70	Relations with Russia	151
Mar 71	House of Lords/Church	138
May 71	Paris Commune	116
Oct 71	*Party politics	193
Oct 71	Church	107
Nov 71	Republican principle	165
Feb 72	Sunday opening of museums	96
Mar 72	India	100
May 72	Votes for women	130
Oct 72	Alsace-Lorraine	122
Nov 72	Corporal punishment	107
Nov 72	Drink	117
Dec 72	Contagious Diseases Act	145
Feb 73	Education of women	108
Mar 73	*Church	185
Oct 73	Party politics	176
Oct 73	Breach of promise law	147
Oct 73	*Rights of women	184
Nov 73	*Home Rule/Irish local government*	53
Feb 74	Party politics	149
Feb 74	Inspection of convents	126
May 74	Cremation	143
Oct 74	Reform of Cambridge	171
Nov 74	Party politics	248
Nov 74	Sunday opening of museums	207
Nov 74	French republic	128
Nov 74	Public Worship Bill	218
Feb 75	Gladstone	193
Feb 75	Votes for women	172
Feb 75	Deceased Wife's Sister	218
Apr 75	*Church	314
May 75	Dr Kenealy	190
May 75	Conscription	122
Oct 75	Party politics	252
Nov 75	Sunday observance	176
Nov 75	House of Lords/life peerages	159
Nov 75	Osborne Morgan's Burials Bill	190
Feb 76	*Church	316

Feb 76	Sunday opening of museums	177
Feb 77	Capital punishment	151
Mar 76	Reform of Cambridge	125
Mar 76	Breach of promise law	142
May 76	Party politics	162
May 76	Votes for women	170
Nov 76	Eastern Question	205
Feb 77	*Church	316
Feb 77	*Home Rule*	106
Apr 77	Party politics	263
May 77	Eastern Question	279
Oct 77	Party politics	256
Dec 77	*Home Rule*	77
Feb 78	Eastern Question	187
Feb 78	*Party politics	284
Feb 78	Osborne Morgan's Burials Bill	199
Oct 78	*Foreign affairs	222
Oct 79	*Party politics	328
Jan 80	Afghanistan	175
Feb 80	*Home Rule*	167
Feb 80	Cremation	166
Mar 80	Monument to the Prince Imperial	211
Apr 80	Church	236
May 80	Women at Cambridge	201
Oct 80	*Party politics	341
Nov 80	*British policy to Ireland*	111
Nov 80	Reform of land laws	310
Dec 80	Votes for women	156
Feb 81	*Coercion*	318
Mar 81	Candahar	215
Mar 81	*Home Rule*	335
Mar 81	Women at Cambridge	268
May 81	*Irish Land Bill*	158
Oct 81	*Irish Land Bill*	274
Nov 81	*Party politics	277
Nov 81	Belief in ghosts	264
Feb 82	*Irish Land/Home Rule*	135
Feb 82	Drink	146
Feb 82	*House of Lords/Irish Land Act*	252
Mar 82	Reform of parliamentary procedure	198
Apr 82	Bradlaugh case	166

Jun 82	Selwyn College	160
Oct 82	Party politics	219
Oct 82	*Home Rule*	145
Nov 82	Women's rights	161
Nov 82	Cambridge University by-election	358
Jan 83	*Coercion*	161
Feb 83	Opium trade	148
Feb 83	Party politics	250
Apr 83	Cambridge proctorial system	229
May 83	Affirmation Bill	342
May 83	House of Lords	300
May 83	*Home Rule*	113
Jun 83	*Party politics	366
Oct 83	Party politics	277
Oct 83	India: Ilbert Bill	224
Nov 83	Drink	179
Nov 83	Church	244
Jan 84	Egypt	163
Feb 84	*Socialism	457
Feb 84	*Irish policy*	207
Mar 84	Profit sharing	183
Mar 84	Party politics	225
May 84	Land nationalisation	187
Jun 84	*Ireland and Franchise Bill*	173
Oct 84	*Party politics	309
Oct 84	Horse racing	194
Nov 84	Church	218
Nov 84	University MPs	159
Nov 84	House of Lords	152
Feb 85	Party politics	239
Feb 85	Votes for women	181
May 85	Student voting rights	181
May 85	*Coercion*	63
Jun 85	Party politics	242
Oct 85	*Party politics	318
Nov 85	Church	267
Jan 86	*Home Rule*	108
Feb 86	Belief in ghosts	141
Mar 86	Votes for women	141
May 86	*Home Rule*	145
Jun 86	*Home Rule*	268[2]

Oct 86	Party politics	160
Oct 86	*Home Rule*	180
Jan 87	*Home Rule*	152
Feb 87	Church	135
May 87	*Coercion*	174
Jun 87	**Home Rule*	271
Oct 87	*Home Rule*	179
Nov 87	State of the Cam	171
Feb 88	Women at Cambridge	190
Feb 88	Belief in ghosts	128
May 88	Party politics	120
Jun 88	*Bacon and Shakespeare	232
Oct 88	*Irish policy*	65
Oct 88	Church	222
Feb 89	Women's rights	126
Feb 89	Cambridge journalism	229
Mar 89	**Irish policy*	425
May 89	Sunday opening of public houses	128
Oct 89	*Sectarian education in Ireland*	92
Oct 89	London County Council	141
Oct 89	Dock strike	190
Nov 89	Fashion	153
Nov 89	Women at Cambridge	192
Nov 89	Hunting	144
Nov 89	*Socialism	254
Feb 90	House of Lords	159
Feb 90	*Home Rule*	180
Mar 90	Democracy	206
Apr 90	*Special Commission*	94
Oct 90	New Trade Unionism	142
Oct 90	Horse racing	147
Nov 90	*Irish policy*	217
Feb 91	Church	164
Feb 91	Women's rights	142
Mar 91	*Party politics	242
May 91	Salvation Army	134
May 91	Opium trade	196
Jun 91	Drink	186
Oct 91	Party politics	230
Jan 92	*University jurisdiction over town	233
Feb 92	Socialism	141

Feb 92	Party politics	147
Mar 92	Church	227
Jun 92	*Ulster resistance to Home Rule*	59
Oct 92	Party politics	187
Oct 92	Drink	190
Nov 92	Modern philanthropy	135
Jan 93	Women at Cambridge	234
Feb 93	*Home Rule	389
Mar 93	Welsh Church	176
May 93	*Ulster*	78
Oct 93	Party politics	181
Oct 93	State ownership of coal mines	164
Oct 93	Church	214
Mar 94	*Home Rule	294
May 94	Welsh Church	146
Jun 94	House of Lords	241
Oct 94	Party politics	183
Oct 94	Church	136
Nov 94	Empire Music Hall	331
Nov 94	House of Lords	179
Feb 95	Church	203
Feb 95	*Home Rule	417[3]
Mar 95	Republican principle	183
Jun 95	Tolerance	144
Oct 95	American democracy	197
Oct 97	Constantinople	145
Nov 95	Democracy	175
Jan 96	Jameson Raid	171
Feb 96	Women at Cambridge	246
Mar 96	*Party politics	397
Jun 96	Party politics	193
Oct 96	Eastern Question	174
Oct 96	Drink	165
Dec 96	Navy	139
Feb 97	*Financial Commission*	94
Mar 97	Party politics	210
Mar 97	Opium trade	136
May 97	Eastern Question	188
May 97	*Women at Cambridge	1221[4]
Nov 97	India	142
Nov 97	*Party politics	344

Nov 97	*Existence of Irish nation*	146[5]
Dec 97	North-west frontier	135
Feb 98	Dreyfus case	211
Feb 98	*Irish local government*	91
Mar 98	Imperialism and nationality	174
May 98	Spanish-American War	201
May 98	Catholic hostel at Cambridge	186
May 98	Party politics	163
Oct 98	Disarmament	181
Oct 98	Dreyfus case	182
Nov 98	Fashoda crisis	147
Nov 98	Drink	136
Dec 98	Kitchener celebrations at Cambridge	157
Mar 99	*International morality	234
May 99	*Catholic university in Ireland*	72
May 99	Party politics	140
Oct 99	*South Africa	239
Nov 99	Closure of Cambridge theatres	212
Nov 99	Trinity College	142
Nov 99	Church	144
Feb 00	South Africa	158
Feb 00	South Africa	185
Mar 00	Diplomacy	162
Mar 00	Cambridge magistrates	166
May 00	British empire and "alien races"	138
Jun 00	Votes for women	124
Oct 00	Party politics	196
Oct 00	*South Africa	212
Nov 00	Imperialism	124
Oct 01	South Africa	112
Nov 01	Censorship of anarchists	116
Nov 01	*Press freedom	155
Jan 02	*Catholic university in Ireland*	114
Feb 02	Drink	117
Mar 02	South Africa	117
May 02	*Coercion*	117
Oct 02	Education Bill	188
Oct 02	Business training	133
Nov 02	Government by party	153
Nov 02	*Landlordism*	149
Nov 02	Party politics	193

Feb 03	Church	176
Feb 03	*Arthur Lynch case*	148
Feb 03	Jury system	129
Feb 03	Votes for women	169
Mar 03	*Party politics	206
May 03	*Home Rule*	108
Jun 03	Party politics	124
Oct 03	Tariff Reform	234
Nov 03	*Tariff Reform	450
Nov 03	Imperialism	154
Dec 03	*Catholic university in Ireland*	151
Feb 04	Compulsory Greek at Cambridge	157
Mar 04	Church	130
May 04	*Home Rule*	117
Jun 04	Tariff Reform	142
Oct 04	Welsh revolt	152
Nov 04	Public schools	188
Nov 04	*Party politics	443[6]
Jan 05	Women at Cambridge	252
Feb 05	Compulsory Greek at Cambridge	267
Mar 05	Party politics	218
May 05	*MacDonnell affair*	88
Oct 05	India	223
Nov 05	Votes for women	155
Nov 05	Party politics	258
Jan 06	Liberal colonial policy	187
Feb 06	Labour Party	229
Mar 06	Party politics	279
May 06	Education Bill	225
Oct 06	*Home Rule*	187
Oct 06	Public schools	157
Oct 06	Socialism	170
Nov 06	Egypt	160
Nov 06	Defence policy	164
Dec 06	Party politics	237
Jan 07	Channel Tunnel	188
Feb 07	Church	216
Feb 07	*House of Lords	307
Feb 07	Votes for women	240
Mar 07	Party politics	194
Mar 07	*Home Rule*	280

Jun 07	Party politics	304
Oct 07	House of Lords	214
Oct 07	State ownership of railways	181
Oct 07	Deceased Wife's Sister	211
Nov 07	India	161
Nov 07	Education Bill	170
Nov 07	Censorship of plays	241
Nov 07	Role of Oxford and Cambridge	175
Dec 07	Party politics	228
Jan 08	Conscription	170
Jan 08	*Irish administration*	135
Feb 08	Church	235
Feb 08	Socialism	304
Mar 08	Imperialism and nationalism	265
May 08	Drink	216
May 08	Tariff Reform	246
May 08	Votes for women	153
Jun 08	*Socialism	310
Oct 08	House of Lords	162
Oct 08	*Home Rule*	142
Nov 08	Land nationalisation	142
Nov 08	Church	207
Dec 08	Votes for women	225
Dec 08	Conscription	239
Jan 09	House of Lords/Drink	155
Jan 09	British Empire	248
Feb 09	Kaiser Wilhelm	160
Feb 09	Women at Cambridge	202
Feb 09	Socialism	248
Mar 09	Dreadnoughts	179
Mar 09	Welsh Church	159
May 09	Conscription	232
May 09	Puritan spirit	152
Jun 09	*Home Rule*	368[7]
Oct 09	House of Lords/Budget	320
Oct 09	Grey's foreign policy	169
Nov 09	Votes for women	344
Nov 09	Censorship of plays	224
Nov 09	Tariff Reform	289
Nov 09	Church	210
Dec 09	*Party politics	340

Jan 10	Party politics	338
Feb 10	Socialism	204
Feb 10	Tariff Reform	335
Mar 10	Poor Law Report	187
May 10	*Home Rule*	112
Oct 10	Land taxation	202
Oct 10	Disarmament	193
Nov 10	Tariff Reform	301
Nov 10	Tariff Reform	301
Nov 10	House of Lords	205
Nov 10	Party politics	343
Dec 10	*Party politics	431
Jan 11	*Home Rule*	234
Feb 11	Socialism	405
Feb 11	Votes for women	138
Feb 11	Government by party	145
Mar 11	Parliament Bill	340
Jun 11	Party politics	203
Oct 11	Labour unrest	249
Oct 11	Canadian general election	189
Oct 11	Churchill at Admiralty	163
Nov 11	Rights of women	294
Dec 11	Party politics	303
Feb 12	Navy	390
Feb 12	Welsh Church	157
Mar 12	*Home Rule*	427
May 12	Women at Cambridge	190
May 12	*Home Rule*	73
Jun 12	Party politics	259
Oct 12	*Bonar Law and Ulster*	247
Nov 12	Votes for women	270
Dec 12	*Party politics	326
Feb 13	Germany	151
Mar 13	*Home Rule*	235
Jun 13	Party politics	214
Oct 13	Labour unrest	153
Oct 13	Lloyd George's land campaign	228
Oct 13	The Stage	189
Nov 13	*Home Rule*	389[8]
Nov 13	Party politics	176
Nov 13	Women's movement	253

Dec 13	Role of Oxford and Cambridge	244
Feb 14	Strikes in South Africa	156
Feb 14	Divorce laws	314
Mar 14	House of Lords/Marconi affair	204
Mar 14	Party politics	280
Apr 14	*Curragh episode*	112
May 14	Socialism	279
Jun 14	Votes for women	145

Notes:

1. Inaugural debate of the new Union building.
2. Visit of John Dillon.
3. Visit of John Redmond.
4. Debate open to all undergraduates.
5. Vote on amendment. Main debate collapsed.
6. Visit of Lloyd George.
7. Visit of John Dillon.
8. Fortieth anniversary of first Home Rule debate.

TABLE 1: CAMBRIDGE UNION DEBATES

ON CATHOLIC EMANCIPATION

1822-1829

Support for Catholic Emancipation barely varied between 1822 and 1829. O'Connell's election for County Clare triggered a larger turn-out, but no major shift in opinion.

Column A: month and year of debate
Column B: numbers voting
Column C: percentage for Catholic Emancipation

Note: in chapters 8-10, percentages have been simplified to the nearest round number.

A	B	C
May 22	62	58.1
Apr 24	104	60.6
May 25	111	53.5
Feb 26	92	56.5
Feb 27	111	54.9
Nov 27	112	60.7
Mar 28	110	59.1
Mar 29	257	55.6

TABLE 2: CAMBRIDGE UNION DEBATES

ON DISESTABLISHMENT   1864-75

The sudden collapse in support for the Irish Church is striking. Yet Cambridge Union opinion remained predominantly Anglican, making it unlikely that the admission of Nonconformists to the University was responsible for the shift in attitudes towards Ireland.

Column A: month and year of debate.
Column B: Church of England or Ireland?
Column C: numbers voting
Column D: Percentage for Established Church

A	B	C	D
Mar 64	Ireland	74	67.6
Mar 65	Ireland	109	50.5
Dec 65	England	163	77.9
Feb 65	Ireland	106	47.2
Nov 69	England	136	74.3
Mar 73	England	185	77.7
Jun 74	England	86	81.3
Apr 75	England	314	80.9

TABLE 3: CONSERVATIVE PARTY SUPPORT

COMPARED WITH OPPOSITION TO HOME RULE

1873-83

Opposition to Home Rule consistently exceeded support for the Conservatives.

Column A: month and year of debate
Column B: numbers voting
Column C: Percentage for Conservatives
Column D: Percentage against Home Rule

A	B	C	D
Oct 73	176	61.4	-
Nov 73	53	-	(32.1)[1]
Feb 74	149	54.4	-
Nov 74	248	60.1	-
May 76	162	54.9	-
Feb 77	106	-	84.9
Apr 77	263	67.7	-
Oct 77	256	64.1	-
Dec 77	77	-	89.6
May 78	145	70.3	-
Oct 79	328	63.7	-
May 80	167	-	74.8
Mar 81	335	-	71.9
Nov 81	277	49.1	-
Feb 82	135	-	73.4
May 82	170	60	-
Oct 82	219	46.1	-
Oct 82	145	-	67.6
May 83	113	-	83.2
Jun 83	366	50.3	-
Oct 83	274	51.1	-

1: The 1873 Home Rule motion was amended to refer more generally to local government.

TABLE 4: CONSERVATIVE PARTY SUPPORT

COMPARED WITH OPPOSITION TO HOME RULE

1885-88

Tables 4 to 6 suggest that, from 1886, Home Rule was a straight party issue.

Column A: month and year of debate
Column B: numbers voting
Column C: Percentage for Conservatives
Column D: Percentage against Home Rule

A	B	C	D
Feb 85	239	62.3	-
Jun 85	142	54.1	-
Oct 85	318	62.6	-
Dec 85	129	56.6	-
Jan 86	108	-	60.2
May 86	145	-	66.2
Jun 86	268	-	56[1]
Oct 86	160	65	-
Oct 86	180	-	58.9
Jan 87	152	-	67.1
Jun 87	271	-	58.3
Oct 87	179	-	69.3
May 88	120	68.3	-

1: Visit of John Dillon.

TABLE 5: CONSERVATIVE PARTY SUPPORT

COMPARED WITH OPPOSITION TO HOME RULE

1888-98

Column A: month and year of debate
Column B: numbers voting
Column C: Percentage for Conservatives
Column D: Percentage against Home Rule

A	B	C	D
May 88	120	68.3	-
Feb 90	180	-	73.9
Mar 91	242	69.4	-
Feb 92	147	67.3	-
Feb 93	389	-	68.6
Oct 92	187	62	-
Oct 93	181	60.2	-
Mar 94	394	-	66.2
Oct 94	183	61.7	-
Feb 95	417	-	56.8[1]
Jun 96	193	64.3	-
Feb 97	94	-	60.6[2]
Mar 97	210	68.6	-
May 98	163	61.4	-

1: Visit of John Redmond

2: The debate was on the Report of the Financial
Commission. Although not formally a Home Rule motion,
it was evidently so interpreted by some participants.

TABLE 6: CONSERVATIVE PARTY SUPPORT

COMPARED WITH OPPOSITION TO HOME RULE

1903-10

Column A: month and year of debate
Column B: numbers voting
Column C: Percentage for Conservatives
Column D: Percentage against Home Rule

A	B	C	D
May 03	108	-	52.8
May 04	117	-	41.9[1]
Nov 04	443	43	-
Mar 05	218	52.3	-
May 05	132	59.1	-
Nov 05	258	53.1	-
Mar 06	279	52.7	-
Oct 06	197	-	56.7
Mar 07	194	43.8	-
Mar 07	280	-	50.7
Jun 07	304	53.9	-
Dec 07	228	53.1	-
Oct 08	142	-	54.2
Nov 08	172	50.6	-
Jun 09	368	-	50[3]
Dec 09	340	52.6	-
Jan 10	338	58.6	-
Mar 10	98	45.9	-
May 10	112	-	50
Nov 10	343	53.4	-
Dec 10	431	54.99	-

1. Visit of Hilaire Belloc
2. Visit of Lloyd George
3. Second visit of John Dillon

TABLE 7: CONSERVATIVE PARTY SUPPORT

COMPARED WITH OPPOSITION TO HOME RULE

AND SUPPORT FOR EXTREME RESISTANCE

1911-14

Some Conservative supporters seem to have distanced themselves from extreme resistance in Ulster.

Column A: month and year of debate
Column B: numbers voting
Column C: Percentage for Conservatives
Column D: Percentage against Home Rule
Column E: Percentage for extreme resistance

A	B	C	D	E
Jun 11	203	45.8	-	-
Dec 11	303	42.2	-	-
Mar 12	427	-	43.1	-
Jun 12	259	54.8	-	-
Oct 12	247	-	-	44.1
Dec 12	326	58.3	-	-
Feb 13	133	-	-	36.1
Nov 13	389	-	(49.6)[1]	
Mar 14	280	57.5	-	-
Apr 14	112	-	-	46.4

1. Composite motion in support of Home Rule but including specific condemnation of Ulster opposition.

TABLE 8: NUMBERS VOTING AT MAIN DEBATE

ON IRELAND AS PERCENTAGE OF MOST POPULAR

DEBATE OF EACH ACADEMIC YEAR

1863-64 TO 1913-14

The Fenians (1867-8) and the Land League (1880-2) pushed Ireland close to the top of the agenda, but it was the three Home Rule episodes that dominated all other issues.

Column A: academic year (October to June) [1]
Column B: non-Irish issue drawing largest vote[2]
Column C: numbers voting in B
Column D: Irish issue drawing largest vote
Column E: numbers voting in D
Column F: E as percentage of C
   (relative importance of Irish issue)

1. Years in which Ireland was not debated are omitted
2. Some issues are simplified. Appendix II supplies more detail.

A	B	C	D	E	F
63/4	Foreign policy	102	Church	74	73.3
64/5	Cambridge issue	191	Church	107	56
65/6	Church	163	Fenians	100	61.4
66/7	Politics[1]	312	Church	106	34
67/8	Votes for women	184	Conciliation	172	98.5
68/9	Cambridge issue	240	Church/Land	75	31.5
69/70	Cambridge issue	143	Land	68	47.6
73/4	Rights of women	184	Home Rule	83	28.8[2]
76/7	Church	316	Home Rule	106	33.5
77/8	Politics	284	Home Rule	77	27.1
79/80	Politics	328	Home Rule	167	50.9
80/1	Politics	341	Coercion	318	98.2
81/2	Politics	277	Land	274	98.9
82/3	Politics	366	Coercion	161	44
83/4	Socialism	57	Irish policy	207	45.3

TABLE 8 (continued)

A	B	C	D	E	F
84/5	Politics	309	Coercion	63	20.4
85/6	Politics	318	Home Rule	268	84.3
86/7	Politics	160	Home Rule	271	169.4
87/8	Shakespeare	232	Home Rule	179	77.1
88/9	Cambridge issue	229	Irish policy	425	185.6
89/90	Socialism	254	Home Rule	180	70.9
90/1	Politics	242	Irish policy	217	89.7
91/2	Cambridge issue	233	Ulster	59	25.3
92/3	Cambridge issue	234	Home Rule	389	166.2
93/4	House of Lords	241	Home Rule	294	121.9
94/5	Empire Music Hall	331	Home Rule	417	126
96/7	Cambridge issue	1221[3]	Finance	94	7.7
97/8	Politics	344	Joke debate[4]	146	44.4
98/9	Foreign policy	234	University	72	30.8
01/2	Press freedom	155	Coercion	117	75.5
02/3	Politics	206	Land	149	72.3
03/4	Tariff Reform	450	University	151	33.6
04/5	Politics	443	MacDonnell	88	19.9
06/7	House of Lords	307	Home Rule	280	91.2
07/8	Socialism	310	Home Rule[5]	135	43.5
08/9	Socialism	248}	Home Rule	368	148.4
	British Empire	248}			
09/10	Politics	340	Home Rule	112	32.9
10/1	Politics	431	Home Rule	234	54.9
11/2	Navy	390	Home Rule	427	109.5
12/3	Politics	326	Ulster	247	72.1
13/4	Divorce	314	Home Rule	389	123.9

1. Inaugural debate of the new Union building
2. Motion amended to remove reference to Home Rule
3. Debate thrown open to all undergraduates
4. The joke does not amuse
5. Motion on Irish administration

TABLE 9: VOTES FOR WOMEN 1866-1886

HOUSE OF COMMONS VOTES COMPARED WITH

DEBATES OF THE CAMBRIDGE UNION

Tables 9 and 10 examine the issue of Votes for Women as a comparison with the Union's attitudes to Ireland. Divisions in the House of Commons were usually based on free votes, independent of party whips, although tactical considerations sometimes intruded (e.g. in 1884, when the attempt to tack on female franchise was a ploy to damage the Reform Bill). Although, as shown in Tables 3 to 6, Liberals made up a substantial minority of every Union audience, young Cambridge males not only exceeded the House of Commons in their opposition to giving the vote to women, but were generally more opposed than the generality of *Conservative* MPs. In comparison, attitudes to Ireland seem almost flexible.

Column A: month and year of debate
Column B: numbers voting in House of Commons
Column C: percentage of House of Commons opposed
Column D: percentage of Conservative MPs opposed
Column E: numbers voting in the Cambridge Union
Column F: percentage of Cambridge Union opposed

Information in Columns A-D derived from Brian Harrison, *Separate Spheres: The Opposition to Women's Suffrage in Britain* (1978), pp, 28-30

A	B	C	D	E	F
Nov 66	-	-	-	178	87.6
May 67	271	72.3	91.3	-	-
Feb 68	-	-	-	184	74.4
Feb 70	-	-	-	115	76.5
May 70	219	42.5	56.9	-	-
May 70	318	69.8	72.9	-	-
May 71	375	59.2	66.9	-	-
May 71	-	-	-	60	86.7
May 72	369	60.7	76.0	-	-

TABLE 9 (continued)

A	B	C	D	E	F
May 72	-	-	-	130	72.3[1]
Apr 73	381	58.8	69.0	-	-
Nov 73	-	-	-	184	64.7[1]
Feb 75	-	-	-	172	81.4
Apr 75	343	55.1	64.6	-	-
Apr 76	394	60.9	71.5	-	-
May 76	-	-	-	200	88
Feb 78	-	-	-	187	72.7
Jun 78	364	61.0	80.1	-	-
Mar 79	324	67.6	84.4	-	-
Dec 80	-	-	-	156	70.5
Nov 82	-	-	-	161	85.7
Jul 83	248	53.2	79.2	-	-
Feb 84	-	-	-	135	71.1
Jun 84	410	66.6	22.8	-	-
Nov 84	41	24.4	66.7	-	-
Feb 85	-	-	-	181	56.9[1]
Feb 86	266	39.1	37.6	-	-
Mar 86	-	-	-	141	58.2
Mar 87	-	-	-	60	58.3

1. motions for restricted franchise only

TABLE 10: VOTES FOR WOMEN 1892-1914

HOUSE OF COMMONS VOTES COMPARED WITH

DEBATES OF THE CAMBRIDGE UNION

For explanation of columns and source of information, see Table 9

A	B	C	D	E	F
Jan 92	-	-	-	60	53.3
Apr 92	331	53.5	50.0	-	-
Jan 94	-	-	-	87	71.3
Feb 95	-	-	-	122	57.4
Dec 96	-	-	-	71	63.4
Feb 97	389	40.9	44.4	-	-
Jun 00	-	-	-	124	69.4
Mar 02	-	-	-	149	75.2
Mar 04	254	27.6	40.9	-	-
Nov 05	-	-	-	155	63.9
Feb 08	367	25.6	66.9	-	-
May 08	-	-	-	153	45.8
Dec 08	-	-	-	225	50.7
Mar 09	283	43.8	98.7	-	-
Nov 09	-	-	-	344	58.1
Jul 10	493	38.9	56.7	-	-
Feb 11	-	-	-	138	55.1
May 11	348	26.1	42.6	-	-
Nov 11	-	-	-	294	49.3
Mar 12	434	51.6	64.2	-	-
Jul 12	512	43.0	100	-	-
Nov 12	459	68.8	54.9	-	-
Nov 12	-	-	-	270	62.3
May 13	490	54.9	83.2	-	-
Jun 14	-	-	-	145	49.7

Sources and Abbreviations

The archives of the Cambridge Union have been deposited on loan to Cambridge University Library. The printed Annual Reports are bound as *Laws and Regulations*. These include the termly Vice-Presidents' Reports (VPR). An accompanying series of Minutes Books (MB) is valuable for the proceedings of business meetings and for debates between 1834 and 1843 for which the printed reports are incomplete. This series is supplemented by the occasional Suggestions Book and, for the later nineteenth century, separate Minute Books for committee proceedings (Secretary's MB).

Biographical information has generally been omitted from the Endnotes, except in cases of direct quotation. The major source for nineteenth-century Cambridge students is the monumental *Alumni Cantabrigienses*, Part II, compiled by J.A. Venn in six volumes between 1940 and 1954. Later personalities often appear in *Who's Who*, and its posthumous compilations, *Who Was Who*. For British and Irish public figures, information has been taken from the *Dictionary of National Biography* (*DNB*) and from H. Boylan, *A Dictionary of Irish Biography* (1978). The source of biographical information can usually be deduced from the context.

Dates of debates are given in the Endnotes in a simple system of day/month/year. A hyphenated date indicates that a debate was adjourned to a second night. In the citation of books, the year of publication is given in the initial reference. The addition of "ed." after the date means that a second or subsequent edition, often in paperback, has been cited. Place of publication has generally been omitted. Frequently used sources are abbreviated as follows:

Alma Mater	[J.F.M Wright], *Alma Mater: or Seven Years at the University of Cambridge* (2 vols, 1827).
Bristed	C.A. Bristed, *Five Years in an English University* (2nd ed., 1852).
Brooke	C.N.L. Brooke, *A History of the University of Cambridge: iv, 1870-1990* (1993).
Catholic Cambridge	M.N.L. Couve de Murville and P. Jenkins, *Catholic Cambridge* (1983).
Cornford	F.M. Cornford, *Microcosmographia Academica: A Guide to the Young Academic Politician* (1908) in G. Johnson, *University Politics: F.M. Cornford's Cambridge* (1994).
Corrie	M. Holroyd, ed., *Memorials of the Life of George Elwes Corrie* (1890).

CR	*Cambridge Review*
Cradock	Percy Cradock, *Recollections of the Cambridge Union 1815-1939* (1953). Pages 1-81 are an evocation of the Union before 1901 by Cradock, followed by reminiscences of twentieth-century Presidents.
Dilke	S. Gwynn and G.M. Tuckwell, *The Life of Sir Charles W. Dilke* (2 vols, 1917).
DNB	*Dictionary of National Biography*
EVC	D.A. Winstanley, *Early Victorian Cambridge* (1955).
Gownsman	G.E. Jackson and P. Vos, eds, *The Cambridge Union Society: Debates April 1910-March 1911* (1911).
Gr	*The Granta*
Gunning	H. Gunning, *Reminiscences of the University, Town and County of Cambridge from the year 1780* (2 vols, 1854).
Hort	A.F. Hort, *Life and Letters of Fenton J.A. Hort* (2 vols, 1896).
Houghton MSS	Trinity College, Wren Library, Houghton MSS (correspondence of Richard Monckton Milnes).
Howarth	*Cambridge Between Two Wars* (1978).
Inaug.	*The Cambridge Union Society: Inaugural Proceedings* (1866).
Johnson	*see* Cornford.
L-G	E. Leedham-Green, *A Concise History of the University of Cambridge* (1966).
LVC	D.A.Winstanley, *Later Victorian Cambridge* (1947).
Lytton	*The Life, Letters and Literary Remains of Edward Bulwer, Lord Lytton by His Son* (2 vols, 1883).
Macaulay	G.O. Trevelyan, *The Life and Letters of Lord Macaulay* (2 vols, 1978 ed.).
MB	Minute Books of the Cambridge Union Society.
Merivale	J.A. Merivale, ed., *Autobiography of Dean Merivale* (1899).
Milnes	T. Wemyss Reid, *The Life, Letters, and Friendships of Richard Monckton Milnes, First Lord Houghton* (2 vols, 1891).
Moultrie	Derwent Coleridge, ed., *Poems of John Moultrie* (2 vols, 1876 ed.).
Oxf. Mag	*Oxford Magazine* (most citations are to the regular Cambridge Letter).

Palmerston-Sulivan Letters

	K. Bourne, ed., *The Letters of the Third Viscount Palmerston to Laurence and Elizabeth Sulivan 1804-1863* (Camden Fourth Series, 1979).
Raikes	H.St.J. Raikes, *The Life and Letters of Henry Cecil Raikes* (1898).
Rom1/Rom2/Rom3	*Romilly's Cambridge Diary*. Volume 1 (1967), covering 1832-42, ed. J.P.T. Bury; vols 2 (1994) and 3 (2000), covering 1842-17 and 1848-64, ed. M.E. Bury and J.D. Pickles.
Searby	P. Searby, *History of the University of Cambridge, iii: 1750-1870* (1997).
Secretary's MB	Secretary's Minute Book, Cambridge Union Society.
Sidgwick	[A. and E.M. Sidgwick], *Henry Sidgwick: A Memoir* (1906).
Sketches of Cantabs	"John Smith" [J.D.Lewis], *Sketches of Cantabs* (1849).
Skipper	J.F. Skipper, *A Short History of the Cambridge University Union* (1878).
Statement	*A Statement Regarding the Union, an Academical Debating Society, which existed at Cambridge from February 13th 1815 to March 24th 1817, When it was Suppressed by the Vice-Chancellor* (1817).
Student's Guide	*The Student's Guide to the University of Cambridge* (2nd ed. 1866).
Thackeray	G.N. Ray, ed., *The Letters and Private Papers of William Makepeace Thackeray, i, 1817-1840* (1945).
VCH	*The Victoria History of the Counties of England: Cambridge iii: Cambridge* (1959).
VPR	Vice-President's Termly Report, Cambridge Union Society. The letters M, L and E which follow stand for the Michaelmas, Lent and Easter Terms.
Whewell	Mrs Stair Douglas, *The Life and Selections from the Correspondence of William Whewell* (1881).

Endnotes

"GONE UP TO JESUS": A NOTE ON TERMINOLOGY

1. C. Hassall, *Rupert Brooke* (1972 ed.), p. 251, in a 1911 parody of A.E. Housman.
2. Leslie Stephen in *National Review*, 42, 1903-4, p. 131.

ENDNOTES TO CHAPTER ONE (pp. 3-25):

THE CAMBRIDGE UNION: SOURCES AND RIVALS

1. For an overview of the history of the Union, Cradock, pp. 1-81.
2. Cradock, p. 10, and see Chapter Five.
3. *Gr*, 25 Feb. 1893, p. 218. Prior to 1914, the magazine was always referred to with the direct article, *The Granta*.
4. Ged Martin, "Parnell and Magdalene: Some New Evidence", *Magdalene College Magazine and Record*, 36, 1992, pp. 37-41 supplements "Parnell at Cambridge: The Education of an Irish Nationalist", *Irish Historical Studies*, 19, 1974, pp. 79-88. But when Cork students were banned from political activity, Parnell praised the Oxford and Cambridge Unions. *Freeman's Journal*, 18 Dec. 1882.
5. MB, 25, fo. 1 (9 June 1892). A contemporary report in *Oxf. Mag.* (10 Feb. 1892, pp. 161-2) suggests that the Cambridge contribution to the Dublin University tercentenary celebrations was the sending of a cricket team.
6. MB, 23, fos 188-9 (5 March 1885).
7. See Chapter Seven
8. *Inaug.*, p. 14 (Lord Houghton, formerly R.M. Milnes)
9. *Statement* (1817).
10. G.O. Trevelyan seems to have had access to a pre-1823 Minute Book for his biography of his uncle, Macaulay (*Macaulay*, i, pp. 74-5).
11. Skipper; Harris (pp. 82-90), McNair (pp. 91-4) and Birkett (pp. 95-105) in Cradock.
12. Leslie Stephen, *The Life of Sir James Fitzjames Stephen* (1895), pp. 98-9; F.W. Maitland, *The Life and Letters of Leslie Stephen (1906)*, p. 46; *Macaulay*, i, pp. 74-5.
13. *Macaulay*, i, p. 75.
14. MB, 5, fo. 52 (17 Feb. 1829)
15. *Gr*, 5 Oct. 1909, p. 501. When the *Gownsman* published an anthology of its Union coverage, the *Cambridge Review* commented that "most of the reports are quite naturally more of a nature of general criticisms than of analyses of arguments". *CR*, 27 April 1911, p. 366.
16. Leslie Stephen, *Sketches from Cambridge* (1865), p. 61.
17. *Inaug.*, p. 6. It was claimed that embarrassment could be caused when successive speakers had memorised the same newspaper article. *Sketches of Cantabs*, pp. 39-41.
18. *Gr*, 26 Feb. 1898, p. 216.

19. *Gr*, 15 Nov. 1902, p. 69.
20. Stephen, *Sketches from Cambridge*, p. 64. Leslie Stephen, who was on the verge of his personal crisis over religion, acknowledged in later life that his *Sketches* were unduly "flippant". Maitland, *Leslie Stephen*, p. 480.
21. *Gr*, 8 March 1889, p. 9. The speaker, E.W. MacBride, appears frequently in Chapter Eight.
22. VPR, M 1887, p. 54.
23. F.A. Rice, ed., *The Granta and its Contributors 1889-1914* (1924), pp. 8-9.
24. Recalled of R.H. Somerset of Queens', the "Heavy Villain", by Birkett in Cradock, pp. 98-9. Somerset had worked in the office of the *Daily Mail* for ten whole weeks, and posed in Cambridge "as a complete man of the world".
25. *The Cambridge Observer* (29 Nov. 1892, p. 1) was struck by "not so much the petty vindictiveness" of MacBride's threat "as by its hopeless silliness".
26. *Gr*, 27 Nov. 1897, pp. 97-8; Rice, ed., *The Granta*, pp. 27-8.
27. *Gr*, 27 Apr 1911, p. 366.
28. *Gr*, 1 Feb. 1908, p. 158.
29. *CR*, 22 Feb. 1893, p. 235.
30. *Gr*, 25 Feb 1893, p. 219.
31. Erskine Childers, *The Framework of Home Rule* (1911), pp. 198-203.
32. H.A. Morrah, *The Oxford Union 1823-1923* (1923); C. Hollis, *The Oxford Union* (1965); D. Walter, *The Oxford Union: Playground of Power* (1984). The high achieving image of the Oxford Union did not always help recruitment in its own university. An objector in 1889 argued there was "no reason why the average undergraduate, who has no expectation of being Prime Minister, or Governor General, or Chancellor of the Exchequer should hasten to enter his name as a member". *Oxf. Mag.*, 27 Oct. 1889, p. 29.
33. *The Penguin Ronald Searle* (1953), unpaginated: "The MP".
34. W. Ellis, *The Oxbridge Conspiracy* (1995 ed.), p. 99.
35. J.S. Mill, *Autobiography* (ed. H.J. Laski, 1924), p. 64.
36. MB 2, 22 Feb. 1825, Wilberforce letter of 15 Feb. 1825 and 2 May 1826, letter from Edward Villiers, Merton College, 28 Apr. 1826. MB 7, 11 Feb. 1832 for extension of membership to the Trinity College Dublin Historical Society. Edinburgh University Union was added in 1894. *Oxf. Mag.*, 16 Nov. 1894, p. 80.
37. Cradock, p. 20.
38. *Inaug.*, p. 12.
39. "Bocardo" and Cardinal Manning in *Pall Mall Gazette* (1866), quoted *Inaug.*, pp. 61, 64. Hallam Tennyson, *Alfred Tennyson: A Memoir* (1906), pp. 31-32 called Sunderland "a very plausible, self-satisfied speaker at the Union Debating Society".
40. M.R.D. Foot, ed., *The Gladstone Diaries, i, 1825-1832* (1968), p. 270.
41. *Milnes*, i, p. 75. Gladstone (*Diaries*, i, p. 271) recorded "I cannot help liking Milnes" although "we scarcely agreed on one point".
42. Allen, *Cambridge Apostles*, p. 54.
43. J. Morley, *The Life of William Ewart Gladstone* (3 vols, 1903);, i, pp. 88-9; R. Shannon, *Gladstone, i: 1809-1865* (1982), pp. 39-40.
44. F.D. Munsell, *The Unfortunate Duke: Henry Pelham, Fifth Duke of Newcastle, 1811-1864* (1985), p. 14.

45. A.G. Gardiner, *The Life of Sir William Harcourt* (2 vols, 1923), i, p. 51.

46. W.M. Thackeray, *The Book of Snobs* (1845), ch. xv. Planning a speech on colonial policy in 1823, Macaulay expected to address a Union audience "composed partly of future senators and planters". T. Penney, ed., *Letters of Thomas Babington Macaulay, i: 1807-February 1831* (1974), pp. 183-4.

47. F.W. Pethick-Lawrence, *Fate Has Been Kind* (1943), p. 36.

48. *Inaug.*, p. 21. In 1891, St John Brodrick offered to bet Arthur Balfour £50 that he could not name four Cambridge graduates from the decade after 1870 who could equal four products of a single Oxford college, Jowett's Balliol. On learning that Brodrick intended to nominate Asquith, Milner, Curzon and Edward Grey, Balfour declined the bet. Earl of Midleton, *Records and Reactions 1856-1939* (1939), pp. 32-3.

49. Bristed, pp. 69-70. The Classical Tripos began in 1824.

50. "Oxford has risen, and we have sunk." *Whewell*, p. 286.

51. S. Walpole, *The Life of Lord John Russell* (2 vols, 1889), i, p. 44.

52. W. Harris, *Life So Far* (1954), p. 61.

53. Harris in Cradock, p. 84. The Union elected its first Jewish President, A.H. Louis, in 1850 and a second, Arthur Cohen, in 1853. The election of individual Jews to the Presidency contrasts with Union opposition to the removal of Jewish disabilities in six of the seven debates on the subject between 1845 and 1857. Louis appears as "Salomons" in *Sketches of Cantabs*, pp, 44-7. According to Geoffrey de Freitas (Cradock, p. 137), members tried (not always successfully) to resist the temptation to engage in Jewish jokes during the nineteen-thirties.

54. Harris in Cradock, p. 87.

55. Maitland, *Leslie Stephen*, p. 35.

56. E. Miller, *Portrait of a College: A History of the College of Saint John the Evangelist Cambridge* (1961), p. 73.

57. Raikes, p. 17.

58. J.R. Seeley, *Lectures and Essays* (1870), p. 290.

59. Brooke, p. 325; *VCH*, p. 284. In 1904, Maitland delivered a similar speech deriding compulsory Greek. "I was ashamed of it afterwards, but I had some fun out of it at the time." C.H.S. Fifoot, ed., *The Letters of Frederick William Maitland* (Selden Society, 1965), p. 334.

60. J.A. Spender, *The Life of the Right Hon. Sir Henry Campbell-Bannerman* (2 vols, 1923), i, p. 19.

61. B.E.C. Dugdale, *Arthur James Balfour* (2 vols, 1936), i, p. 28, quoting Walter Durnford.

62. Lord Crewe, *Lord Rosebery* (2 vols, 1931), i, p. 42.

63. K. Middlemas and J. Barnes, *Baldwin: A Biography* (1969), pp. 15-18.

64. S. Baldwin, *On England and Other Addresses* (1937 ed.), p. 102; R.A. Butler in Cradock, p. 116; Anthony Howard, *RAB: The Life of R.A. Butler* (1988 ed.), p. 24. "Rab" appreciated that Baldwin's parting gift was "a vicarious tit for tat" against his own great-uncle. *The Art of the Possible. The Memoirs of Lord Butler* (1972 ed.), p. 16.

65. VPR, E 1895.

66. Lytton, i, p. 235; VPR, E 1908.

67. J. Joliffe, *Raymond Asquith: Life and Letters* (1980), pp. 67-8.
68. The account that follows is based on Martin Ceadel, "The 'King and Country' Debate, 1933: Student Politics, Pacifism and the Dictators", *Historical Journal*, 22, 1979, pp. 397-422.
69. W.S. Churchill, *The Gathering Storm* (1960 ed.), pp. 85-6.
70. A.J.P. Taylor, *English History, 1914-1945* (1965), p. 362; A.J.P. Taylor, *A Personal History* (1994 ed.), p. 92.
71. A.M. Ramsey in Cradock, p. 127; Howarth, pp. 147-8.
72. Geoffrey Shakespeare in Cradock, p. 107.
73. Howarth, p. 228.
74. De Freitas in Cradock, p. 139. Whereas Oxford fostered the King and Country myth, the Cambridge establishment tended to denigrate its Union. In 1943, T.R. Glover of St John's wrote contemptuously that the Cambridge Union had "decayed ... abandoned very largely to Indians and Communists". T.R. Glover, *Cambridge Retrospect* (1943), p. 113.
75. Allen, *Cambridge Apostles*; P. Levy, *Moore: G.E. Moore and the Cambridge Apostles* (1981 ed.); W.C. Lubenow, *The Cambridge Apostles 1820-1914* (1998).
76. Bristed (p. 122) did not regard the Apostles as a secret society.
77. In fact, Roby was a notable public figure, who contributed substantially to the development of English education, as shown by his contribution to the quasi-official Cambridge handbook, the *Student's Guide*, and his entry in the *Dictionary of National Biography*.
78. Levy, *Moore*, p. 66.
79. Stephen, *Fitzjames Stephen*, p. 103.
80. *Fraser's Magazine*, quoted *Macmillan's Magazine*, 11, 1865, p. 18.
81. Bristed, p. 121.
82. Allen, *Cambridge Apostles*, p. 4, quoting *Sidgwick*, p. 32n..
83. C.L. Ferguson, *A History of the Magpie and Stump Debating Society 1866-1926* (1931), p. 7.
84. [Bertrand Russell], *The Autobiography of Bertrand Russell, i: 1872-1914* (1967), pp. 68-70, 73-4; Leonard Woolf, *Sowing: An Autobiography of the Years 1880 to 1904* (1988 ed.), pp. 129-30, 150-1.
85. Levy, *Moore*, pp. 143-146.
86. Ramsey in Cradock, pp. 125-6.
87. Stephen, *Sketches from Cambridge*, p. 64.
88. Lubenow, *Cambridge Apostles*.
89. Edith Lyttelton, *Alfred Lyttelton: An Account of his Life* (1917), p. 77.
90. M. Cox, *M.R. James: An Informal Portrait* (1983), p. 58.
91. Allen, *Cambridge Apostles*, p. 22,
92. Leslie Stephen, *National Review*, 42, 1903-4, p. 141.
93. Stephen, *Fitzjames Stephen*, p. 106.
94. *Sidgwick*, p. 63.
95. *Richard Chenevix Trench Archbishop: Letters and Memorials* (2 vols, 1881), i, p. 2.
96. Apostles are listed in Levy, *Moore*, pp. 300-11; officers of the Union in Cradock, pp. 169-85.
97. Bristed, p. 125.

ENDNOTES TO CHAPTER TWO (pp. 26-47):

THE TOWN AND THE UNIVERSITY

1. The principal histories of the University for this period are the volumes by Searby and Brooke, two older and more detailed studies by Winstanley (*EVC* and *LVC*), and more recent general overviews by L-G and Johnson.
2. Bristed, pp. 1-2.
3. *Alma Mater*, i, p. 185n; *Rom3*, p. 104 (13 May 1852). The calendar had been reformed exactly a century earlier, in September 1752. Gwen Raverat, *Period Piece: A Cambridge Childhood* (1960 ed.), p. 47. As a child, Raverat, who was born in 1885, believed that the 23rd Psalm ("on pastures green ... the quiet waters by") was set on Sheep's Green, just a quarter of a mile from the centre of the town (p. 42).
4. Merivale, p. 57; *Oxf. Mag.*, 24 May 1895, p. 389; *Thackeray*, p. 59; R.J. White, *Cambridge Life* (1960), p. 10 and L. & H. Fowler, comps, *Cambridge Commemorated: An Anthology of University Life* (1984), p. 179. A guidebook of 1861 admitted that the appearance of Cambridge was "generally disappointing, and below what might be anticipated, but it is rapidly improving". Quoted, *Rom3*, p. xii. According to Alec Clifton-Taylor, "Cambridgeshire must be regarded as among the least fortunate of English counties" for building materials. N. Pevsner, *The Buildings of England: Cambridgeshire* (1970 ed.), p. 289.
5. *Whewell*, pp. 15-16.
6. MB7, 21 Feb. 1832, fo. 68.
7. *Rom1*, p. 4.
8. Pethick-Lawrence, *Fate Has Been Kind*, p. 32.
9. Ferguson, *Magpie and Stump*, pp. 28-9.
10. *Whewell*, p. 9
11. R. Southey, *Letters from England* (1807, ed. J. Simmons, 1984), p. 271.
12. Pevsner, *Cambridgeshire*, p. 451; Leslie Stephen in *National Review*, 42, 1903-4, p. 131.
13. "Cave Canem" in *Cambridge Chronicle*, 30 June 1866
14. 15/11/87.
15. A robust exception was Gwen Raverat, *Period Piece*, p. 34. Thomas Carlyle's *The Life of John Sterling* (1851, various editions, ch. 4) transmits alarm at the story of the sickly young man wading into the river to fill buckets at the end of a chain of fire-fighters, but Carlyle did not explain that the river was a sewer. According to Raverat, a Cambridge story had Queen Victoria asking Whewell why there were so many piece of paper floating in the Cam. With great presence of mind, he assured her that they were notices banning bathing.
16. *Sidgwick*, p. 554. For some colleges, such as Magdalene, the cost of the sewerage scheme was a major burden. Ronald Hyam in P. Cunich, et al., *A History of Magdalene College Cambridge 1428-1988* (1994), p. 224. For recreation on the Cam, Searby, pp. 678-80. An illustration of 1793 seems to show punting on the Cam: White, *Cambridge Life*, facing p. 112.
17. A. Gray, *Cambridge and its Story* (1912), p. 8.

18. H. Tennyson, *Tennyson*, p. 29.
19. Thackeray, p. 59; C.E. Stephen, *The Right Honourable Sir James Stephen: Letters with Biographical Notes* (1906), p. 141. But Thackeray thought Coton attractive and "there are a number of quaint old buildings, and pretty bits scattered about" (pp. 44, 59).
20. *Moultrie*, p, 419. The countryside had other attractions. Moultrie and his friend Derwent Coleridge enjoyed "Our mid-day luncheon in the village inn/ Served haply by the fair domestic hands/ Of her, the maid of Quy – that saint whose shrine/ By many a Cantabrigian pilgrimage/ (By none more zealous or more pure than ours)/ Was, in those days, frequented!" (p. 420).
21. Maitland, *Leslie Stephen*, p. 191.
22. *Whewell*, p. 367.
23. Searby, p. 102.
24. Leslie Stephen, *National Review*, 42, 1903-4, p. 135.
25. M.R. James in G.M. Trevelyan, ed., *Fifty Years: Memories and Contrasts* (1932), p. 94.
26. *EVC*, pp. 1-7; *VCH*, pp. 487-8.
27. Lytton, i, p. 228.
28. For C.H. de Thierry, see *Dictionary of New Zealand Biography, i: 1769-1869* (1990), p. 533. Recent scholarship has scaled down his North Island purchase. De Thierry claimed 40,000 acres and was eventually awarded 800.
29. *Whewell*, p. 297.
30. Leslie Stephen in *National Review*, 42, 1903-4, p. 136.
31. 13/2/00.
32. *Student's Guide*, p. 44.
33. Harris in Cradock, p. 82.
34. *Student's Guide*, p. 96.
35. Merivale, p. 67; Cornford in Johnson, p. 108.
36. Bristed, p. 100.
37. C.V. Stanford, *Pages from an Unwritten Diary* (1914), p. 126. The Trinity-Magdalene link was in fact even more narrowly specific. By the eighteen-fifties, Trinity supported two rowing clubs, First and Third (Second Trinity having disappeared at an early stage). It was the academically challenged members of Third Trinity who made the transpontine migration. A notable refugee was Jack Hall, who transferred in 1855. In 1856, he "contested the captaincy [of the Boat Club] with a genuine Magdalene man and was elected". Hall was "compelled to remain an undergraduate for seven years owing to difficulties with his examiners" but used his adopted college as a platform for his rowing activities. Meanwhile, "the mere fact that the boat representing Magdalene was really a Third Trinity boat tended to make the rest of the College lose interest". *The Magdalene Boat Club 1828-1928* (1930), pp. 15-16. Jesus was another small college where incomers from Trinity seem to have been regarded with some reserve. One refugee was said to have been greeted at his first appearance in chapel with a hymn that began: "Ashamed of Jesus! Can it be?/ A mortal man ashamed of thee!". (The lines represent a loose conflation of a hymn by the eighteenth-century Presbyterian minister, Joseph Grigg.) B. and P. Russell, eds, *The Amberley Papers: Bertrand Russell's Family Background* (2 vols,

1937), i, p. 227. Except for the recruitment of non-collegiate students, inter-college migration largely disappeared in the later nineteenth century as overall academic standards improved.

38. *Rom1*, pp. 86, 227; *Rom2*, p. 196. "I thank my Fortune daily I was not a Johnian," rejoiced Thackeray. "It is the lowest, most childish, piggish punning place." *Thackeray*, p. 107.

39. *Rom3*, p. 391 (27 Sept. 1861).

40. 21/11/99.

41. Bristed, p. 331.

42. A.F. Wratislaw in *EVC*, p. 151.

43. *Whewell*, p. 92.

44. *Whewell*, p. 497.

45. *DNB*, "Thompson, William Hepworth".

46. *Autobiography of Bertrand Russell*, i, p. 67. Russell's view of Trinity Fellows was coloured by their hostility to his pacifist stand in the First World War.

47. *LVC*, pp. 318, 206n.

48. Spender, *Campbell-Bannerman*, ii, p. 343.

49. *Mandragora* (1914), pp. 38-42; T. Thornely, *Cambridge Memories: (The Lighter Side of Long Ago)* (1936), pp. 115-16.

50. *Student's Guide*, p. 99.

51. A.C. Benson, *From a College Window* (1906), pp. 6-7. Walter Besant, a Christ's undergraduate in the eighteen-fifties, was "strongly of opinion that a very large college, such as Trinity, Cambridge, does not offer anything like the social and educational advantages of a small college". *Autobiography of Walter Besant* (1902), p. 79.

52. Pethick-Lawrence, *Fate Has Been Kind*, p. 34.

53. M.R. James in Trevelyan, ed., *Fifty Years*, p. 95.

54. *Inaug.*, p. 2.

55. J.R.M. Butler, *Henry Montagu Butler, Master of Trinity College, Cambridge, 1886-1918: A Memoir* (1925), p. 114. I owe this reference to Ronald Hyam.

56. Miller, *Portrait of a College*, p. 100. K.O. Morgan, *Wales 1880-1980: Rebirth of a Nation* (1982 ed.), p. 139.

57. *Oxf. Mag.*, 16 March 1892, pp. 250-1.

58. *VCH*, p. 489.

59. Tense adapted from Brooke, p. 44. *Rom3*, p. 133 reveals that that there was opposition to the appointment among the Fellows of Magdalene. But Latimer Neville was one of a minority of eight Heads of Houses to attend the banquet that inaugurated the Union extension in 1886. In 1915, his successor, S.A. Donaldson, became the first Head of House to speak in a Union debate when he urged support for wartime temperance legislation.

60. Oscar Browning, *Memories of Sixty Years at Eton, Cambridge and Elsewhere* (1910), p. 30. "A few men belonged to the Union," Walter Besant recalled of Christ's in 1855, "but not many." *Autobiography of Walter Besant*, p. 89.

61. *Whewell*, p. 61.

62. Johnson, p. 55.

63. Bristed, p. 10.

64. N. Harte, *The University of London* (1986), p. 73.

65. Leslie Stephen, *National Review*, 42, 1903-4, p. 134.

66. A. Gray, *Cambridge and its Story*, p. 318. "As regards science, their contempt was as colossal as their ignorance," wrote Besant of the Fellows of Christ's in the eighteen-fifties. *Autobiography of Walter Besant*, p. 81. A century later, it was a Fellow of Christ's, C.P. Snow, who coined the term "The Two Cultures" to describe the gulf between science and the humanities. However, in the first half of the nineteenth century, disciplines were not simply compartmentalised to the exclusion of the sciences. Rather, perceptions of science had to be shoe-horned into a universal system of understanding centred upon revealed religion. M.M. Garland, *Cambridge Before Darwin: The Ideal of a Liberal Education 1800-1860* (1980), esp. pp. 90-112,

67. A. Gray, *Cambridge and its Story*, p. 318 and cf. Johnson, p. 39.

68. Johnson, p. 54.

69. C.W. Scott-Giles, *Sidney Sussex College: A Short History* (1975), p. 103. On the strength of Sidney's capacity to offer training in chemistry, college mythology has toyed with the possibility that T.S. Holmes, who matriculated in 1871, was the original of Sherlock Holmes. One can only sympathise.

70. Johnson, p. 53. Cambridge had considered an alumni appeal as early as 1890. *Oxf. Mag.*, 22 Oct. 1890, pp. 31-2. It was not that the university was wealthy in comparison with the colleges, but rather that centralisation was required for efficiency. In a parliamentary debate on Cambridge in 1876, a former President of the Union, Spencer Walpole, had reported that the University's annual income from property (i.e. in the modern sense, its endowment income) was £24,000, while the combined income of the colleges from the same source was £264,000. Another ex-President, Charles Dilke, described this as "a flea-bite". *Parliamentary Debates*, 230, 6 July 1876, cols 1052, 1058.

71. Gray, *Cambridge and its Story*, p. 126.

72. Cornford in Johnson, p. 95. Johnson, pp. 40-1 for maps showing the development of the New Museums and Downing Sites, and cf. *VCH*, facing p. 274.

73. Leslie Stephen in *National Review*, 42, 1903-4, p. 136.

74. Searby, pp. 420, 289.

75. Leslie Stephen in *National Review*, 42, 1903-4, p. 136. But Smyth had abandoned lecturing some years before Stephen's time. *Rom1*, pp, 41-2 suggests that he was a better performer than legend allowed, as does his memorial tablet in Norwich Cathedral.

76. *Corrie*, p. 277; F.E. Kingsley, *Charles Kingsley: His Letters and Memories of His Life* (1904 ed.). p. 240.

77. Seeley, *Lectures and Essays*, p. 290. As late as the eighteen-seventies, professorships were still often regarded as irrelevancies. Dilke poked fun at them in the parliamentary debate of 1876, reporting that one resident don "wished to see a Chair of critical journalism founded to expose the errors of the daily Press". *Parliamentary Debates*, 230, 6 July, col. 1059. Academic prejudice against media studies evidently has a long history.

78. Brooke, p. 458; Howarth, p. 118.

79. H. Reeve, ed., *The Greville Memoirs: A Journal of the Reigns of George IV and*

William IV (3 vols, 1875), iii, p. 73.

80. Johnson, p. 9.

81. *Oxf. Mag.*, 20 Nov. 1889, p. 102; Johnson, p. 64.

82. Queens' has a President; King's a Provost. Catharine Hall, Clare Hall and Pembroke Hall each adopted the title "College" during the nineteenth century, leaving only Trinity Hall to use the older form to distinguish itself from Trinity College. Unlike Oxford, Cambridge made no distinction of status between Colleges and Halls. (The name "Clare Hall" was revived in 1966 for a graduate society.) St Benet's College became more formally known as Corpus Christi, while St Peter's College settled down in Cambridge parlance to Peterhouse. Perhaps the most eccentric Cambridge nomenclature is that of Jesus College. Dedicated to the Blessed Virgin Mary, St John the Evangelist and the Glorious Virgin St Radegund, it apparently borrowed its popular name from a monastery in Rotherham.

83. *EVC*, p. 58.

84. D.A. Winstanley, *Unreformed Cambridge* (1935), p. 16.

85. A.C. Benson, *Memories and Friends* (1924), p. 274.

86. *EVC*, pp. 139-47.

87. *Whewell*, p. 288.

88. *Westminster Review*, 35, 1841, p. 468.

89. D. Hudson, *Munby: Man of Two Worlds* (1972), p. 15.

90. Palmerston's supporters insisted that all electors take the oath against bribery, implying that opponents had been paid to come and vote. K. Bourne, *Palmerston: The Early Years 1784-1841* (1982), pp. 245-7.

91. *LVC*, p. 306.

92. *LVC*, pp. 306-7.

93. *British and Foreign Review*, 5, 1837, p. 201.

94. Corrie, pp. 271-2 and cf. A. Gray and F. Brittain, *A History of Jesus College Cambridge* (1988 ed.), p. 165 and White, *Cambridge Life*, p. 34; *Oxf. Mag.*, 30 April 1890, p. 281.

95. Maitland, *Leslie Stephen*, p. 176. Cf. Ged Martin, "The Cambridge American Lectureship of 1866", *Journal of American Studies*, 7, 1973, pp. 17-29.

96. Howarth, p. 42. The mob destroyed Newnham's Memorial Gates. A similar victory demonstration in 1897 had been foiled in the attempt to burn an effigy of a woman graduate in the Newnham grounds.

97. *LVC*, p. 306.

98. Cornford in Johnson, p. 107.

99. Benson, *From a College Window*, p. 160.

100. Johnson, p. 18.

101. Cox, *M.R. James*, p. 101.

102. *Whewell*, p. 264. Thackeray (p. 58) attempted to think in Greek. In 1891, it was reported that "[t]he rowing coaches went solid for compulsory Greek". *Oxf. Mag.*, 4 Nov. 1891, p. 52.

103. Leslie Stephen, *National Review*, 42, 1903-4, p. 134.

104. Harris, *Life So Far*, p. 44.

105. Merivale, p. 59. According to Merivale, the examination on Paley was "merely ... an exercise of memory" (p. 62). Cambridge became increasingly uneasy about its

reliance upon Paley: Garland, *Cambridge Before Darwin*, pp. 62-79. Parnell claimed that reading Paley "upset his faith". T.M. Healy, *Letters and Leaders of My Day* (2 vols, 1928), ii, p. 367. A.G.L. Haigh has pointed to increasing reluctance among the ablest Cambridge graduates to take orders in the Church of England from the eighteen-sixties. However, as late as 1903-7, one quarter of candidates for the Pass degree became clergyman. There was therefore some justification for retaining the undemanding Paley in the curriculum. A.G.L. Haigh, "The Church, the Universities and Learning in Later Victorian England", *Historical Journal*, 29, 1986, pp. 187-201; *VCH*, p. 288.

106. *LVC*, p. 358.
107. *LVC*, p. 294.
108. A.C. Benson, *From a College Window*, p. 38.
109. J.R. Honey, *Tom Brown's Universe* (1977), pp. 116-17. "If I may judge from myself", wrote Walter Besant, "the effect of Cambridge upon the youth of the time was wholly and unreservedly beneficial." *Autobiography of Walter Besant*, p. 98. As the late Eric Morecambe used to say, there is no answer to that.

ENDNOTES TO CHAPTER THREE (pp.48-75):

THE UNDERGRADUATE WORLD

1. Brooke, p. 287n challenges the notion that "student" was not traditionally a Cambridge term. The mid-Victorian founding of the *Student's Guide* suggests that emphasis upon the term "undergraduate" was a device to arrogate special status to the Oxbridge experience in the face of the rise of newer universities. Cf. Fowler, comp., *Cambridge Commemorated*, p. 266, for 1901.
2. *Sidgwick*, pp. 46-7 (letter of 18 Feb. 1860).
3. L-G, pp. 161, 191.
4. *Alma Mater*, ii, p. 198.
5. Gunning, ii, p. 349. Some privileges could still be claimed on the basis of royal lineage. *Rom3*, pp. 5, 325.
6. Searby, p. 71; *Student's Guide*, p. 48. "The sizars at Cambridge do not live luxuriously", wrote Whewell – an ex-sizar himself – in 1843; "many of them live as frugally and simply as can be desired." *Whewell*, p. 298. Of undergraduates admitted to the University in November 1851, 390 were pensioners and 43 sizars. In 1856, the numbers were 376 pensioners and 35 sizars (of whom 28 were at Trinity and St John's). Thus by mid-century, sizars accounted for around ten percent of undergraduate numbers. *Rom3*, pp. 95, 261.
7. G.P. Gooch, *Life of Lord Courtney* (1920), pp. 20-28.
8. *Alma Mater*, i, p. 61 and cf. Searby, p. 69.
9. A. Balfour, *Chapters of Autobiography* (ed. E. Dugdale, 1930), pp. 26-7.
10. Hudson, *Munby*, p. 270. Numbers had been in decline for some years. Romilly wrote that "the race of Fellow Commoner is nearly extinguished" when only five were admitted to the University in 1852. *Rom3*, p. 120.
11. *Milnes*, i, pp. 53-4.
12. *Rom2*, p. 113.

13. Rice, ed., *The Granta*, p. 33.
14. *Whewell*, p. 115 (1827). Almost a century later, as an undergraduate at Trinity, the Duke of York (and future king George VI) was "progged" and fined the standard six shillings and eightpence for smoking in academical dress. He described the cigarette as "one of the most expensive I have ever sampled". The confession came in a contribution to the (delayed) centenary celebrations of the Cambridge Union in 1921, an ordeal for a young man who suffered from a speech impediment. A survivor of the battle of Jutland, he told J.R.M. Butler that the speech was "the most frightening occasion of his life". J.W. Wheeler-Bennett, *King George VI: His Life and Reign* (1958), pp. 132-3. Neither the *Cambridge Review* nor the *Granta* reported the Duke's speech.
15. H. Tennyson, *Tennyson*, p. 28.
16. *LVC*, pp. 94-143; *Rom3*, p. 199.
17. *Student's Guide*, p. 8.
18. *Autobiography of Bertrand Russell*, i, p. 67.
19. 24/4 /83; 26/1/92; 6/3/93; 19/2 /01.
20. Statistics compiled by Venn are given in J.R. Tanner, ed., *The Historical Register of the University of Cambridge ... to 1910* (1917), p. 990 and ... *Supplement 1907-1920* (1922), p. 198. Graph in L-G, p. 181. Cf. Searby, p. 61; Brooke, pp. 593-5.
21. G. Stephen, *The Jesuit at Cambridge* (2 vols, 1847), i, pp. 113-14. For Parnell and Magdalene, see Chapter 1, note 4. R.B. O'Brien, *The Life of Charles Stewart Parnell 1846-1891* (2 vols, 1891) relied for Parnell's Cambridge experience on an account by a Fellow of Magdalene, Wilfred Gill, who had not been in residence at the time (i, pp. 40-3). On 17 Nov. 1866, the *Cambridge Chronicle* reported the admission of 517 new students and a total undergraduate population of 2039. The multiplier of almost four to one cannot be entirely accounted for by tenth-term "questionists" returning for part of the fourth year for Honours examinations. However, it does point to the inefficient use of student accommodation caused by the ten-term Tripos requirement.
22. Pevsner, *Cambridgeshire*, pp. 35-6 and *passim* for the link between matriculations and construction.
23. Searby, pp. 65-7.
24. Bristed, p. 278.
25. *The Times*, 26 Jan. 1825. "In consequence of the overflow of students at both our Universities, it is in contemplation to found a third University in the neighbourhood of York, towards which the venerable and excellent Earl Fitzwilliam has promised to subscribe £50,000."
26. The Union resolved by 54 votes to 10 in May 1826 that "a University in London" should not "possess any exclusive privileges or endowments", and in May 1834 opposed the grant of a charter by 26 votes to 9. A motion to present the collected works of Newton "to the London University" was rejected in a business meeting on 27 May 1827. MB 4, fo. 43.
27. Bristed, p. 271.
28. L. Stone, "The Size and Composition of the Oxford Student Body 1580-1910", in Stone, ed., *The University in Society* (2 vols, 1975), i, pp. 5-6; R. Anderson, "Universities and Elites in Modern Britain", *History of Universities*, 10, 1991, pp.

225-50.

29. T.W. Moody, "The Irish Universities Question in the Nineteenth Century", *History*, 43, 1958, pp.90-109.

30. T.W. Moody and J.C. Beckett, *Queen's Belfast 1845-1949: The History of the University* (2 vols, 1959.

31. J.A. Murphy, *The College: A History of Queen's/University College Cork 1845-1995* (1995), pp. 109, 151, 63-4.

32. VPR, E 1865

33. In 1884, before the extension, there were 203 new members and 973 matriculations to the University (21%), in 1905 381 against 1067 (36%) and in 1911 406 out of 1156 (35%).

34. Brooke, pp. 44, 51-2, 86-7; *LVC*, p. 272; G.P. Browne, *The Recollections of a Bishop* (1915), pp. 229-30 for the plans to merge King's and St Catharine's. For Lord Edmond Fitzmaurice's proposal to close Sidney (along with All Souls, Oxford), *Parliamentary Debates*, 230, 6 July 1876, col. 1893.

35. *VCH*, pp. 497-8 and W.W. Grave, *Fitzwilliam College Cambridge 1869-1969* (1983).

36. Grave, *Fitzwilliam College*, pp. 67-8.

37. Grave, *Fitzwilliam College*, p. 149.

38. Support fell from 38 percent (55-21 in May 1868) to 29 percent (93-38 in November).

39. Johnson, pp. 25-7; Brooke, pp. 92-5; 5/11/78; 16/8/81 (19-11 against); 6/6/82 (amendment rejected, 69-44).

40. Brooke, pp. 91-2; Honey, *Tom Brown's Universe*, pp. 75-8, quoting *Pall Mall Gazette*, 20 Sept. 1887 at p. 80; P. Searby, "A Failure at Cambridge: Cavendish College 1877-1892", *Proceedings of the Cambridge Antiquarian Society*, 72, 1982-3, pp. 106-20; *Oxf. Mag.*, 20 Nov. 1889, p.102. Honey, p. 356, points out that Cavendish was only about one-third cheaper than the regular colleges.

41. Gunning, ii, p. 170.

42. Maitland, *Leslie Stephen*, p. 156. The writer John Cowper Powys received a "frightful" shock as an undergraduate at Corpus in the early eighteen-nineties when a fellow student informed him "with lurid realism of the hemorrhages [sic] that women have to suffer from the revolutions of the moon". Unofficial sex education at Corpus sounds to have been only marginally accurate in its understanding of the causes of menstruation. J.C. Powys, *Autobiography* (1934), p. 191.

43. O. Teichman, ed., *The Cambridge Undergraduate 100 Years Ago* (1926), p. 36.

44. Hugh Dalton, *Call Back Yesterday: Memoirs 1887-1931* (1953), p. 37.

45. E.F. Benson, *David of King's* (1924), p. 175.

46. Howarth, p. 44. See more generally R. McWilliams Tullberg, *Women at Cambridge* (1988 ed.) and her "Women and Degrees at Cambridge" in M. Vicinus, ed., *A Widening Sphere: Changing Roles of Victorian Women* (1980 ed.), p. 295. For summaries, L-G, pp. 175-8 and Brooke, pp. 301-30.

47. L. & H. Fowler, comps, *Cambridge Commemorated*, p. 239.

48. *Sidgwick*, p. 247.

49. McWilliams Tullberg, "Women and Degrees", p. 295. Kingsley attributed this verdict on the beneficial effects of childbearing to his wife.

50. 18/12/63; 28/5/67.
51. 2/6/68; 7/12/69; 24/1/93. The 1893 motion was debated again in 1915, probably as an attempt at light-heartedness in wartime. It was again rejected, by an almost identical percentage, 68 votes to 43 (the anti-feminist 37 percent of 1893 rising to 39 percent in 1915). *CR*, 15 May 1915, p. 293.
52. Brooke, pp. 301-30; *Oxf. Mag.*, 11 June 1891, p. 281.
53. J.R.M. Butler, *H.M. Butler*, pp.29-31. The Master of Trinity insisted that it was "her goodness, not her Greek and Latin, which have stolen my heart".
54. D. Newsome, *On the Edge of Paradise: A.C. Benson The Diarist* (1980), p. 120.
55. *Autobiography of Bertrand Russell*, i, p. 66.
56. Another Trinity offered a partial solution. Cambridge women were able to trade their notional qualifications for Dublin degrees.
57. 30/1/77; 13/5/79; 28/11/76.
58. 25/5/80; 24/8/87; 29/3/81.
59. 7/2/88.
60. 12/11/89: "That this House would welcome the admission of Women (who keep terms and pass qualifying examinations) to the Bachelor Degrees"; 8/12/91: "That the time has come for women to be admitted to degrees". Support fell from 47 to 37 percent.
61. 12/2/89; 17/2/91; 30/1/94. But "the gradual extension to Women of the Parliamentary Franchise" was rejected on 7/6/92 by only 32 votes to 28.
62. 11/5/96.
63. Brooke, pp. 324-7; Johnson, pp. 33-8. It was claimed that there had been no such mass protest among undergraduates since 1771 when there had been a petition against subscription to the Thirty-Nine Articles of the Church of England, *Gr*, 8 May 1897, p. 300. But there had been attempts to circulate petitions for and against Catholic Emancipation in 1829.
64. *Gr*, 15 May 1897, pp. 311-12; 317, 322-4.
65. *Gr*, 24 April 1897, p. 264. G.P. Browne of St Catharine's, who drafted the compromise proposal, thought it would be in "the best interests of the higher education of women ... that it should be left to expand independently of the higher education of men". Browne, *Recollections of a Bishop*, pp. 309-10. It was an attitude not confined to Cambridge. The Principal of Edinburgh University condemned the idea of integrating women into male universities as "mistaken ... though undoubtedly women should have facilities for a University education, it should probably be one cast on different lines from the present University system for men". A. Grant, *The Story of the University of Edinburgh During its First Three Hundred Years* (2 vols, 1884), ii, p. 159.
66. J.P. Thompson in *Gr*, 15 May 1897, pp. 322-4. Thompson had recently entered the Indian Civil Service.
67. *Gr*, 15 May 1897, p. 315.
68. *Gr*, 15 May 1897, pp. 322-4.
69. *Gr*, 24 April 1897, p. 264.
70. *Gr*, 15 May 1897, pp. 322-4.
71. *Gr*, 24 April 1897, p. 264. "As long as the University [of Edinburgh] is overflowing with male Students, and every class-room is over-crowded", wrote Principal Grant

in 1884, "it is of course impossible to think of admitting a number of ladies in addition." Grant, *Story of the University of Edinburgh*, ii, p. 159.

72. *Gr*, 15 May 1897, pp. 322-4.
73. Pethick-Lawrence, *Fate Has Been Kind*, p. 35.
74. *Inaug.*, pp. 34-5.
75. 7/3/37. Twenty members were present, and the motion passed on the casting vote of the President.
76. VPR, E 1892.
77. *CR*, 25 Feb. 1897, p. 260 (and cf. *Gr*, 27 Feb. 1897, pp. 218-20).
78. *Gr*, 24 April 1897, p. 263.
79. *Gr*, 15 May 1897, pp. 322-4.
80. 30/1/05; 9/2/09.
81. *The Times*, 25 Feb. 1886.
82. 14/5/12; *CR*, 16 May 1912, p. 444. The speaker was Aubrey Attwater.
83. Howarth, p. 169.
84. Brooke, pp. 324-7, L-G, pp. 192-3. For the abbreviation, Howarth, pp. 41-2.
85. Balfour, *Chapters of Autobiography*, pp. 52-3.
86. L. Stephen, *Life of Fitzjames Stephen*, p. 93.
87. *British and Foreign Review*, 5, 1837, p. 180.
88. Barry O'Brien, *Parnell*, i, p. 41.
89. Pethick-Lawrence, *Fate Has Been Kind*, p. 31.
90. 22/10/01.
91. E. Waugh, *A Little Learning* (1983 ed.), p. 139. Defenders of the proposed Lectureship in American History in 1866 challenged critics to explain why the Cambridge curriculum gave so much attention to the republican institutions of Greece and Rome. Ged Martin, "Cambridge Lectureship of 1866", p. 25.
92. Gunning, i, p. 19; *Rom2*, p. 179n.
93. 10/2/91; *Oxf. Mag.*, 19 Feb. 1891, pp. 220-1. MacBride was regarded as "a prominent representative of the Scientific Course". (11 Feb. 1891, p. 205).
94. Johnson, p. 11.
95. *VCH*, p. 282.
96. *Student's Guide*, pp.97-8. A critic of Oxford and Cambridge pointed out that such arguments would imply that similar educational benefit would be obtained "if the same number of young men were to live in any two cities, as York and Exeter ... for the same period". *Westminster Review*, 15, 1841, p. 65.
97. A.C. Benson, *From a College Window*, p. 167.
98. 2/4/78; 25/2 /79; *Oxf. Mag.*, 12 Nov. 1890, p. 88.
99. Johnson, p. 65. But as an undergraduate Jebb had denounced "those wretched Classics, which I now almost detest". C. Jebb, *Life and Letters of Richard Claverhouse Jebb* (1907), p. 35.
100. 26/11/78; 22/4/04; 23/2/05; 27/5/13; Johnson, pp. 65-6.
101. 1/3 /92.
102. 9-15/5/49.
103. 5/6/88.
104. Bristed, p. 104.
105. Cradock, p. 66; *Oxf. Mag.*, 16 Nov. 1892, 8 Feb. 1893, pp. 91, 208-9.

106. D. Newsome, *Godliness and Good Learning: Four Studies on a Victorian Ideal* (1964), pp. 104-5; Bristed, p. 423.
107. Honey, *Tom Brown's Universe*, p. 35. However, Eton was poor at preparing students for the study of mathematics.
108. *LVC*, p. 357. Macaulay defended the Maynooth grant by reminding the House of Commons of Protestant appropriation of the medieval endowments of Catholicism. *Macaulay*, ii, p.102n.
109. Brooke, p. 113.
110. "Magdalene in the Sixties", *Magdalene College Magazine*, March 1910, p. 68. Magdalene discontinued chapel fines in 1902 on ethical grounds, sacrificing on principle vitally needed income. Cunich et al, eds, *History of Magdalene*, p. 217.
111. Searby, pp. 268-73; *Rom1*, p. 162; W.W. Rouse Ball, *Cambridge Papers* (1918), pp. 71-83. In fact the young Australian, John Lang, went on to read for the Bar in London.
112. 6/12/64; 24/4/66; 24/3/68; 1/3/70; 23/4/72.
113. *EVC*, p. 83n.
114. Pethick-Lawrence, *Fate Has Been Kind*, p. 32.
115. Johnson, pp. 28-30 and Cornford in Johnson, p. 100.
116. Blunt, *Land War*, p. 165. The student cannot be identified from Blunt's description, although Goldsworthy Lowes Dickinson is a possibility. This is the sole allusion to hallucinogenic drugs at Cambridge encountered during this study.
117. H. Dalton, *Call Back Yesterday*, p. 37.
118. *LVC*, p. 41.
119. Cradock, pp. 17-18; Thackeray, p. 38.
120. H. Montgomery Hyde, *Norman Birkett: The Life of Lord Birkett of Ulverston* (1964), p. 31. The switch in Birkett's career plans coincided with the announcement by the Master of Emmanuel that he (the Master) had become an atheist. Brooke, pp. 123-6.
121. Birkett in Cradock, p. 96.
122. Thackeray, *The Book of Snobs* (1993 ed.), p. 59 (ch. 14).
123. S. Rothblatt, *The Revolution of the Dons: Cambridge and Society in Victorian England* (1968), pp. 48-93.
124. *Student's Guide*, p. 73; Rothblatt, *Revolution of the Dons*, pp. 65-72. For wages, G. Best, *Mid-Victorian Britain 1851-74* (1973 ed.), pp. 116-17. A "steady reading man" was estimated to spend £100 a year at Magdalene in 1852. At St John's in 1867, "a poor person" could survive on £80 a year, whereas at Trinity "a few men live for as little as £150 a year ... including tradesmen's bills and everything, but the majority spend from £150 to £300 a year". By 1914, minimum annual costs were estimated at anything from £110 to £225. *Parliamentary Papers*, 1852-3, 44, p. 412; 1867, 13, questions 571, 1628; *VCH*, p. 285. A glance at *Whitaker's Almanack* for 1914 puts these figures into some context. The Housing Manager of the London County Council received £800 a year. Second-class clerks in the Land Registry in London were paid on a scale of between £250 and £400 a year. For District Inspectors in the Royal Irish Constabulary, the scale began at £125 and rose to £300 a year. The Clerk in charge of Minor Staff at the Reformatory and Industrial Schools section at Dublin Castle was paid up to £350: he held a Doctorate in Laws. Parents who groan at the

cost of higher education today may wish to reflect on these figures.

125. A.C. Benson, *The Life of Edward White Benson Sometime Archbishop of Canterbury* (2 vols, 1988) i, p. 74. Despite financial pressures, E.W. Benson joined the Union.

126. Gray and Brittain, *History of Jesus College*, p. 175. Cf. Searby, pp. 74-5; Brooke, pp. 240-54.

127. Rothblatt, *Revolution of the Dons*, pp. 78-80.

128. W. Harris, *Life So Far*, p. 45.

129. *Autobiography of Bertrand Russell*, i, p. 57. Crompton Llewelyn Davies later had links with Sinn Féin and Russell claimed that he drafted the 1921 Treaty "though this was never publicly known" (p. 59). The story seems unlikely.

130. *Gr*, 26 Jan. 1907, pp. 159-60.

131. 2/5 /11; Annual Report 1914.

132. *Rom3*, p. 159; Cunich et al., *History of Magdalene*, p. 231.

133. A. Fox, *Dean Inge* (1960), pp. 203.

134. Fox, *Dean Inge*, p. 202.

135. Howarth, p. 66. Cambridge incorporated a number of Latin terms into its day-to-day vocabulary. "In loco parentis" was the counterpart of "in statu pupillari", meaning that college and university authorities assumed a parental responsibility for (and control over) undergraduates. Permission to go out of residence (i.e. to leave college for a few days or at the end of term) was conveyed in an "exeat" ("let him go forth"). Offered the chance of a ride in a balloon, Monckton Milnes dutifully sought permission from his tutor, William Whewell, who invented a new document, an "ascendat".

ENDNOTES TO CHAPTER FOUR (pp. 76-95):

CAMBRIDGE, CATHOLICISM AND THE IRISH

1. *The Cam: A May Week Magazine*, 9 June 1892, p. 19.

2. Gray, *Cambridge and its Story*, p. 1. Regulations for the appointment of official peace-keepers in 1268 imply the presence at Cambridge of students from Scotland, Wales and Ireland, but these perhaps owed inspiration to Paris, where the university was organised into "nations". English *county* identities were important at individual colleges, but it is noteworthy that Cambridge did not develop a structure based on "nations". L-G, p. 12n.

3. Ged Martin, "Cambridge Lectureship of 1866", p. 24.

4. John Buchan surprised Hensley Henson in 1934 by referring to himself as "an *Englishman*", adding "I have no use at all for the silly affectation of substituting Briton for Englishman when speaking of Scots". H.H. Henson, *Retrospect of an Unimportant Life* (2 vols, 1943 ed.), ii, p. 354. Like Cosmo Lang, who went on to become Archbishop of Canterbury, Buchan was a former President of the Oxford Union.

4. Scott-Giles, *Sidney Sussex*, p. 36.

5. *Alma Mater*, ii, p. 134.

7. Bristed, p. 279.

8. *Alma Mater*, ii, pp. 135, 137. Beresford Hope (former President of the Union and MP for Cambridge University) defined the difference between the older English universities and their Scots counterparts in 1876: "the Scotch universities, with their Professorships and spacious lecture rooms, take up the members of the middle and lower classes, educate them, and leave them members of the middle and poorer classes still". Cambridge and Oxford, on the other hand, "take the same classes, and by their system …[of examinations and awards] … raise them to the rank of that best of aristocracies, the aristocracy of respect, of influence, and of power". He was replying to criticisms from the Scot, Lyon Playfair (a self-styled "outer barbarian") that Oxford University had an annual income of £400,000 compared to £23,000 for Edinburgh, "and yet the number of their students is almost equal". *Parliamentary Debates*, 230, 6 July 1876, cols 1081, 1068-71.
9. *Moultrie*, i, pp. viii, ii, xxxi-iii; *Corrie*, p. 114.
10. Lord Huntly was so badly beaten that one witness assumed he was dead. Although the local magistrates condemned the assault as "gross", they angered student opinion by imposing a derisory fine of ten shillings upon his assailant. *Cambridge Chronicle*, 10, 17 Nov. 1866.
11. 31/10/71 (the Archbishop was supported by 77 votes to 30); 3/2/85 ("the condition of the Scotch crofters calls for an instant and radical reform of the rights possessed by landed proprietors", opposed by W.F. Scott but carried by 70 votes to 54); 15/7 /02; 10/7/11.
12. G. Williams, *Renewal and Reformation: Wales c. 1415-1642* (1993 ed.), p. 434.
13. Cunich et al., *History of Magdalene*, p. 85.
14. L. &. H. Fowler, comps, *Cambridge Commemorated*, pp. 70-1.
15. Morgan, *Wales: Rebirth of a Nation*, p. 100.
16. P. Hollis, *Eton: A History* (1960), p. 232.
17. "His Welsh intonation was most attractive", Birkett recalled of Evans. Cradock, p. 103.
18. 11/3/09; 28/1/13; 18/10/04.
19. E. Longford, *Wellington: Years of the Sword* (1971 ed.), p. 171.
20. Moody and Beckett, *Queen's Belfast*, i, pp. xlii-xliv.
21. Gray and Brittain, *History of Jesus*, pp. 174-6.
22. Bourne, *Palmerston: The Early Years*, p. 15.
23. J. Pope-Hennessy, *Monckton Milnes: The Years of Promise 1809-1851* (1949), p. 18.
24. Bristed, p. 281, recorded another case, from the eighteen-forties, of an Irish Protestant student who went over to Rome "leaving an Orange father to bewail his untimely fate".
25. T.F.R. McDonnell was President in 1898; M.F.J. McDonnell in 1904. R.F. Foster, *Charles Stewart Parnell: The Man and his Family* (1979), pp. 54-64.
26. *DNB*, "Lynch, Thomas Kerr".
27. *Gr*, 2 May 1914, p. 279.
28. L. & H. Fowler, comps, *Cambridge Commemorated*, p. 173.
29. *Rom1*, p. 48.
30. *Rom1*, p. 72.
31. *Rom2*, p. 127; *Rom1*, p. x. In 1859, the Queen's University in Ireland, representing

the Colleges at Belfast, Cork and Galway, requested the same privilege, that its graduates be admitted to Cambridge degrees "ad eundem". The application was refused, since "Dublin [i.e. Trinity College] does not recognise these Queen's degrees any more than we recognise the degrees of the London University". *Rom3*, p. 337. As late as the nineteen-sixties, Cambridge staff with London doctorates were still sometimes formally referred to (if male) as "Mr".

32. *Catholic Cambridge*, pp. 100-124 (esp. p. 120) and cf. Brooke, pp. 388-91.
33. *Catholic Cambridge*, pp. 104-5; *Rom3*, p. 112 (9 Aug. 1863, presumably a reference to migrant harvest workers).
34. *Catholic Cambridge*, pp. 106-7. Oxford had lost twice as many converts to Rome.
35. *Catholic Cambridge*, p. 114-15. Protestant Cambridge delighted in the story that the benefactor was the widow of a man who had made his money from the manufacture of dolls' eyes. When it was falsely reported that the Union had voted in favour of an Irish Catholic university in 1889, Anglican opinion in Cambridge was quick to see "the first manifestation of the machinations of the new cathedral". *Oxf. Mag.*, 23 Oct 1889, p. 29. The first official recognition of the Hills Road Catholic church was probably in June 1902, when the Vice-Chancellor gave formal notice of a requiem mass for Lord Acton. There was a respectable turn-out of official Cambridge, but H.M. Butler "was about the only Anglican parson" among the mourners. Fifoot, ed., *Letters of Maitland*, p. 246.
36. *Catholic Cambridge*, pp. 100, 134; *Rom1*, p. 70.
37. Magdalene became less welcoming to Catholics as the nineteenth century progressed, and declined to admit the future Regius Professor, Lord Acton, nephew of the Cardinal. But arguably he became a better historian through missing Cambridge. Cf. Cunich et al., *History of Magdalene*, p. 204; Brooke, pp. 405-6. Christ's was also open to Catholics. *EVC*, p. 83n.
38. *Rom2*, p, 180. F.A. Paley later returned to Cambridge and worked as a coach (i.e. free-lance tutor, "a crammer for the Classical Tripos") between 1860 and 1874, when he became a Professor at Manning's unsuccessful Catholic University in Kensington. *Rom3*, p. 435.
39. Gray and Brittain, *History of Jesus*, p. 165.
40. 22/4 /45. Lord Bernard Howard was the younger son of the 13th Duke of Norfolk (who briefly seceded from the Catholic Church in protest against the re-establishment of the hierarchy in 1851). Lord Bernard had been a member of the Speculative Society at Edinburgh. He died in December 1846, shortly before his 21st birthday. For the Synod of Thurles and the Queen's Colleges (an issue that divided the Irish bishops), E. Larkin, *Making of the Roman Catholic Church in Ireland 1850-1860* (1980), pp. 27-57.
41. Gavin Souter, *Lion and Kangaroo* (1976), p. 206. The governor-general of Australia, Sir Ronald Munro-Ferguson, thought Strickland "obsessed by petty personal ambition" and barely sane.
42. 21/11/86. D. Cannadine, *Aspects of Aristocracy: Grandeur and Decline in Modern Britain* (1994), pp. 109-29.
43. *Catholic Cambridge*, pp. 121-2.
44. *Catholic Cambridge*, p. 123.
45. Johnson, pp. 27-8, L-G, p. 175. After the First World War, the University's Catholic

community rented a house in Round Church Street from the Union for use as a chapel prior to the acquisition of Fisher House.

46. Annual Report, 1851, p. 127.
47. 26/5/29; 3/12 /44; 4 /3/62; 8/12/74; 10/5/98. The 1829 discussion of the Jesuits was "but a poor debate" which "did not last more than half an hour". *Thackeray*, p. 80. Venn, usually so helpful, offers no information on Seyyid Ben-Yusuf.
48. MB2, Easter Term 1825 (no pagination).
49. MB2, report received 5 Dec. 1825.
50. MB3, report by R. Hutt, 14 Nov. 1826, fo. 53.
51. MB3, letter from M. Boylan, Johnstown [Drogheda], 4 Nov. 1826, fos. 71-2.
52. MB4, fos 6-7.
53. MB3, M. Boylan to J. Jordan, Johnstown, 4 Jan. 1827, fos 86-7.
54. 6/4/24; 26/4-3/5/25. Boylan spoke tenth out of eleven in criticism of English rule in Ireland (before 1800) on 23/11/24.
55. 19-26/3/33. Sir Thomas Redington failed to persuade Cullen to accept the post of Visitor at Queen's College Belfast. E. Larkin, *The Making of the Roman Catholic Church in Ireland, 1850-1860*, pp. 37-8.
56. 5/3/39. Trollope made Phineas a member of the debating society at Trinity College Dublin. Like Phineas, Ball was Under-Secretary for Colonies. Like Phineas, he took an interest in the development of the Canadian prairies, and was largely responsible for the despatch of the expedition under Captain John Palliser in 1857. Ball was a founder of the Alpine Club. Plantagenet Palliser first appears in *The Small House at Allington*, written in 1862 at about the time Trollope became a member.
57. J.A.Venn, comp., *Alumni Cantabrigienses*, Part ii, iv (1951), pp. 499-500.
58. *DNB*, "Murphy, Robert".
59. 4/2/90; 10/6/ 90.
60. C.H.Cooper, *Annals of Cambridge*, i (1892), p. 181.
61. C.H. Cooper, *Annals of Cambridge*, iii (1895), p. 644.
62. Cambridge University Library, James Stephen Papers, MS7349/1, James Stephen to James Fitzjames Stephen (aged 7), 2 Dec. 1836.
63. Merivale, p. 314.
64. *Whewell*, pp. 173, 177 (8 May 1835). It is noteworthy that when Whewell revisited Ireland in 1857, he does not seem to have been so struck by poverty (p. 496). This may perhaps be explained by the fact that he based himself at Malahide Castle.
65. *Rom1*, p. 97 (28 Feb. 1836).
66. *Corrie*, pp. 50-2.
67. *Corrie*, pp. 122-31.
68. *Corrie*, pp. 72-3, 89.
69. Kingsley, *Charles Kingsley* (1883 ed.), p. 236. In 1866, Kingsley wrote that "some races, e.g. the Irish Celts, seem quite unfitted for self-government ... because they regard freedom and law ... merely as weapons to be used for their own private interests and passions". (p. 278). In 1861, G.O. Trevelyan went to Mayo as part of a "reading party" (a group of students who based themselves in a remote location to engage in energetic recreation and intensive study). "The accommodation was miserable, even for an Irish wilderness" and they were confined to their "porous cottage" by heavy rain. However, the capacity of the stranded undergraduates to

empathise with the Mayo peasantry was considerably diminished by the fact that they had each brought along "a hamper from Fortnum and Mason". Jebb, *Life of Jebb*, p. 53.

70. G.F. Lewis, ed., *Letters of the Right Hon. George Cornewall Lewis, Bart., to Various Friends* (1870), pp. 40-41.

71. R. Hyam, *Britain's Imperial Century 1815-1914* (1976 ed.), p. 88.

72. *CR*, 14 March 1907, pp. 327-8.

73. Cradock, p. 145; *Gr*, 6 May 1890, p. 298

75. *CR*, 25 Nov. 1897, p. 112. The most that can be said in defence of this sentiment, which was surely unsavoury even at the time, is that it was not original. It can be traced to the medieval historian, E.A. Freeman, who had visited the United States in 1881. "Very many approved when I suggested that the best remedy for whatever was amiss would be if every Irishman should kill a negro [sic] and be hanged for it." Freeman's opinion was unpopular in Rhode Island, which had abolished the death penalty, while some of his hosts objected "that if there were no Irish and no negroes, they would not be able to get any domestic servants". E.A. Freeman, *Some Impressions of the United States* (1883), p. 138. The publication of Freeman's biography in 1895 may have drawn further attention to the remark. W.R.W. Stephens, *The Life and Letters of Edward A. Freeman* (2 vols, 1895), ii, p. 242. Perhaps unexpectedly, Freeman supported Home Rule in 1886, on the unusual but probably accurate assessment that it would create for the first time "a real Imperial relation[ship]" by removing Irish MPs from Westminster. "I should have thought one main object of the whole thing was to get rid of them." (ii, p. 346). I am obliged to Owen Dudley Edwards for this identification.

76. R.W. Pfaff, *Montague Rhodes James* (1980), p. 99. Henry Bradshaw, University Librarian, from 1867 to 1886, was a notable figure in Celtic scholarship.

77. A.M. Sullivan, *The New Ireland* (1884 ed.), p. 42.

ENDNOTES TO CHAPTER FIVE (pp. 99-117):

THE EARLY YEARS OF THE CAMBRIDGE UNION

1. At the first debate, on 20 February 1815, a house of 68 decided by a majority of two votes that the Whig opposition had been justified in refusing to join the ministry three years earlier.

2. *Statement*, p. vii. Cf. Cradock, pp. 3-6; Searby, pp. 718-19.

3. Lord Teignmouth, *Reminiscences of Many Years* (2 vols, 1878), i, p. 47. This anecdote does not appear in Cradock.

4. *Alma Mater*, i, pp. 202-3.

5. *Autobiographical Reminiscences of George Pryme* (ed. A. Bayne, 1870), p. 117. In 1816, Pryme began to lecture on Political Economy, even though it formed part of no degree curriculum. In 1828 the University awarded him a Personal Chair. Thackeray in 1829 commented that "his delivery is very bad but his [subject] matter is excellent as it ought to be" (*Thackeray*, p. 71). In 1861 it was reported that he had "a prodigious class and is most popular, for he plucks [fails] nobody". Pryme began

his lectures with the statement "Gentlemen, Political Economy is a noble science", to which his class responded "So it is − 3 cheers for the Professor". By this time, classical Cambridge had nicknamed him "Priam", after the elderly and gentle king of Troy in Homer's *Iliad*. "Old Pryme told me that he meant to lecture as long as life was in him, " Romilly noted that October, adding "he is past 80 & looks good for 10 years more." In fact he resigned two years later, after the Senate had agreed to continue his Chair. Detractors likened the length of his nose to the length of his prose. Pryme died in 1868. *Rom3*, pp. 381-2, 393, 403, 446.

6. The original Union rooms were probably not the usually quoted "cavernous, tavernous" extension at the back of the Red Lion, as was made clear by Professor William Selwyn in *Inaug.*, p. 25. Two fragments of verse suggest that the Society originally occupied a room at the front of the Red Lion on an upper floor, where debates "with languid roar/ Of cheers had shaken Petty Cury's roofs". *Moultrie*, p. 420 and cf. Searby, p. 718. See also the squib by M. Lawson in Teichman, *The Cambridge Undergraduate 100 Years Ago*, p. 86, picturing a member of the Union in 1817: "At a window, which on high/ Frowns o'er the market-place below". However, this is puzzling, since no part of the Red Lion could provide an easy line of vision to Market Hill. In the absence of any Minute Books before 1823, the mystery cannot be resolved. By the time Bulwer Lytton became a member, in 1823, the Union was located at the back of the Red Lion.

7. *Palmerston-Sulivan Letters*, pp. 8-12. The suggested explanation for the nickname made by the editor, Kenneth Bourne, is implausible.

8. *Palmerston-Sulivan Letters*, p. 11. Whewell in 1822 called Bankes " a very remarkable man" and "one of the most entertaining persons I have ever met with", but regretted his "bigoted intolerance towards Papists". But J.C. Hobhouse was less impressed on encountering Bankes, for the first time in twenty years, during the hard-fought Cambridge election of 1826. "He is exactly the same rattling grinning fellow as ever and he talked … the same sort of nonsense as he used when a pupil at College." *Whewell*, pp. 73-4; Bourne, *Palmerston: The Early Years*, p. 247.

9. *Palmerston-Sulivan Letters*, pp. 11-12.

10. Allen, *Cambridge Apostles*, pp. 38-42, 51. In an appropriately Apostolic parallel, R.C. Trench, later Archbishop of Dublin, likened Sunderland to Judas.

11. *EVC*, pp. 58-60.

12. *Alma Mater*, i, p. 203.

13. *Inaug*, p. 83, letter to *The Times* from "The First Secretary and Third President of the Union" (i.e. C.J. Shore).

14. C. Hollis, *Eton: A History*, pp. 208-9.

15. W.E. Gladstone, *Autobiographical Memoranda, iv, 1868-1894* (1981), p. 102 (29 June 1894).

16. D.T. Andrew, ed., *London Debating Societies 1776-1799* (1994), pp. vii-xi; J. Money, "Taverns, Coffee Houses and Clubs: Local Politics and Popular Articulacy in the Birmingham Area in the Age of the American Revolution", *Historical Journal*, 14, 1971, pp. 15-48; M. Thales, "London Debating Societies in the 1790s", *Historical Journal*, 32, 1989, pp. 57-86.

17. Thales, "London Debating Societies", pp. 72, 78.

18. *Parliamentary Debates*, 36, 28 April 1817, cols. 17-21.

19. *Autobiographical Reminiscences of George Pryme*, pp. 65-6; 117.
20. *Statement*, p. x.
21. *Palmerston-Sulivan Letters*, p. 38 (5 March 1805).
22. *History of the Speculative Society of Edinburgh from its Institution in MDCCLXIV* (1845), p. 20; *The History of the Speculative Society 1764-1904* (1905); A.G. Fraser, *The Building of the Old College: Adam, Playfair & the University of Edinburgh* (1989), pp. 43, 93-4, 212-13. For an outline history of debating societies at Edinburgh, see Grant, *The Story of the University of Edinburgh*, ii, pp. 485-6. By 1884, there was a five-guinea (£5.25) entrance fee to join the Speculative "which alone is a bar to the majority of Students, and it is rather for young advocates". Undergraduate debaters joined either the Dialectic Society (founded in 1787) or the Diagnostic, which began in 1816. In addition, there was the Philomathic, established in 1858 for freshmen.
23. *Palmerston-Sulivan Letters*, p. 177.
24. *Statement*, Appendix. Members were fined one shilling and sixpence if absent from any meeting, and all members were to take their turns at opening a subject. By 1817, there were 187 members on the Society's books, although some would have left Cambridge by then. F. J. A. Hort reported in 1846 to his father, a member active in 1816, that the fines of his day had disappeared. Hort, p. 44.
25. Skipper, p. 5, accepted by Tanner, *Historical Register of the University of Cambridge*, p. 991. Bickersteth was a member of an earlier debating society at Cambridge – possibly the Speculative – but his biographer made no reference to the Union. In any case, Bickersteth left Cambridge soon after taking his BA in 1808. T.D. Hardy, *Memoirs of the Right Honourable Henry Lord Langdale* (2 vols, 1852), i, p. 232.
26. Palmerston's term in *Palmerston-Sulivan Letters*, p. 70.
27. *The Times*, 31 March 1817.
28. *Thackeray*, p. 56.
29. Cunich et al., *History of Magdalene*, p. 191.
30. *EVC*, pp. 18-25.
31. Gunning, ii, pp. 278-9.
32. *EVC*, p. 24.
33. I am grateful to Dr Ronald Hyam for a transcript of the memorial inscription, which was incorporated to the new St John's chapel built in the eighteen-sixties.
34. *DNB*, "Maitland, James".
35. B. Lenman, *Integration, Enlightenment, and Industrialization: Scotland 1760-1832* (1981), p. 112.
36. Teignmouth, *Reminiscences*, i, p. 47.
37. Winstanley, *Unreformed Cambridge*, p. 208. Dr Leedham-Green informs me that the Union Coffee House had disappeared by 1800.
38. For Peel's membership, see N. Gash, *Mr Secretary Peel* (2nd ed., 1985), p. 266.
39. *Dilke*, i, p. 31.
40. Ferguson, *Magpie and Stump*, p. 28.
41. E.g. *Rom1*, pp. 157, 159, 167, 185. Information from the late R.F. Thompson.
42. F.D. Cartwright, ed., *The Life and Correspondence of Major Cartwright* (2 vols, 1826, facsimile 1969), ii, p. 376.

43. E.P. Thompson, *The Making of the English Working Class* (1968 ed.), pp. 676, 678, 691, 788.

44. *Statement*, p. vii.

45. *Inaug.*, pp. 26-7. The story is briefly mentioned in the biography by Mrs Stair Douglas (*Whewell*, p. 41), and is specifically credited by I. Todhunter, *William Whewell Master of Trinity College Cambridge* (2 vols, 1876), i, p. 8. Cf. Allen, *Cambridge Apostles*, p. 13 for Whewell, and *EVC*, p. 26; Searby, p. 319.

46. Morrah, *Oxford Union*, pp. 27-8. Samuel Wilberforce was speaking in hired rooms at the Freemasons' Hall when the Oxford proctors "demanded a dispersal". The Union replied: "this house has received the proctors' message, and will send an answer to the summons by an officer of its own". The leader of resistance was Metcalf of Magdalen, described as an "Irishman of excellent humour and racy character". However, this jovial Irishman seems to have come from Burton-on-Trent.

47. *Alma Mater*, i, p. 204.

48. *Statement*, p. viii.

49. *Statement*, p. ix.

51. *Alma Mater*, i, p. 202; Gray, *Cambridge and its Story*, p. 316; Searby, p. 316n.

52. *Statement*, p. x.

53. *Alma Mater*, i, p. 205.

54. *EVC*, p. 26. For Winstanley, see the note by G.M. Trevelyan in *LVC*, pp. v-vii and G.M. Trevelyan, *An Autobiography & Other Essays* (1949), pp. 235-7.

55. *Statement*, p. xi.

56. J.E. Cookson, *Lord Liverpool's Administration 1815-1822* (1975), pp. 102-16. There was some doubt about the alleged assassination attempt: C. Hibbert, *George IV* (1976 ed.), p. 493.

57. *The Times*, 22 Feb. 1817.

58. Thompson, *Making of the English Working Class*, pp. 711-12.

59. *The Times*, 22 Feb. 1817.

60. *Parliamentary Debates*, 35, 21 Feb. 1817, cols 472-91. Cf. Cartwright, *Life and Correspondence of Major Cartwright*, ii, p. 129.

61. Thompson, *Making of the English Working Class*, p. 694.

62. *The Times*, 12 March 1817, quoting *Leeds Mercury*.

63. *The Times*, 1 April 1817.

64. Gunning, i, pp. 211-15 is dismissive of Christian; Searby, p. 562.

65. Gunning, ii, pp. 303-4, presented at Carlton House, 18 Feb. 1817.

66. 11/11/16; 10/3/17. Connop Thirlwall, later Bishop of St David's, opposed this motion; 17/3/17; 24/3/17. This last motion was "Negatived" but understandably no vote was recorded.

67. Samuel Bamford, *Passages in the Life of a Radical* (3rd ed., n.d.), p. 9 for a list of Lancashire reformers whose background resembled that of Whewell.

68. Cornford in Johnson, p. 106.

69. *Statement*, pp. x-xi.

70. *The Times*, 31 March, 17 April 1817.

71. *Parliamentary Debates*, 34, 28 April 1817, cols. 20-1.

72. *EVC*, p. 123.

73. Gunning, ii, pp. 314-16.
74. *VCH*, pp. 26, 44, 75.
75. *EVC*, p. 123; L-G, p. 181; Searby, p. 93.
76. *Parliamentary Debates*, 36, 28 April 1817, cols 17-21.
77. Cradock, p. 9, following *Laws and Transactions of the Union Society MDCCCXXII* (1822), p. 134; *EVC*, p. 27; L-G, p. 139; Searby, p. 719.
78. Cookson, *Lord Liverpool's Administration*, p. 111; *Alma Mater*, i, pp. 52, 203; *Palmerston-Sulivan Letters*, p. 12. Wood on horseback was known as "St John's head on a charger".
79. *Autobiographical Recollections of George Pryme*, p. 118.
80. Verse by Lawson in Teichmann, ed., *The Cambridge Undergraduate*, p. 87.
81. *Alma Mater*, i, p. 204. Arthur Thistlewood was executed for treason in 1820. His conduct on the scaffold was flamboyant.
82. Thales, "London Debating Societies", pp. 67, 71.
83. *Statement*, p. v.
84. *Macaulay*, pp. 74-5.
85. *Statement*, p. vi. This claim was hardly borne out by the printed list of debates.
86. *Laws and Regulations of the Union Society MDCCCXXI* (1821), Laws 1 and 24 and cf. *Laws and Transactions* (1822), p. 134.

ENDNOTES TO CHAPTER SIX (pp. 118-138):

THE UNION AND ITS DEBATES 1821-1914

1. *The Times*, 25 Feb. 1886.
2. Harris, *Life So Far*, p. 60. Rupert Brooke never spoke in a debate, but he used Union Society notepaper when writing to Katherine Cox, the love of his life. G. Knights, ed., *The Letters of Rupert Brooke* (1968), p. 324.
3. It is not easy to interpret early Union accounts, since Treasurers seem to have employed different accounting periods, and some figures simply do not add up. Between 16 December 1824 and 26 March 1825, income was £252-11-6 and total expenditure £153-1-8, of which £73-11-3 went on newspapers, plus a further £43-12-5 that was overdue. On 7 October 1831, income for the preceding but unspecified period was reported to be £325-9-3 and expenditure £242-7-3. The Union was thus a substantial business enterprise, but run on largely amateur lines until a clerk was hired in 1831.
4. Allen, *Cambridge Apostles*, p. 43. In the early years, members spoke from their places, not from the despatch box. Backbench speakers were sometimes inaudible. *Sketches of Cantabs*, p. 48.
5. MB1, 16 Dec. 1823.
6. MB3, 22 May 1826, fos 38-9.
7. MB3, 12 Feb. 1827; MB4, 27 Nov. 1827, fo. 69.
8. *Inaug.*, p. 8; *VCH*, p. 115.
9. MB3, 11 Dec. 1826, fo. 80.
10. *Laws and Transactions* (1822), pp. 35-40.
11. MB3, 28 Nov. 1826, fo. 68.

12. MB3, 30 Oct. 1826, fo. 34.
13. MB4, 10 March 1828, fos 100-2.
14. MB3, 30 Oct. 1826, fo. 34; MB6, 8 Feb. 1831, fo. 105.
15. MB2, 9 Feb. 1825.
16. MB2, April 1825.
17. MB6, 16 Nov. 1830, fo. 60. The post had been filled by 8 Feb. 1831 when "the Clerks Dinner time" was fixed from 12.30 to 2, fo. 105.
18. MB3, 29 Oct. 1827, fos 49-50.
19. MB3, 2 May 1826, 29 Oct. 1827, fos 49-50.
20. MB5, 18 Nov. 1828, fo. 16.
21. MB6, 16 Nov. 1830, fo. 60.
22. MB6, 6 Dec. 1830, fos 86-7.
23. Bristed, p. 118.
24. Hort, p. 44. Cf. *Sketches of Cantabs*, p. 35 for a description of the Union's club facilities c. 1846.
25. MB15, fos 55-65. *VCH*, p. 137. In 1854, Homersham Cox published *The British Commonwealth: or a Commentary on the Institutions and Principles of British Government*.
26. Annual Report, 1851, pp. 124-5 (26/11/50). The officers and committee had failed to turn up the previous week.
27. Leslie Stephen in *Saturday Review*, quoted *Inaug.*, pp. 43-4.
28. *Inaug.*, p. 19
29. *Dilke*, i, p. 31.
30. VPR E 1860.
31. *Inaug.*, p. 63. The historian of the finances of St John's states that "it was not the policy of the College to dispose of its land [in the town of Cambridge] in the absence of some specially strong reason for this course". A town centre site was sold in the mid-Victorian period for the Divinity Schools, a project also associated with William Selwyn. The same authority also states that "no steps were taken by the College to provide for the balance of the cost [of the new Chapel] until after the work had been completed" in 1871. However, since the total cost was £98,649, it seems reasonable to assume that the sale of the Round Church site to the Union was partly motivated by the growing financial burden. A benefactor agreed to contribute £1000 a year during his lifetime towards the cost of the tower, but he was killed soon afterwards in a train crash. H.F. Howard, *An Account of the Finances of the College of St John the Evangelist* (1935), pp. 201-2, 209-12.
32. *Dilke*, i, pp. 50-1. If the Peto family did advise on the project, the Union was lucky with its timing for Sir Samuel Morton Peto went bankrupt in 1866.
33. *Inaug.*, pp. xiii-xv. "There are few who would have given it the time and attention which Mr Waterhouse has done" (p. xii).
34. *Inaug.*, p. 40.
35. *Inaug.*, pp. xiii, 84.
36. *The Times*, 25 Feb. 1886
37. Bristed, p. 118; *Cambridge Observer*, 22 Nov. 1892, p. 2.
38. *Student's Guide*, pp. 52, 70-1.
39. *Laws and Transactions* (1822), pp. 29-30.

40. MB5, 24 Feb. 1829, fo. 58.
41. *Laws and Transactions* (1822), pp. 40-43.
42. MB3, fo. 27 (Easter Term 1827); MB5, 9 Feb. 1829, fo. 35; Merivale, pp. 59-60. See also MB6, 11 Feb. 1832, fo. 71.
43. MB6, 1 Nov. 1830, fo. 42.
44. Suggestions Book (c. 1854), undated.
45. MB2, 16 May 1826, fo. 12.
46. Skipper, p. 16. Nineteenth-century Cambridge memoirs do not suggest that individual students bought many newspapers. Thackeray received newspapers from home, but in his day they were expensive items. For Walter Besant in the eighteen-fifties, Sunday breakfast included the treat of reading the controversial *Saturday Review*. Thackeray, p. 63; *Autobiography of Walter Besant*, p. 94. Bristed (p. 328) commented on the lethargy of the average undergraduate "for at least two hours" after dinner (which, in the mid-nineteenth century, was usually served around 4 p.m.). "The most he will do is lounge to the Union and read the papers".
47. MB3, 22 May 1827, fo. 27.
48. *CR*, 23 May, 1912, p. 459.
49. VPR E 1870.
50. VPR M 1895.
51. VPR M 1897.
52. MB2, 14 Nov. 1823.
53. *Sketches of Cantabs*, p. 37, also quoted Cradock, p. 44.
54. E.F. Benson, *David of King's*, pp. 237-8.
55. *Gr*, 9 Feb. 1895, p. 176. The *Granta* contested this criticism.
56. MB5, 18, 25 Nov. 1828, fos 18-21.
57. MB5, fo. 21; Cradock, p.20.
58. MB5, 2 Dec. 1828, fos 23-25 indicates that 247 members were present; 9 Feb. 1829, fo. 36.
59. C. Whibley, *Lord John Manners and His Friends* (2 vols, 1925), i, p. 59.
60. Quoted W.F. Monypenny, *The Life of Benjamin Disraeli Earl of Beaconsfield*, ii (1912), pp. 162-3.
61. *DNB*, "Vaughan, Charles John". In a remarkable "Establishment" cover-up, the story did not reach the public domain until the publication of Phyllis Grosskurth's biography of John Addington Symonds in 1964.
62. Cradock, pp. 29-30.
63. Bristed, p. 120. Bristed's annoyance is partly explained by the fact that he was similarly defeated for the Presidency.
64. Raikes, pp. 18-19. The future Archbishop was W. Saumarez Smith, who launched the Union's Building Fund (*Inaug.*, p. xi).
65. *Laws and Transactions* (1822), pp. 26-7 (29 May 1821).
66. Cradock, p. 36; Hort, p. 58; Skipper, pp. 13-14.
67. *Oxf. Mag.*, 13 May 1891, pp. 363-4; 28 Feb. 1894, p. 243.
68. Milnes, p. 58 (8 Dec. 1828); *The Times*, 25 Feb. 1886. The award of "Blues" for sporting achievement is a survival of this fancy dressing.
69. Dalton, *Call Back Yesterday*, p. 43.
70. *Alma Mater*, i, p. 62. The Atheist Club was inspired by Voltaire, whose influence in

Cambridge was understandably limited.

71. *Student's Guide*, p. 72.
72. Newsome, *On the Edge of Paradise*, p. 35. The Union had opposed the award of an honorary degree to Browning, 12/3/67.
73. A. Gray, *Cambridge Revisited* (1921), pp. 137-50.
74. J. Nehru, *An Autobiography* (1962 ed.), p. 21; Dalton, *Call Back Yesterday*, p. 51; P. Spear, *The Oxford History of Modern India 1740-1947* (1965), p. 363.
75. E.F. Benson, *David of King's*, p. 277. The Pitt Club settled in Jesus Lane in 1863.
76. Searby, pp. 711-18.
77. B. Holland, *The Life of Spencer Compton, Eighth Duke of Devonshire* (2 vols, 1912), i, pp. 14-15; Searby, p. 712 and note; A.C. Benson, *Edward White Benson*, i, pp. 74-5; Oliver Lyttelton, *The Memoirs of Lord Chandos* (1962), pp. 18-19. In the early eighteen-sixties, the Athenaeum seems to have passed through a serious phase. B and P. Russell, eds, *The Amberley Papers*, i, p. 230.
78. *Autobiography of Bertrand Russell*, i, p. 73; E.F. Benson, *David of King's*, p. 294. Whewell, who was an energetic rather than a competent horseman, claimed to have "personally measured the depth of every ditch in the neighbourhood of Cambridge by tumbling into it" (*Whewell*, p. 190). A guide to night-climbing on the roofs of Trinity was published in 1899.
79. Bristed, p. 343. Nehru (*Autobiography*, p. 20) wrote of his Cambridge days, "in spite of our brave talk, most of us were rather timid where sex was concerned".
80. Lyttelton, *Alfred Lyttelton*, p. 54.
81. Leslie Stephen in *National Review*, 42, 1903-4, p. 145.
82. MB3, 7/12 May 1827, fos 125-6.
83. Annual Report 1855, p. 49.
84. *CR*, 16 June 1892, p. 392; *Gr*, 2 May 1914, pp. 278-9.
85. *CR*, 6 Nov. 1890, p. 68.
86. *Laws and Transactions* (1823), 18 March 1823.
87. MB, i, fo. 44, 30 March, 25 May 1824.
88. C.H. Cooper, *Annals of Cambridge*, iv (1902), pp. 517, 524, 530, 537, 541 (and 546 for March 1826).
89. MB2, 13 Feb. 1825.
90. E.g. the debate of 17/2/24 specifically asked: "Is the present system of Game Laws deserving of the support of Parliament?" Despite criticism from Praed, the Union decided by 85-68 that it did. But members voted by 62 to 5 in favour of "a reform in the present system of the Game Laws" on 19/4/25. The debate on the same subject on 20/5/28 was also present-focused. The irrelevance of the restriction may be seen from the decision of 27 Feb. 1827 (MB3, fo. 11) to debate parliamentary reform at the next meeting. The motion, on 13/3/27, included the "twenty year" provision, apparently *pro forma*.
91. MB6, 9, 11 Nov. 1830, fos 52, 55-7.
92. MB6, fo. 57.
93. *Parliamentary Debates*, 20, 24 March 1829, cols 1413-17. For Kerry, see *Milnes*, i, p. 57 and *Macaulay*, i, p. 142: "I do not know when I have taken so much to so young a man", wrote Macaulay in February 1830, calling Kerry "kind, lively, intelligent, modest ... without the least affectation". He died in 1836. In 1856,

Romilly was surprised to find that Lord Lansdowne, although an elder statesman, was poor at spelling, *Rom3*, p. 263.

94. *Laws and Transactions* (1834), p. 66.
95. MB6, 16 Nov. 1830, fo. 60.
96. MB6, 22 Nov. 1830, fo. 75.
97. MB6, Nov. 1830, fo. 83.
98. MB7, 8 Nov. 1831, fo. 39. For "little Wentworth", see Trinity College, Houghton MSS 35/100, family letter of 10 March 1829 by R.M. Milnes.
99. MB7, 29 Nov. 1831, fos 51-4.
100. Lytton, i, p. 233.
101. Bristed, p. 118.
102. Stephen, *Sketches from Cambridge*, p. 59. In 1903, Stephen admitted in 1902 that his Sketches had been "very flippant". Maitland, *Leslie Stephen*, p. 480. Stephen claimed that if the origins were traced of the archetypal "stupendous bore" who addressed the Social Science Association, "you will find that in his earlier days he spoke at the Union ... generously bestow[ing] his tediousness upon the debating society". "The bore who has just chipped the egg-shell is as like the full-fledged bore of later life as a grampus to a whale." None the less, Union debates were "often highly amusing". Stephen, *Sketches from Cambridge*, pp. 59-61.
103. *National Review*, 42, 1903-4, p. 104.
104. W. Everett, *On The Cam* (1865), pp. 106-8. Cambridge seems to have treated Everett's account with some indulgence. "I rate its uses and especially its debates far higher than our young cousin from the New World", said Lord Powys at the inauguration of the new debating chamber. *Inaug.*, pp. 2-3. The *Cambridge Chronicle*, 7 April 1866, called Everett "a clever man and a keen observer" and welcomed news of the publication of the "frank and candid" lectures on the University that he had delivered in Boston.
105. The impression of a golden age relies upon accounts of the Union c. 1823 and again c.1827-9. However, numbers voting at debates fell away sharply around 1826.
106. Bristed, p. 118.
107. Whibley, *Lord John Manners and His Friends*, i, p. 58.
108. *Inaug.*, p. 3.
109. The point was made by the leading article in *The Times*, 25 Feb. 1886.
110. Whibley, *Lord John Manners and His Friends*, i, p. 66.
111. 27/2-5/3/44. The Evangelical, George Stephen, claimed in 1847 to be "familiar with the present tone of feeling among the junior classes at Cambridge ... a very large majority of those who affect conversion to Tractarian principles, are led away either by the seduction of pious romance, or by the far less excusable impulse of a love of notoriety". G. Stephen, *The Jesuit at Cambridge*, ii, pp. 325-6. His son was an undergraduate at that time.
112. Allen, *Cambridge Apostles*, pp. 53-4.
113. H. Tennyson, *Tennyson*, p. 32.
114. Allen, *Cambridge Apostles*, p. 54.
115. Bristed, p. 118.
116. Bristed, pp. 125, 188-19.
117. H.S. Jones, "Student Life and Sociability, 1860-1930: Comparative Reflections",

History of Universities, 14, 1995-6, pp. 225-46.
118. Cradock, pp. 99-100.
119. Grave, *Fitzwilliam College*, pp. 122-3.
120. See the foolish motion moved by T.F.R. McDonnell in 1897, discussed in Chapter Eight.
121. See the dismal account in *Gr*, 21 Nov. 1896, p. 81, reprinted in Rice, comp., *The Granta*, pp. 294-6. In clique-ridden King's, freshmen in 1889 formed a debating society called "The Cigarettes", *Gr*, 8 March 1889, p. 7.
122. Ferguson, *Magpie and Stump*, p. 14.
123. Miller, *Portrait of a College*, p. 108.
124. Ferguson, *Magpie and Stump*, pp. 9-10, 38-9.
125. J.R.M. Butler, *H. M. Butler*, p. 14; *Oxf. Mag.*, 9 March 1892, p. 233.
126. Ferguson, *Magpie and Stump*, pp. 17-34.
127. Nehru, *Autobiography*, p. 21.
128. MB2, 18/25 April 1826. Holt was protesting against the omission of his name from the membership list.
129. MB6, 7 Dec. 1830, fos 94, 96. The incident happened on the night Smith O'Brien was elected President.
130. MB14, 27 Nov. 1849, fos 231-2; L. Stephen, *Fitzjames Stephen*, pp. 98-9; *Rom3*, pp. 83, 118, 209, 450-1.
131. Dick Sedgwick had initially refused to go to Dent, but accepted the living in 1859 probably to assure his bachelor uncle of a home in eventual retirement, *Rom3*, pp. 312-13; *Gr*, 24 Oct. 1891, p. 29. Sedgwick appears at "Tickler" in *Sketches of Cantabs*, pp. 36-50, from which it appears that he spoke with a lisp ("I would weform these wadical cowwuptions.")
132. Bristed, p. 119.
133. Allen, *Cambridge Apostles*, p. 54.
134. MB3, 21 Nov. 1826, fo. 47.
135. MB7, 8 March 1831, fo. 2.
136. *Gr*, 20 May 1899, p. 329.
137. *Gr*, 11 Feb. 1899, pp. 178-9.
138. Bristed, p. 118.
139. *The Snarl*, 21 Oct. 1899, p. 3.

ENDNOTES TO CHAPTER SEVEN (pp. 139-159):

ORATORY AND OPINION

1. White, *Cambridge Life*, p. 137.
2. VPR E 1891.
3. *Oxf. Mag.*, 7 Dec. 1892, p. 151; *Gr*, 20 May 1899, p. 329.
4. Praed's squib, quoted *Macaulay*, i, p. 75n; *Inaug.*, p. 50.
5. *CR*, 8 May 1902, p. 300.
6. Lytton, i, pp. 246-7; Merivale, p. 65. Praed satirised the different speaking styles of his Union contemporaries in the early eighteen-twenties: S. Waterlow, ed., *In Praise*

of Cambridge (1912), pp.104-13. Cf. R.A. Butler in Cradock, p. 119: "In Parliament one is apt to hear it said that a speech full of quips, jokes, and aphorisms is typical of the Union style." But Butler did not recall such speaking at Cambridge.

7. *Gr*, 16 May 1903, p. 294; Harris in Cradock, p. 86; A.F.W. Plumtre, "Keynes at Cambridge", *Canadian Journal of Economics and Political Science*, 13, 1947, p. 368.

8. *Gr*, 16 June 1892, p. 399.

9. Cradock, p. 98; *Gr*, 20 Oct. 1906, pp. 21-2.

10. *Inaug.*, p. 15. Lord Houghton (Monckton Milnes) went on to rebut this charge.

11. Merivale, p. 98 (letter of 11 March 1827); Praed in Waterlow, ed., *In Praise of Cambridge*, p. 110; *Gr*, 20 May 1899, p. 329.

12. *The Times*, 25 Feb. 1886.

13. Dalton, *Call Back Yesterday*, pp. 51-2.

14. *Milnes*, i, p. 51; *Thackeray*, p. 38.

15. *Dilke*, i, p. 31.

16. 28-29/10/62; 27/10/63. By 14-21/2/65, when the South was clearly losing the Civil War, the vote was still 76 to 29, a 72 percent level of support for the Confederates. Given the regular turnover in the student population, few would have attended all three debates.

17. Raikes, p. 18 (letter of 10 Nov. 1857, referring to 27/10/57).

18. This episode is discussed in Chapter Eight.

19. *Inaug.*, pp. 45-6.

20. *Gr*, 8 Feb. 1890, p. 185.

21. *CR*, 12 Feb. 1903, p. 185. The death sentence had already been commuted to imprisonment by the time of the debate.

22. A.M. Ramsey in Cradock, p. 125.

23. 12/5/74.

24. 5-12/2/84. The 58 votes for socialism were balanced by a massive 399 against. Moreover, one of Hyndman's supporters, F.S. Oliver, later became an exponent of consumerist capitalism as an employee of Debenham and Peabody, and switched his intellectual enthusiasm to imperialism. As the first leader of a British socialist party, Hyndman had plenty of scope for disappointment in life. It is striking that he recorded his greatest regret as his failure to play cricket for Cambridge. "I declare that I feel at this moment, fifty years later, my not playing for Cambridge against Oxford in the University Cricket Match as a far more unpleasant and depressing experience than infinitely more depressing failures have been to me since." H.M. Hyndman, *The Record of an Adventurous Life* (1911), p. 20. It is a statement that surely merits inclusion in any discussion of the failure of the British Revolution.

25. Morrah, *Oxford Union*, pp. 265-6.

26. *CR*, 14 March 1889, p. 272.

27. The episode is discussed in Chapter Eight.

28. *Gr*, 2 March 1895, p. 231.

29. Hollis, *Oxford Union*, p. 143.

30. See Appendix II and Table 5.

31. Gokhale was an early Indian nationalist. His visit on 31/10/05 resulted in a 72 percent vote in favour of "Government on more popular lines" (161-62). An

undergraduate debate (5/11/07) on a motion supporting the "movement towards associating the people of India with the management of their own affairs" produced a 60 percent affirmative vote (96-65).

32. Walter, *Oxford Union: Playground of Power*, p. 39.
33. Ceadel, "King and Country Debate", p. 400.
34. Harris in Cradock, p. 90.
35. Secretary's MB 1885-87, 31 Jan., 30 May 1887.
36. Secretary's MB 1885-87, 8 June 1887.
37. *Gr*, 18 May 1901, p. 335.
38. Harris in Cradock, p. 88.
39. Arnold McNair in Cradock, p. 92: "our main function was to afford adequate opportunity to our own members to debate".
40. A story by Birkett illustrates just how profound was this "prefectorial" form of deference. An announcement by the joint Emmanuel and Caius debating society that the American anti-alcohol campaigner, Mrs Carrie Nation, would address a debate drew a large audience. It soon became clear that the purported Mrs Nation was a Caius undergraduate in drag, and the audience began to barrack. The President of the Union, Arnold McNair, who was privy to the plot, tried to save the day by rebuking the audience for its discourtesy to a lady. "Such was the position of McNair that when he said those words I felt suddenly ashamed myself – but it *was* a Caius undergraduate all the time." (Cradock, pp. 99-100).
41. *Autobiography of Bertrand Russell*, i, p. 63. According to his own account (p. 56), Russell was unusually deficient in social skills. As a scholarship candidate at Trinity in December 1889, he "was too shy to enquire the way to the lavatory". Consequently he walked each morning over a mile to perform the necessary bodily functions at the railway station before returning to tackle his examination papers.
42. Harris in Cradock, p. 83. Encountering the "sour-faced" Edwin Montagu at a reception in Trinity in 1905, Leonard Woolf was tempted to take him aside "and inform him that he is not another Dizzy [Disraeli]". Woolf, *Sowing: An Autobiography of the Years 1880 to 1904*, p. 199.
43. Birkett in Cradock, p. 96.
44. As late as 1938, the public school ethos was so oppressive at Clare that a disgruntled member of the college predicted the introduction of staircase prefects. Howarth, p. 157.
45. Merivale, p. 65; Lytton, i, pp. 232-3 (18/2/23).
46. Lytton, i, p. 233 (14/12/24).
47. 20/5/08; 22/2/10; Birkett in Cradock, p. 97.
48. 8/11/10; 3/11/03.
49. *CR*, 30 Jan. 1908, p. 200.
50. McNair in Cradock, p. 93; *CR*, 19 June 1909, p. 484.
51. *Gr.*, 7 May 1910, p. 349.
52. Appendix II and Tables 6 and 7, pp. 271-2.
53. *Dilke*, i, p. 33. "Oratory and debating are very different things," noted Tim Healy on an American fund-raising tour in 1882, a year after his election to the House of Commons. Healy, *Letters and Leaders* i, p. 149.

54. *Gr.*, 9 Feb. 1895, p. 178.
55. Harris in Cradock, p. 90. "Thousands" was an exaggeration.
56. *Inaug.*, pp. 15-16.
57. *Inaug.*, p. 20. G.F. Browne recalled Fawcett as "a sledge-hammer orator at the Union". Leslie Stephen thought Fawcett's Union experience helped him to overcome a "boyish tendency to stilted rhetoric". Browne, *Recollections of a Bishop*, p. 231; L. Stephen, *Life of Henry Fawcett* (1885), p. 30.
58. Lytton, i, p. 231.
59. *Inaug.*, p. 50.
60. *Pall Mall Gazette*, quoted in *Inaug.*, p. 72.
61. *Inaug.*, p. 4.
62. Whibley, *Lord John Manners and His Friends*, i, p. 54. Recalling his undergraduate days in the eighteen-eighties, T.R. Glover wrote that "men cultivated style and in some cases learnt to speak in such a way that their rising was not followed by the immediate exit of the assembly ... the Union too was education". Glover, *Cambridge Retrospect*, pp. 131-2.
63. J.K. Chapman, *The Career of Arthur Hamilton Gordon First Lord Stanmore 1829-1912* (1964), p. 5. He appears in *Sketches of Cantabs* as "Alexis Gorgon".
64. [R.C. Lehmann], *Harry Fludyer at Cambridge* (1890), p. 15. Lehmann was President of the Union in 1876.
65. Lytton, i, p. 231.
66. Trinity College, Houghton MSS 35/88, undated family letter, cf. *Milnes*, i, p. 53.
67. *Thackeray*, p.p. 45-6 (family letter, 22 March 1829).
68. Gardiner, *Harcourt*, i, p. 36. Harcourt's maiden speech in the House of Commons in 1869 does not support the argument that the Cambridge Union was an effective training ground for statesmen. One journalist criticised his "tedious" delivery and complained that "his apparent confidence in himself verges upon ... self-conceit" (i, p. 211).
69. A.L. Thorold, *The Life of Henry Labouchere* (1913), p. 21. After two years at Cambridge, Labouchere had gambled away £6000. He contemptuously defied University regulations by passing a note to a friend during his Little-Go examination (on which he was said to have placed a £300 bet that he would pass) and haughtily insisted that it was insulting to be asked to explain his behaviour. He conducted himself "in a reckless discreditable manner" when summoned before the Vice-Chancellor's court, and was suspended for two years, effectively a sentence of expulsion from Cambridge. Thorold, *Life of Labouchere*, pp. 21-5; *Rom3*, p. 102.
70. VPR M 1898.
71. VPR M 1898.
72. *Gr*, 23 April 1892, p. 272. Wilson Harris made his maiden speech during his second term at Cambridge, in the Arthur Lynch debate. Nervous, Harris spoke too fast. As the *Granta* reported: "Mr Harris passed and who shall measure his speed?" But it was from such unpromising novices that the Union culled its future stars. Just over two years later, Harris was elected President.
73. Lytton, i, p. 231.
74. *Inaug.*, p. 5.
75. *Gr*, 9 February 1895, p. 178.

76. *Gr*, 15 Nov. 1902, pp. 69-70. Chapter Ten suggests that other factors may have influenced the outcome of the debate. Despite Geary's surname, no immediate family link to Ireland has been traced.
77. *Inaug.*, p. 47.
78. *The Times*, 25 Feb. 1886.
79. Birkett in Cradock, p. 102.
80. A.M. Ramsey in Cradock, p. 122.
81. *Dilke*, i, p. 34 (1898).
82. Hort, i, p. 106.
83. *Inaug.*, p. 49.
84. *CR*, 14 May 1903, p. 298.
85. Trinity College, Houghton MSS 35/153, family letter of Feb. 1829, and cf. *Milnes*, i, pp. 60-1 where Kemble is given as "Campbell". The debate took place on 17/2/29. Cf. *Inaug.*, p. 26.
86. Memorandum of 17 Nov. 1841 on dealing with the legislature of New Brunswick, P. Knaplund, *James Stephen and the British Colonial System* (1953), p. 260. In 1920, a speech by Kingsley Martin was criticised as "a series of superior sneers". C.H. Rolph, *Kingsley: The Life, Letters and Diaries of Kingsley Martin* (1973), p. 75.
87. Bourne, *Palmerston: The Early Years*, p. 29.
88. Report in *Gownsman*, pp. 67-8.
89. *CR*, 26 Jan. 1887, p. 165.
90. The following section is based upon R.M. Worcester, *British Public Opinion: A Guide to the History and Methodology of Public Opinion Polling* (1991), esp. pp. 121-80. Cambridge Union voting did not always eliminate "don't-know" voting. Thackeray cast a vote in a debate on the French Revolution "[t]hough in truth I knew little about it". *Thackeray*, p. 42.
91. White, *Cambridge Life*, p. 140.
92. R.A. Butler in Cradock, p. 120.
93. VPR M 1860.
94. VPR E 1883.
95. 28/4/91. The motion was defeated by 42 votes to 35.
96. VPR M 1860.
97. Everett, *On the Cam*, pp. 106-8.
98. VPR E 1864.
99. Morrah, *Oxford Union*, pp. 106-7, 113-14; Hollis, *Oxford Union*, pp. 72-3. The point at issue was not whether money should be raised for Famine relief, but whether the funds of a society dedicated to entirely different aims should be voted for that purpose. Dufferin was able to raise about £1000 in direct subscriptions from his Oxford friends, and contributed a further £1000 himself. A. Lyell, *The Life of the Marquis of Dufferin and Ava* (1905), ch. 2.
100. 28/11/71.
101. Leslie Stephen in *National Review*, 42, 1903-4, pp. 140-1; 26/10/52; 9/11/52.
102. Lines by Praed, quoted Lytton, i, p. 239 and in Waterlow, ed., *In Praise of Cambridge*, p. 104.

ENDNOTES TO CHAPTER EIGHT (pp. 162-187):

THE IRISH DEBATES 1816-1885

1. 18/3/16. Records were admitted to be defective as early as 1818 (*Statement*, p. xii) because a page had been accidentally ripped from the now-lost first Minute Book. However, the University was closed for much of the summer of 1815 on health grounds, and in later years debates rarely began before November. Thus the debate on Ireland in February 1816 was probably the first.
2. Gash, *Mr Secretary Peel*, p. 175.
3. 25/11/16.
4. 6/12/25.
5. 9/12/28; 19-26/3/33.
6. 14/2/37.
7. 15/3/30.
8. 4/12/21.
9. 11/2/23; 23/11/24; 1/5/27.
10. "The so-called Catholic Emancipation" as Charles Merivale remembered it, Merivale, p. 65. Debates and votes were as follows: 7/5/22 (36-26); 6/4/24 (63-41); 26/4-3/5/25 (54-47); 14/2/26 (52-40); 13-20/2/27 (61-50); 6/11/27 (68-44); 4/3/28 (85-55); 3-10/3/29 (143-114).
11. 26/5/29; 8/2/31; 4/12/31. Cf. Chapter Four, note 47 for the 1829 debate. The Jesuits were again condemned (by 30 votes to 5) on 3/12/44.
12. *Milnes*, i, p. 50, wrongly printed as "Campbell".
13. Houghton MSS 35/88, family letter of 7 Nov. 1827.
14. Allen, *Cambridge Apostles*, pp. 43-4, from *The Athenaeum*, 14 June 1829. The author was given as "E.B. of Christ's". But no member of Christ's spoke on the Catholic issue. For Norreys, see Hollis, *Eton*, p. 217.
15. *Palmerston-Sulivan Letters*, p. 177.
16. Gash, *Mr Secretary Peel*, pp. 556-63; Houghton MSS, 35/100, family letter of 10 March 1829; MB5, fos 64, 69. The result as announced on the night was 157 votes to 121.
17. *Globe*, 11, 12 March 1829; Houghton MSS 35/100; *Thackeray*, p. 38.
18. *Globe*, 13 March 1829. The Secretary, P.H. Crutchley of Magdalene, tried without success to make it "illegal for any member to take upon himself to publish the proceedings of the Society" although officers would retain "the power of contradicting any statements which might appear, whenever they might think it necessary to do so". MB5, fo. 71, 21 March 1829.
19. *Parliamentary Debates*, 20, 24 March 1829, cols. 1413-17; *Thackeray*, pp. 47-50. George Law was the brother of the High Tory politician, Lord Ellenborough.
20. 5/5/29; 22/4/28. Thackeray (p. 70) missed the debate on the Irish forty-shilling freeholders because he mistook the date. Thus poor organisation may partly explain the low turn-out.
21. 8/12/35; 7/4/40; *Corrie*, p. 73.
22. *Whewell*, pp. 213, 214-15. Julius Hare had spoken in the Union in 1816, opposing Latin American independence.

23. 16/11/41.
24. 8/11/42; 16/11/52.
25. 5-12/11/33; 1/5/27; 23/11/24.
26. 19-26/3/33; 5-12/11/33; 18/3-25/4/35.
27. 17/11/35.
28. 8/11/36.
29. 28/2/37; *Whewell*, p. 173.
30. 25/4-2, 5/5/37.
31. 12/2/39.
32. Bristed, p. 245.
33. 9/2/36; 6-13/12/36; 5/3/39; 22/4/28; 11/3/34.
34. 3/4/38; 19/2/38. Charles Greville, ed. Henry Reeve, *A Journal of the Reign of Queen Victoria from 1837 to 1852* (3 vols, 1885), i, pp. 67-8.
35. 6-13/12/36; 17/11/40; 3/12/39. Cf. George Corrie, then a tutor at St Catharine's, in 1837: "who can suppose that Ireland will not be thrown into the hands of the Papists, as to secure a permanent majority in the House of Commons efficient only for mischief?" (*Corrie*, p. 73).
36. N. Gash, *The Life of Sir Robert Peel after 1830* (1972), pp. 404-9.
37. 7-14/11/43.
38. 22-23/4/45; *DNB*, "Hallam, Henry".
39. 1/11/51.
40. 13/5/45; 3-10/11/46. Reeve, ed., *Greville Journal 1837-1852*, ii, p. 41. The son was seen as the mouthpiece for the father, iii, p. 89.
41. 21-28/11/48.
42. 16/3/47.
43. C. Woodham-Smith, *The Great Hunger: Ireland 1845-1849* (1962), p. 336. Large sums were collected in Cambridge churches in January 1847, the Nonconformists outstripping the Anglicans. Fellows of Trinity were among those who contributed generously to the appeal for Ireland: Whewell gave £50. Cambridge also marked the national day of humiliation for the Famine in March 1847, although at least one local cleric used the occasion to preach against the Maynooth Grant. *Rom2*, pp. 191, 203. Less pleasant is the "conundrum" later recorded by Romilly: Q: "What is the cause of the potato disease?" A: "The rot-tatory motion of the earth." The sole plea in mitigation is that Romilly, who delighted in puns, did not encounter this one until 1856. *Rom3*, p. 235.
44. 28/3/48. It was almost certainly this debate which is referred to in *Sketches of Cantabs*, pp. 37-8, in which a "Unionic" orator is portrayed asking a friend for a crash course in Irish history since "of course it won't do for me to be deficient in the minutest particular". Defenders of the Irish Church included Lord Alwyne Compton, who became Bishop of Ely in 1886.
45. 16/4/50.
46. 8/2/59.
47. *DNB*, "Raikes, Henry Cecil".
48. 8/3/64.
49. 14-21/3/65.
50. Lowry-Corry was MP for Tyrone from 1873 to 1880, surviving a [Protestant]

tenants' revolt when he defended his seat in 1874. J. Bardon, *A History of Ulster* (1994 ed.), pp. 357-8.

51. 5/2/67. The motion was carried by 56 votes to 50.
52. J.A. Venn, *Alumni Cantabrigienses*, part ii, ii, p. 284.
53. Quoted, Shannon, *Gladstone*, i, p. 538.
54. 4/12/65; 30/11/69 and Table 2.
55. 31/10/65; 19/3/67. 156 members voted on the Jamaica issue on 28/1/67.
56. 4/2/68; 25/2/68.
57. 17-18/3/68.
58. 18-19/5/69. The motion against the convents was defeated by 42 votes to 16 on 27/4/69.
59. He was A.P. Graves, Scholar of the University of Dublin 1868 and BA 1872.
60. 8/2/70.
61. 4-11/11/73. J.G. Swift MacNeill, *What I Have Seen and Heard* (1925), p. 99, and see Table 3.
62. 13/2/77. The Church of England had been upheld by 246 votes to 70, a 78 percent majority, on 6/2/77.
63. 4/12/77.
64. 17/2/80. British policy towards Afghanistan was condemned on 3/1/80 by 103 votes to 72.
65. 1/3/81.
66. 7/2/81.
67. 3/10/82.
68. 1/5/83.
69. 18/3/84.
70. Austen Chamberlain spoke against Coercion on 30/1/83 and 26/5/85. For the Political Society, I. Anstruther, *Oscar Browning: A Biography* (1983), pp. 85-87 and A. Chamberlain, *Politics from Inside: An Epistolatory Chronicle 1906-1914* (1936), p. 116. Chamberlain was reminded of the episode on being shown a record of the meeting when revisiting Cambridge in 1908. Lowes Dickinson, a fellow member of the Political Society, recalled Austen Chamberlain as "friendly and honourable" but "perhaps not the most intelligent of men". E.M. Forster, *Goldsworthy Lowes Dickinson* (1934). p. 31. For his father's attitude to Irish devolution before 1886, C.H.D. Howard, "Joseph Chamberlain, Parnell and the Irish 'central board' scheme, 1884-5", *Irish Historical Studies*, 8, 1953, pp. 324-61.
71. 24/8/80. Long Vacation meetings were rarely well attended. This, and the 1881 debate, produced an unusually good turn-out.
72. 2/11/80.
73. 8/2/81.
74. 3/5/81.
75. 23/8/81.
76. 25/10/81.
77. 25/10/81.
78. 28/2/82.
79. 7/2/82.
80. 3/5/81; 28/2/82.

81. 30/1/83; 26/5/85.
82. 19/2/84; 16/10/84; 11/3/84 and see Table 3.
83. 3/2/85. Only 63 members voted on Irish Coercion in May 1885 but "the Union always slacks off a good deal in the summer term", *Oxf. Mag.*, 11 May 1893, pp. 350-1.
84. 21/10/84; 25/11/84; 3/6/84.

ENDNOTES TO CHAPTER NINE (pp. 189-211):

GLADSTONIAN HOME RULE 1886-1898

1. Maitland, *Leslie Stephen*, p. 388 (6 May 1886). Stephen thought the Home Rule Bill "about the most insane contrivance that anybody ever blundered into. But what is a poor radical to do?" But in October 1881 he had expressed "a devout wish that the Irish might be left to settle their own quarrels and see how they liked it. I should repeal the Union to-morrow, but people here do not seem to be of my way of thinking just yet." (pp. 388-9; 345).
2. *Gr*, 8 Mar 1889, pp. 3-4.
3. 26/1-2/2/86, *CR*, 27 Jan. 1886, pp. 168-9. At Edinburgh on 18 March 1886, students in the Dialectic Society unsuccessfully tried to block a motion censuring the Liberal government by moving an amendment calling for suspension of judgement "till Mr Gladstone's scheme for the pacification of Ireland is before Parliament and the country". *History of the Dialectic Society* (1887), p. 130.
4. Published in *The Times*, 4 May 1886 and quoted A.B. Cooke and J. Vincent, *The Governing Passion: Cabinet Government and Party Politics in Britain 1885-86* (1974), p. 411.
5. *CR*, 26 Jan. 1887, pp. 164-7.
6. Morley, *Gladstone*, iii, pp. 345-6; H. Pelling, *Social Geography of British Elections 1885-1910* (1967), p. 415. Constituency results of the 1886 general election are taken from J. Vincent and M. Stenton, eds., *McCalmont's Parliamentary Poll Book: British Election Results, 1832-1918* (1971).
7. 8-15/6/86; *CR*, 7 June 1886, p. 372.
8. So Rosebery believed. Cooke and Vincent, *Governing Passion*, p. 434.
9. Blunt, *Land War*, p. 34 (5 March 1886).
10. R.F. Foster, *Lord Randolph Churchill: A Political Life* (1988 ed.), pp. 220, 322; W.S. Churchill, *Lord Randolph Churchill* (1951 ed.), pp. 231, 256-7.
11. Blunt, *Land War*, p. 34.
12. He ostentatiously nominated Oscar Browning for the post of Provost of Eton despite the fact that he was a Harrovian himself and would almost certainly have known that Browning had been eased out of his post at the school because of his suspected homosexuality. Hollis, *Eton*, pp. 281-4.
13. Blunt, *Land War*, p. 144.
14. F.S.L. Lyons, *Parnell* (1978 ed.), p. 353; O'Brien, *Life of Parnell*, ii, pp. 155-7. Parnell told Barry O'Brien: "we cannot persuade the English people. They will only do what we force them to do." Davitt felt that Parnell "had neglected the English democracy" – but the Cambridge Union was on odd place to start reversing the

process.

15. Blunt, *Land War*, pp. 144-5.
16. *CR*, 9 June 1886, p. 373.
17. Blunt, *Land War*, pp. 144-5.
18. F.S.L. Lyons, *John Dillon: A Biography* (1968), p. 79.
19. H.C.G. Matthew, ed., *The Gladstone Diaries*, xi (1990), p. 585 (8 July 1886).
20. 24/8/86.
21. 26/10/86. See Table 5.
22. 25/1/87. *CR*, 26 Jan. 1887, p. 165.
23. 7-14/6/87.
24. 18/10/87.
25. 3-10/5/87.
26. *CR*, 26 Jan. 1887, p. 164.
27. Secretary's MB, 1885-7, Private Business Meeting, 31 Jan. 1887.
28. P. Lewsen, ed., *Selections from the Correspondence of John X. Merriman 1890-1898* (Van Riebeeck Society, 1963), p. 242. Cf. E. Pakenham, *Jameson's Raid* (1960), p. 252. E.T. Cook, *Edmund Garrett: A Memoir* (1909) gives a more favourable picture, but says little about his Cambridge days.
29. Browning, *Memories of Sixty Years*, pp. 317-19. Known as the "O.B.", Browning was an early version of a publicity-seeking media-don. After losing his post at Eton, he did useful work at Cambridge in the development of teacher training and in cultivating friendly relations (for whatever motives) with students. Undergraduates liked but did not respect him. As E.F. Benson put it, "it was impossible not to be aware that he was a buffoon". (E.F. Benson, *As We Were: A Victorian Peep-Show* (1971 ed.), p. 129.) Browning's increasing tendency to put on weight, which caused him to waddle rather than walk, literally made him a figure of fun: a Cambridge rhyme punningly warned him against becoming "too obese". He was sometimes mistaken for his namesake, the poet, but not by Tennyson. "I'm Browning", the O.B. said by way of introduction. "You're not", replied Tennyson in an unambiguous put-down. Although a prolific rather than a profound historian, Oscar Browning was thought to be in the running for the Regius Chair in 1895. "O.B. or not O.B, that is the question", remarked Maitland in a faint attempt to find the threat amusing. Fifoot, ed., *Letters of Maitland*, p. 130. Happily for History at Cambridge, Lord Acton was appointed instead.
30. Stanford, *Passages from an Unwritten Diary*, pp. 254-7.
31. Secretary's MB, 1887-9, 5 May 1887.
32. Secretary's MB, 1887-9, 30 May, 1, 8 June 1887. Officially, canvassing in Union elections was banned, but the prohibition was often ingeniously or even blatantly evaded. *Oxf. Mag.*, 11 March 1891, p. 280.
33. *DNB* 1922-1930 (1937), p. 805.
34. *CR*, 15 June 1887, pp. 385-7.
35. *CR*, 25 Oct. 1888, pp. 40-1; 23/10/88; cf. 16/10/88.
36. *CR*, 7, 14 March 1888, pp. 272-3, 260-1; *Gr*, 8 March, p. 8; 15 March 1889, pp. 8-9; 5-12/3/89. For Lehmann, see Searby, pp. 664-5. Tanner defended boycotting, pointing out "that his fashionable practice in Cork had been ruined when he became a Nationalist politician. If the classes boycotted, why not the masses?" When the

O'Shea divorce case revealed that Parnell had used the alias "Mr Fox", Tanner pursued him through the North Kilkenny by-election campaign shouting "Tally-ho!". T.P. O'Connor, *Memories of an Old Parliamentarian* (2 vols, 1929), ii, pp. 158-9; F. Callanan, *The Parnell Split* (1992), pp. 66-7.

37. 4/2/90. *CR*, 6 Feb. 1890, pp. 188-9; *Gr*, 8 Feb. 1890, p. 185.

38. Lyons, *Parnell*, p. 472.

39. 29/4/90; *CR*, 1 May 1890, pp. 292-3; *Gr*, 6 May 1890, pp. 297-8. It is possible that the proposer was related to Sir Thomas Newenham Deane, the architect of the National Library in Dublin, who came from a Cork Protestant family. The Cambridge Union's handling of the Special Commission may seem petty, but it was mild in comparison with that of the Oxford Union. There Lord Hugh Cecil successfully proposed a motion insisting that "the great prevalence of crime and outrage in Ireland from the year 1878 to the year 1888 was chiefly due to the wicked and criminal acts, speeches and conduct of Mr. Parnell and his associates". *Oxf. Mag.*, 5, 12 March 1890, pp. 246-7, 264-5.

40. 4-11/11/90; *Gr*, 8 Nov. 1890; *CR*, 6 Nov. 1890, pp. 68-9. The Cambridge correspondent of the *Oxford Magazine* sarcastically reported that the Union was "so excited by the novelty of the subject that it adjourned the debate". J.K. Stephen died in 1892. An obituary praised his "brilliant oratory and fascinating wit" as well as his "indefinable personal magnetism". *Oxf. Mag.*, 12 Nov. 1890, p. 88; 10 Feb. 1892, pp. 161-2.

41. An Oxford visitor who contributed to the debate, H.E.A. Cotton, was identified by the *Granta* as an Irishman whose "native county was Killarney [sic]". *Gr*, 15 Nov. 1890, pp. 70-1; *Oxf. Mag.*, 19 Nov. 1890, p. 105.

42. 14/6/92; *Gr*, 16 June 1892, pp. 398-9.

43. 9/5/93; *CR*, 11 May 1893, p. 331; *Gr*, 13 May 1893, pp. 315-16; *Oxf. Mag.*, 17 May 1893, p. 376.

44. 21/2/93; *Gr*, 25 Feb. 1893, pp. 218-19; *CR*, 25 Feb. 1893, pp. 234-5.

45. *CR*, 8 March 1894, p. 272; Lord Crewe, *Lord Rosebery*, ii, pp. 444-5.

46. *Gr*, 10 March 1894, p. 245.

47. 6/3/94. *CR*, 8 March 1894, pp. 272-3.

48. 26/2/95; *Gr*, 2 March 1895, pp. 231-2; *CR*, 28 Feb. 1895, p. 228; *Oxf. Mag.*, 6 March 1895, p. 277.

49. 23/2/97; *CR*, 25 Feb. 1897, p. 260; *Gr*, 27 Feb. 1897, pp. 218-20.

50. 23/11/97; *Gr*, 27 Nov. 1897, pp. 106-7; *CR*, 25 Nov. 1897, pp. 112-13.

51. 22/2/98. *CR*, 24 Feb. 1898, pp. 247-8; *Gr*, 26 Feb. 1898, pp. 215-16. The joke about the Maxim gun might suggest the influence of Hilaire Belloc's sardonic comment on Britain's growing empire in Africa: "Whatever happens we have got/ The Maxim Gun, and they have not." In this case, however, the young Cambridge orator can be acquitted of plagiarism, for Belloc's *The Modern Traveller* did not appear until November 1898. I am grateful to Peter B. Freshwater for this information.

ENDNOTES TO CHAPTER TEN (pp. 212-233):

IRELAND IN THE NEW CENTURY

The chapter title derives from the amusing and insightful book by Sir Horace Plunkett, published in 1904.

1. E. O'Halpin, *The Decline of the Union: British Government in Ireland 1892-1920* (1987), p. 35.
2. 15/10/89. *CR*, 17 Oct. 1889. Cf. Chapter Four, note 35 for the false report that the motion had been passed.
3. 16/5/99; *CR*, 18 May 1899, p. 342.
4. 25/1/02; *CR*, 30 Jan. 1902, p. 155; *Gr*, 1 Feb. 1902, pp. 166-8.
5. 1/12/03; *Gr*, 5 Dec. 1903; *CR*, 3 Dec. 1903, pp. 121-2.
6. 13/05/02; *Gr*, 17 May 1902, pp. 311-12.
7. 11/11/02; *CR*, 13 Nov. 1902, pp. 72-3; *Gr*, 15 Nov. 1902, pp. 69-70.
8. 10/2/03; *CR*, 12 Feb. 1903, p. 185. Arnold's speech is discussed in Chapter Seven. Lynch's sentence had already been commuted to life imprisonment. He was pardoned in 1907 and re-elected to parliament as a Nationalist in 1909. During the First World War, he recruited for the Allied cause in Ireland and became a Colonel in the British army. In 1923 he published a textbook on psychology which he predicted would remain an intellectual beacon "when the British Empire itself is forgotten". The *Dictionary of National Biography* adds: "This judgement has not received general endorsement." *DNB* 1931-1940 (1949), pp. 551-2.
9. See Table 6.
10. 12/5/03. *Gr*, 17 May 1902. p. 313; *CR*, 14 May 1903, pp. 297-8; *Gr*, 16 May 1903, pp. 294-5.
11. 31/5/04. Of Belloc, *CR*, 2 June 1904, p. 343: "it is some time since the Union has listened to so delightful a speaker". McDonnell described Home Rule as "that ideal which of all political ideals is dearest to him", *Gr*, 4 June 1904, pp. 342-3. Cf. M.F.J. McDonnell, *Ireland and the Home Rule Movement* (1908).
12. 9/5/05; *CR*, 11 May 1905, pp. 296-7; *Gr*, 13 May 1905, pp. 261-2.
13. *Gr*, 20 Jan. 1907, p. 160. Selwyn later became a noted Anglo-Catholic theologian. A.R. Vidler, *The Church in an Age of Revolution: 1789 to the Present Day* (1971 ed.), p. 198.
14. 16/10/06; *CR*, 18 Oct. 1906, p. 12; *Gr*, 20 Oct. 1906, pp. 21-2.
15. 12/3/07; *CR*, 14 March 1907, pp. 327-8. In June 1891, the Union had dismissed by 64 votes to 20 a motion claiming that it was "the function of the Celt to rule the Saxon". On 28/1/08, the Union condemned "the administration of the Government in Ireland" by 88 votes to 47. The focus of the debate is not wholly clear from reports. The proposer of the motion "belched forth terrific adjectives", denounced the Liberals for failing to invoke Coercion and generally warned that clouds were gathering and floodgates opened. *CR*, 30 Jan. 1908, pp. 199-200.
16. 27/10/08. *Gr*, 31 Oct. 1908, pp. 36-7; *CR*, 29 Oct. 1908, pp. 43-4.
17. 8/06/09. *CR*, 17 June 1909, pp. 483-4. Dillon's comment in Cradock, p. 93

(McNair). Unluckily there is no *Granta* report for this debate.

18. 3/5/10; *Gr*, 7 May 1910, pp. 348-9; *Gownsman*, pp. 5-9. In contrast to the *Granta*, the *Gownsman* thought it "a dull debate ...enlivened by a few bright speeches". For Roxburgh, see Birkett in Cradock, p. 101 and N. Annan, *Roxburgh of Stowe* (1965), p. 28. For the "Grand Dukes", *CR*, 18 Oct. 1906, p. 12.

19. *Gr*, 7 May 1909, p. 349.

20. 22/11/10; 29/11/10.

21. 24/1/11; *Gr*, 28 Jan. 1911, pp. 188-9; *Gownsman*, pp. 67-75. Gwynn's impact is discussed in Chapter Seven.

22. 12/3/12; *CR*, 14 March 1912, pp. 357-8 and cf. *Gr*, 12 March 1912, pp. 296-7.

23. 21/5/12; *Gr*, 25 May 1912, pp. 402-3; *CR*, 23 May 1912, p. 464. Alan O'Day, *Irish Home Rule 1867-1921* (1998), pp. 249-50; Childers, *Framework of Home Rule*, pp. 198-203.

24. 22/10/12; 11/2/13; *Gr*, 26 Oct. 1913, p. 24. R. Blake, *The Unknown Prime Minister: The Life and Times of Andrew Bonar Law 1858-1923* (1955), p. 130.

25. James placed Dillon in the elusive category of gentleman, calling him "an honest man but a fanatic". Cox, *M.R. James*, p. 107.

26. 4/3/13; *CR*, 6 March 1913, pp. 353-4; *Gr*, 7 March 1913, pp. 253-4.

27. D.E. Butler, *The British General Election of 1955* (1955), p. 1.

28. 4/11/13; *Gr*, 8 Nov. 1913, pp. 56-7; *CR*, 6 Nov. 1913, pp. 84-5; MacNeill, *What I Have Seen and Heard*, pp. 99-100; H. Macmillan, *Winds of Change 1914-1939* (1966), p. 44. For Swift MacNeill as a Victorian, see M. Manning, *James Dillon: A Biography* (1999), p. 21. (He denounced the 1916 rebels as "*rascals*", apologising for the vehemence of his language.) O'Connor, *Memoirs of an Old Parliamentarian*, ii, pp. 45-53 gives a portrait of his eccentricities.

29. 28/4/14; *CR*, 29 April 1914, p. 391; *Gr*, 2 May 1914, pp. 278-9.

30. A. Gray, *Cambridge University: An Episodical History* (1926), p. 297.

31. *Mandragora* (Cambridge), May Week 1914, p. 34.

32. *CR*, 17 June 1914, p. 544.

33. *Mandragora*, pp. 38-42.

34. VPR L 1914

35. 26/10/09; 25/11/13; 15/2/10; 15/5/06; 14/11/05; 2/2/09 (and cf. Birkett in Cradock, pp. 95-6); 31/10/11; 4/2/13; 26/5/14; 19/5/14. "The threat of German aggression had hardly been realized", McNair recalled, adding that "a straight debate on a question of Foreign Policy would have attracted only a small house". (Cradock, p. 92).

36. *CR*, 27 May 1914, p. 469. I am grateful to Dr Elisabeth Leedham-Green for information on von Lubtow.

37. For the list of candidates, *CR*, 10 June 1914, p. 512, and for Durrant, *CR*, 29 April 1914, p. 391. Casualties are recorded in G.V. Carey, ed., *The War List of the University of Cambridge 1914-1918* (1921).

38. Gray, *Cambridge University: An Episodical History*, pp. 297-8. Cf. Brooke, pp. 331-40 and Howarth, p. 16.

39. *Gr*, May Week 1914, pp. 37-8; Birkett in Cradock, pp. 96, 101-2. Allen was killed on 21 June 1915.

40. *CR*, 7 June 1916, p. 352 and cf. 20 Jan. 1915, pp. 136-7; 1 Dec. 1915, p. 132; 23 Feb. 1916, p. 223; Heitland, *After Many Years*, p. 214; *Historical Register of the*

University of Cambridge Supplement 1911-1920, p. 200.
41. *CR*, 29 Nov. 1916, p. 124.
42. M.R. James addressed the Tipperary Club in 1915. Pfaff, *Montague Rhodes James*, p. 245.

ENDNOTES TO CHAPTER ELEVEN (pp. 234-253):

CONCLUSION

1. *CR*, 9 June 1886, p. 393; *CR*, 14 March 1912, p. 358; Cradock, p. 80.
2. Childers, *Framework of Home Rule*, p. 148.
3. F. Pakenham, *Peace by Ordeal* (1951 ed.), p. 33.
4. McDonnell, *Ireland and the Home Rule Movement*, pp. x-xi.
5. *CR*, 14 March 1912, p. 358.
6. K. Rose, *King George V* (1983), p. 242. As Duke of York, George V had been present in the gallery of the House of Commons to hear Gladstone introduce the Second Home Rule Bill in 1893 in "a beautiful speech". However, in 1913, he was "assured by resident landowners in the South and West of Ireland that their tenants, while ostensibly favourable to Home Rule, are no longer enthusiastic about it". H. Nicolson, *King George V: His Life and Reign* (1952), pp. 48, 227.
7. Lyons, *Parnell*, p. 260.
8. *Gr*, 23 Feb. 1893, p. 219; Childers, *Framework of Home Rule*, pp. 203, 201.
9. *CR*, 23 Feb. 1893, p. 235.
10. Cradock, p. 143.
11. 14/3/82.
12. A. Jones, *Politics of Reform 1884* (1972), pp. 18-20; Matthew, *Gladstone*, pp. 206-7.
13. J. Pope, *Memoirs of the Right Honourable Sir John Alexander Macdonald* (2 vols, 1894), ii, pp. 222-7; Merivale, p. 66; W.S. Churchill, *Lord Randolph Churchill* (1951 ed.), p. 488.
14. Stephen, *The Jesuit at Cambridge*, i, p. 251.
15. 13/11/66. A. Rosen, *Rise Up Women!* (1974), p. 6.
16. R. Taylor, *Lord Salisbury* (1975), p. 4 (and only just: young Cecil is elected on line 4!); G.M. Young, *Stanley Baldwin* (1952), p. 25 (text begins on p. 17).
17. Merivale, p. 66. This recollection seems unreliable. Reform may have been "in the background" at Westminster, but surviving accounts of debates from the eighteen-twenties suggest that it was a staple of Cambridge oratory.
18. *Gownsman*, p. 6.
19. *Rom1*, pp. 226-7; M. & E. Brock, eds, *H.H. Asquith's Letters to Venetia Stanley* (1982), p. 122 (24 July 1914). "Cushion-thumper" was contemporary slang for a clergyman, usually of a fashionable kind, who preached violent sermons.
20. E.g. J.J. Lee, *Ireland 1912-1985: Politics and Society* (1989), pp. 1, 4; P. Travers, *Settlements and Divisions: Ireland 1870-1922* (1988), pp. 69-71.
21. Childers, *Framework of Home Rule*, p. 172.

ENDNOTES TO APPENDIX I (pp. 254-260):

THE TROUBLES 1919-21

1.   Howarth, p. 57.
2.   Shakespeare in Cradock, pp. 107-9. Howarth, p. 23, points out that the audience was equal to about one-fifth of the undergraduate population of Cambridge.
3.   *CR*, 19 March 1919, pp. 261-2.
4.   *Gr*, 15 May 1919, pp. 50-1.
5.   *CR*, 30 Jan. 1920, p. 133.
6.   16/3/1920.*CR*, 19 May 1919, pp. 312-13; *Gr*, 15 May 1919, pp. 50-1.
7.   27/1/1920. *CR*, 30 Jan. 1920, pp. 173-4; *Gr*, 30 Jan. 1920, pp. 166-7.
8.   26/10/1920. *CR*, 29 Oct. 1920, pp. 50-1; *Gr*, 29 Oct. 1920, pp. 48-9 and cf. W.D. Johnston in *CR*, 11 Nov. 1921, pp. 84-5.
9.   10/5/1921. *CR*, 13 May 1921; *Gr*, 13 May 1921, p. 390.
10. 8/11/1921. *CR*, 11 Nov. 1921, pp. 84-5; *Gr*, 11 Nov. 1921, pp. 82-3.
11. *Gr*, 11 Nov. 1921, pp. 82-3; A. Howard, *RAB*, p. 16.
12. *CR*, 11 Nov. 1921, p. 84.
13. *CR*, 16 May 1919, pp. 312-13; *Gr*, 15 May 1919, pp. 50-1.
14. *CR*, 30 Jan. 1920, pp. 173-4.
15. *CR*, 29 Oct. 1920, pp. 50-1. Macpherson's namesake, Lloyd George's Chief Secretary for Ireland, does not appear to have been related.
16. *Gr*, 29 Oct. 1920, pp. 48-9.
17. *CR*, 30 Jan. 1920, p. 174.
18. O'Connor, *Memoirs of an Old Parliamentarian*, ii, p. 218.
19. *CR*, 30 Jan. 1920, pp. 173-4.
20. *CR*, 16 May 1919, p. 312-13. The *Cambridge Review* praised him for raising the quality of debate.
21. *Gr*, 15 May 1919, pp. 50-1.
22. *CR*, 29 Oct. 1920, p. 51.
23. *CR*, 11 Nov. 1921, pp. 84-5.
24. *CR*, 29 Oct. 1920, p. 50.
25. *CR*, 20 Oct. 1920, p. 51.
26. *CR*, 13 May 1921, pp. 365-6.
27. *CR*, 29 Oct. 1920, p. 50.
28. M. Hopkinson, *Green Against Green: The Irish Civil War* (1988), p. 32.
29. F. Pakenham, *Peace by Ordeal* (1935), p. 298, quoting from notes by Austen Chamberlain.
30. *Gr*, 30 Jan. 1920, p. 165 ("Those in Authority").
31. G. Shakespeare, *Let Candles Be Brought In* (1949), p. 22. His father, Dr J.H. Shakespeare, was a member of a key committee established in July 1918 to plan Coalition Liberal election strategy. T. Wilson, *The Downfall of the Liberal Party 1914-1935* (1968 ed.), p. 151.
32. Shakespeare, *Let Candles Be Brought In*, pp. 87-8; Pakenham, *Peace by Ordeal*, p. 301.

33. Pakenham, *Peace by Ordeal*, p. 301.
34. Pakenham, *Peace by Ordeal*, p. 302.
35. Shakespeare, *Let Candles Be Brought In*, pp. 89-91.

St John's College Gates, The Backs

Index

Index

Conventional abbreviations are used for Cambridge colleges. In addition, officials of the Union are indicated by P (President). T (Treasurer). V (Vice-President and S (Secretary.)